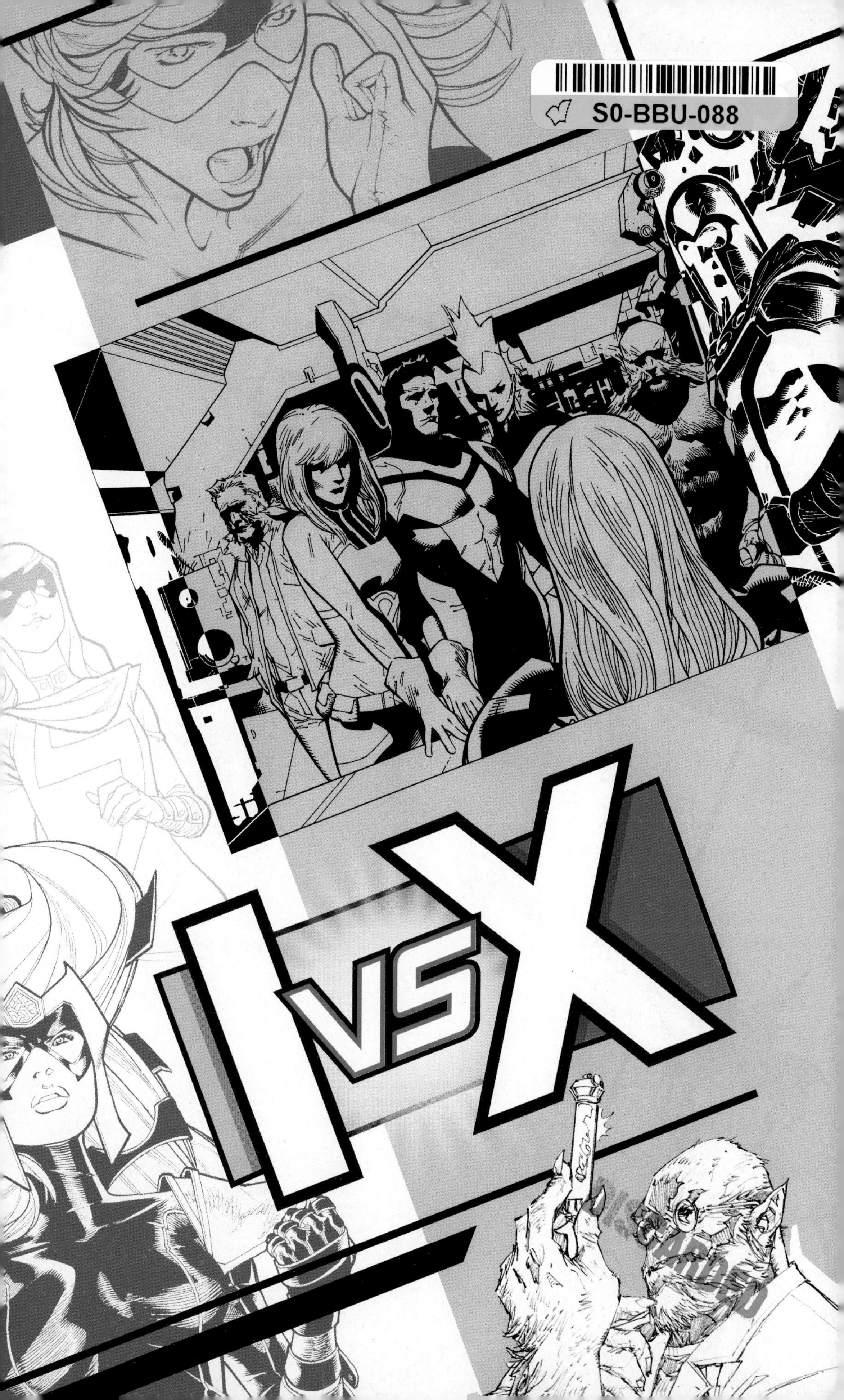
I vs X

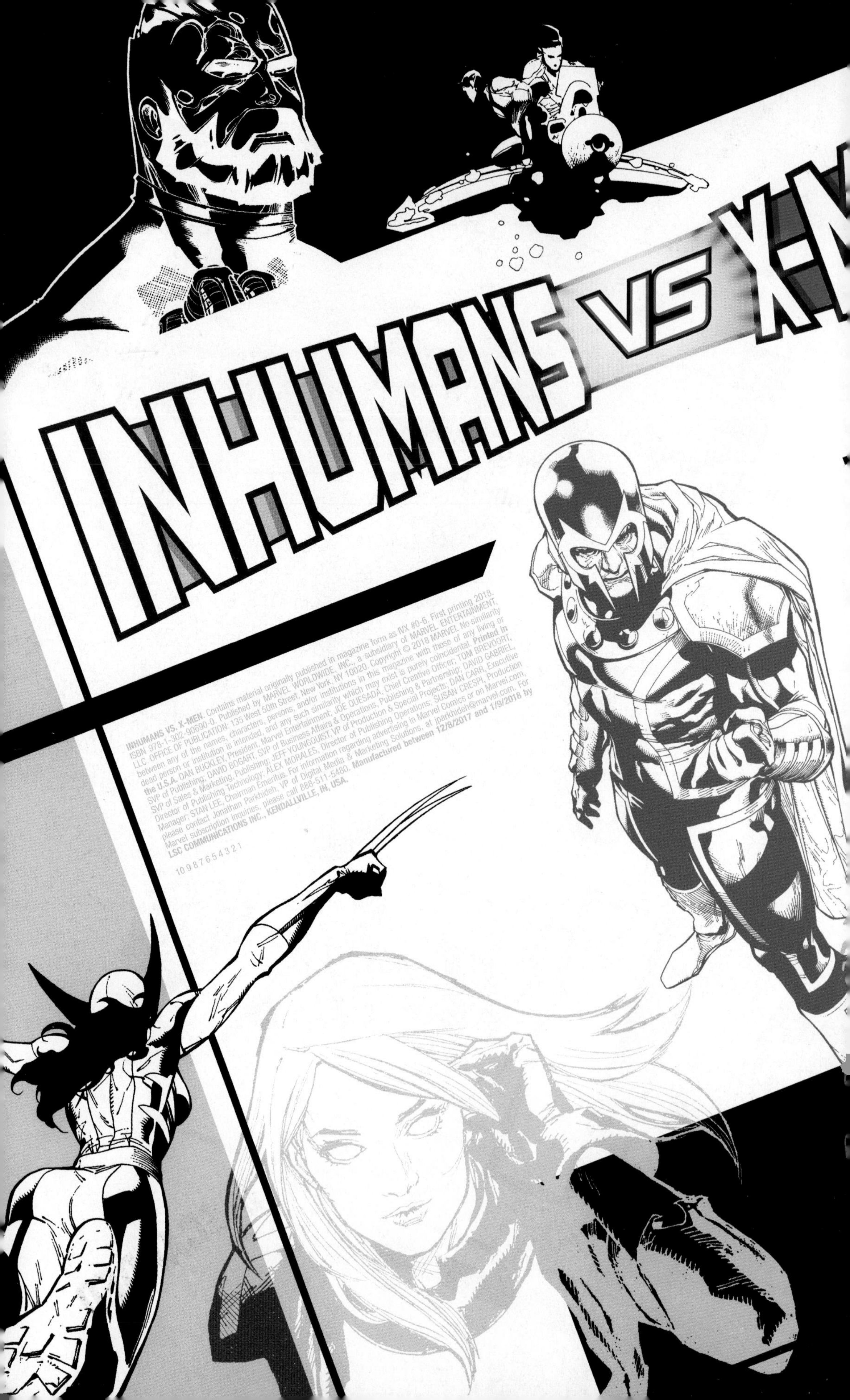
INHUMANS VS X-M

INHUMANS VS. X-MEN. Contains material originally published in magazine form as IVX #0-6. First printing 2018. ISBN 978-1-302-90690-0. Published by MARVEL WORLDWIDE, INC., a subsidiary of MARVEL ENTERTAINMENT, LLC. OFFICE OF PUBLICATION: 135 West 50th Street, New York, NY 10020. Copyright © 2018 MARVEL No similarity between any of the names, characters, persons, and/or institutions in this magazine with those of any living or dead person or institution is intended, and any such similarity which may exist is purely coincidental. **Printed in the U.S.A.** DAN BUCKLEY, President, Marvel Entertainment; JOE QUESADA, Chief Creative Officer; TOM BREVOORT, SVP of Publishing; DAVID BOGART, SVP of Business Affairs & Operations, Publishing & Partnership; DAVID GABRIEL, SVP of Sales & Marketing, Publishing; JEFF YOUNGQUIST, VP of Production & Special Projects; DAN CARR, Executive Director of Publishing Technology; ALEX MORALES, Director of Publishing Operations; SUSAN CRESPI, Production Manager; STAN LEE, Chairman Emeritus. For information regarding advertising in Marvel Comics or on Marvel.com, please contact Jonathan Parkhideh, VP of Digital Media & Marketing Solutions, at jparkhideh@marvel.com. For Marvel subscription inquiries, please call 888-511-5480. **Manufactured between 12/8/2017 and 1/9/2018 by LSC COMMUNICATIONS INC., KENDALLVILLE, IN, USA.**

10 9 8 7 6 5 4 3 2 1

Charles Soule (#0-6) & Jeff Lemire (#1-6)
WRITERS

ISSUE #0

Kenneth Rocafort
ARTIST

Dan Brown
COLORIST

ISSUES #1-2 & #6

Leinil Francis Yu
PENCILER

Gerry Alanguilan with
Leinil Francis Yu (#6)
INKERS

David Curiel
COLORIST

ISSUES #3-5

Javier Garrón
ARTIST

Andres Mossa (#3),
Jay David Ramos (#3)
& David Curiel (#4-6)
COLORISTS

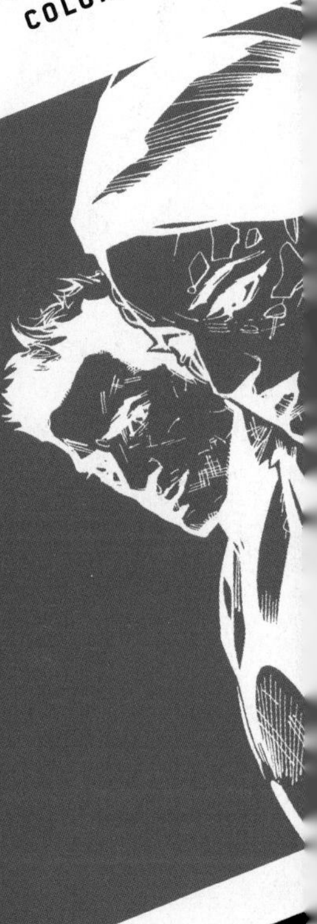

VC's Clayton Cowles
LETTERER

Kenneth Rocafort (#0), Leinil Francis Yu (#1)
and Leinil Francis Yu & David Curiel (#2-6)
COVER ART

Charles Beacham & Chris Robinson
ASSISTANT EDITORS

Wil Moss & Daniel Ketchum
EDITORS

Mark Paniccia
X-MEN GROUP EDITOR

Nick Lowe
EXECUTIVE EDITOR

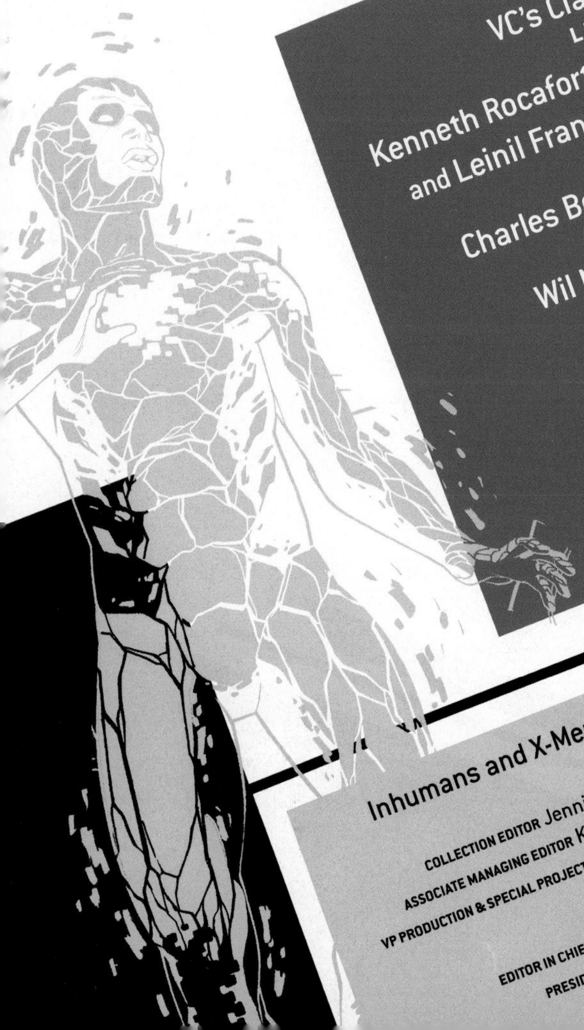

Inhumans and X-Men created by Stan Lee & Jack Kirby

COLLECTION EDITOR Jennifer Grünwald | ASSISTANT EDITOR Caitlin O'Connell
ASSOCIATE MANAGING EDITOR Kateri Woody | EDITOR, SPECIAL PROJECTS Mark D. Beazley
VP PRODUCTION & SPECIAL PROJECTS Jeff Youngquist | SVP PRINT, SALES & MARKETING David Gabriel
BOOK DESIGNER Jay Bowen

EDITOR IN CHIEF C.B. Cebulski | CHIEF CREATIVE OFFICER Joe Quesada
PRESIDENT Dan Buckley | EXECUTIVE PRODUCER Alan Fine

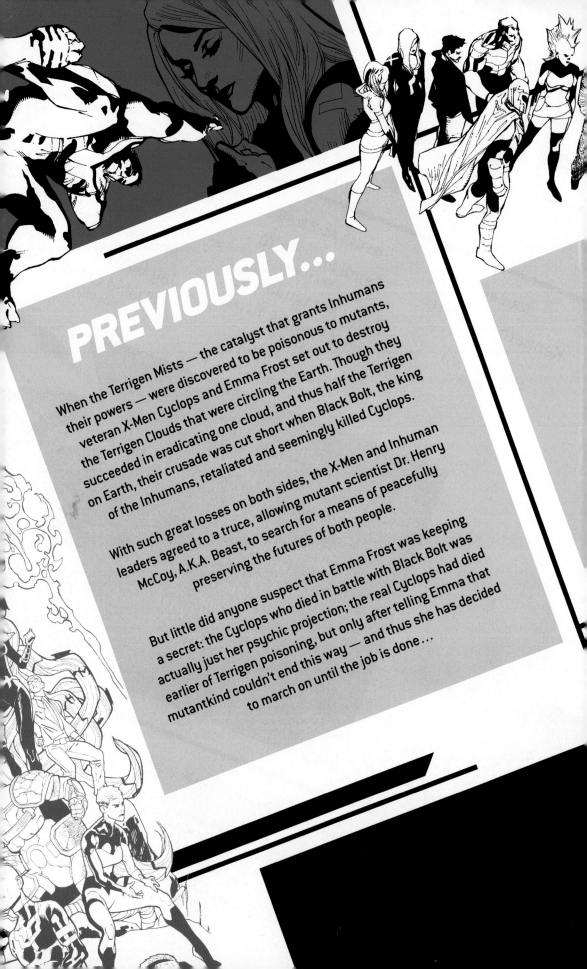

PREVIOUSLY...

When the Terrigen Mists — the catalyst that grants Inhumans their powers — were discovered to be poisonous to mutants, veteran X-Men Cyclops and Emma Frost set out to destroy the Terrigen Clouds that were circling the Earth. Though they succeeded in eradicating one cloud, and thus half the Terrigen on Earth, their crusade was cut short when Black Bolt, the king of the Inhumans, retaliated and seemingly killed Cyclops.

With such great losses on both sides, the X-Men and Inhuman leaders agreed to a truce, allowing mutant scientist Dr. Henry McCoy, A.K.A. Beast, to search for a means of peacefully preserving the futures of both people.

But little did anyone suspect that Emma Frost was keeping a secret: the Cyclops who died in battle with Black Bolt was actually just her psychic projection; the real Cyclops had died earlier of Terrigen poisoning, but only after telling Emma that mutantkind couldn't end this way — and thus she has decided to march on until the job is done...

INHUMANS

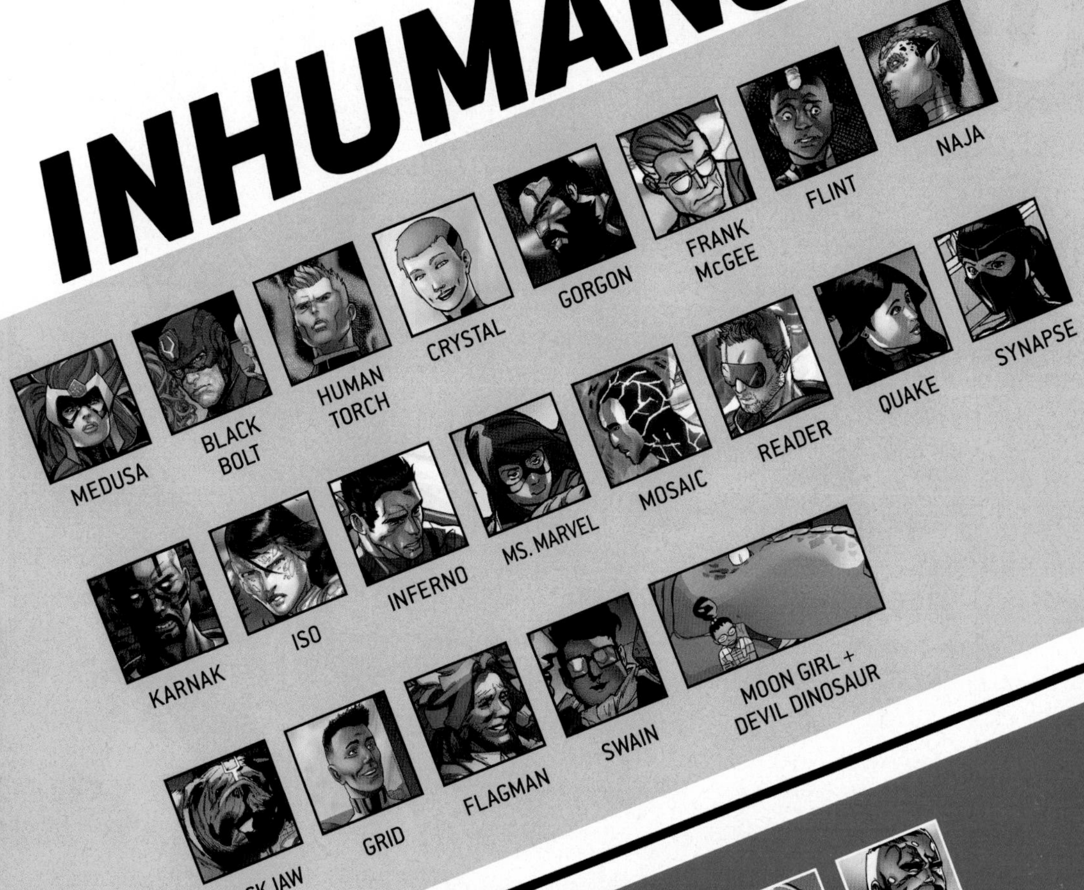

MEDUSA
BLACK BOLT
HUMAN TORCH
CRYSTAL
GORGON
FRANK McGEE
FLINT
NAJA
KARNAK
ISO
INFERNO
MS. MARVEL
MOSAIC
READER
QUAKE
SYNAPSE
LOCKJAW
GRID
FLAGMAN
SWAIN
MOON GIRL + DEVIL DINOSAUR

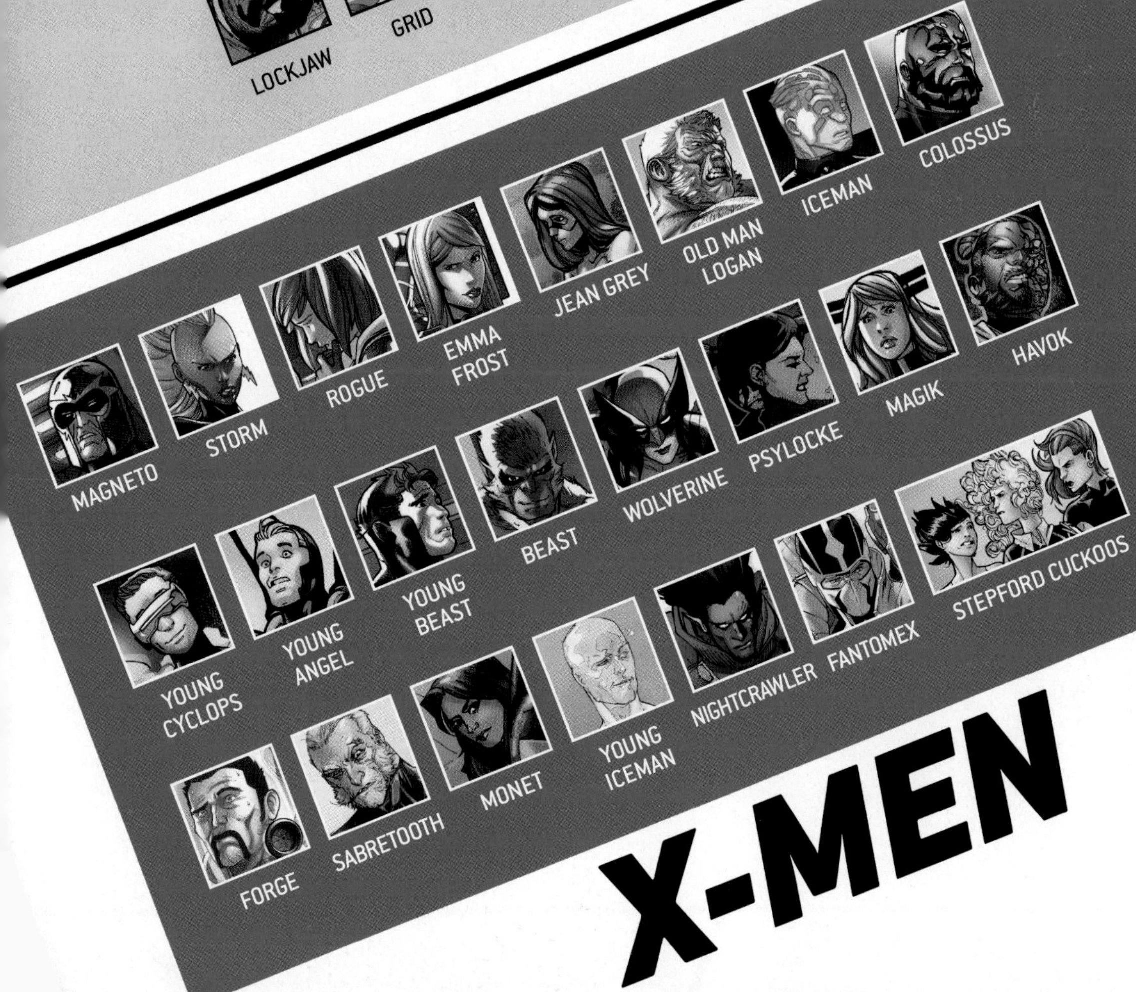

MAGNETO
STORM
ROGUE
EMMA FROST
JEAN GREY
OLD MAN LOGAN
ICEMAN
COLOSSUS
YOUNG CYCLOPS
YOUNG ANGEL
YOUNG BEAST
BEAST
WOLVERINE
PSYLOCKE
MAGIK
HAVOK
FORGE
SABRETOOTH
MONET
YOUNG ICEMAN
NIGHTCRAWLER
FANTOMEX
STEPFORD CUCKOOS

X-MEN

0

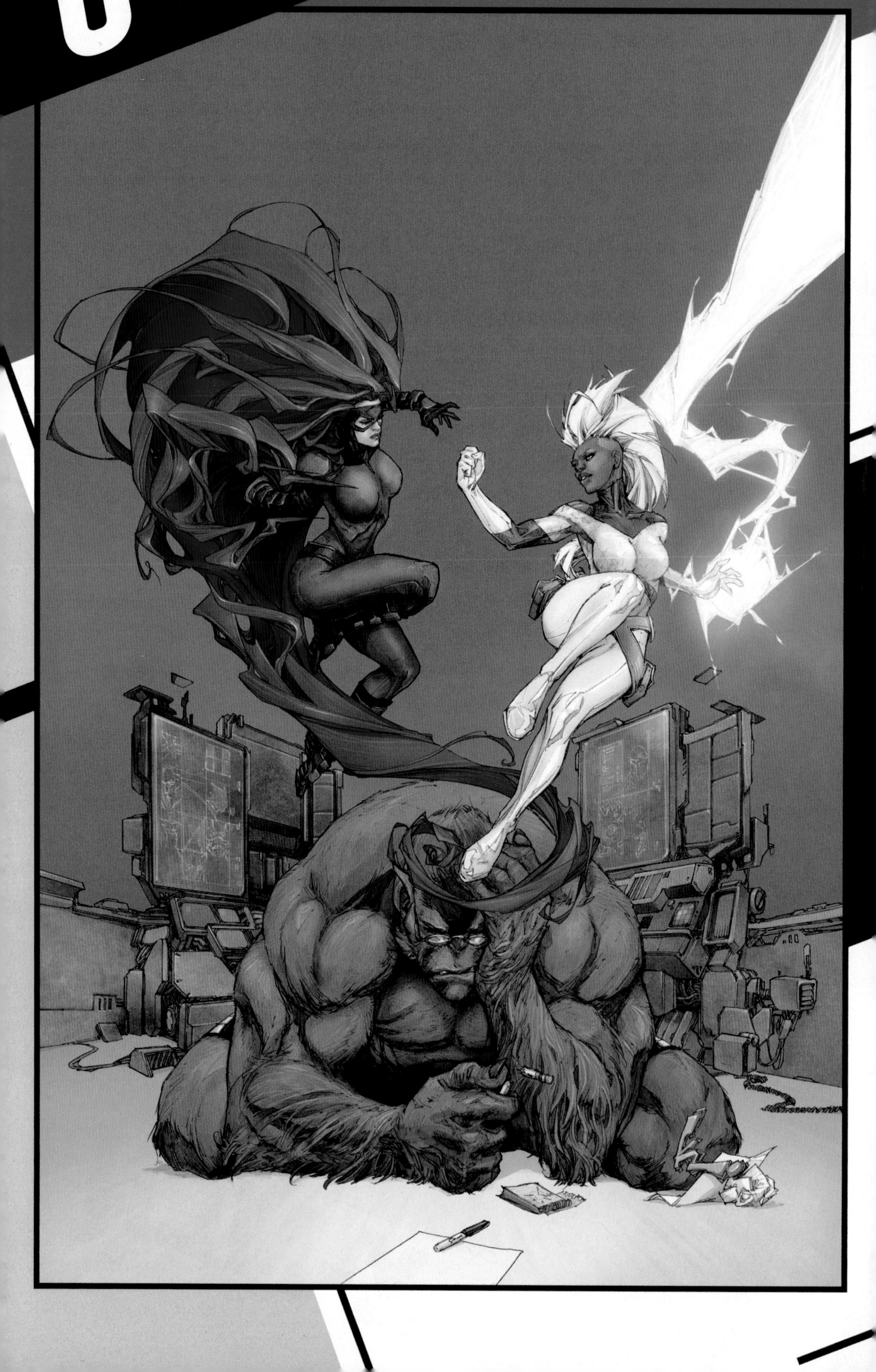

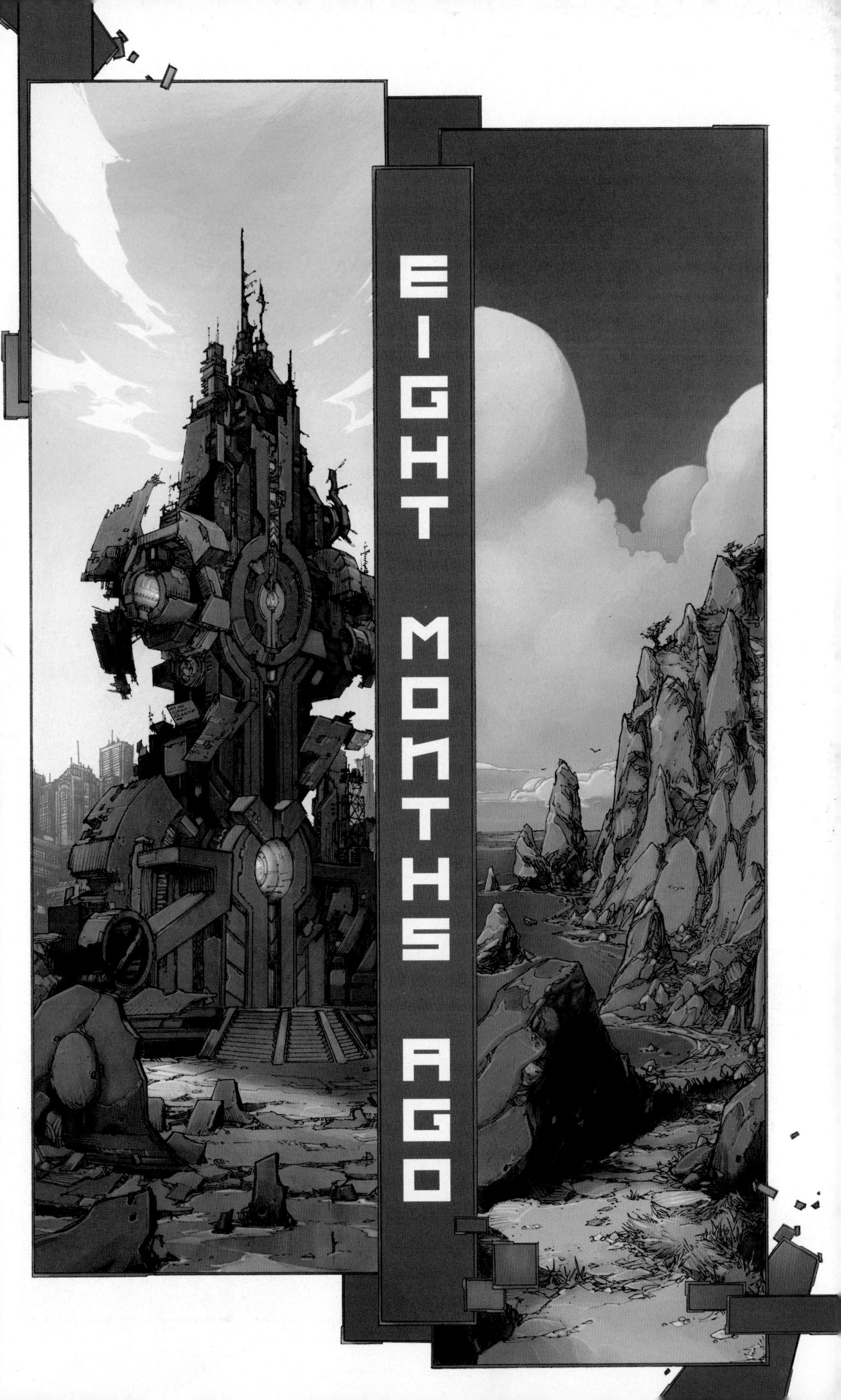
EIGHT MONTHS AGO

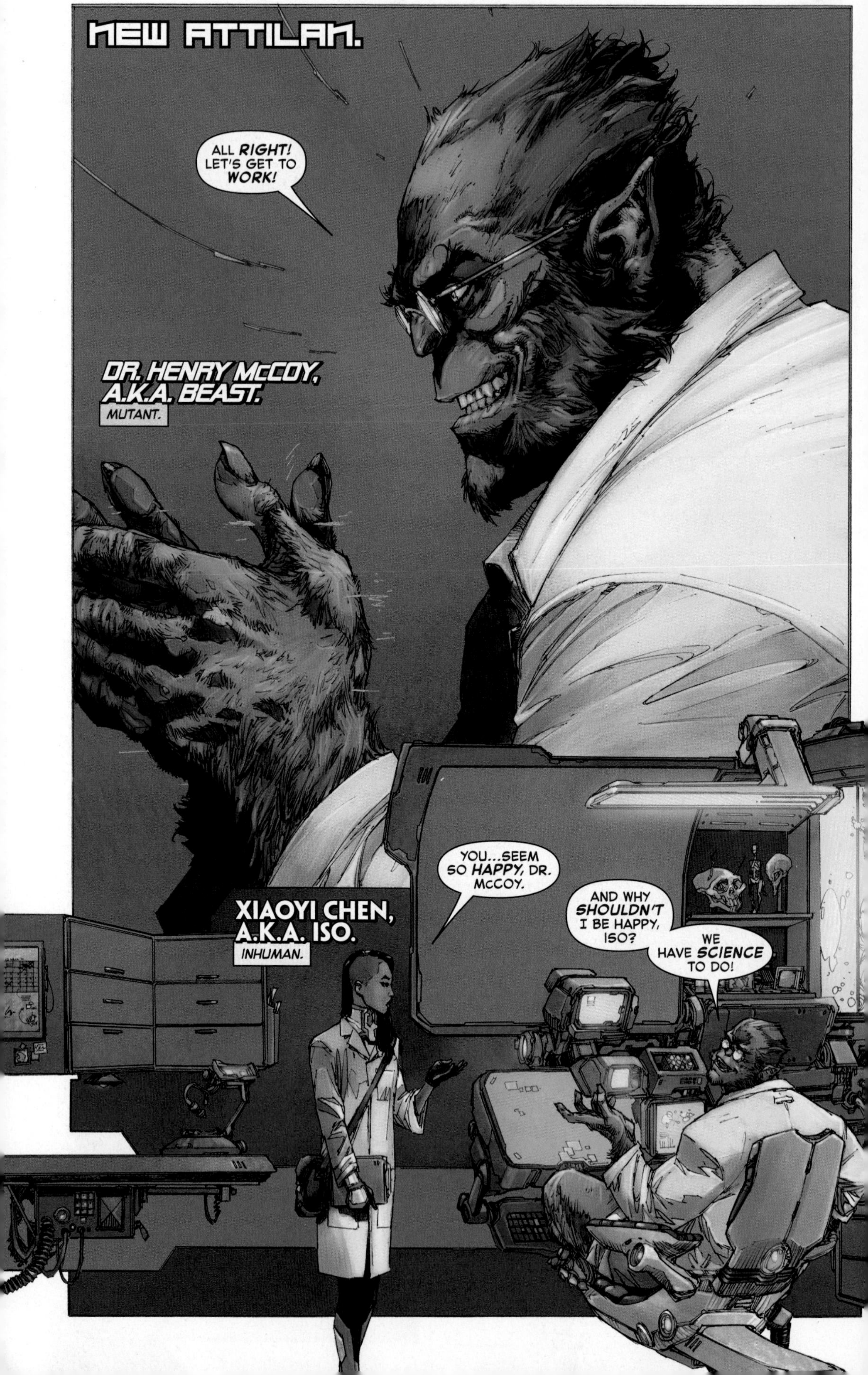
NEW ATTILAN.
ALL RIGHT! LET'S GET TO WORK!
DR. HENRY McCOY, A.K.A. BEAST.
MUTANT.
XIAOYI CHEN, A.K.A. ISO.
INHUMAN.
YOU...SEEM SO HAPPY, DR. McCOY.
AND WHY SHOULDN'T I BE HAPPY, ISO?
WE HAVE SCIENCE TO DO!

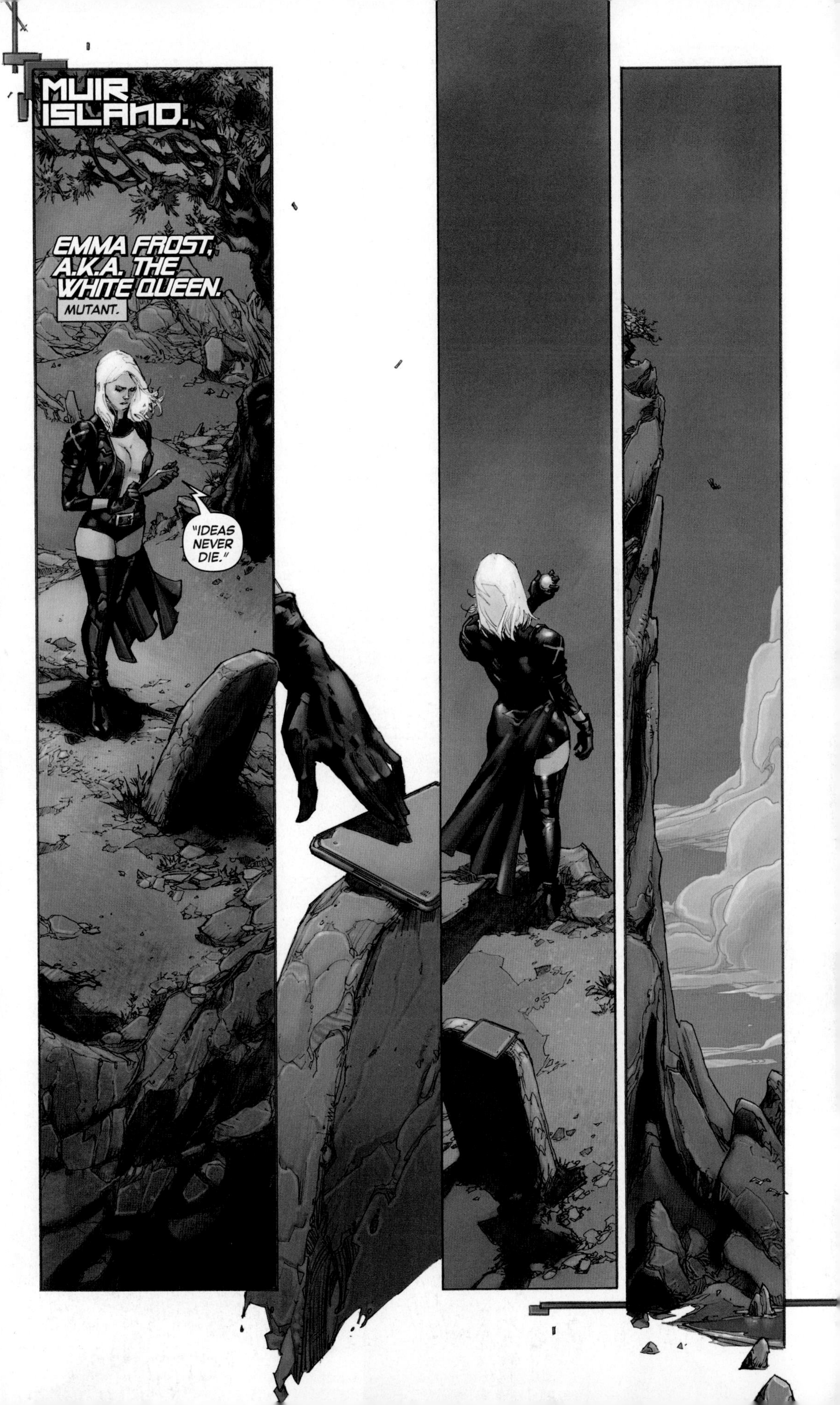
MUIR ISLAND.
EMMA FROST, A.K.A. THE WHITE QUEEN.
MUTANT.
"IDEAS NEVER DIE."

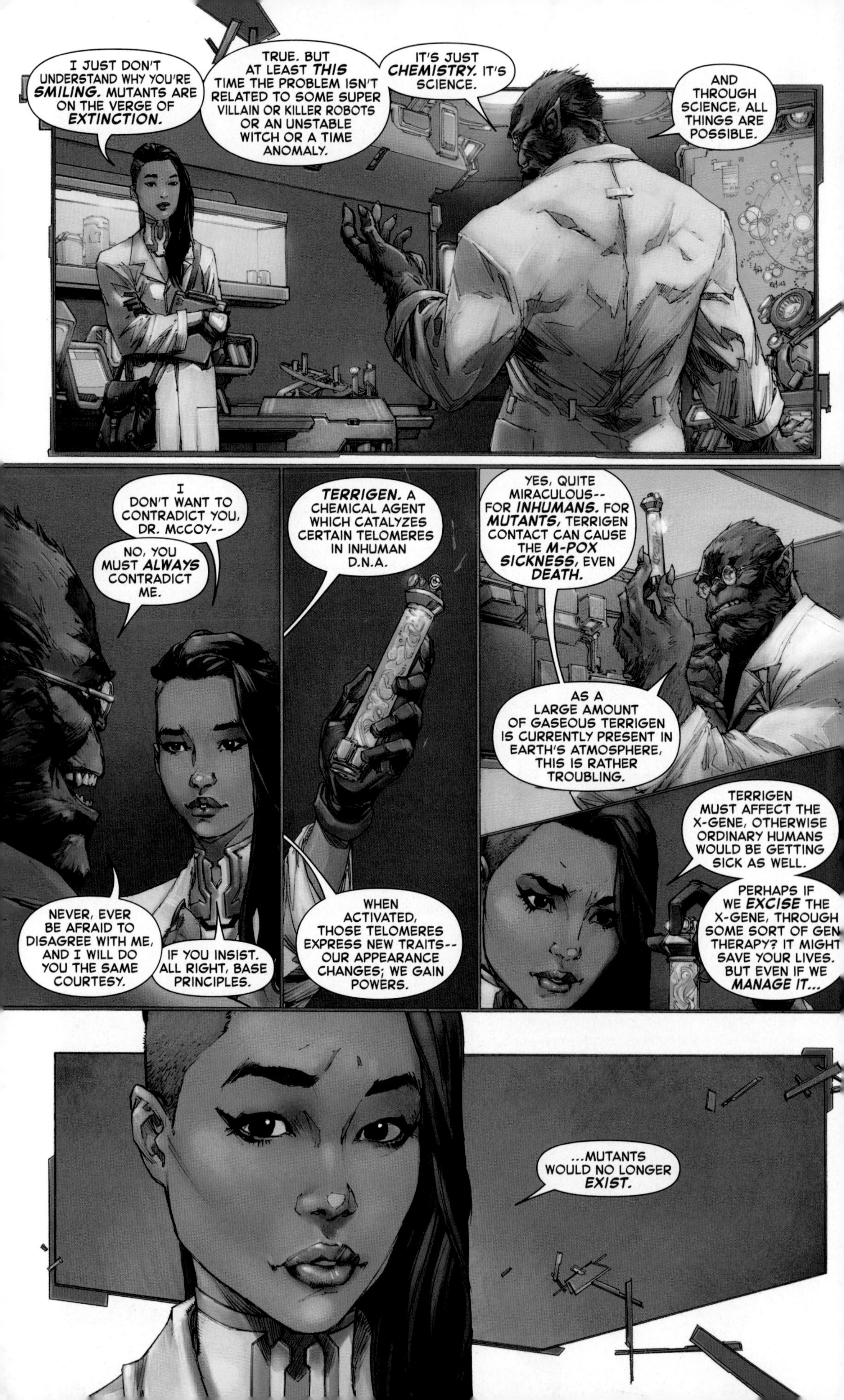
I JUST DON'T UNDERSTAND WHY YOU'RE SMILING. MUTANTS ARE ON THE VERGE OF EXTINCTION.
TRUE. BUT AT LEAST THIS TIME THE PROBLEM ISN'T RELATED TO SOME SUPER VILLAIN OR KILLER ROBOTS OR AN UNSTABLE WITCH OR A TIME ANOMALY.
IT'S JUST CHEMISTRY. IT'S SCIENCE.
AND THROUGH SCIENCE, ALL THINGS ARE POSSIBLE.
I DON'T WANT TO CONTRADICT YOU, DR. McCOY--
NO, YOU MUST ALWAYS CONTRADICT ME.
NEVER, EVER BE AFRAID TO DISAGREE WITH ME, AND I WILL DO YOU THE SAME COURTESY.
IF YOU INSIST. ALL RIGHT, BASE PRINCIPLES.
TERRIGEN. A CHEMICAL AGENT WHICH CATALYZES CERTAIN TELOMERES IN INHUMAN D.N.A.
WHEN ACTIVATED, THOSE TELOMERES EXPRESS NEW TRAITS--OUR APPEARANCE CHANGES; WE GAIN POWERS.
YES, QUITE MIRACULOUS--FOR INHUMANS. FOR MUTANTS, TERRIGEN CONTACT CAN CAUSE THE M-POX SICKNESS, EVEN DEATH.
AS A LARGE AMOUNT OF GASEOUS TERRIGEN IS CURRENTLY PRESENT IN EARTH'S ATMOSPHERE, THIS IS RATHER TROUBLING.
TERRIGEN MUST AFFECT THE X-GENE, OTHERWISE ORDINARY HUMANS WOULD BE GETTING SICK AS WELL.
PERHAPS IF WE EXCISE THE X-GENE, THROUGH SOME SORT OF GEN THERAPY? IT MIGHT SAVE YOUR LIVES. BUT EVEN IF WE MANAGE IT...
...MUTANTS WOULD NO LONGER EXIST.

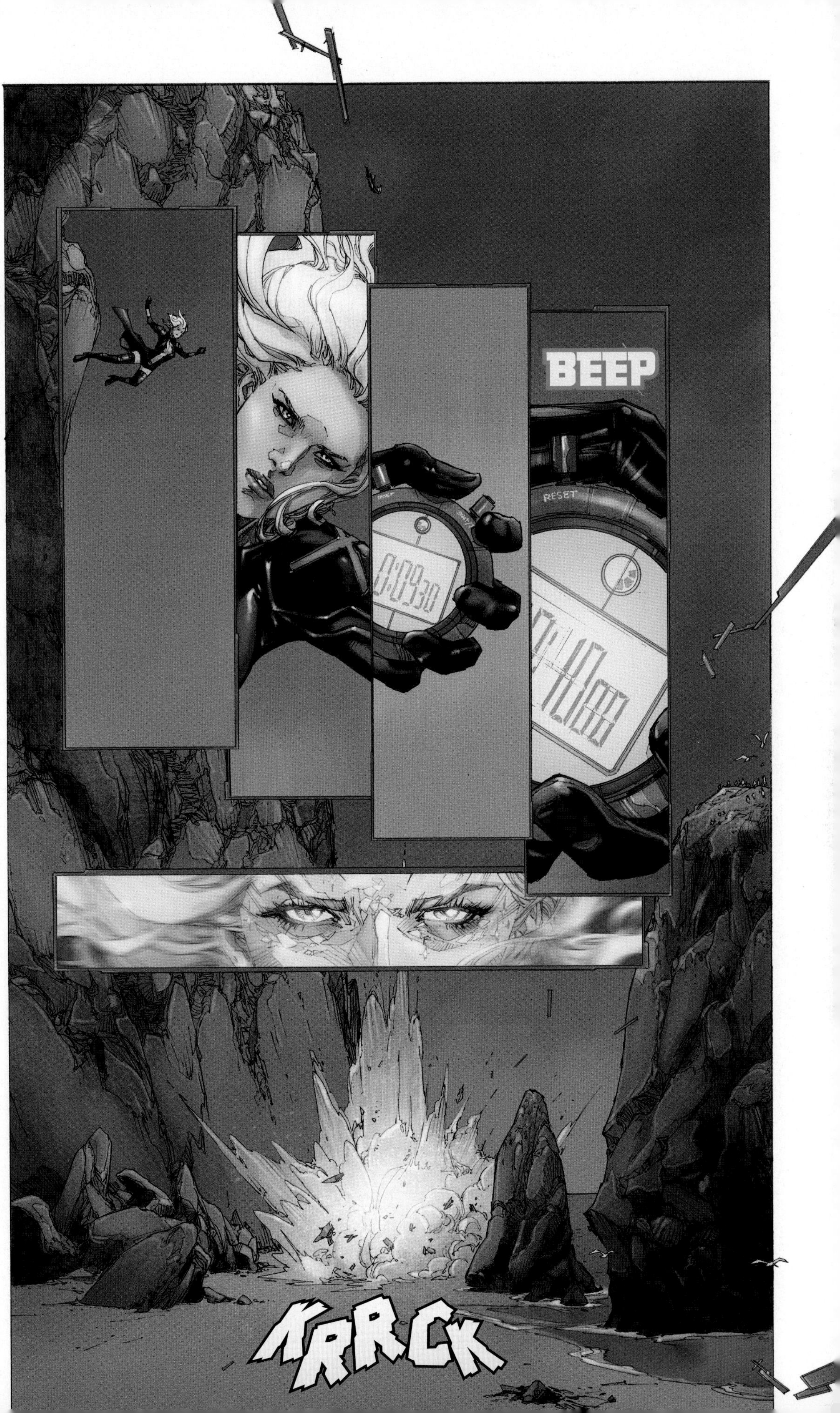
BEEP
KRRCK

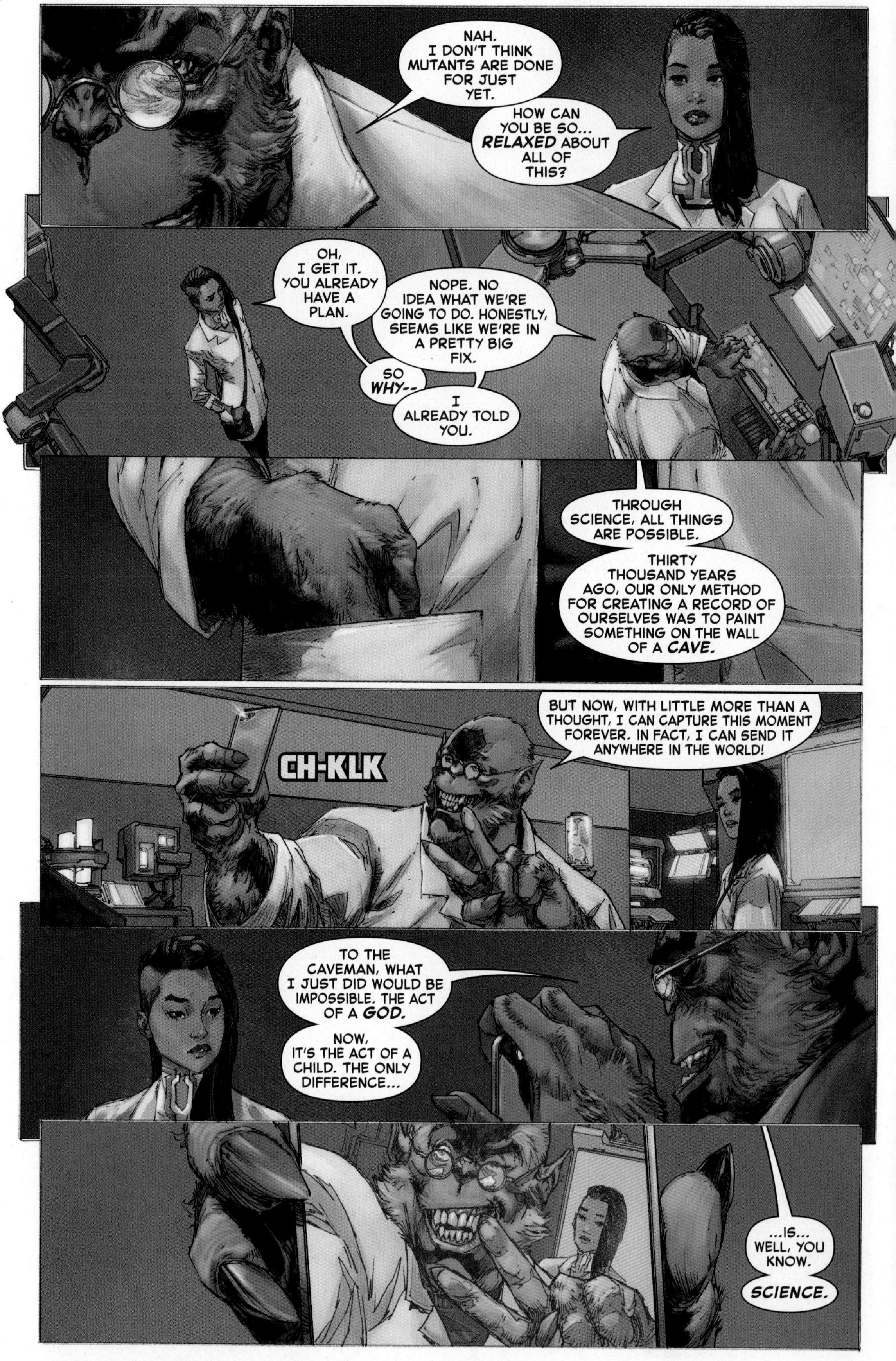
NAH. I DON'T THINK MUTANTS ARE DONE FOR JUST YET.
HOW CAN YOU BE SO... RELAXED ABOUT ALL OF THIS?
OH, I GET IT. YOU ALREADY HAVE A PLAN.
NOPE. NO IDEA WHAT WE'RE GOING TO DO. HONESTLY, SEEMS LIKE WE'RE IN A PRETTY BIG FIX.
SO WHY--
I ALREADY TOLD YOU.
THROUGH SCIENCE, ALL THINGS ARE POSSIBLE.
THIRTY THOUSAND YEARS AGO, OUR ONLY METHOD FOR CREATING A RECORD OF OURSELVES WAS TO PAINT SOMETHING ON THE WALL OF A CAVE.
CH-KLK
BUT NOW, WITH LITTLE MORE THAN A THOUGHT, I CAN CAPTURE THIS MOMENT FOREVER. IN FACT, I CAN SEND IT ANYWHERE IN THE WORLD!
TO THE CAVEMAN, WHAT I JUST DID WOULD BE IMPOSSIBLE. THE ACT OF A GOD.
NOW, IT'S THE ACT OF A CHILD. THE ONLY DIFFERENCE...
...IS... WELL, YOU KNOW.
SCIENCE.

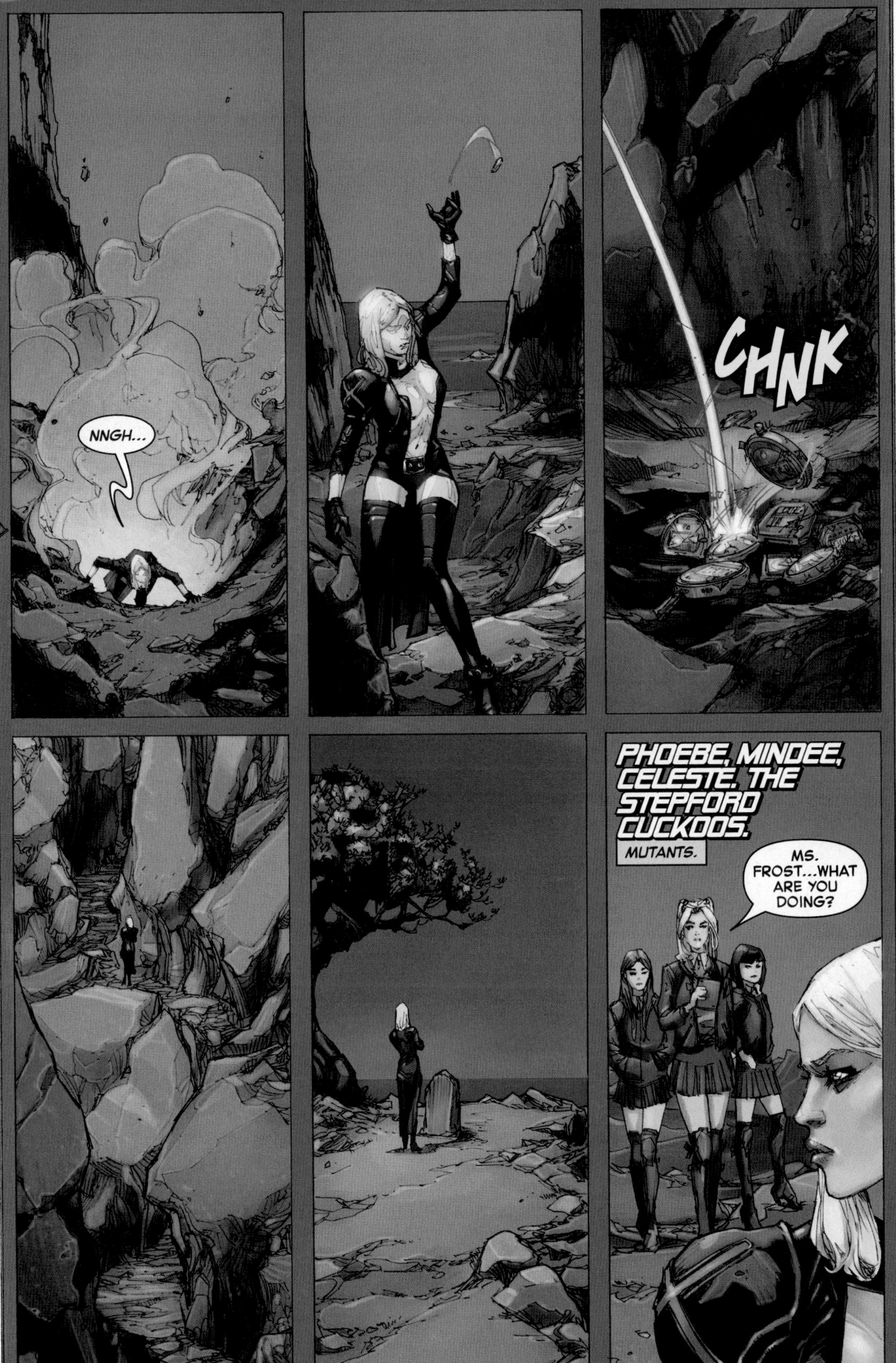
NNGH...
CHNK
PHOEBE, MINDEE, CELESTE. THE STEPFORD CUCKOOS.
MUTANTS.
MS. FROST...WHAT ARE YOU DOING?

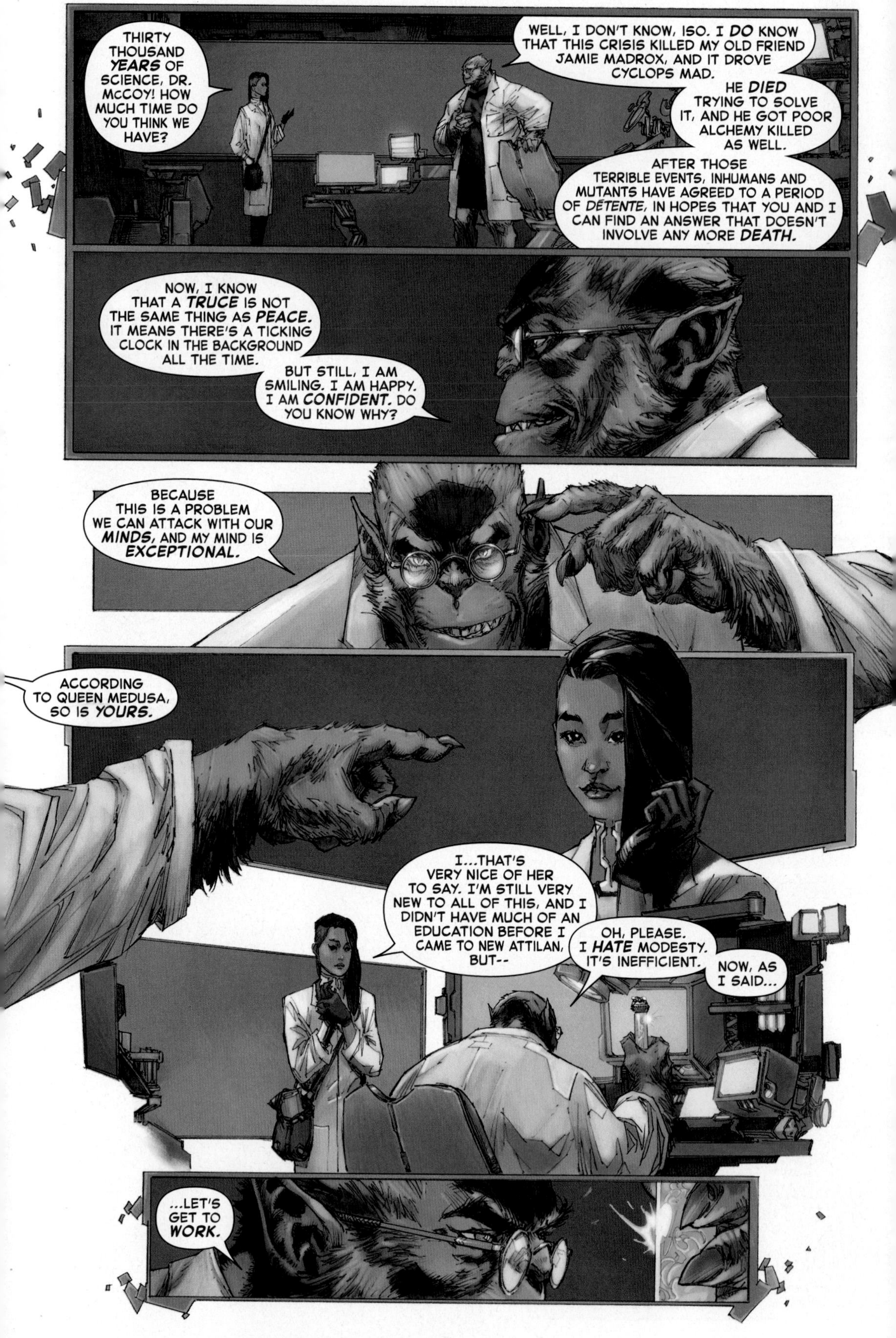
THIRTY THOUSAND YEARS OF SCIENCE, DR. McCOY! HOW MUCH TIME DO YOU THINK WE HAVE?
WELL, I DON'T KNOW, ISO. I DO KNOW THAT THIS CRISIS KILLED MY OLD FRIEND JAMIE MADROX, AND IT DROVE CYCLOPS MAD.
HE DIED TRYING TO SOLVE IT, AND HE GOT POOR ALCHEMY KILLED AS WELL.
AFTER THOSE TERRIBLE EVENTS, INHUMANS AND MUTANTS HAVE AGREED TO A PERIOD OF DÉTENTE, IN HOPES THAT YOU AND I CAN FIND AN ANSWER THAT DOESN'T INVOLVE ANY MORE DEATH.
NOW, I KNOW THAT A TRUCE IS NOT THE SAME THING AS PEACE. IT MEANS THERE'S A TICKING CLOCK IN THE BACKGROUND ALL THE TIME.
BUT STILL, I AM SMILING. I AM HAPPY. I AM CONFIDENT. DO YOU KNOW WHY?
BECAUSE THIS IS A PROBLEM WE CAN ATTACK WITH OUR MINDS, AND MY MIND IS EXCEPTIONAL.
ACCORDING TO QUEEN MEDUSA, SO IS YOURS.
I...THAT'S VERY NICE OF HER TO SAY. I'M STILL VERY NEW TO ALL OF THIS, AND I DIDN'T HAVE MUCH OF AN EDUCATION BEFORE I CAME TO NEW ATTILAN, BUT--
OH, PLEASE. I HATE MODESTY. IT'S INEFFICIENT.
NOW, AS I SAID...
...LET'S GET TO WORK.

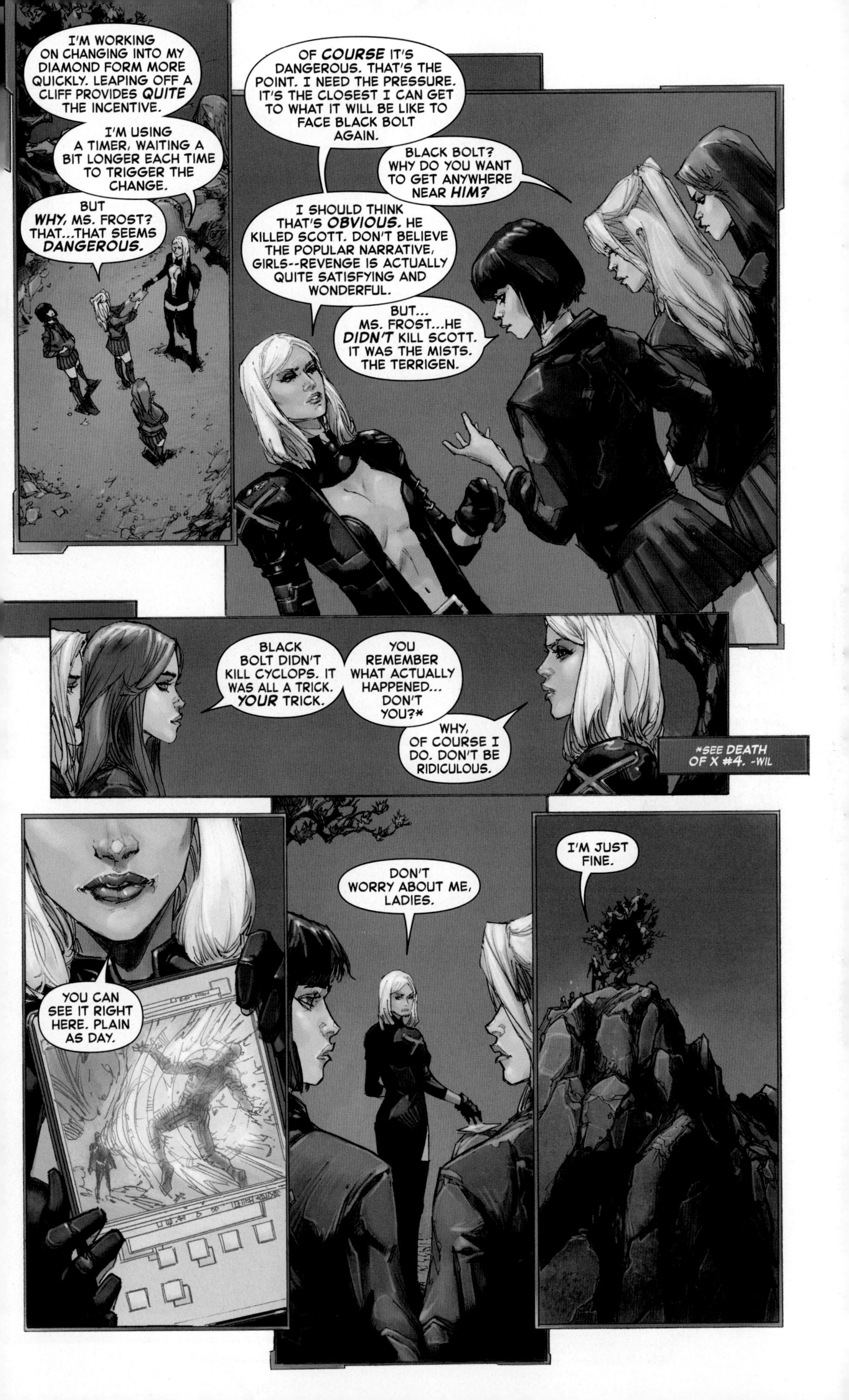
I'M WORKING ON CHANGING INTO MY DIAMOND FORM MORE QUICKLY. LEAPING OFF A CLIFF PROVIDES QUITE THE INCENTIVE.
I'M USING A TIMER, WAITING A BIT LONGER EACH TIME TO TRIGGER THE CHANGE.
BUT WHY, MS. FROST? THAT...THAT SEEMS DANGEROUS.
OF COURSE IT'S DANGEROUS. THAT'S THE POINT. I NEED THE PRESSURE. IT'S THE CLOSEST I CAN GET TO WHAT IT WILL BE LIKE TO FACE BLACK BOLT AGAIN.
BLACK BOLT? WHY DO YOU WANT TO GET ANYWHERE NEAR HIM?
I SHOULD THINK THAT'S OBVIOUS. HE KILLED SCOTT. DON'T BELIEVE THE POPULAR NARRATIVE, GIRLS--REVENGE IS ACTUALLY QUITE SATISFYING AND WONDERFUL.
BUT... MS. FROST...HE DIDN'T KILL SCOTT. IT WAS THE MISTS. THE TERRIGEN.
BLACK BOLT DIDN'T KILL CYCLOPS. IT WAS ALL A TRICK. YOUR TRICK.
YOU REMEMBER WHAT ACTUALLY HAPPENED... DON'T YOU?*
WHY, OF COURSE I DO. DON'T BE RIDICULOUS.
*SEE DEATH OF X #4. -WIL
YOU CAN SEE IT RIGHT HERE. PLAIN AS DAY.
DON'T WORRY ABOUT ME, LADIES.
I'M JUST FINE.

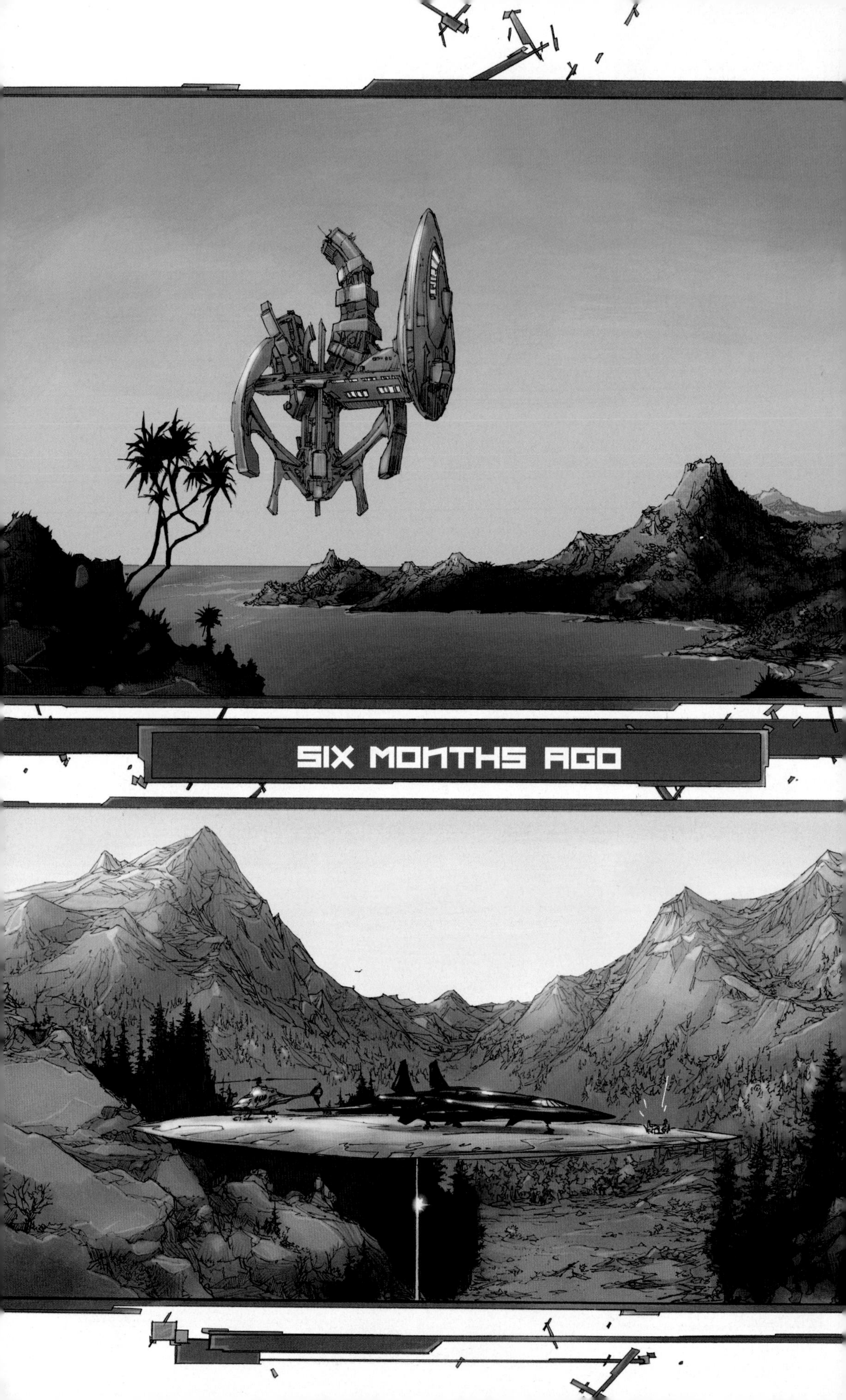
SIX MONTHS AGO

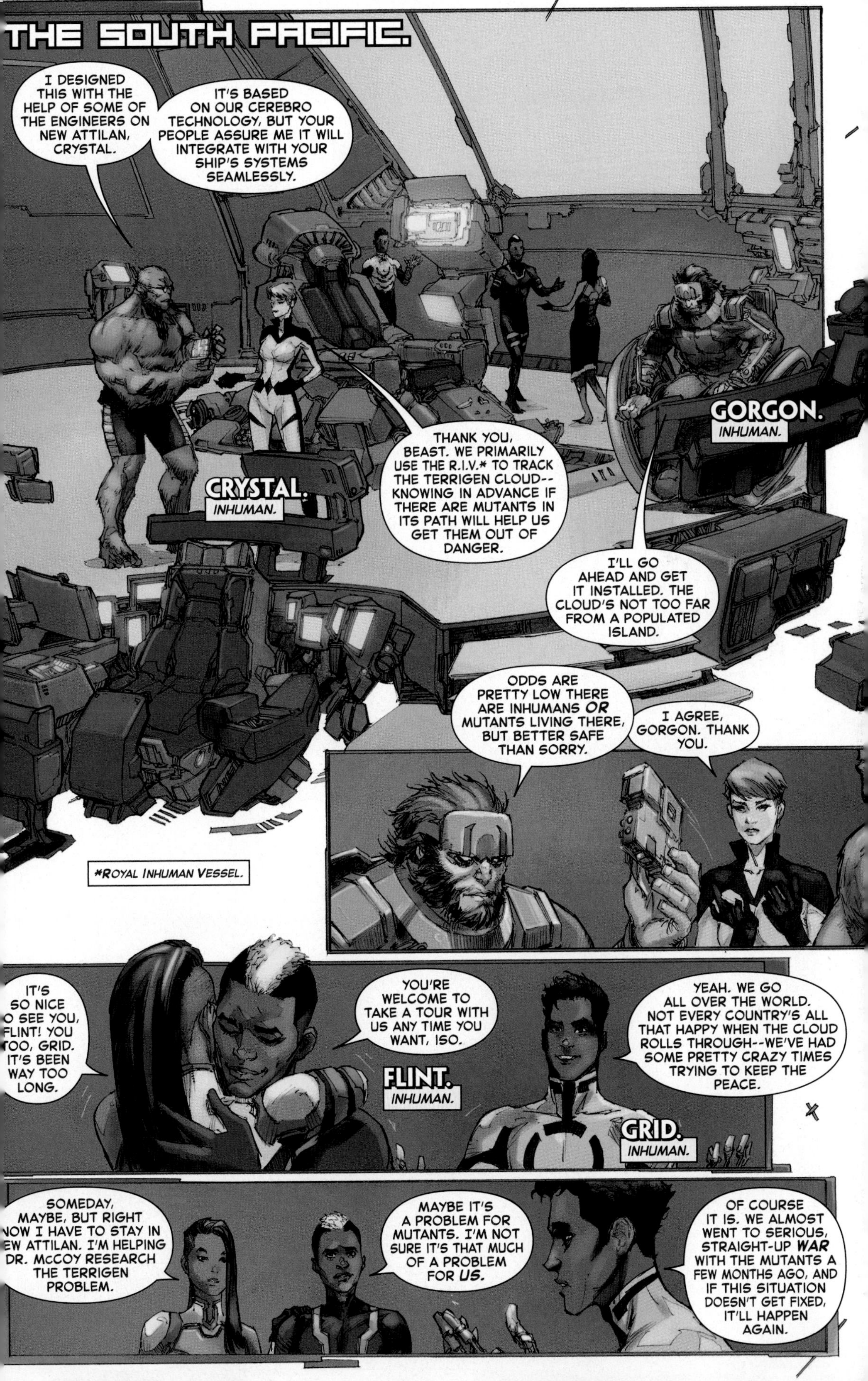

THE SOUTH PACIFIC.
I DESIGNED THIS WITH THE HELP OF SOME OF THE ENGINEERS ON NEW ATTILAN, CRYSTAL.
IT'S BASED ON OUR CEREBRO TECHNOLOGY, BUT YOUR PEOPLE ASSURE ME IT WILL INTEGRATE WITH YOUR SHIP'S SYSTEMS SEAMLESSLY.
CRYSTAL. INHUMAN.
THANK YOU, BEAST. WE PRIMARILY USE THE R.I.V.* TO TRACK THE TERRIGEN CLOUD--KNOWING IN ADVANCE IF THERE ARE MUTANTS IN ITS PATH WILL HELP US GET THEM OUT OF DANGER.
GORGON. INHUMAN.
I'LL GO AHEAD AND GET IT INSTALLED. THE CLOUD'S NOT TOO FAR FROM A POPULATED ISLAND.
*ROYAL INHUMAN VESSEL.
ODDS ARE PRETTY LOW THERE ARE INHUMANS OR MUTANTS LIVING THERE, BUT BETTER SAFE THAN SORRY.
I AGREE, GORGON. THANK YOU.
IT'S SO NICE O SEE YOU, FLINT! YOU TOO, GRID. IT'S BEEN WAY TOO LONG.
YOU'RE WELCOME TO TAKE A TOUR WITH US ANY TIME YOU WANT, ISO.
FLINT. INHUMAN.
YEAH. WE GO ALL OVER THE WORLD. NOT EVERY COUNTRY'S ALL THAT HAPPY WHEN THE CLOUD ROLLS THROUGH--WE'VE HAD SOME PRETTY CRAZY TIMES TRYING TO KEEP THE PEACE.
GRID. INHUMAN.
SOMEDAY, MAYBE, BUT RIGHT NOW I HAVE TO STAY IN EW ATTILAN. I'M HELPING DR. McCOY RESEARCH THE TERRIGEN PROBLEM.
MAYBE IT'S A PROBLEM FOR MUTANTS. I'M NOT SURE IT'S THAT MUCH OF A PROBLEM FOR US.
OF COURSE IT IS. WE ALMOST WENT TO SERIOUS, STRAIGHT-UP WAR WITH THE MUTANTS A FEW MONTHS AGO, AND IF THIS SITUATION DOESN'T GET FIXED, IT'LL HAPPEN AGAIN.

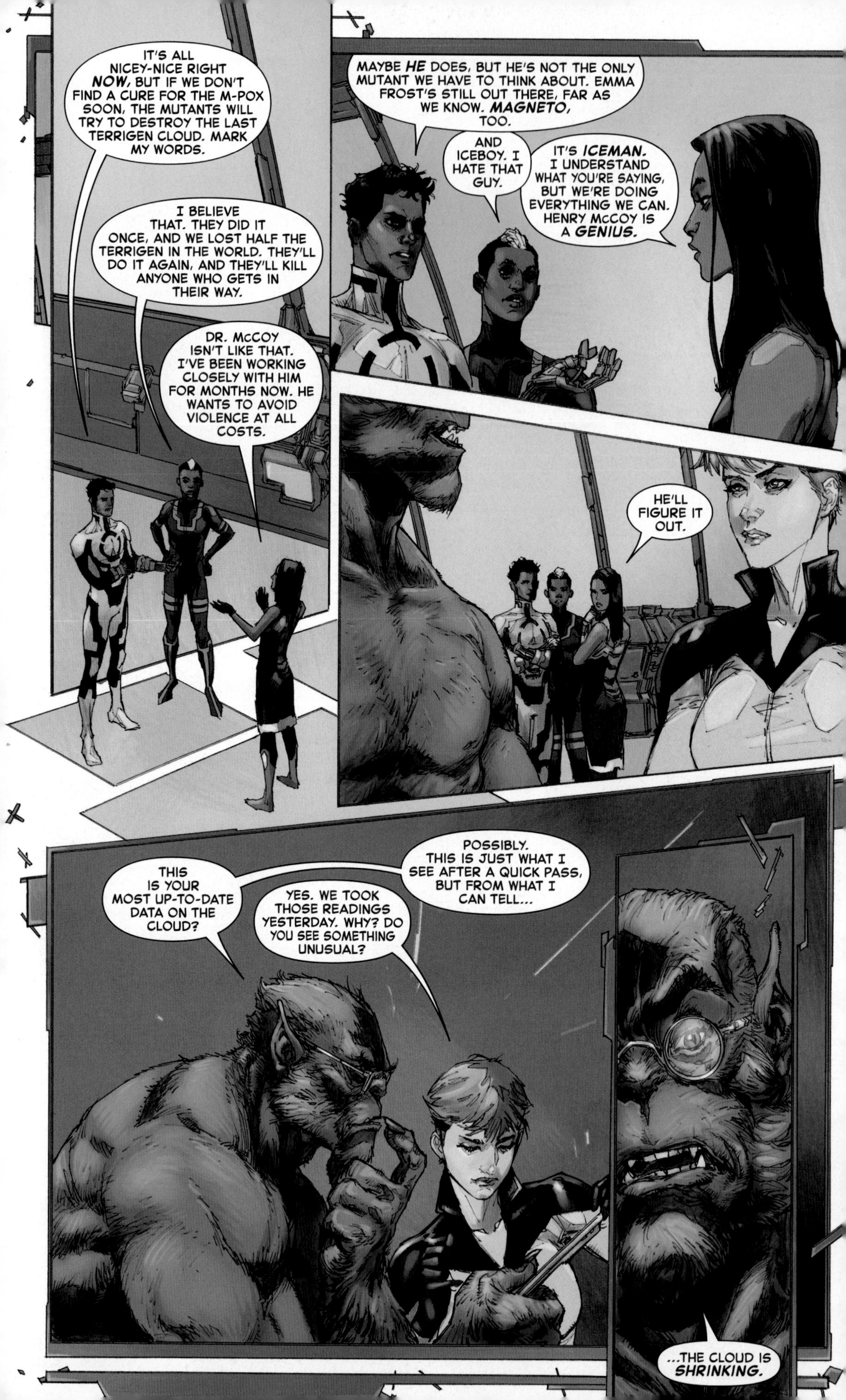

IT'S ALL NICEY-NICE RIGHT NOW, BUT IF WE DON'T FIND A CURE FOR THE M-POX SOON, THE MUTANTS WILL TRY TO DESTROY THE LAST TERRIGEN CLOUD. MARK MY WORDS.
I BELIEVE THAT. THEY DID IT ONCE, AND WE LOST HALF THE TERRIGEN IN THE WORLD. THEY'LL DO IT AGAIN, AND THEY'LL KILL ANYONE WHO GETS IN THEIR WAY.
DR. McCOY ISN'T LIKE THAT. I'VE BEEN WORKING CLOSELY WITH HIM FOR MONTHS NOW. HE WANTS TO AVOID VIOLENCE AT ALL COSTS.
MAYBE HE DOES, BUT HE'S NOT THE ONLY MUTANT WE HAVE TO THINK ABOUT. EMMA FROST'S STILL OUT THERE, FAR AS WE KNOW. MAGNETO, TOO.
AND ICEBOY. I HATE THAT GUY.
IT'S ICEMAN. I UNDERSTAND WHAT YOU'RE SAYING, BUT WE'RE DOING EVERYTHING WE CAN. HENRY McCOY IS A GENIUS.
HE'LL FIGURE IT OUT.
THIS IS YOUR MOST UP-TO-DATE DATA ON THE CLOUD?
YES. WE TOOK THOSE READINGS YESTERDAY. WHY? DO YOU SEE SOMETHING UNUSUAL?
POSSIBLY. THIS IS JUST WHAT I SEE AFTER A QUICK PASS, BUT FROM WHAT I CAN TELL...
...THE CLOUD IS SHRINKING.

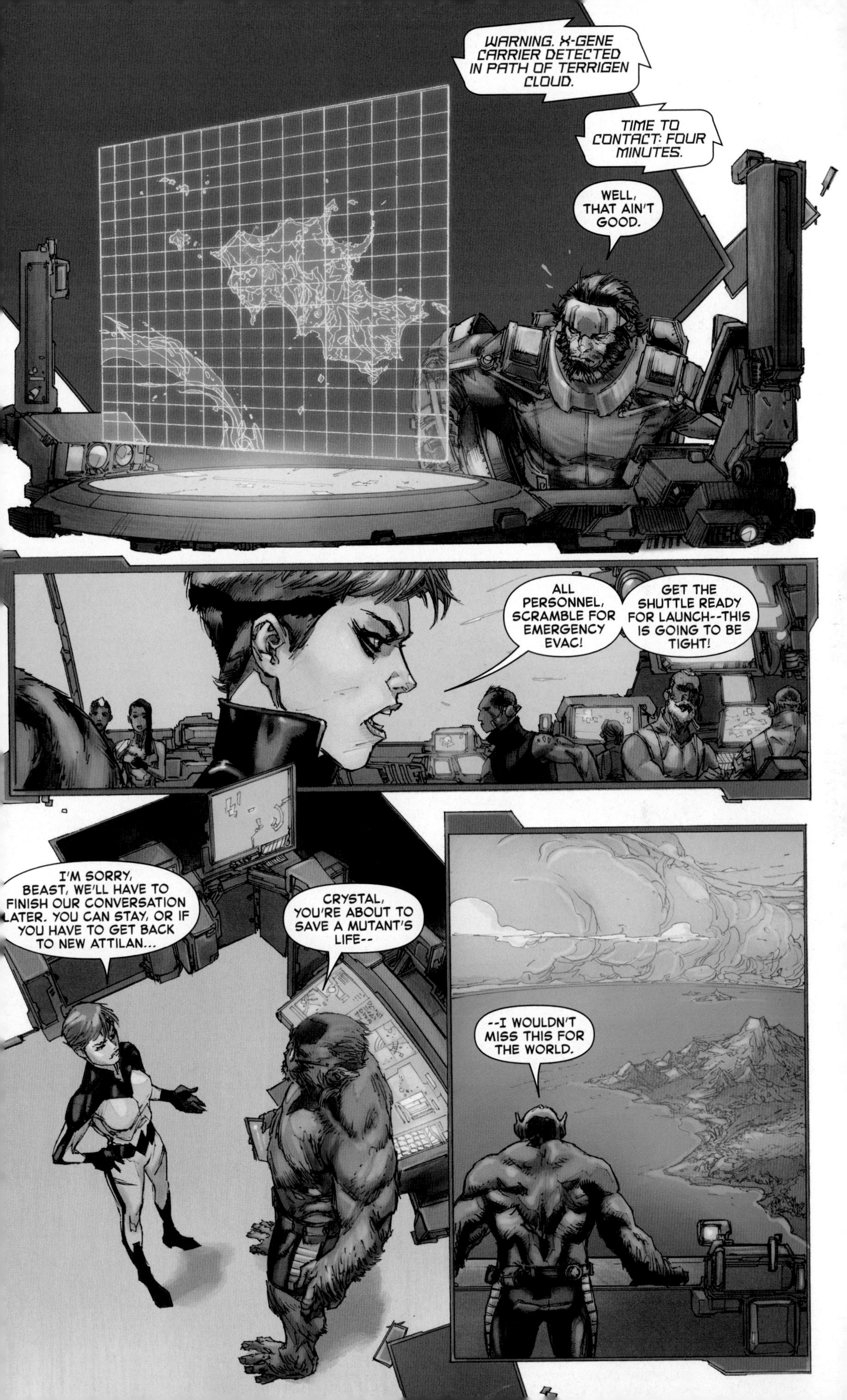
WARNING. X-GENE CARRIER DETECTED IN PATH OF TERRIGEN CLOUD.
TIME TO CONTACT: FOUR MINUTES.
WELL, THAT AIN'T GOOD.
ALL PERSONNEL, SCRAMBLE FOR EMERGENCY EVAC!
GET THE SHUTTLE READY FOR LAUNCH--THIS IS GOING TO BE TIGHT!
I'M SORRY, BEAST, WE'LL HAVE TO FINISH OUR CONVERSATION LATER. YOU CAN STAY, OR IF YOU HAVE TO GET BACK TO NEW ATTILAN...
CRYSTAL, YOU'RE ABOUT TO SAVE A MUTANT'S LIFE--
--I WOULDN'T MISS THIS FOR THE WORLD.

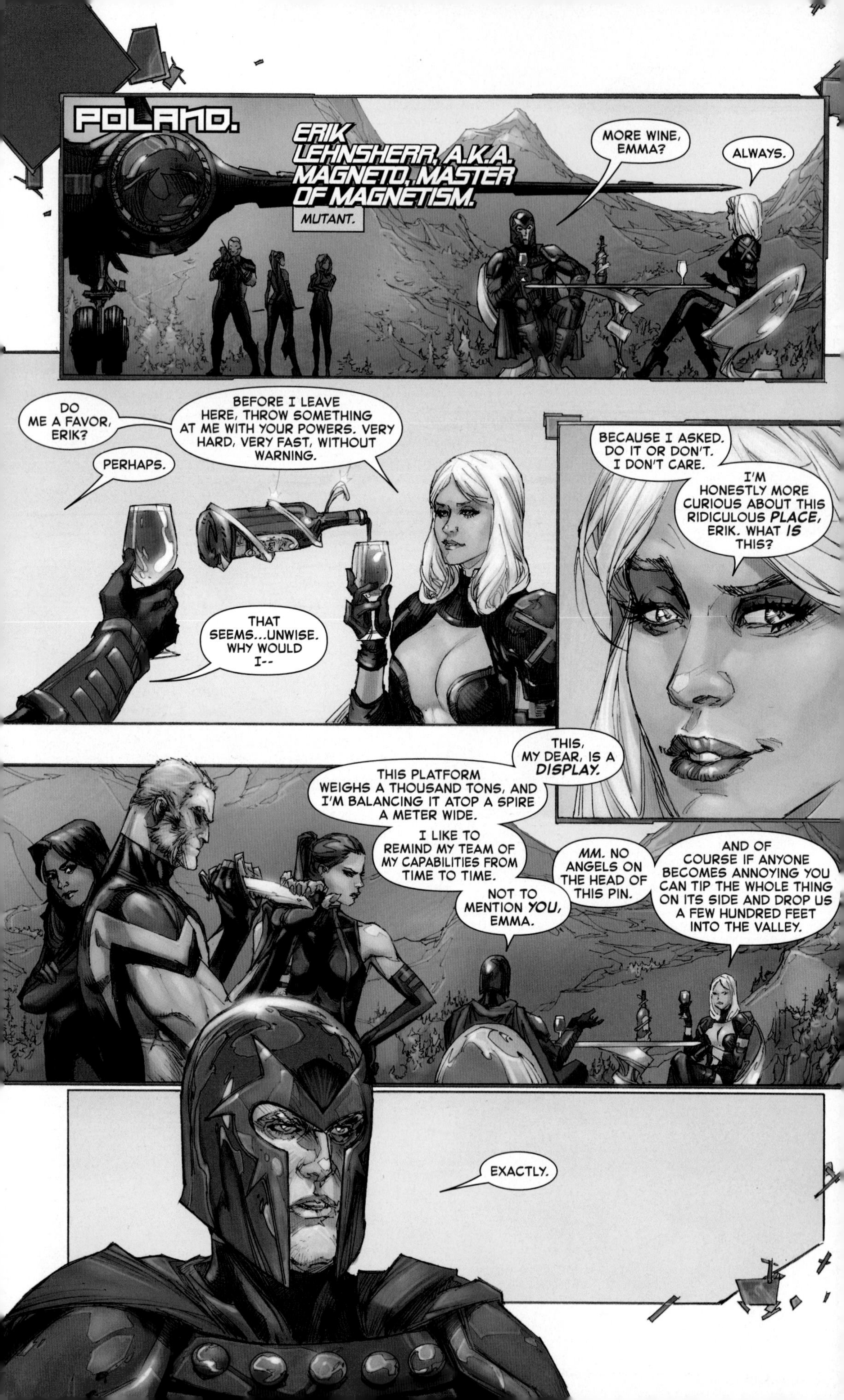
POLAND.
ERIK LEHNSHERR, A.K.A. MAGNETO, MASTER OF MAGNETISM.
MUTANT.
MORE WINE, EMMA?
ALWAYS.
DO ME A FAVOR, ERIK?
BEFORE I LEAVE HERE, THROW SOMETHING AT ME WITH YOUR POWERS. VERY HARD, VERY FAST, WITHOUT WARNING.
PERHAPS.
THAT SEEMS...UNWISE. WHY WOULD I--
BECAUSE I ASKED. DO IT OR DON'T. I DON'T CARE.
I'M HONESTLY MORE CURIOUS ABOUT THIS RIDICULOUS PLACE, ERIK. WHAT IS THIS?
THIS, MY DEAR, IS A DISPLAY.
THIS PLATFORM WEIGHS A THOUSAND TONS, AND I'M BALANCING IT ATOP A SPIRE A METER WIDE.
I LIKE TO REMIND MY TEAM OF MY CAPABILITIES FROM TIME TO TIME.
NOT TO MENTION YOU, EMMA.
MM. NO ANGELS ON THE HEAD OF THIS PIN.
AND OF COURSE IF ANYONE BECOMES ANNOYING YOU CAN TIP THE WHOLE THING ON ITS SIDE AND DROP US A FEW HUNDRED FEET INTO THE VALLEY.
EXACTLY.

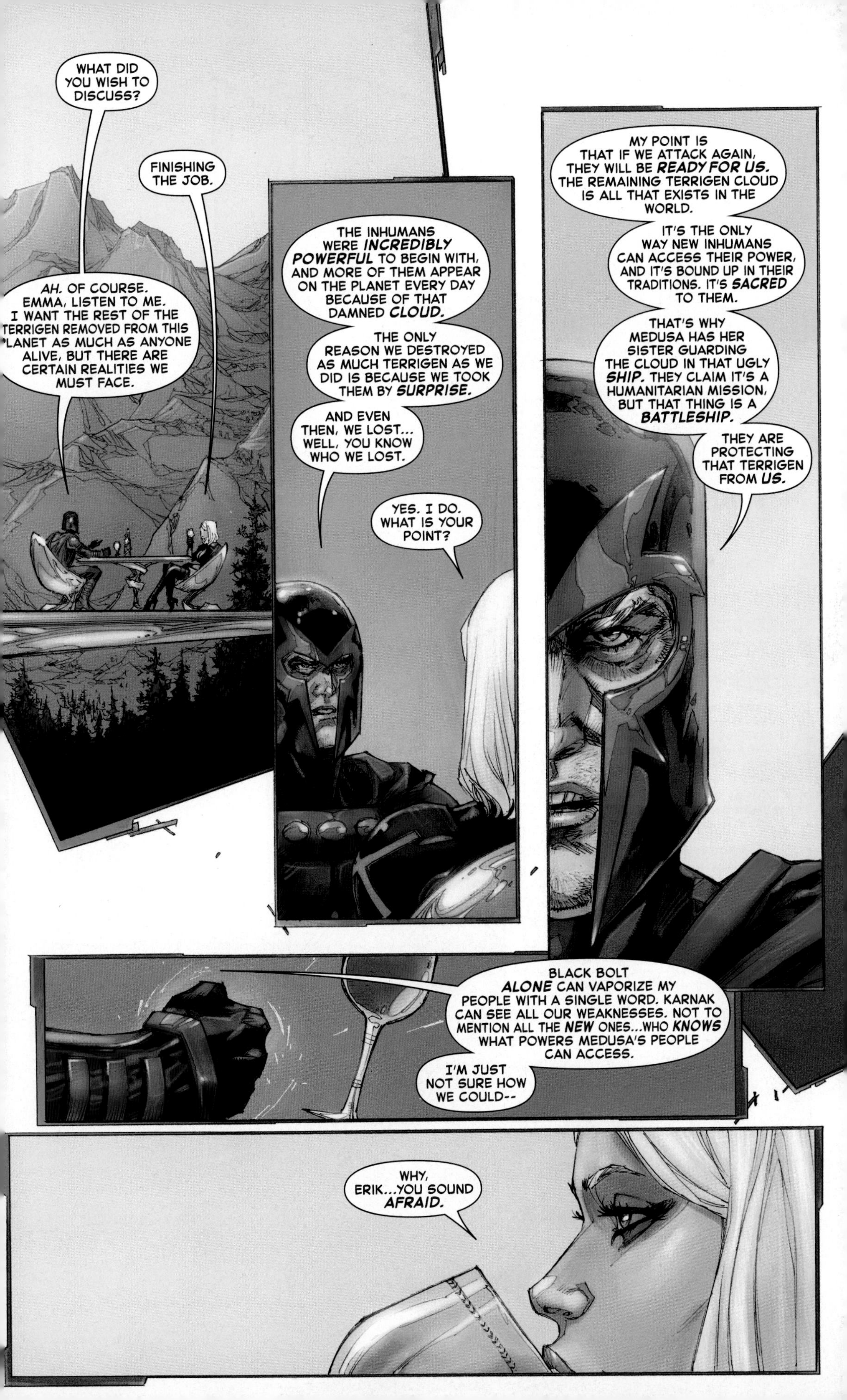
WHAT DID YOU WISH TO DISCUSS?
FINISHING THE JOB.
AH. OF COURSE. EMMA, LISTEN TO ME. I WANT THE REST OF THE TERRIGEN REMOVED FROM THIS PLANET AS MUCH AS ANYONE ALIVE, BUT THERE ARE CERTAIN REALITIES WE MUST FACE.
THE INHUMANS WERE INCREDIBLY POWERFUL TO BEGIN WITH, AND MORE OF THEM APPEAR ON THE PLANET EVERY DAY BECAUSE OF THAT DAMNED CLOUD.
THE ONLY REASON WE DESTROYED AS MUCH TERRIGEN AS WE DID IS BECAUSE WE TOOK THEM BY SURPRISE.
AND EVEN THEN, WE LOST... WELL, YOU KNOW WHO WE LOST.
YES. I DO. WHAT IS YOUR POINT?
MY POINT IS THAT IF WE ATTACK AGAIN, THEY WILL BE READY FOR US. THE REMAINING TERRIGEN CLOUD IS ALL THAT EXISTS IN THE WORLD.
IT'S THE ONLY WAY NEW INHUMANS CAN ACCESS THEIR POWER, AND IT'S BOUND UP IN THEIR TRADITIONS. IT'S SACRED TO THEM.
THAT'S WHY MEDUSA HAS HER SISTER GUARDING THE CLOUD IN THAT UGLY SHIP. THEY CLAIM IT'S A HUMANITARIAN MISSION, BUT THAT THING IS A BATTLESHIP.
THEY ARE PROTECTING THAT TERRIGEN FROM US.
BLACK BOLT ALONE CAN VAPORIZE MY PEOPLE WITH A SINGLE WORD. KARNAK CAN SEE ALL OUR WEAKNESSES. NOT TO MENTION ALL THE NEW ONES...WHO KNOWS WHAT POWERS MEDUSA'S PEOPLE CAN ACCESS.
I'M JUST NOT SURE HOW WE COULD--
WHY, ERIK...YOU SOUND AFRAID.

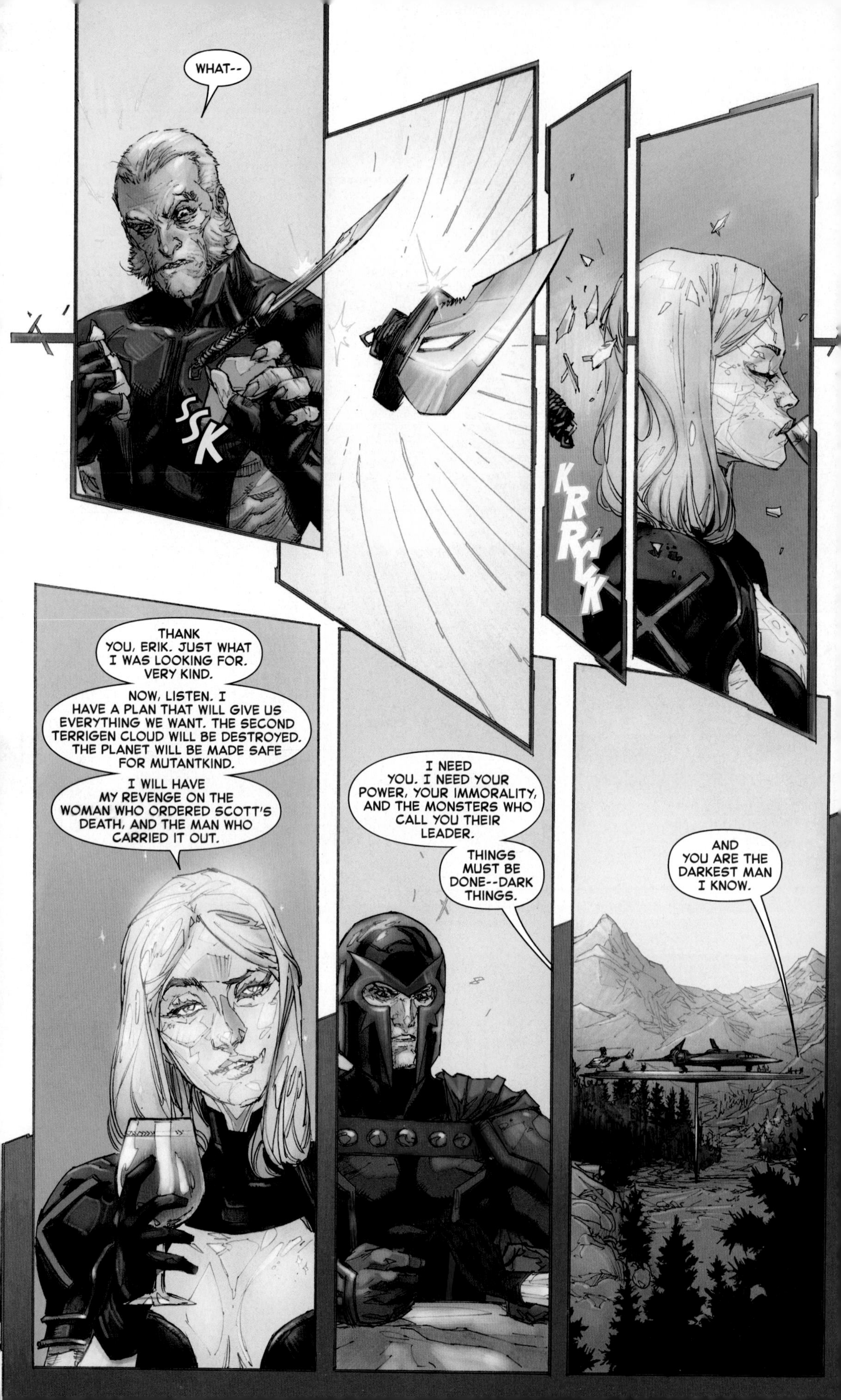
WHAT--
SSK
KRRK
THANK YOU, ERIK. JUST WHAT I WAS LOOKING FOR. VERY KIND.
NOW, LISTEN. I HAVE A PLAN THAT WILL GIVE US EVERYTHING WE WANT. THE SECOND TERRIGEN CLOUD WILL BE DESTROYED. THE PLANET WILL BE MADE SAFE FOR MUTANTKIND.
I WILL HAVE MY REVENGE ON THE WOMAN WHO ORDERED SCOTT'S DEATH, AND THE MAN WHO CARRIED IT OUT.
I NEED YOU. I NEED YOUR POWER, YOUR IMMORALITY, AND THE MONSTERS WHO CALL YOU THEIR LEADER.
THINGS MUST BE DONE--DARK THINGS.
AND YOU ARE THE DARKEST MAN I KNOW.

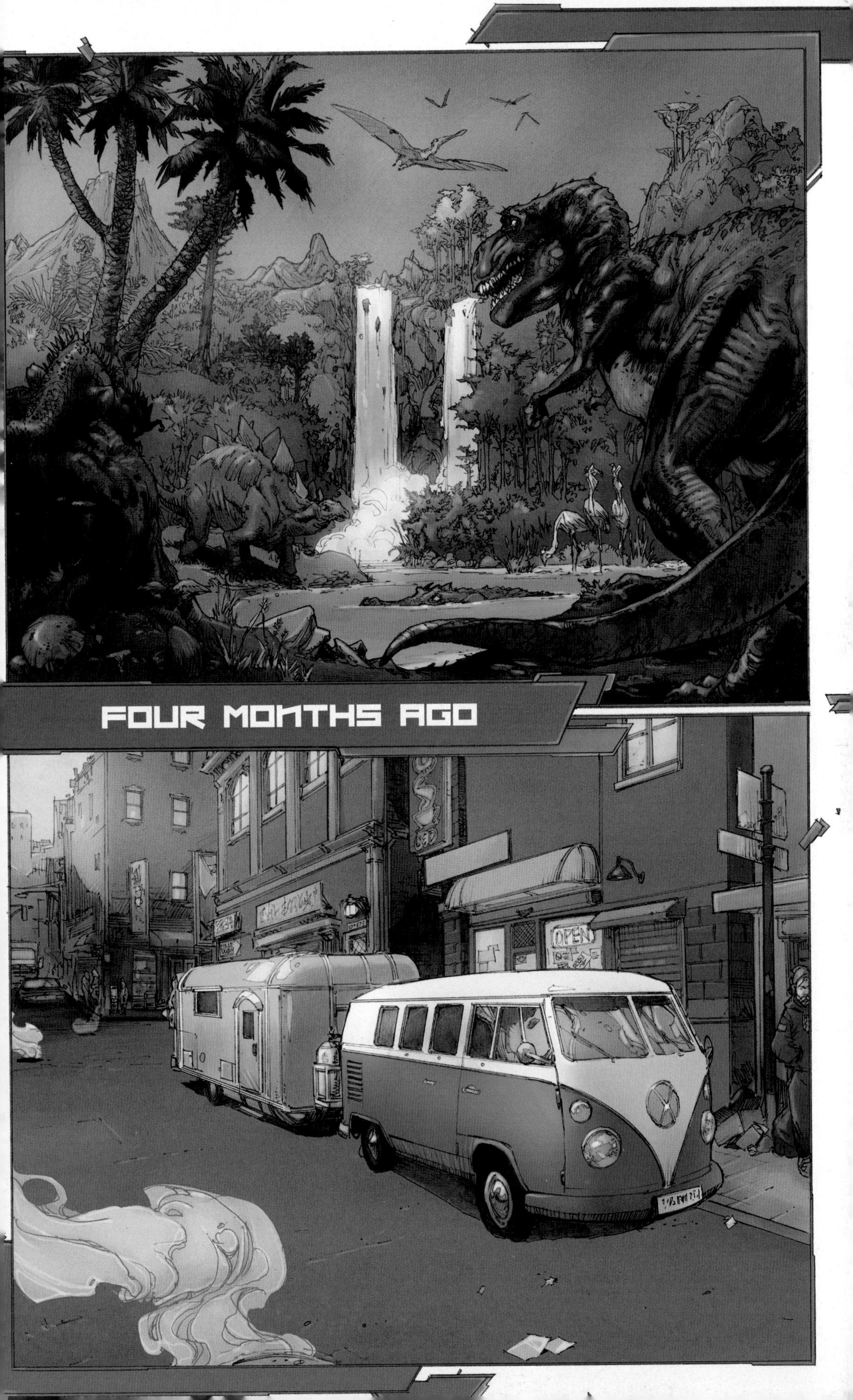
FOUR MONTHS AGO
OPEN

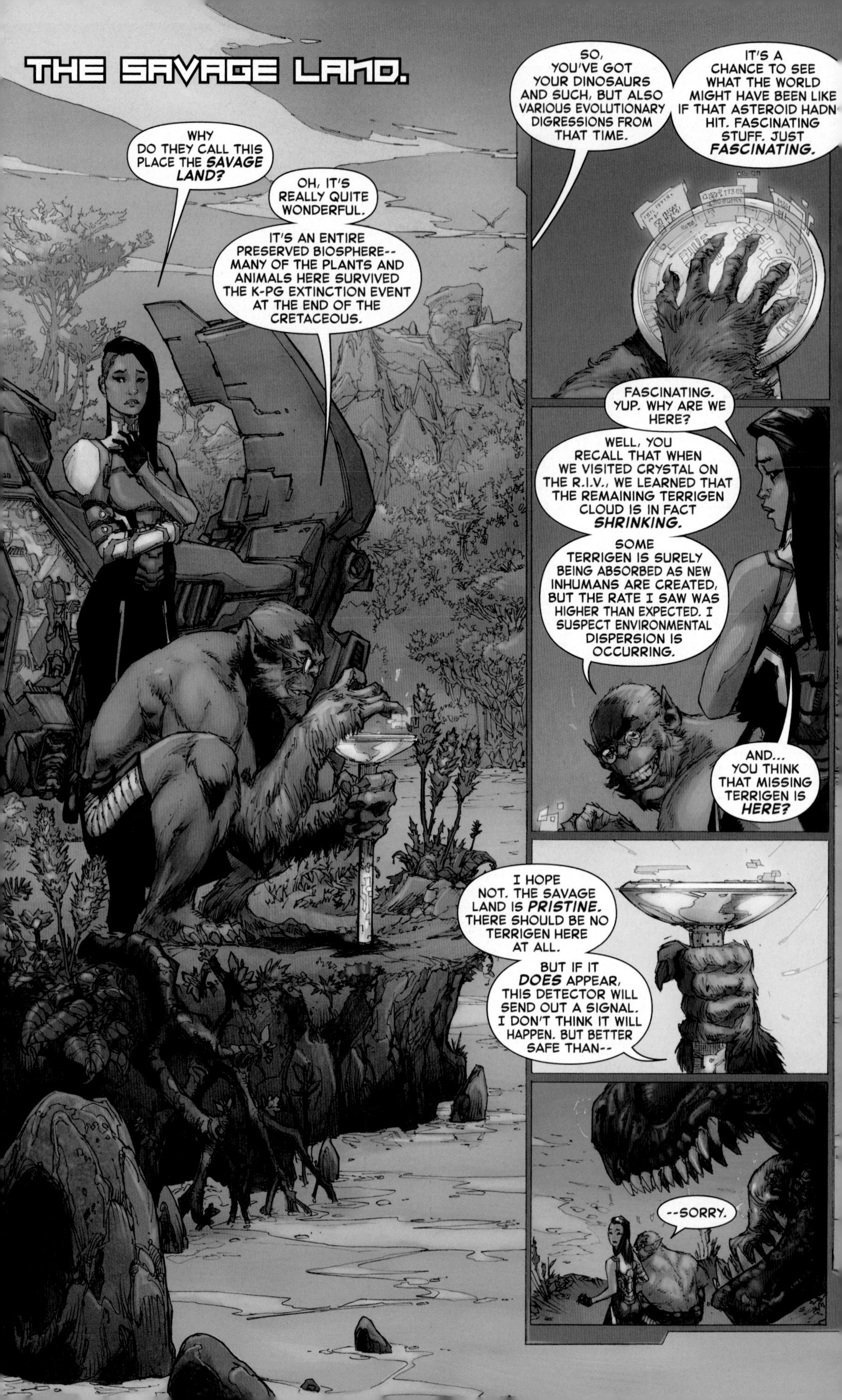

THE SAVAGE LAND.
WHY DO THEY CALL THIS PLACE THE SAVAGE LAND?
OH, IT'S REALLY QUITE WONDERFUL.
IT'S AN ENTIRE PRESERVED BIOSPHERE-- MANY OF THE PLANTS AND ANIMALS HERE SURVIVED THE K-PG EXTINCTION EVENT AT THE END OF THE CRETACEOUS.
SO, YOU'VE GOT YOUR DINOSAURS AND SUCH, BUT ALSO VARIOUS EVOLUTIONARY DIGRESSIONS FROM THAT TIME.
IT'S A CHANCE TO SEE WHAT THE WORLD MIGHT HAVE BEEN LIKE IF THAT ASTEROID HADN'T HIT. FASCINATING STUFF. JUST FASCINATING.
FASCINATING. YUP. WHY ARE WE HERE?
WELL, YOU RECALL THAT WHEN WE VISITED CRYSTAL ON THE R.I.V., WE LEARNED THAT THE REMAINING TERRIGEN CLOUD IS IN FACT SHRINKING.
SOME TERRIGEN IS SURELY BEING ABSORBED AS NEW INHUMANS ARE CREATED, BUT THE RATE I SAW WAS HIGHER THAN EXPECTED. I SUSPECT ENVIRONMENTAL DISPERSION IS OCCURRING.
AND... YOU THINK THAT MISSING TERRIGEN IS HERE?
I HOPE NOT. THE SAVAGE LAND IS PRISTINE. THERE SHOULD BE NO TERRIGEN HERE AT ALL.
BUT IF IT DOES APPEAR, THIS DETECTOR WILL SEND OUT A SIGNAL. I DON'T THINK IT WILL HAPPEN. BUT BETTER SAFE THAN--
--SORRY.

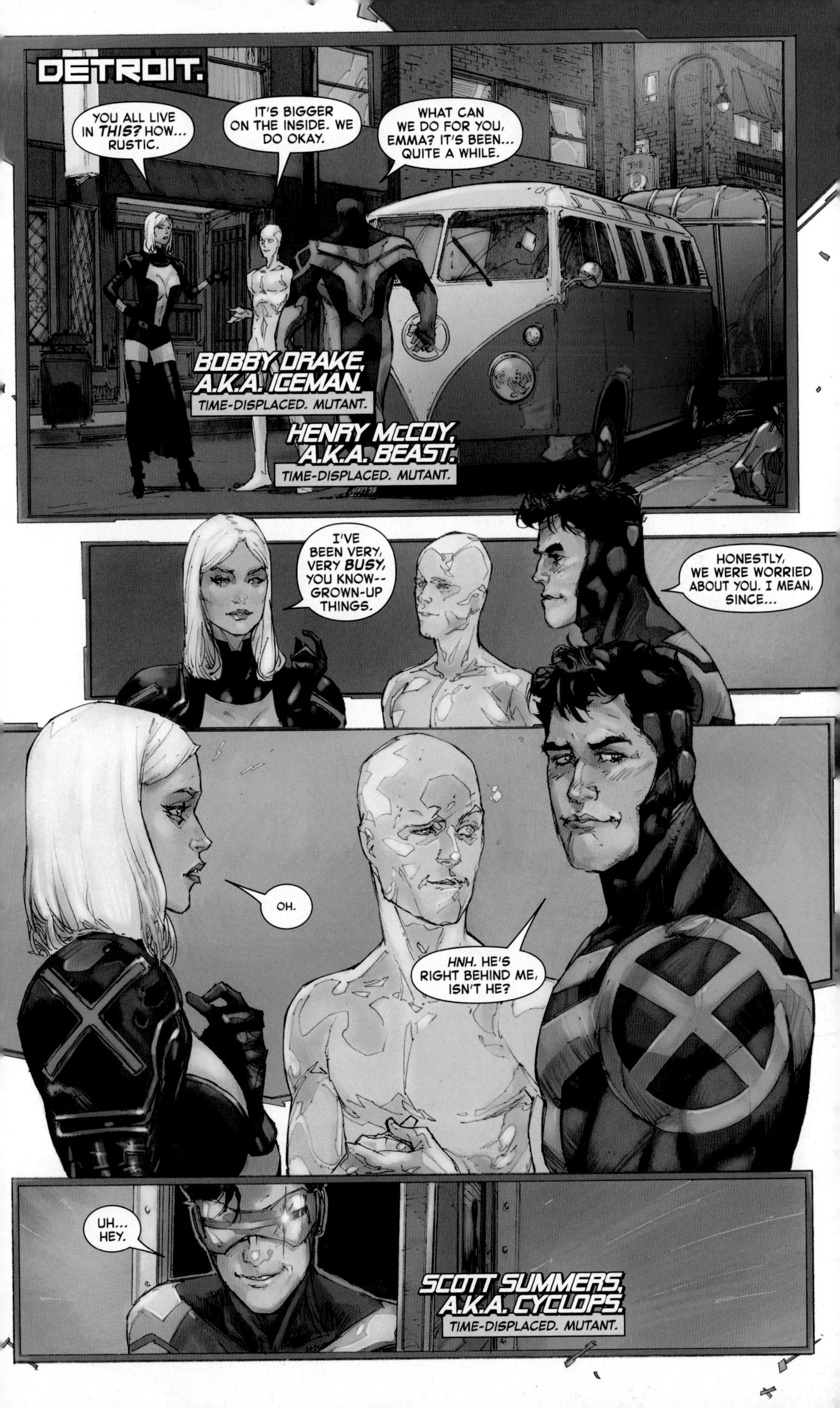
DETROIT.
YOU ALL LIVE IN THIS? HOW... RUSTIC.
IT'S BIGGER ON THE INSIDE. WE DO OKAY.
WHAT CAN WE DO FOR YOU, EMMA? IT'S BEEN... QUITE A WHILE.
BOBBY DRAKE, A.K.A. ICEMAN.
TIME-DISPLACED. MUTANT.
HENRY McCOY, A.K.A. BEAST.
TIME-DISPLACED. MUTANT.
I'VE BEEN VERY, VERY BUSY, YOU KNOW-- GROWN-UP THINGS.
HONESTLY, WE WERE WORRIED ABOUT YOU. I MEAN, SINCE...
OH.
HNH. HE'S RIGHT BEHIND ME, ISN'T HE?
UH... HEY.
SCOTT SUMMERS, A.K.A. CYCLOPS.
TIME-DISPLACED. MUTANT.

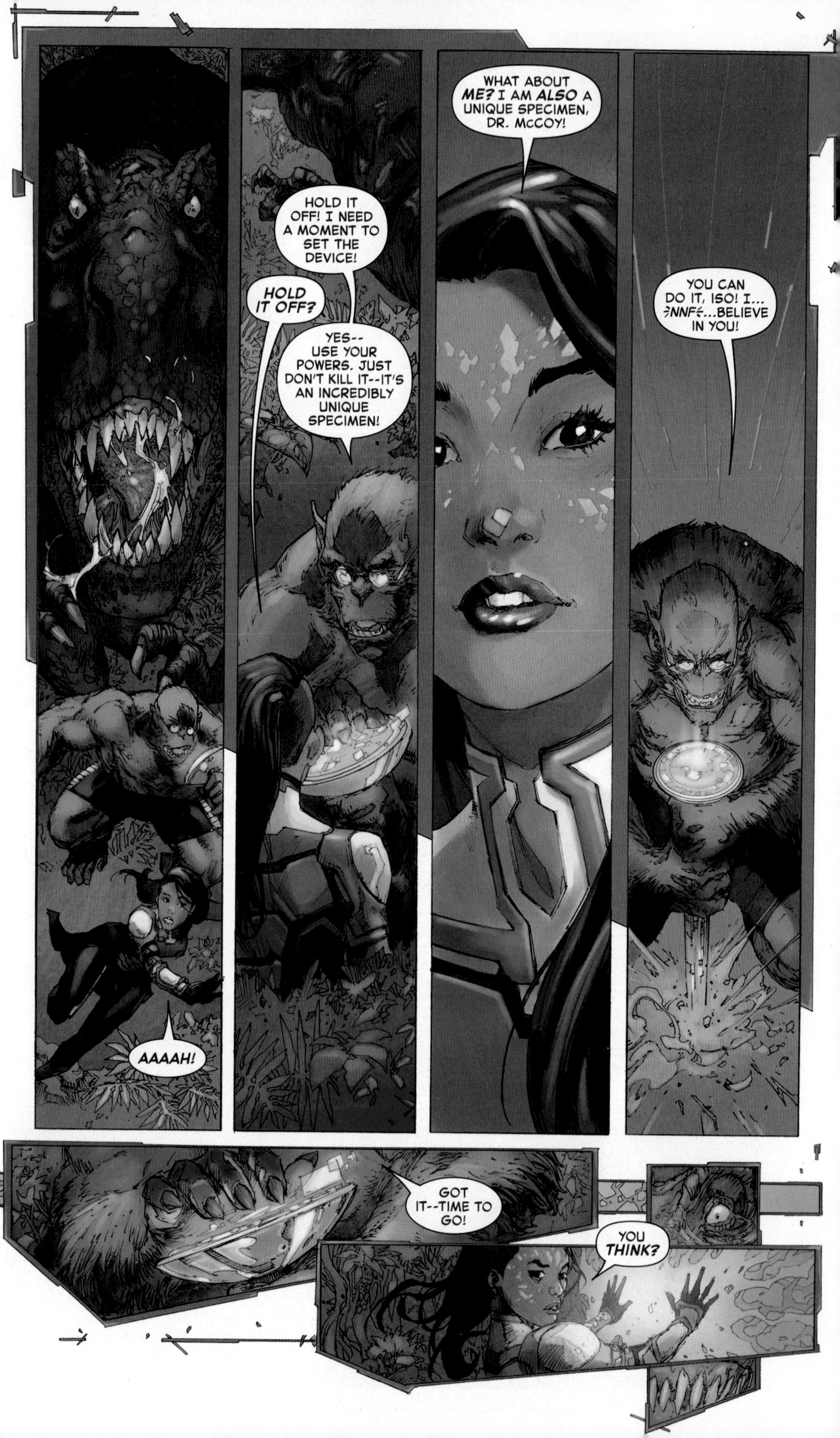

HOLD IT OFF! I NEED A MOMENT TO SET THE DEVICE!
HOLD IT OFF?
YES-- USE YOUR POWERS. JUST DON'T KILL IT--IT'S AN INCREDIBLY UNIQUE SPECIMEN!
AAAAH!
WHAT ABOUT ME? I AM ALSO A UNIQUE SPECIMEN, DR. McCOY!
YOU CAN DO IT, ISO! I... NNF... BELIEVE IN YOU!
GOT IT--TIME TO GO!
YOU THINK?

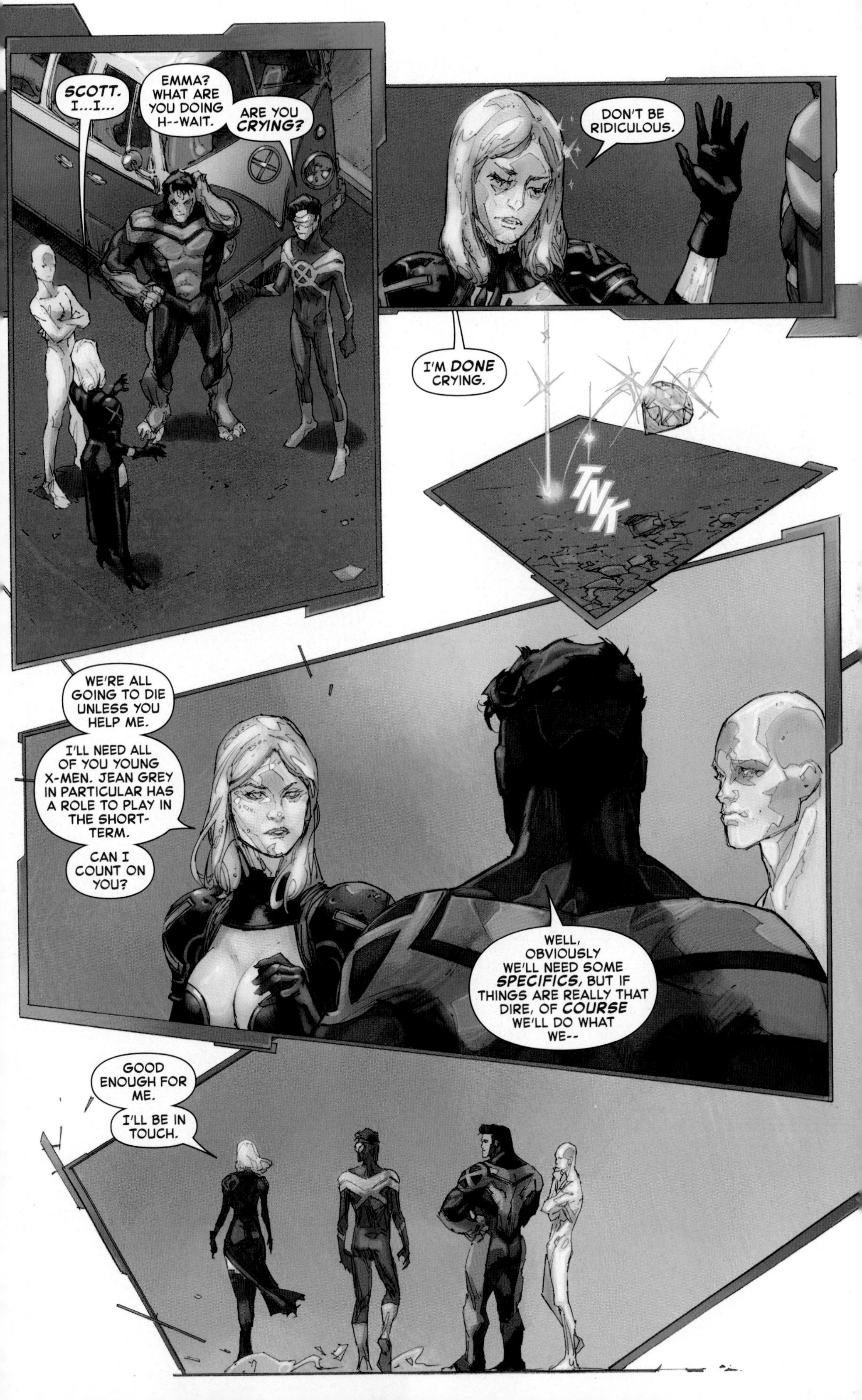
SCOTT. I...I...
EMMA? WHAT ARE YOU DOING H--WAIT.
ARE YOU CRYING?
DON'T BE RIDICULOUS.
I'M DONE CRYING.
TNK
WE'RE ALL GOING TO DIE UNLESS YOU HELP ME.
I'LL NEED ALL OF YOU YOUNG X-MEN. JEAN GREY IN PARTICULAR HAS A ROLE TO PLAY IN THE SHORT-TERM.
CAN I COUNT ON YOU?
WELL, OBVIOUSLY WE'LL NEED SOME SPECIFICS, BUT IF THINGS ARE REALLY THAT DIRE, OF COURSE WE'LL DO WHAT WE--
GOOD ENOUGH FOR ME.
I'LL BE IN TOUCH.

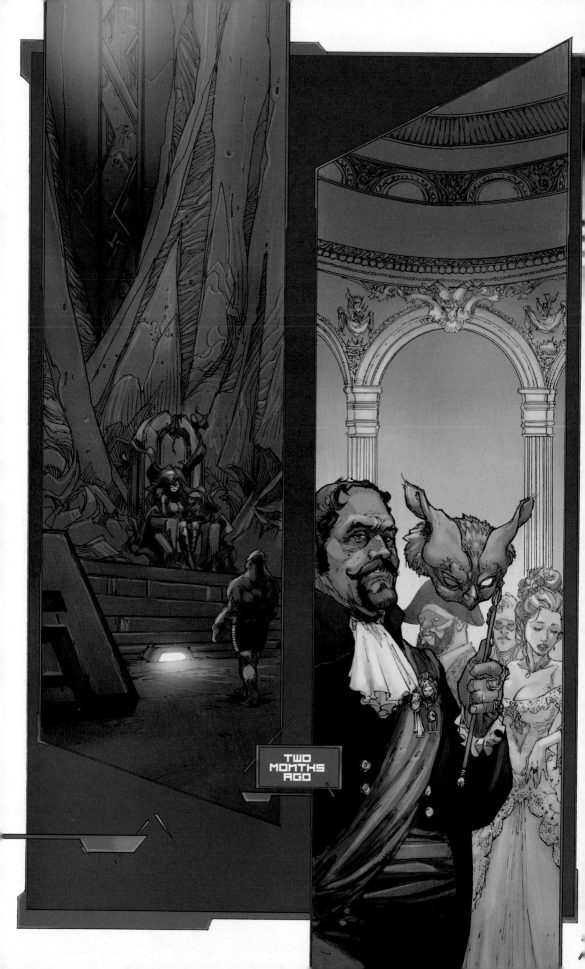

TWO
MONTHS
AGO

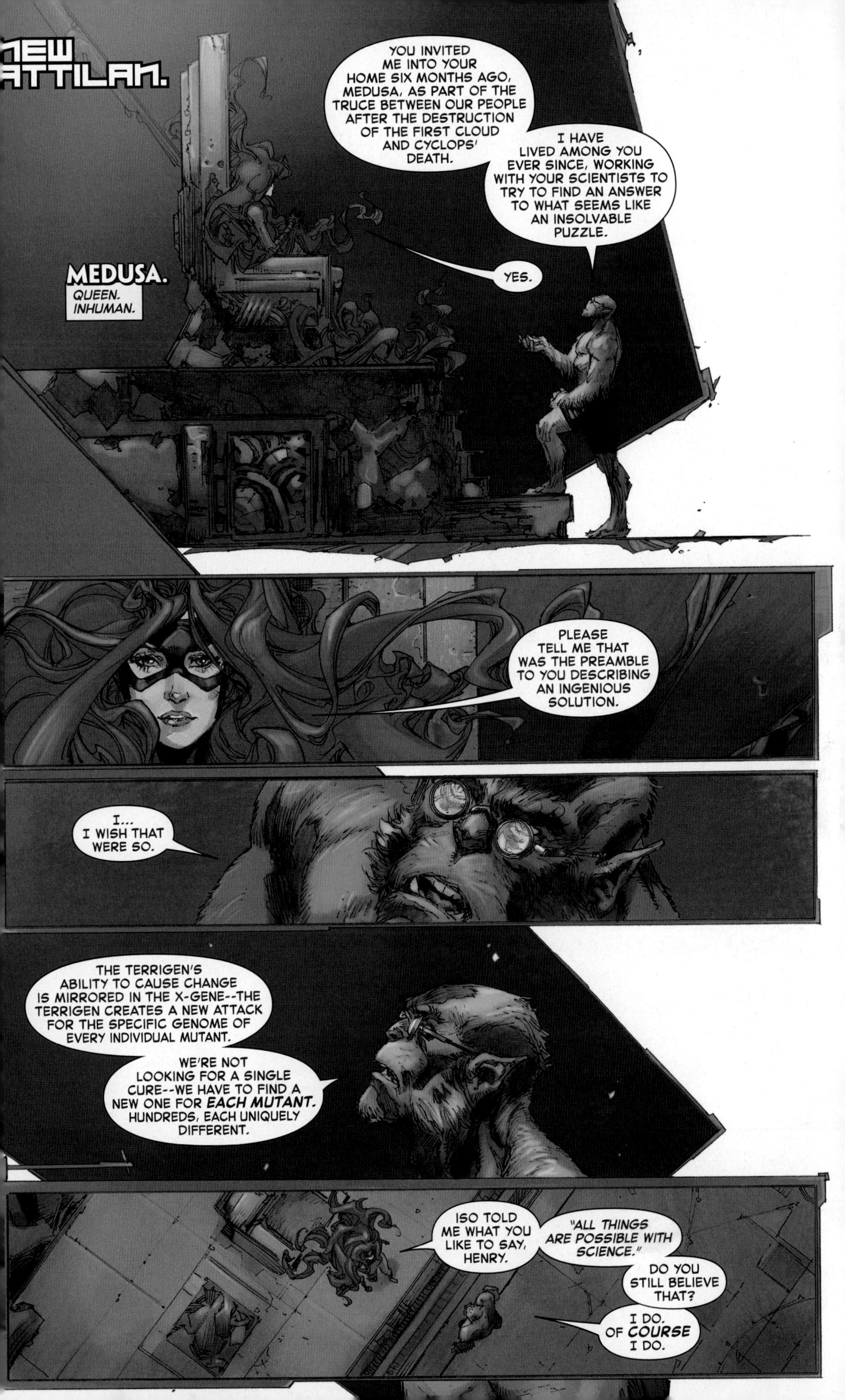
NEW ATTILAN.
MEDUSA.
QUEEN. INHUMAN.
YOU INVITED ME INTO YOUR HOME SIX MONTHS AGO, MEDUSA, AS PART OF THE TRUCE BETWEEN OUR PEOPLE AFTER THE DESTRUCTION OF THE FIRST CLOUD AND CYCLOPS' DEATH.
I HAVE LIVED AMONG YOU EVER SINCE, WORKING WITH YOUR SCIENTISTS TO TRY TO FIND AN ANSWER TO WHAT SEEMS LIKE AN INSOLVABLE PUZZLE.
YES.
PLEASE TELL ME THAT WAS THE PREAMBLE TO YOU DESCRIBING AN INGENIOUS SOLUTION.
I... I WISH THAT WERE SO.
THE TERRIGEN'S ABILITY TO CAUSE CHANGE IS MIRRORED IN THE X-GENE--THE TERRIGEN CREATES A NEW ATTACK FOR THE SPECIFIC GENOME OF EVERY INDIVIDUAL MUTANT.
WE'RE NOT LOOKING FOR A SINGLE CURE--WE HAVE TO FIND A NEW ONE FOR EACH MUTANT. HUNDREDS, EACH UNIQUELY DIFFERENT.
ISO TOLD ME WHAT YOU LIKE TO SAY, HENRY.
"ALL THINGS ARE POSSIBLE WITH SCIENCE."
DO YOU STILL BELIEVE THAT?
I DO. OF COURSE I DO.

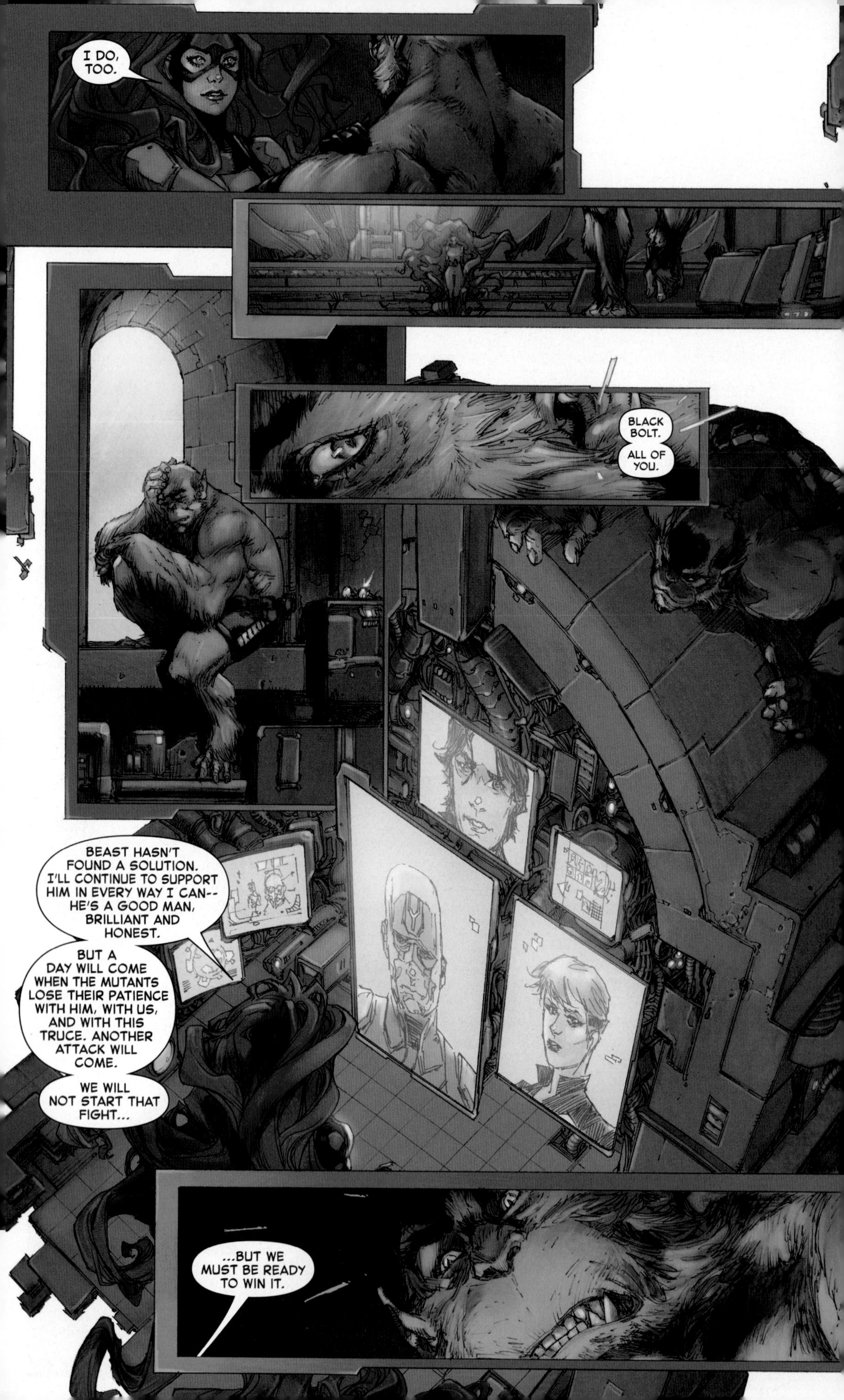
I DO, TOO.
BLACK BOLT.
ALL OF YOU.
BEAST HASN'T FOUND A SOLUTION. I'LL CONTINUE TO SUPPORT HIM IN EVERY WAY I CAN-- HE'S A GOOD MAN, BRILLIANT AND HONEST.
BUT A DAY WILL COME WHEN THE MUTANTS LOSE THEIR PATIENCE WITH HIM, WITH US, AND WITH THIS TRUCE. ANOTHER ATTACK WILL COME.
WE WILL NOT START THAT FIGHT...
...BUT WE MUST BE READY TO WIN IT.

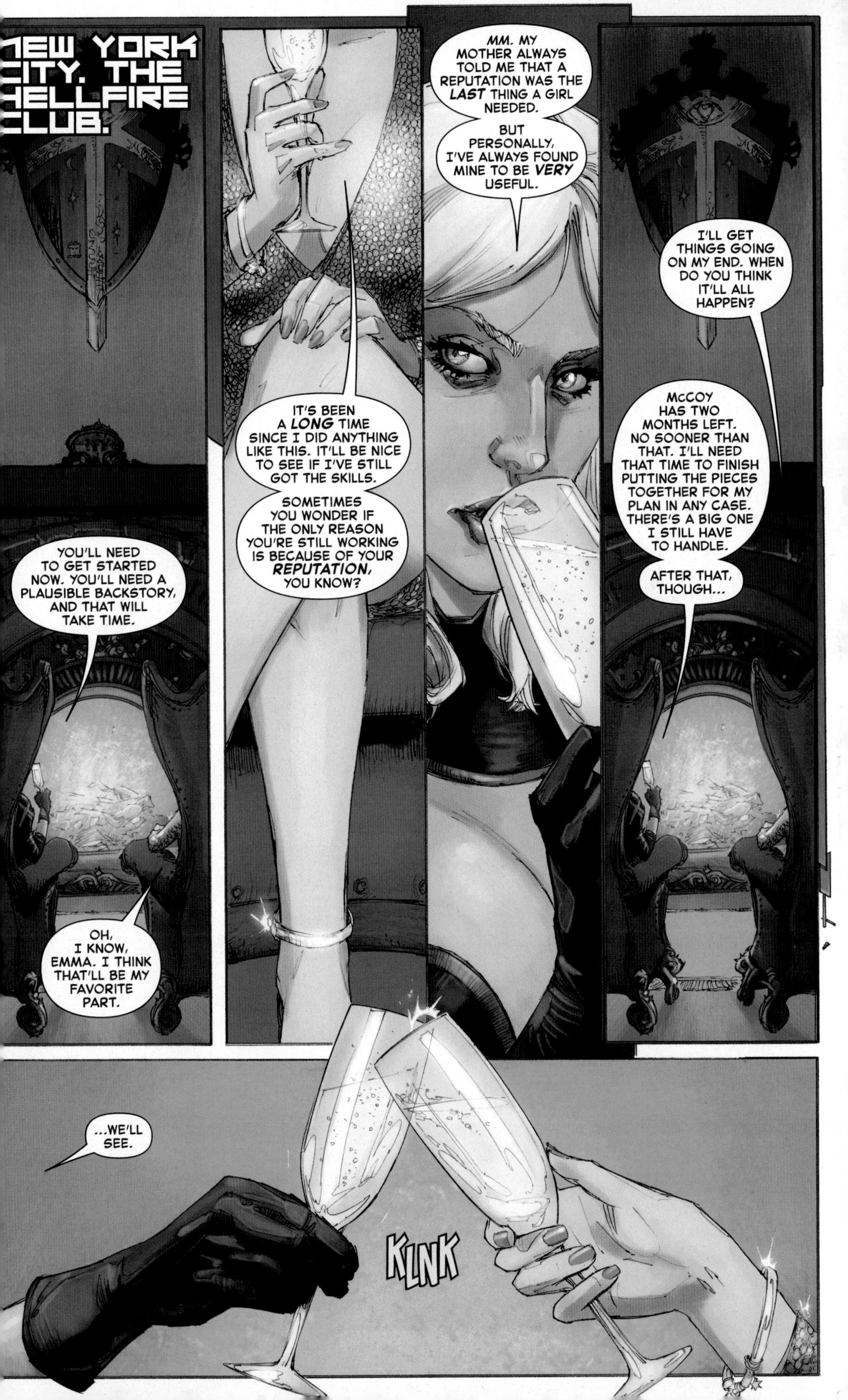
NEW YORK CITY. THE HELLFIRE CLUB.
YOU'LL NEED TO GET STARTED NOW. YOU'LL NEED A PLAUSIBLE BACKSTORY, AND THAT WILL TAKE TIME.
OH, I KNOW, EMMA. I THINK THAT'LL BE MY FAVORITE PART.
IT'S BEEN A LONG TIME SINCE I DID ANYTHING LIKE THIS. IT'LL BE NICE TO SEE IF I'VE STILL GOT THE SKILLS.
SOMETIMES YOU WONDER IF THE ONLY REASON YOU'RE STILL WORKING IS BECAUSE OF YOUR REPUTATION, YOU KNOW?
MM. MY MOTHER ALWAYS TOLD ME THAT A REPUTATION WAS THE LAST THING A GIRL NEEDED.
BUT PERSONALLY, I'VE ALWAYS FOUND MINE TO BE VERY USEFUL.
I'LL GET THINGS GOING ON MY END. WHEN DO YOU THINK IT'LL ALL HAPPEN?
McCOY HAS TWO MONTHS LEFT. NO SOONER THAN THAT. I'LL NEED THAT TIME TO FINISH PUTTING THE PIECES TOGETHER FOR MY PLAN IN ANY CASE. THERE'S A BIG ONE I STILL HAVE TO HANDLE.
AFTER THAT, THOUGH...
...WE'LL SEE.
KLNK

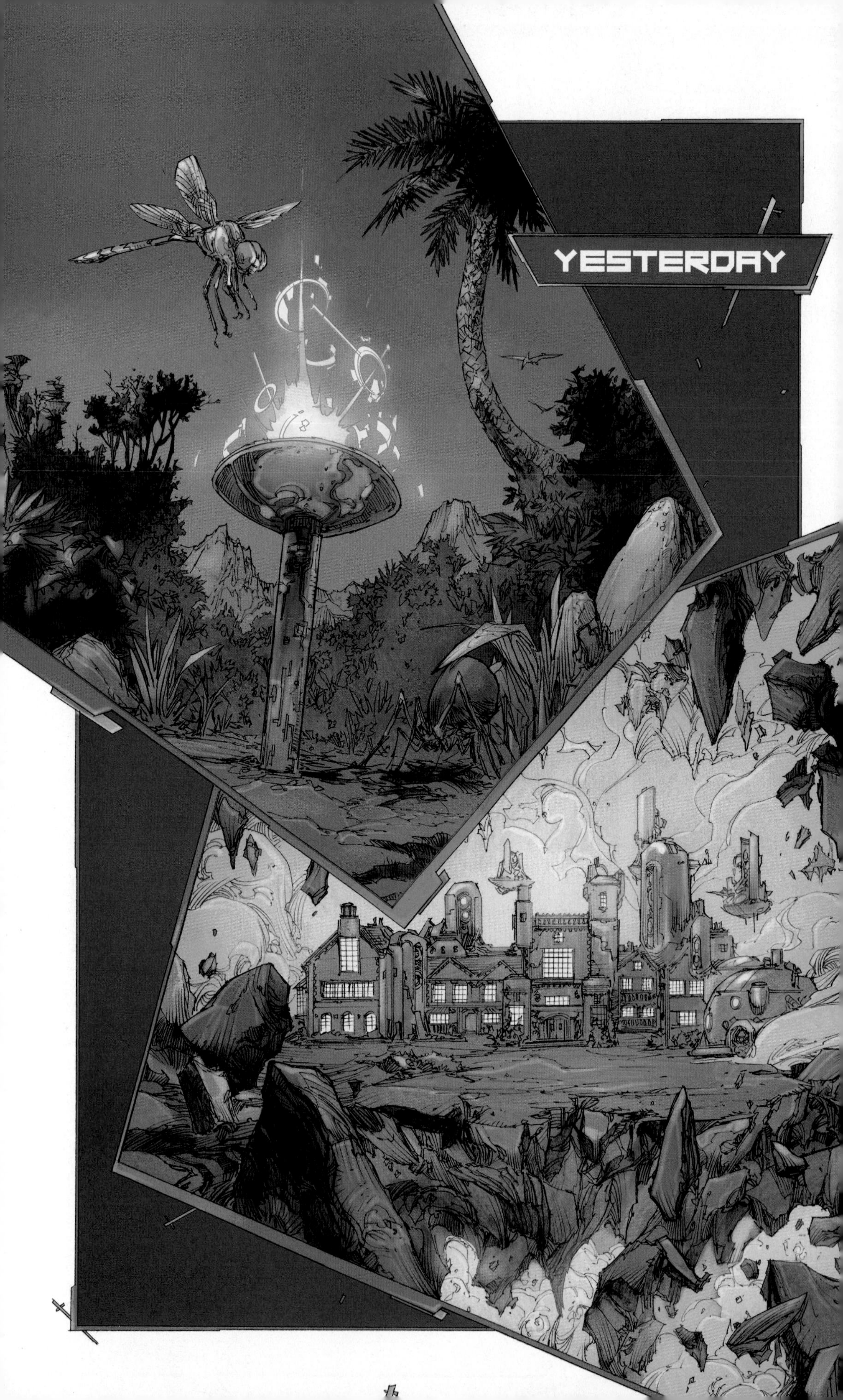
YESTERDAY

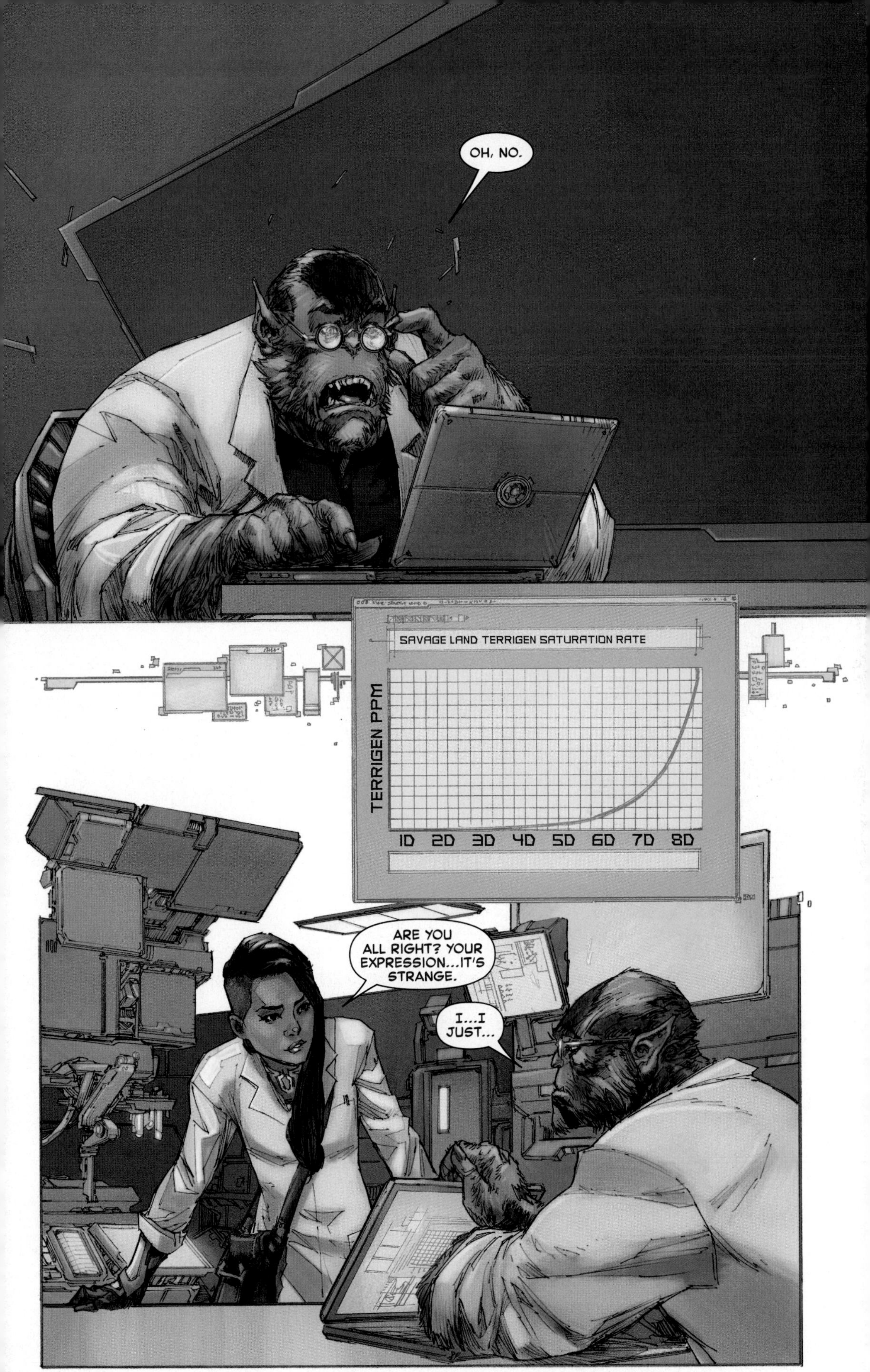
OH, NO.
SAVAGE LAND TERRIGEN SATURATION RATE
TERRIGEN PPM
1D 2D 3D 4D 5D 6D 7D 8D
ARE YOU ALL RIGHT? YOUR EXPRESSION...IT'S STRANGE.
I...I JUST...

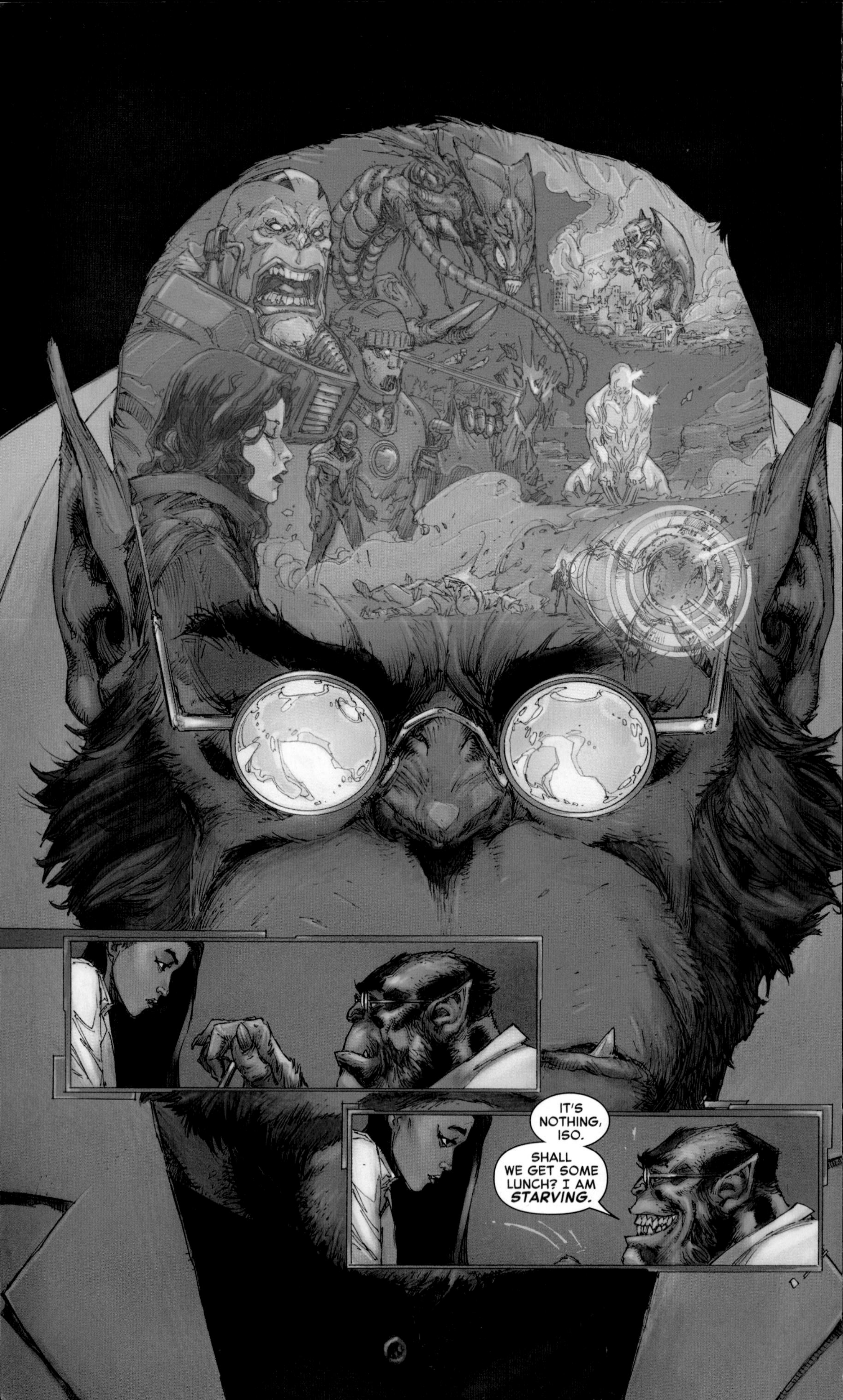
IT'S NOTHING, ISO.
SHALL WE GET SOME LUNCH? I AM *STARVING.*

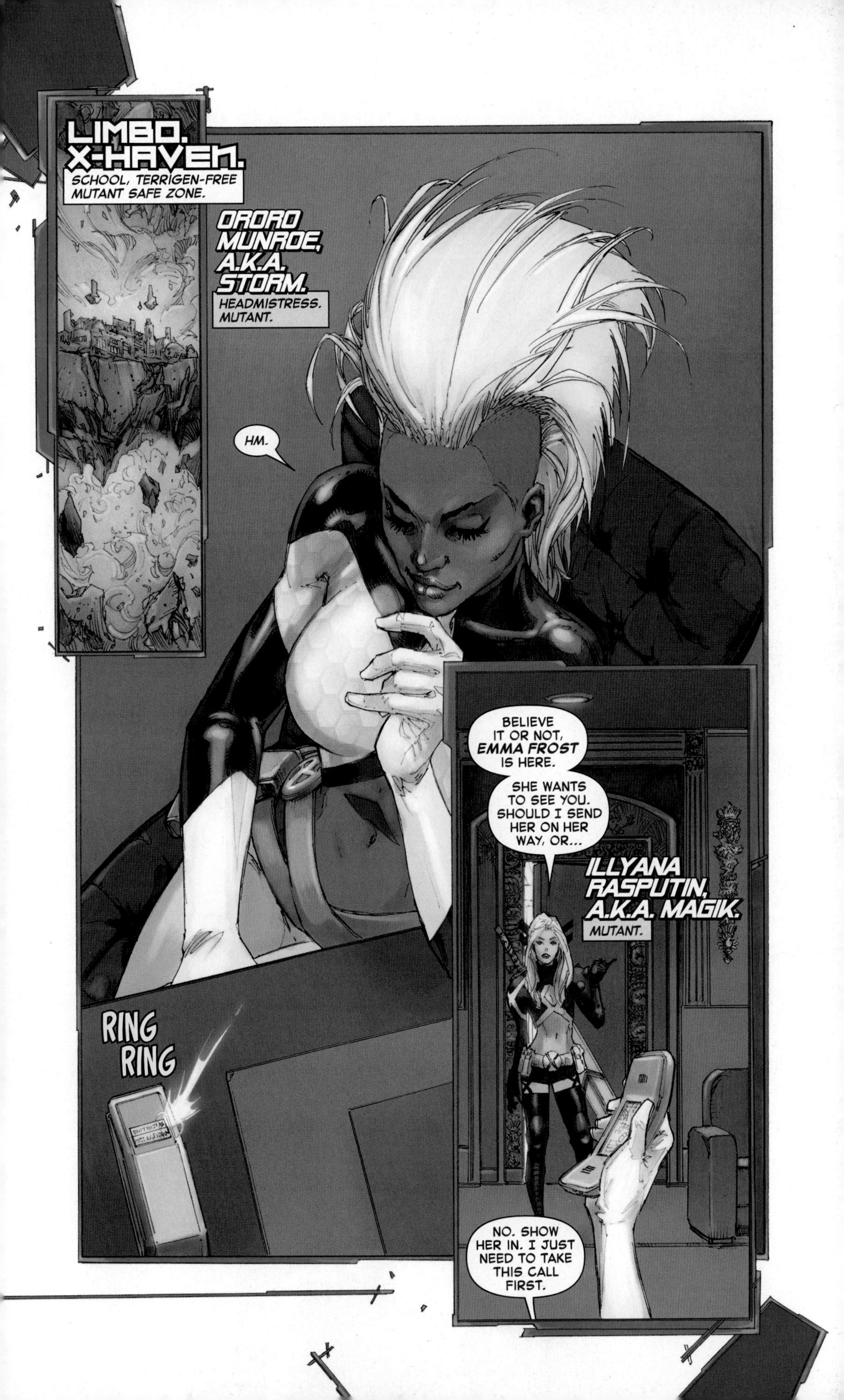
LIMBO.
X-HAVEN.
SCHOOL, TERRIGEN-FREE MUTANT SAFE ZONE.
ORORO MUNROE, A.K.A. STORM.
HEADMISTRESS. MUTANT.
HM.
RING RING
BELIEVE IT OR NOT, EMMA FROST IS HERE.
SHE WANTS TO SEE YOU. SHOULD I SEND HER ON HER WAY, OR...
ILLYANA RASPUTIN, A.K.A. MAGIK.
MUTANT.
NO. SHOW HER IN. I JUST NEED TO TAKE THIS CALL FIRST.

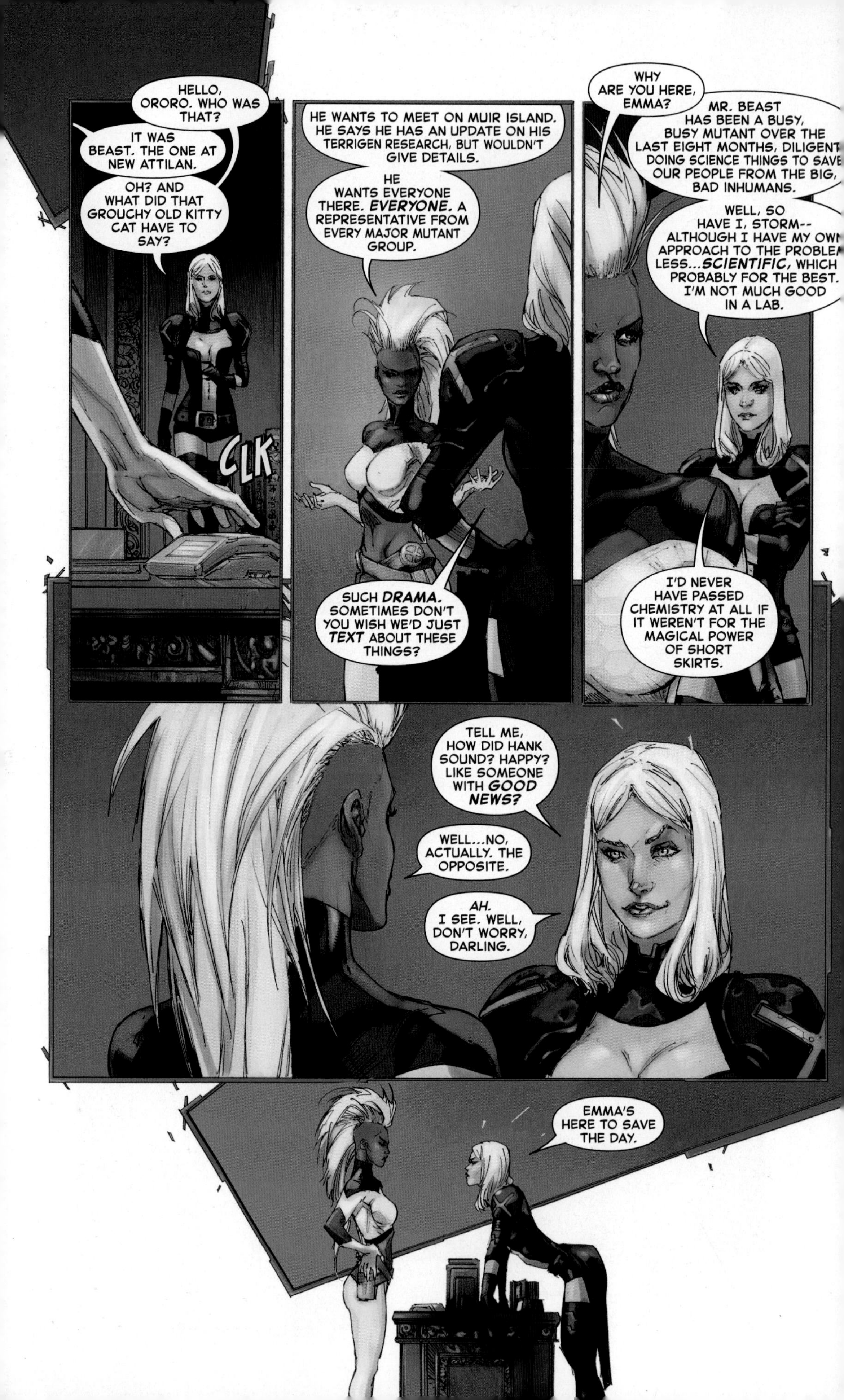
HELLO, ORORO. WHO WAS THAT?
IT WAS BEAST. THE ONE AT NEW ATTILAN.
OH? AND WHAT DID THAT GROUCHY OLD KITTY CAT HAVE TO SAY?
CLK
HE WANTS TO MEET ON MUIR ISLAND. HE SAYS HE HAS AN UPDATE ON HIS TERRIGEN RESEARCH, BUT WOULDN'T GIVE DETAILS.
HE WANTS EVERYONE THERE. EVERYONE. A REPRESENTATIVE FROM EVERY MAJOR MUTANT GROUP.
SUCH DRAMA. SOMETIMES DON'T YOU WISH WE'D JUST TEXT ABOUT THESE THINGS?
WHY ARE YOU HERE, EMMA?
MR. BEAST HAS BEEN A BUSY, BUSY MUTANT OVER THE LAST EIGHT MONTHS, DILIGENT DOING SCIENCE THINGS TO SAVE OUR PEOPLE FROM THE BIG, BAD INHUMANS.
WELL, SO HAVE I, STORM-- ALTHOUGH I HAVE MY OWN APPROACH TO THE PROBLEM LESS...SCIENTIFIC, WHICH PROBABLY FOR THE BEST. I'M NOT MUCH GOOD IN A LAB.
I'D NEVER HAVE PASSED CHEMISTRY AT ALL IF IT WEREN'T FOR THE MAGICAL POWER OF SHORT SKIRTS.
TELL ME, HOW DID HANK SOUND? HAPPY? LIKE SOMEONE WITH GOOD NEWS?
WELL...NO, ACTUALLY. THE OPPOSITE.
AH. I SEE. WELL, DON'T WORRY, DARLING.
EMMA'S HERE TO SAVE THE DAY.

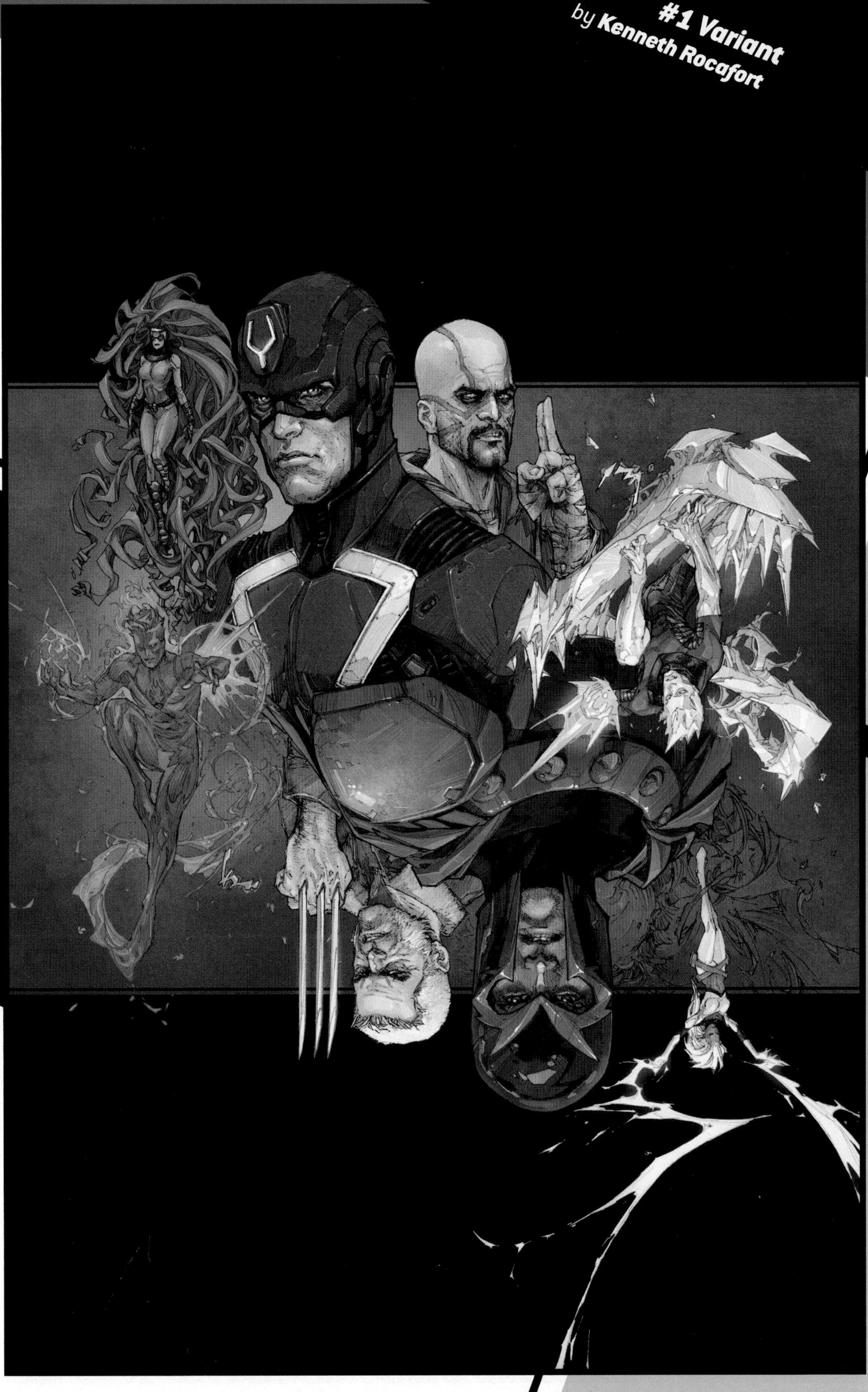

#1 Variant
by Kenneth Rocafort

1

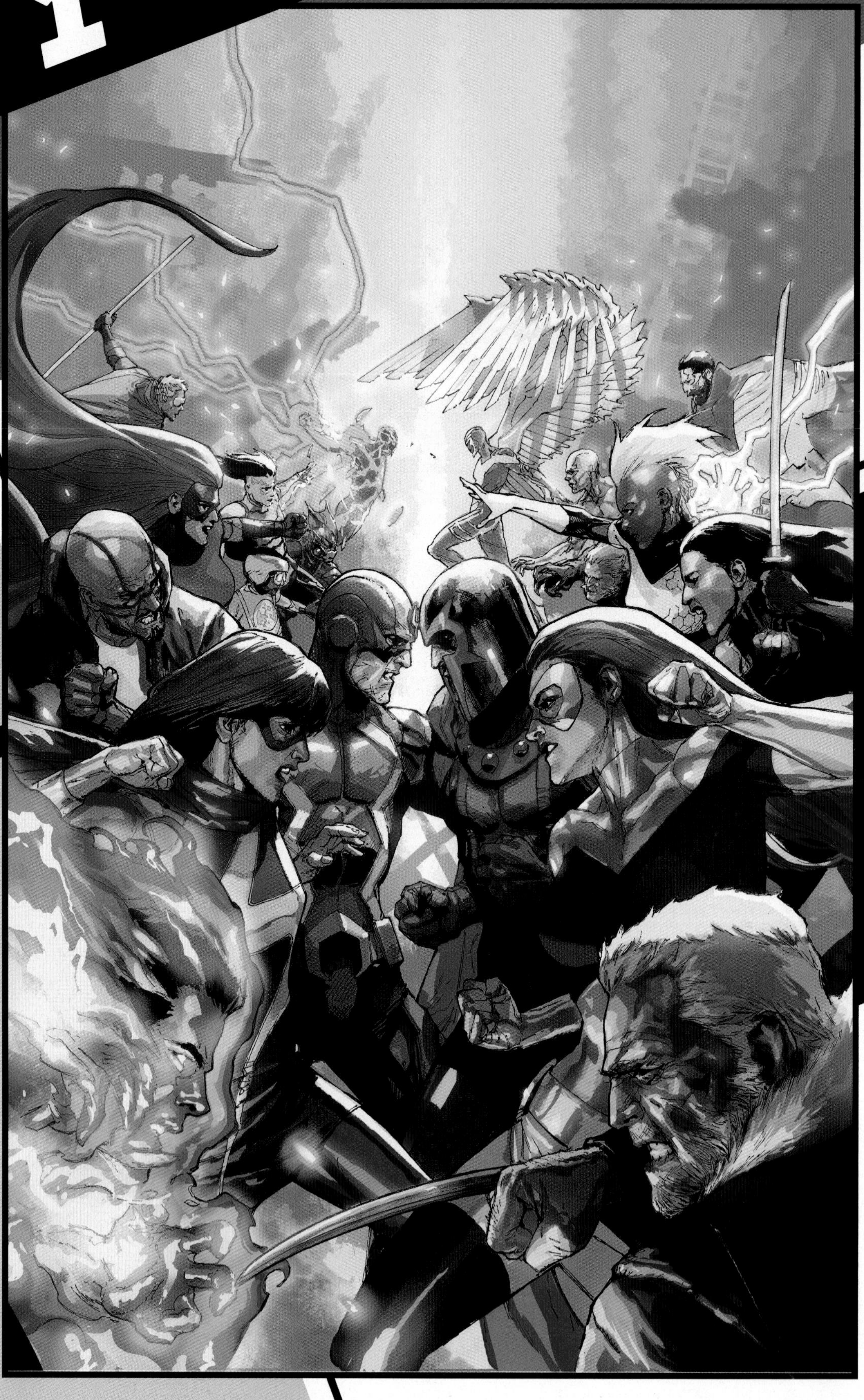

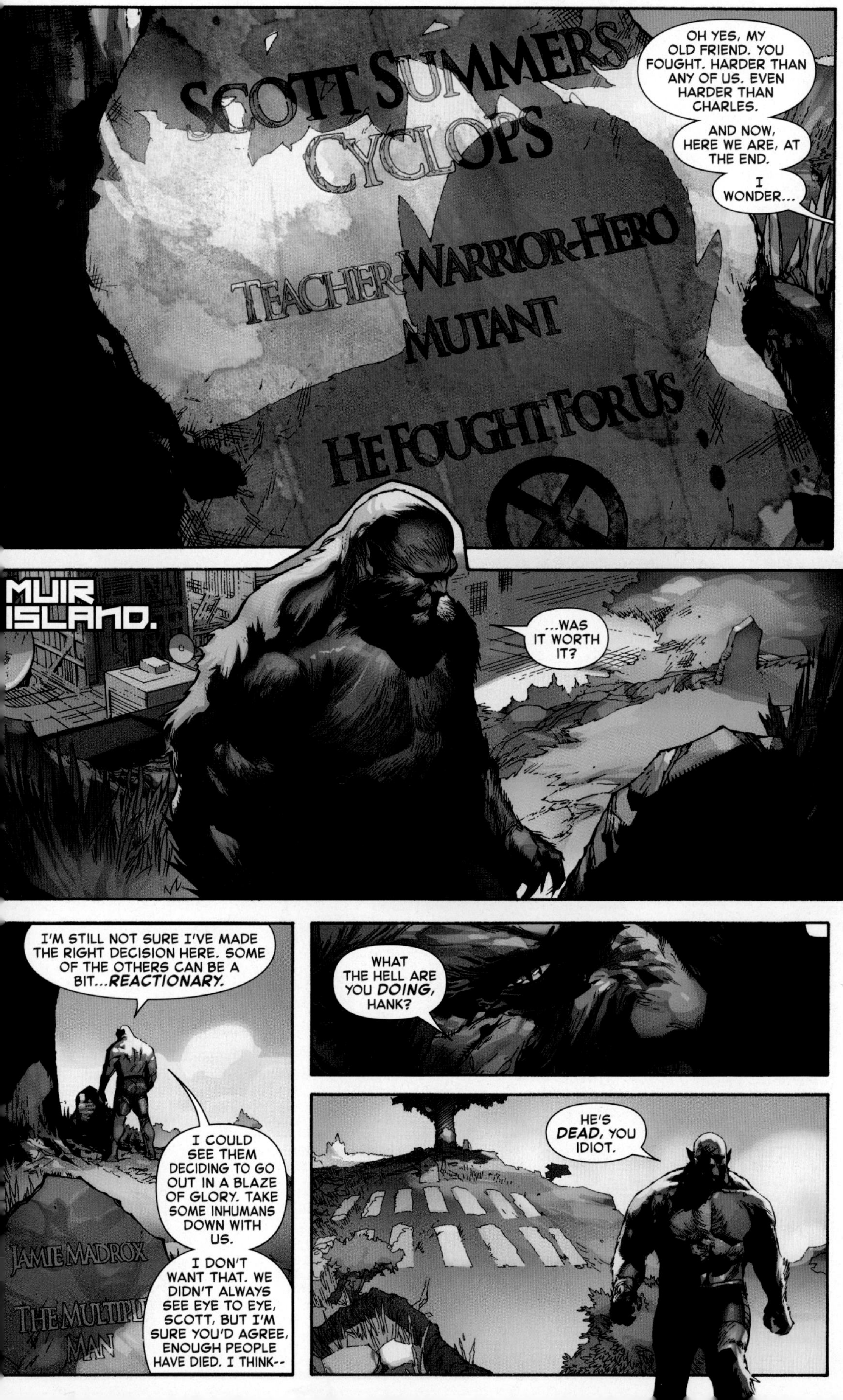
SCOTT SUMMERS
CYCLOPS
TEACHER-WARRIOR-HERO
MUTANT
HE FOUGHT FOR US
OH YES, MY OLD FRIEND. YOU FOUGHT. HARDER THAN ANY OF US. EVEN HARDER THAN CHARLES.
AND NOW, HERE WE ARE, AT THE END.
I WONDER...
MUIR ISLAND.
...WAS IT WORTH IT?
I'M STILL NOT SURE I'VE MADE THE RIGHT DECISION HERE. SOME OF THE OTHERS CAN BE A BIT...REACTIONARY.
I COULD SEE THEM DECIDING TO GO OUT IN A BLAZE OF GLORY. TAKE SOME INHUMANS DOWN WITH US.
I DON'T WANT THAT. WE DIDN'T ALWAYS SEE EYE TO EYE, SCOTT, BUT I'M SURE YOU'D AGREE, ENOUGH PEOPLE HAVE DIED. I THINK--
JAMIE MADROX
WHAT THE HELL ARE YOU DOING, HANK?
HE'S DEAD, YOU IDIOT.

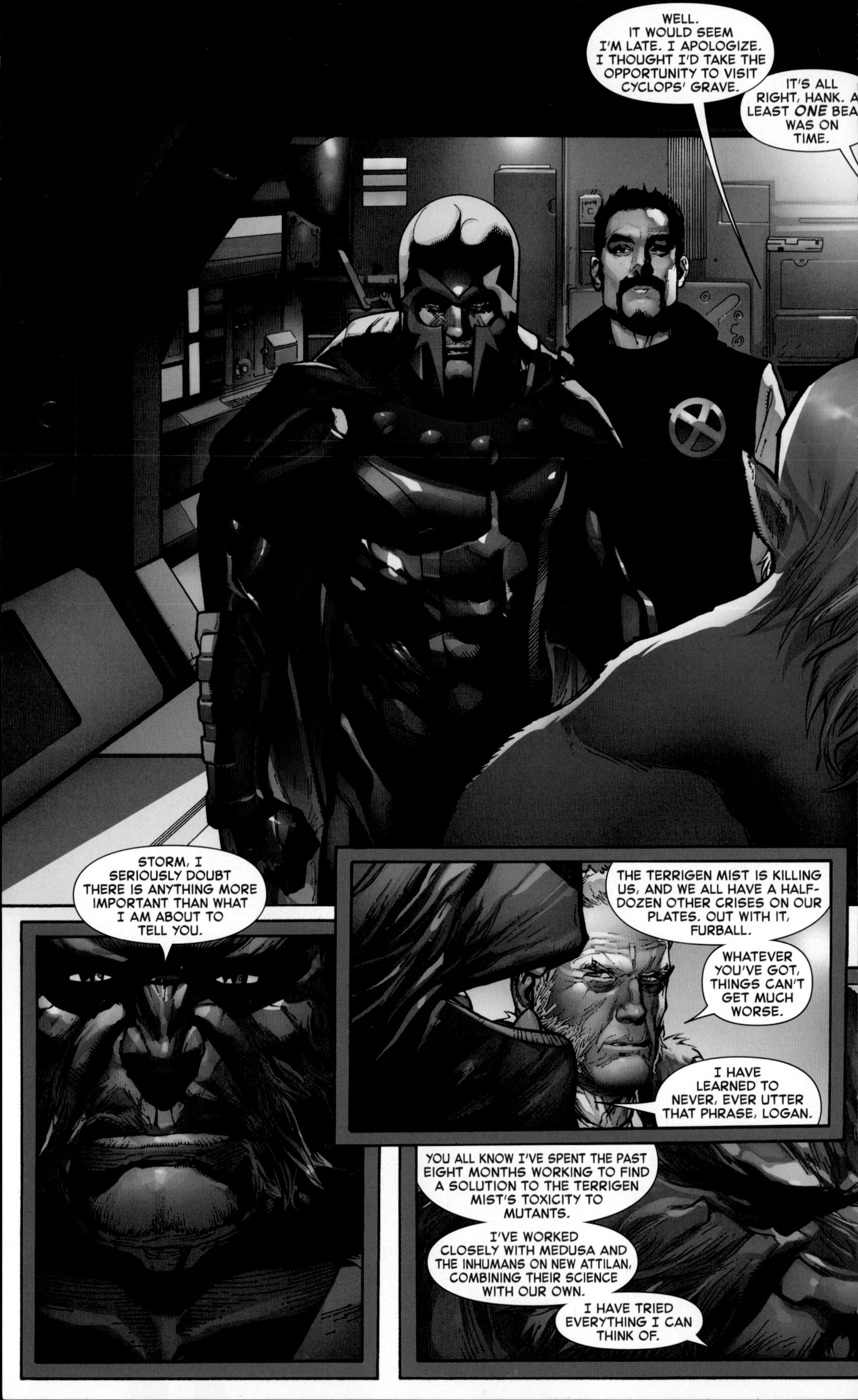
WELL. IT WOULD SEEM I'M LATE. I APOLOGIZE. I THOUGHT I'D TAKE THE OPPORTUNITY TO VISIT CYCLOPS' GRAVE.
IT'S ALL RIGHT, HANK. A LEAST ONE BEA WAS ON TIME.
STORM, I SERIOUSLY DOUBT THERE IS ANYTHING MORE IMPORTANT THAN WHAT I AM ABOUT TO TELL YOU.
THE TERRIGEN MIST IS KILLING US, AND WE ALL HAVE A HALF-DOZEN OTHER CRISES ON OUR PLATES. OUT WITH IT, FURBALL.
WHATEVER YOU'VE GOT, THINGS CAN'T GET MUCH WORSE.
I HAVE LEARNED TO NEVER, EVER UTTER THAT PHRASE, LOGAN.
YOU ALL KNOW I'VE SPENT THE PAST EIGHT MONTHS WORKING TO FIND A SOLUTION TO THE TERRIGEN MIST'S TOXICITY TO MUTANTS.
I'VE WORKED CLOSELY WITH MEDUSA AND THE INHUMANS ON NEW ATTILAN, COMBINING THEIR SCIENCE WITH OUR OWN.
I HAVE TRIED EVERYTHING I CAN THINK OF.

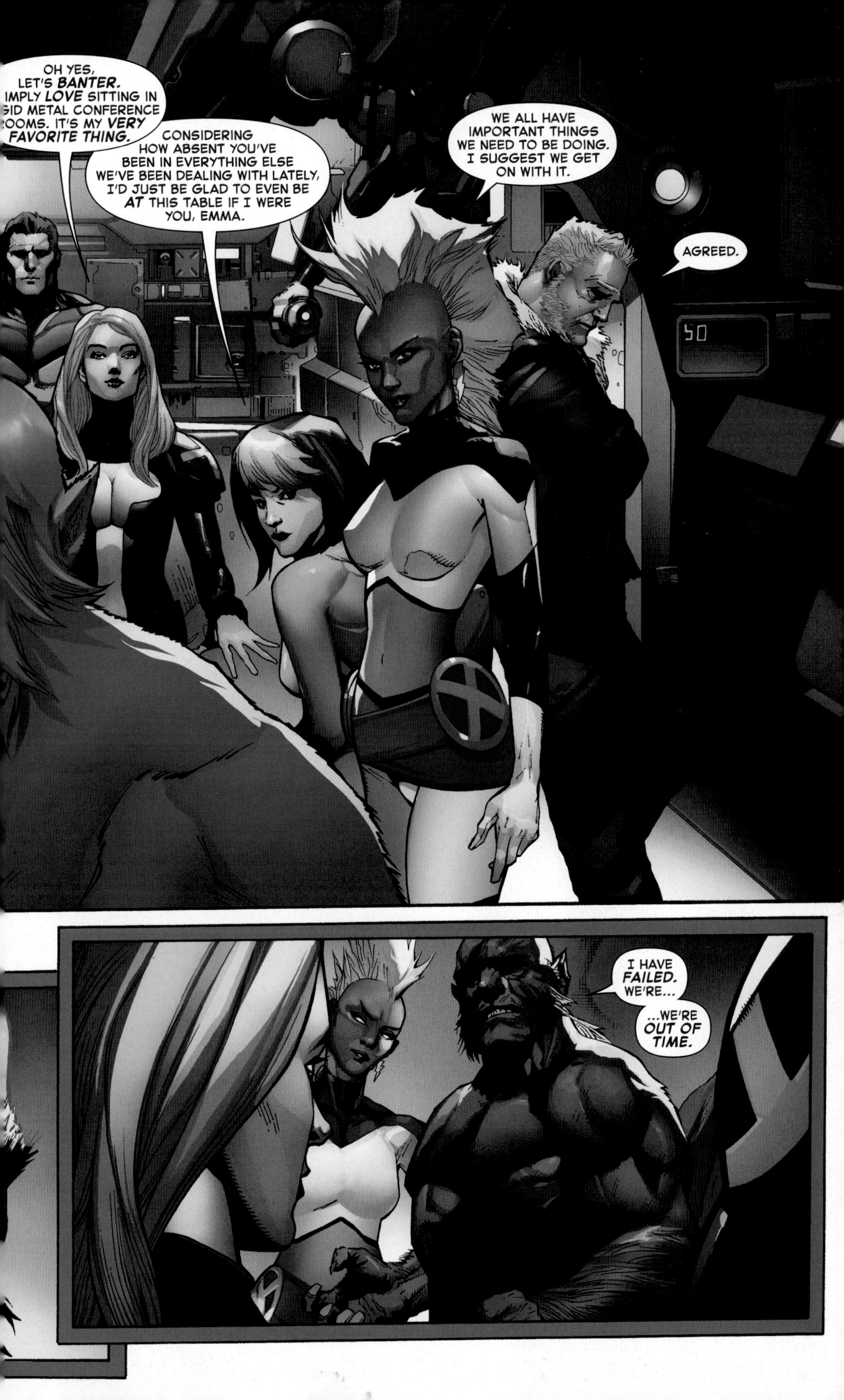

OH YES, LET'S BANTER. IMPLY LOVE SITTING IN GID METAL CONFERENCE OOMS. IT'S MY VERY FAVORITE THING.
CONSIDERING HOW ABSENT YOU'VE BEEN IN EVERYTHING ELSE WE'VE BEEN DEALING WITH LATELY, I'D JUST BE GLAD TO EVEN BE AT THIS TABLE IF I WERE YOU, EMMA.
WE ALL HAVE IMPORTANT THINGS WE NEED TO BE DOING. I SUGGEST WE GET ON WITH IT.
AGREED.
I HAVE FAILED. WE'RE...
...WE'RE OUT OF TIME.

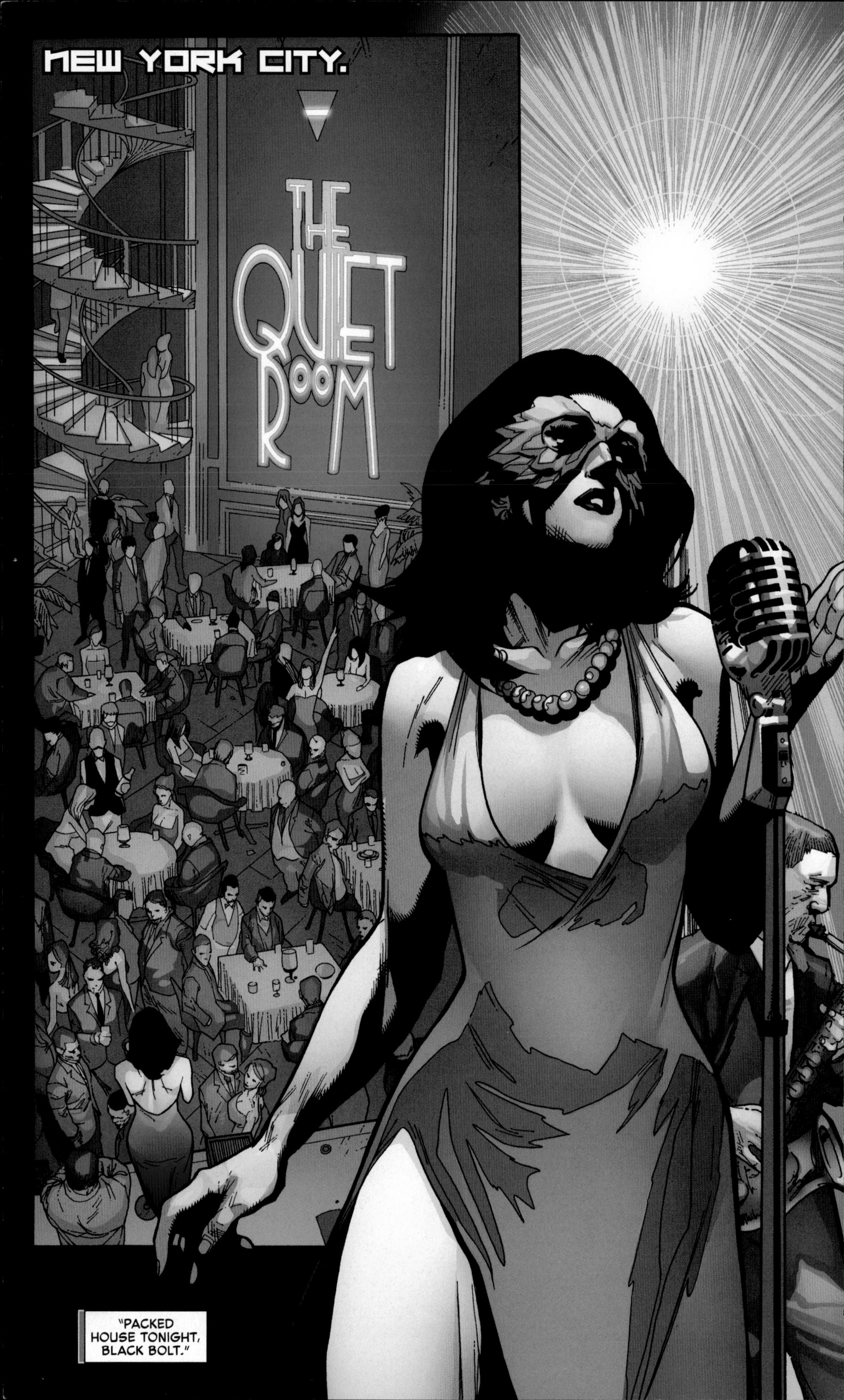
NEW YORK CITY.
THE QUIET ROOM
"PACKED HOUSE TONIGHT, BLACK BOLT."

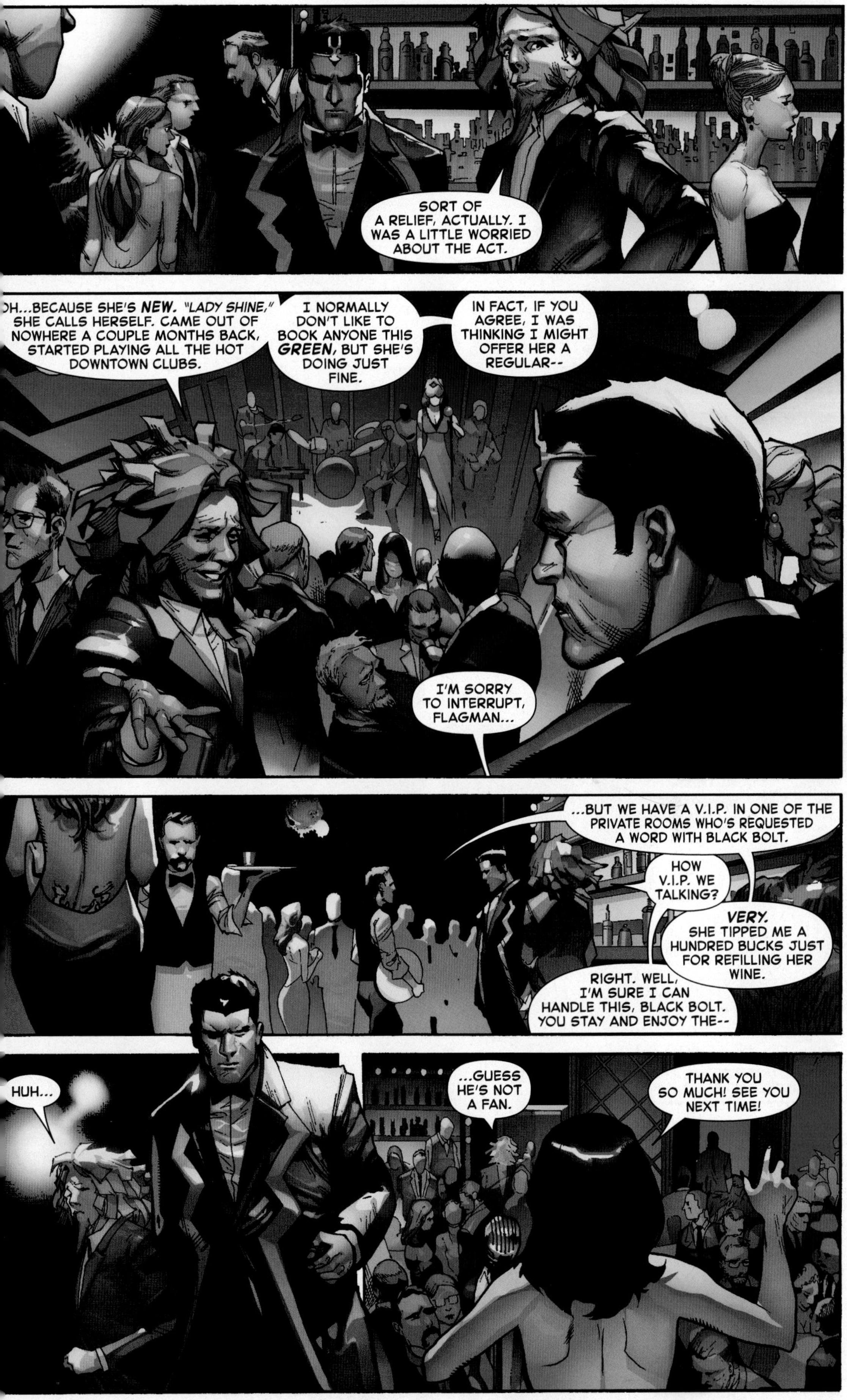
SORT OF A RELIEF, ACTUALLY. I WAS A LITTLE WORRIED ABOUT THE ACT.
OH...BECAUSE SHE'S NEW. "LADY SHINE," SHE CALLS HERSELF. CAME OUT OF NOWHERE A COUPLE MONTHS BACK, STARTED PLAYING ALL THE HOT DOWNTOWN CLUBS.
I NORMALLY DON'T LIKE TO BOOK ANYONE THIS GREEN, BUT SHE'S DOING JUST FINE.
IN FACT, IF YOU AGREE, I WAS THINKING I MIGHT OFFER HER A REGULAR--
I'M SORRY TO INTERRUPT, FLAGMAN...
...BUT WE HAVE A V.I.P. IN ONE OF THE PRIVATE ROOMS WHO'S REQUESTED A WORD WITH BLACK BOLT.
HOW V.I.P. WE TALKING?
VERY. SHE TIPPED ME A HUNDRED BUCKS JUST FOR REFILLING HER WINE.
RIGHT. WELL, I'M SURE I CAN HANDLE THIS, BLACK BOLT. YOU STAY AND ENJOY THE--
HUH...
...GUESS HE'S NOT A FAN.
THANK YOU SO MUCH! SEE YOU NEXT TIME!

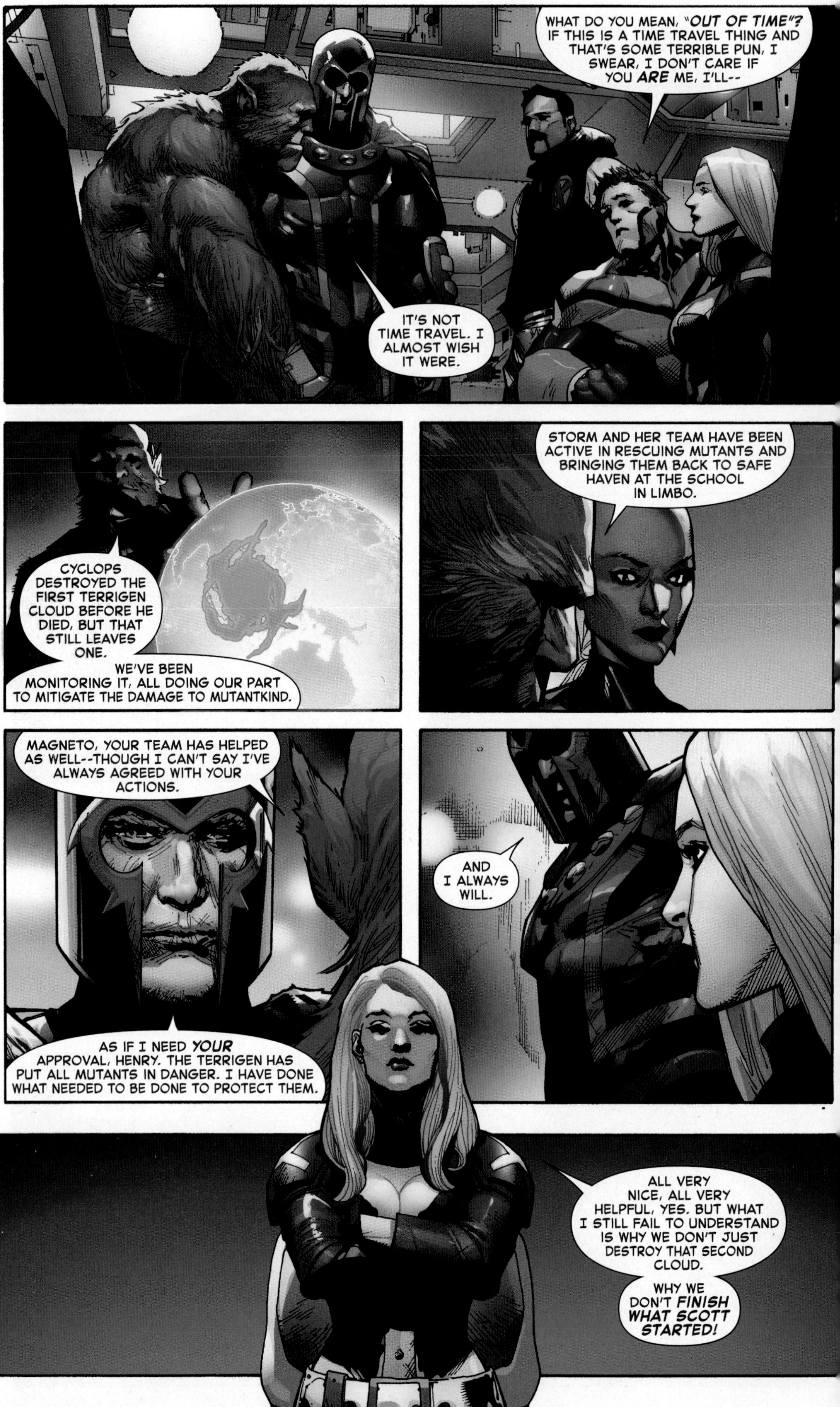
WHAT DO YOU MEAN, "OUT OF TIME"? IF THIS IS A TIME TRAVEL THING AND THAT'S SOME TERRIBLE PUN, I SWEAR, I DON'T CARE IF YOU ARE ME, I'LL--
IT'S NOT TIME TRAVEL. I ALMOST WISH IT WERE.
CYCLOPS DESTROYED THE FIRST TERRIGEN CLOUD BEFORE HE DIED, BUT THAT STILL LEAVES ONE.
WE'VE BEEN MONITORING IT, ALL DOING OUR PART TO MITIGATE THE DAMAGE TO MUTANTKIND.
STORM AND HER TEAM HAVE BEEN ACTIVE IN RESCUING MUTANTS AND BRINGING THEM BACK TO SAFE HAVEN AT THE SCHOOL IN LIMBO.
MAGNETO, YOUR TEAM HAS HELPED AS WELL--THOUGH I CAN'T SAY I'VE ALWAYS AGREED WITH YOUR ACTIONS.
AS IF I NEED YOUR APPROVAL, HENRY. THE TERRIGEN HAS PUT ALL MUTANTS IN DANGER. I HAVE DONE WHAT NEEDED TO BE DONE TO PROTECT THEM.
AND I ALWAYS WILL.
ALL VERY NICE, ALL VERY HELPFUL, YES. BUT WHAT I STILL FAIL TO UNDERSTAND IS WHY WE DON'T JUST DESTROY THAT SECOND CLOUD.
WHY WE DON'T FINISH WHAT SCOTT STARTED!

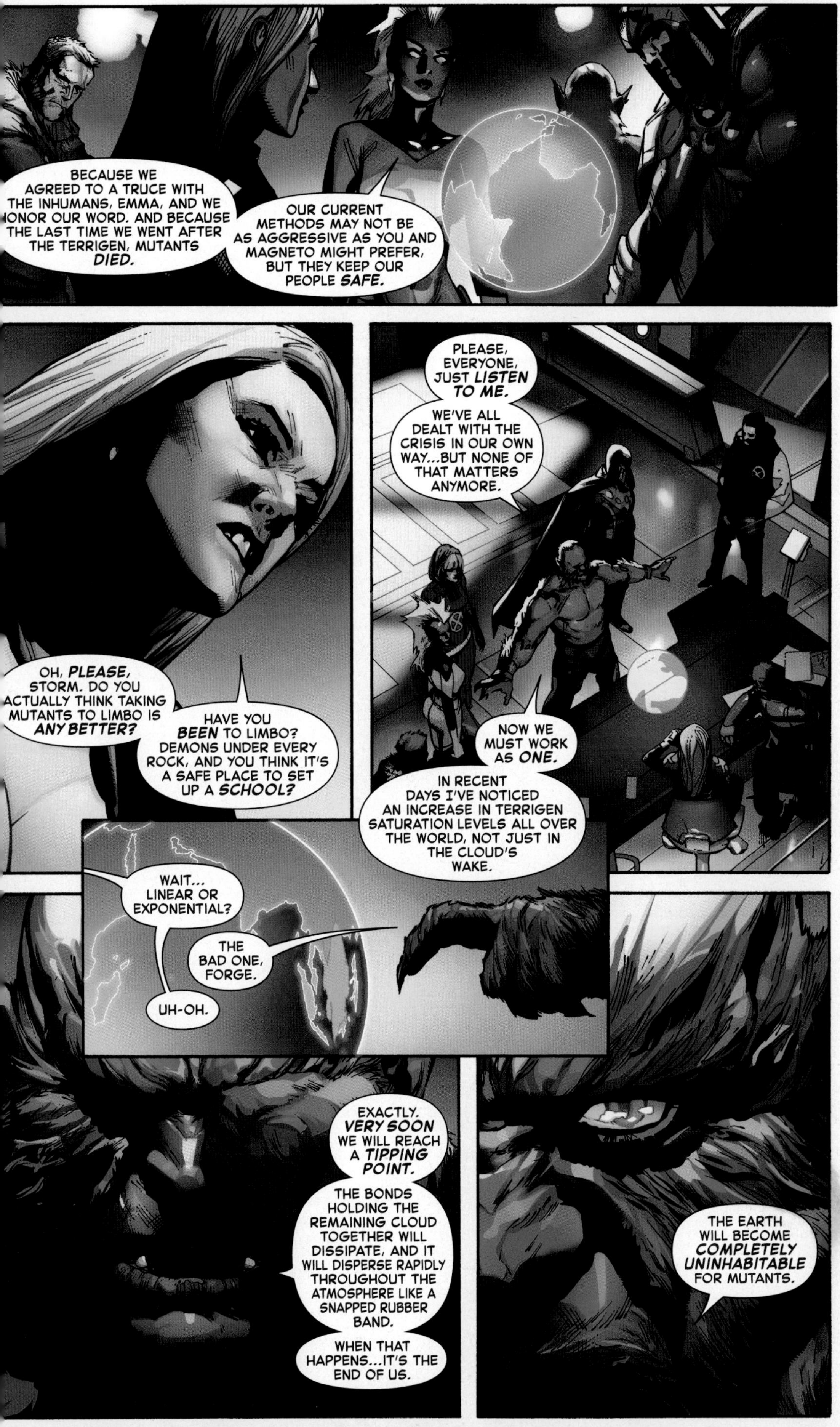
BECAUSE WE AGREED TO A TRUCE WITH THE INHUMANS, EMMA, AND WE HONOR OUR WORD. AND BECAUSE THE LAST TIME WE WENT AFTER THE TERRIGEN, MUTANTS DIED.
OUR CURRENT METHODS MAY NOT BE AS AGGRESSIVE AS YOU AND MAGNETO MIGHT PREFER, BUT THEY KEEP OUR PEOPLE SAFE.
OH, PLEASE, STORM. DO YOU ACTUALLY THINK TAKING MUTANTS TO LIMBO IS ANY BETTER?
HAVE YOU BEEN TO LIMBO? DEMONS UNDER EVERY ROCK, AND YOU THINK IT'S A SAFE PLACE TO SET UP A SCHOOL?
PLEASE, EVERYONE, JUST LISTEN TO ME.
WE'VE ALL DEALT WITH THE CRISIS IN OUR OWN WAY...BUT NONE OF THAT MATTERS ANYMORE.
NOW WE MUST WORK AS ONE.
IN RECENT DAYS I'VE NOTICED AN INCREASE IN TERRIGEN SATURATION LEVELS ALL OVER THE WORLD, NOT JUST IN THE CLOUD'S WAKE.
WAIT... LINEAR OR EXPONENTIAL?
THE BAD ONE, FORGE.
UH-OH.
EXACTLY. VERY SOON WE WILL REACH A TIPPING POINT.
THE BONDS HOLDING THE REMAINING CLOUD TOGETHER WILL DISSIPATE, AND IT WILL DISPERSE RAPIDLY THROUGHOUT THE ATMOSPHERE LIKE A SNAPPED RUBBER BAND.
WHEN THAT HAPPENS...IT'S THE END OF US.
THE EARTH WILL BECOME COMPLETELY UNINHABITABLE FOR MUTANTS.

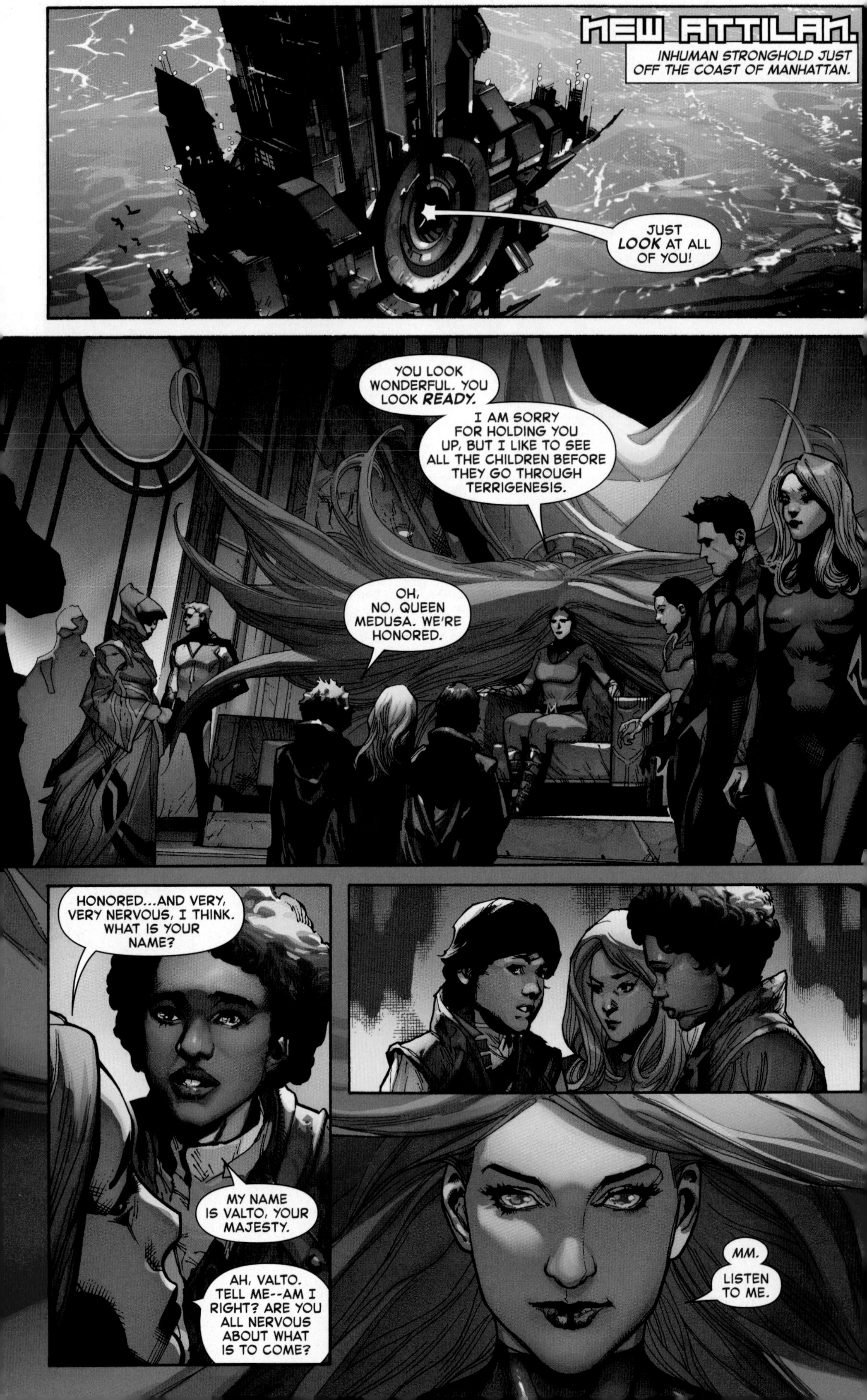
NEW ATTILAN.
INHUMAN STRONGHOLD JUST OFF THE COAST OF MANHATTAN.
JUST LOOK AT ALL OF YOU!
YOU LOOK WONDERFUL. YOU LOOK READY.
I AM SORRY FOR HOLDING YOU UP, BUT I LIKE TO SEE ALL THE CHILDREN BEFORE THEY GO THROUGH TERRIGENESIS.
OH, NO, QUEEN MEDUSA. WE'RE HONORED.
HONORED...AND VERY, VERY NERVOUS, I THINK. WHAT IS YOUR NAME?
MY NAME IS VALTO, YOUR MAJESTY.
AH, VALTO. TELL ME--AM I RIGHT? ARE YOU ALL NERVOUS ABOUT WHAT IS TO COME?
MM.
LISTEN TO ME.

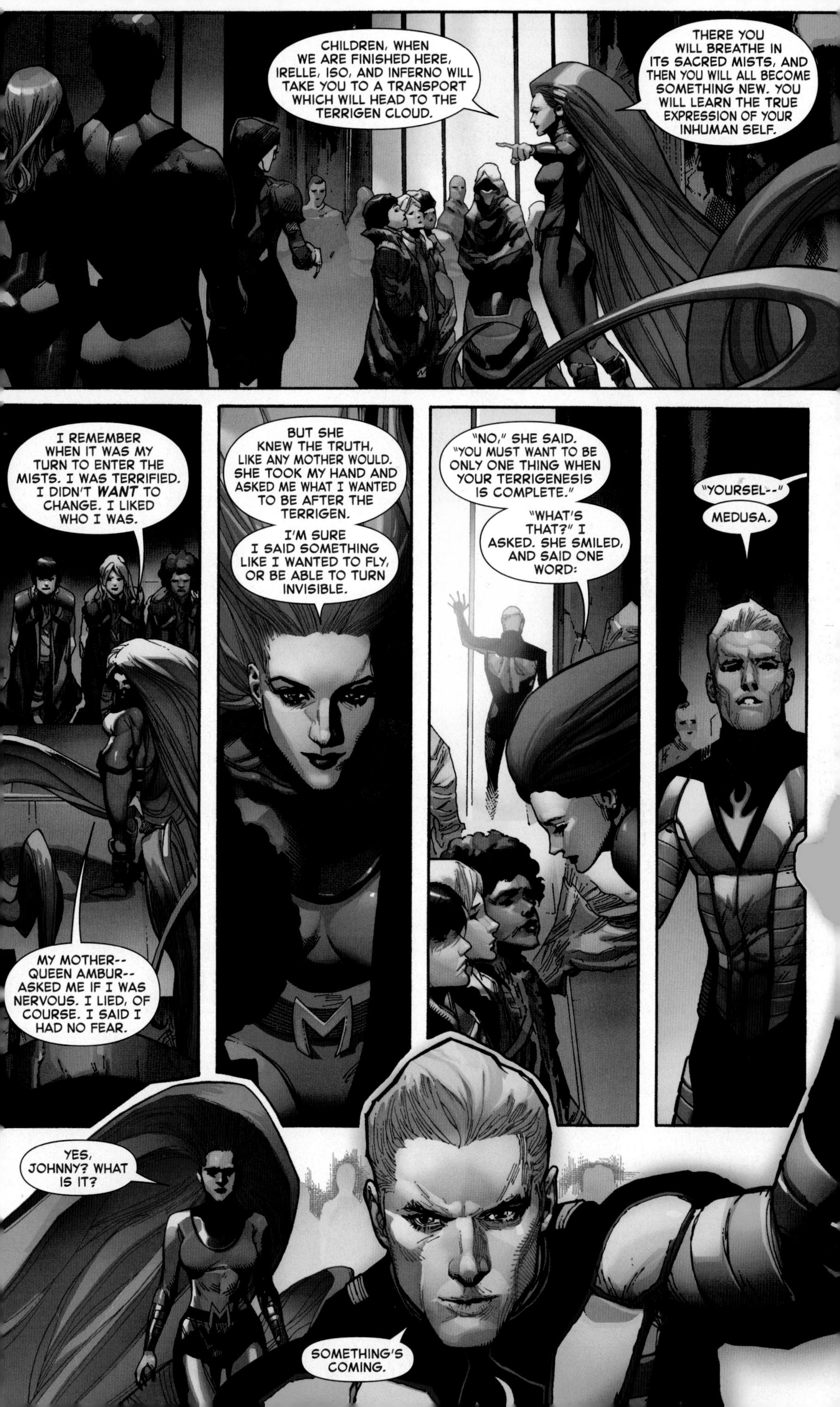
CHILDREN, WHEN WE ARE FINISHED HERE, IRELLE, ISO, AND INFERNO WILL TAKE YOU TO A TRANSPORT WHICH WILL HEAD TO THE TERRIGEN CLOUD.
THERE YOU WILL BREATHE IN ITS SACRED MISTS, AND THEN YOU WILL ALL BECOME SOMETHING NEW. YOU WILL LEARN THE TRUE EXPRESSION OF YOUR INHUMAN SELF.
I REMEMBER WHEN IT WAS MY TURN TO ENTER THE MISTS. I WAS TERRIFIED. I DIDN'T *WANT* TO CHANGE. I LIKED WHO I WAS.
MY MOTHER-- QUEEN AMBUR-- ASKED ME IF I WAS NERVOUS. I LIED, OF COURSE. I SAID I HAD NO FEAR.
BUT SHE KNEW THE TRUTH, LIKE ANY MOTHER WOULD. SHE TOOK MY HAND AND ASKED ME WHAT I WANTED TO BE AFTER THE TERRIGEN.
I'M SURE I SAID SOMETHING LIKE I WANTED TO FLY, OR BE ABLE TO TURN INVISIBLE.
"NO," SHE SAID. "YOU MUST WANT TO BE ONLY ONE THING WHEN YOUR TERRIGENESIS IS COMPLETE."
"WHAT'S THAT?" I ASKED. SHE SMILED, AND SAID ONE WORD:
"YOURSEL--"
MEDUSA.
YES, JOHNNY? WHAT IS IT?
SOMETHING'S COMING.

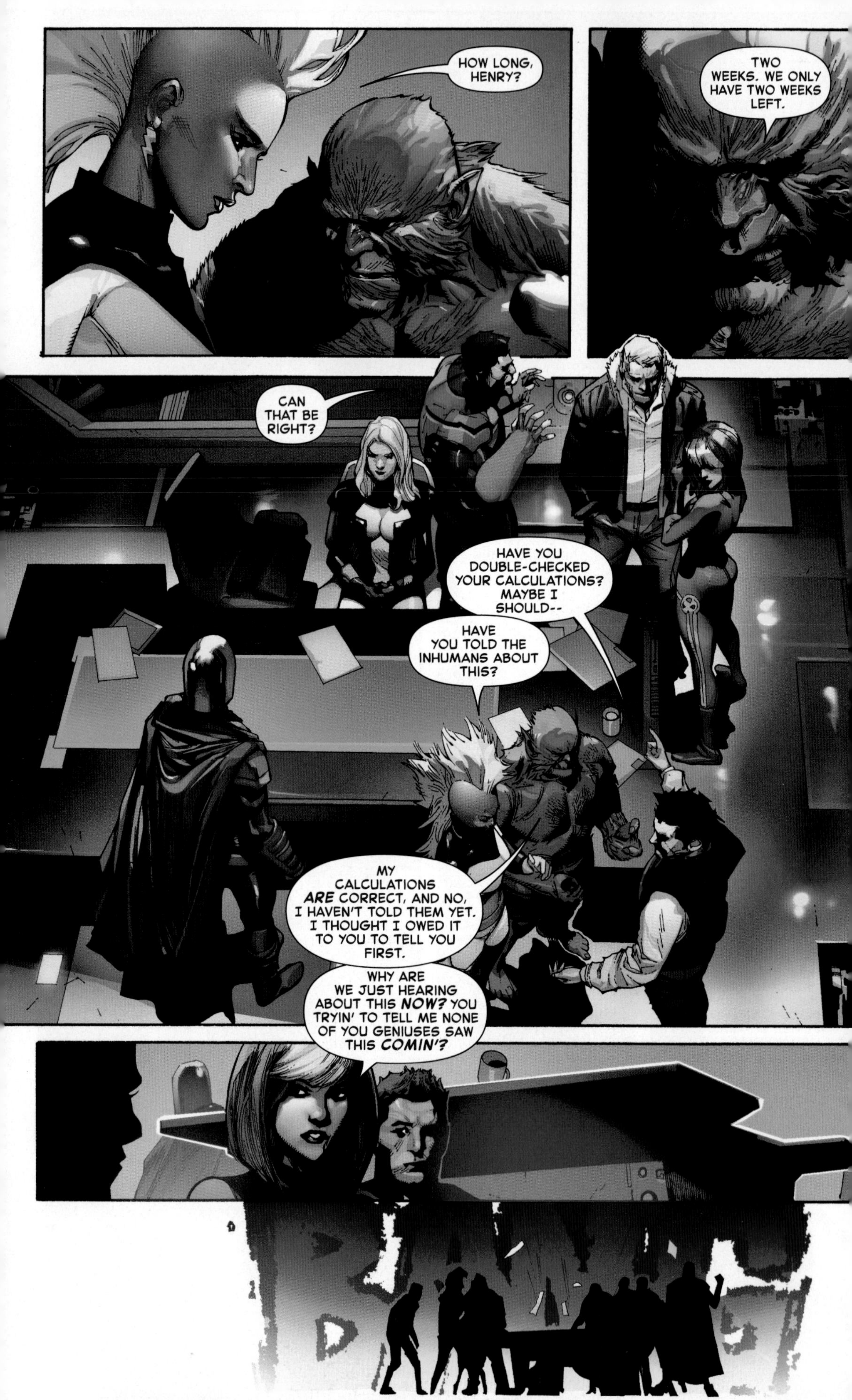

HOW LONG, HENRY?
TWO WEEKS. WE ONLY HAVE TWO WEEKS LEFT.
CAN THAT BE RIGHT?
HAVE YOU DOUBLE-CHECKED YOUR CALCULATIONS? MAYBE I SHOULD--
HAVE YOU TOLD THE INHUMANS ABOUT THIS?
MY CALCULATIONS ARE CORRECT, AND NO, I HAVEN'T TOLD THEM YET. I THOUGHT I OWED IT TO YOU TO TELL YOU FIRST.
WHY ARE WE JUST HEARING ABOUT THIS NOW? YOU TRYIN' TO TELL ME NONE OF YOU GENIUSES SAW THIS COMIN'?

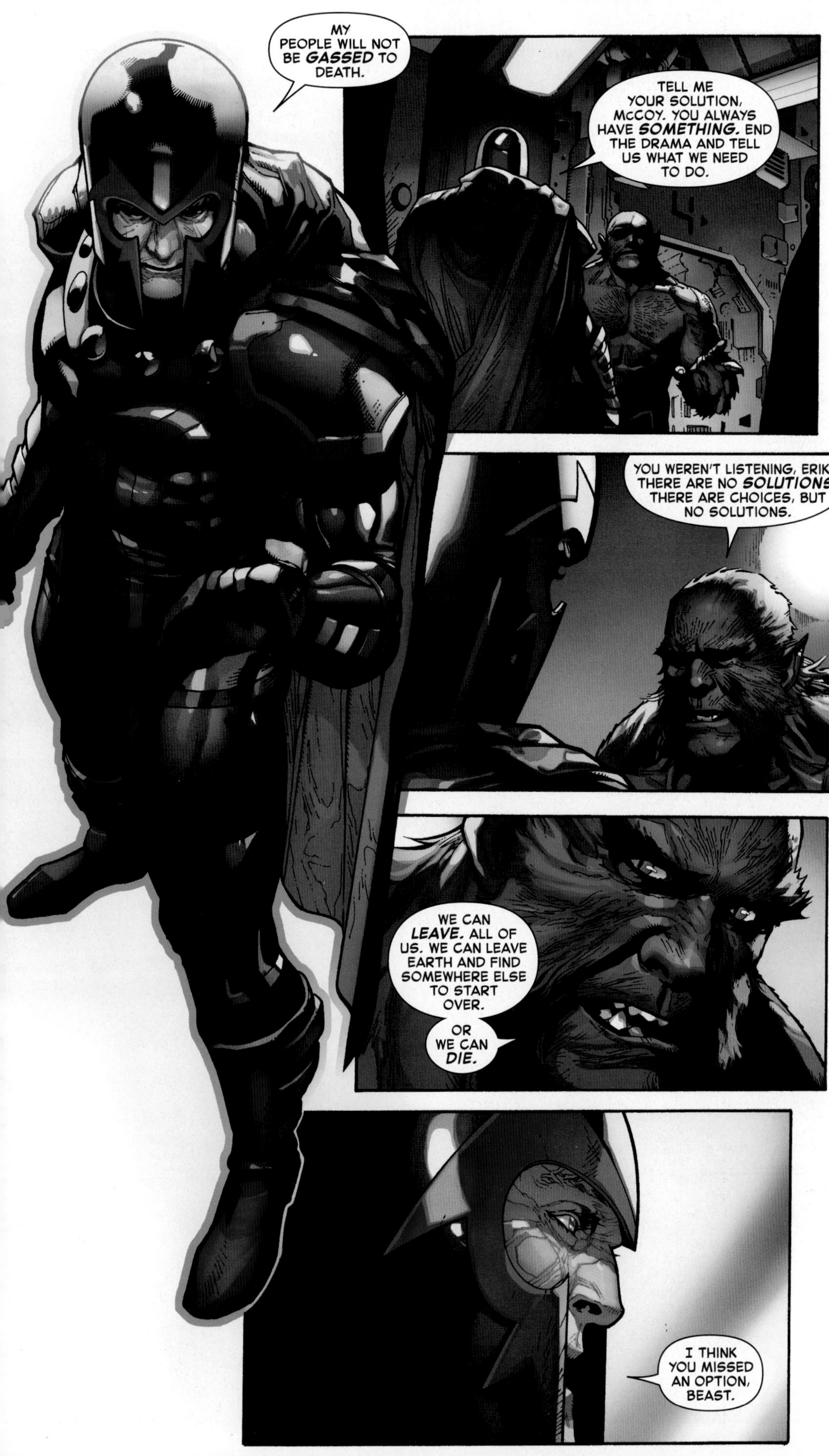
MY PEOPLE WILL NOT BE GASSED TO DEATH.
TELL ME YOUR SOLUTION, McCOY. YOU ALWAYS HAVE SOMETHING. END THE DRAMA AND TELL US WHAT WE NEED TO DO.
YOU WEREN'T LISTENING, ERIK-- THERE ARE NO SOLUTIONS. THERE ARE CHOICES, BUT NO SOLUTIONS.
WE CAN LEAVE. ALL OF US. WE CAN LEAVE EARTH AND FIND SOMEWHERE ELSE TO START OVER.
OR WE CAN DIE.
I THINK YOU MISSED AN OPTION, BEAST.

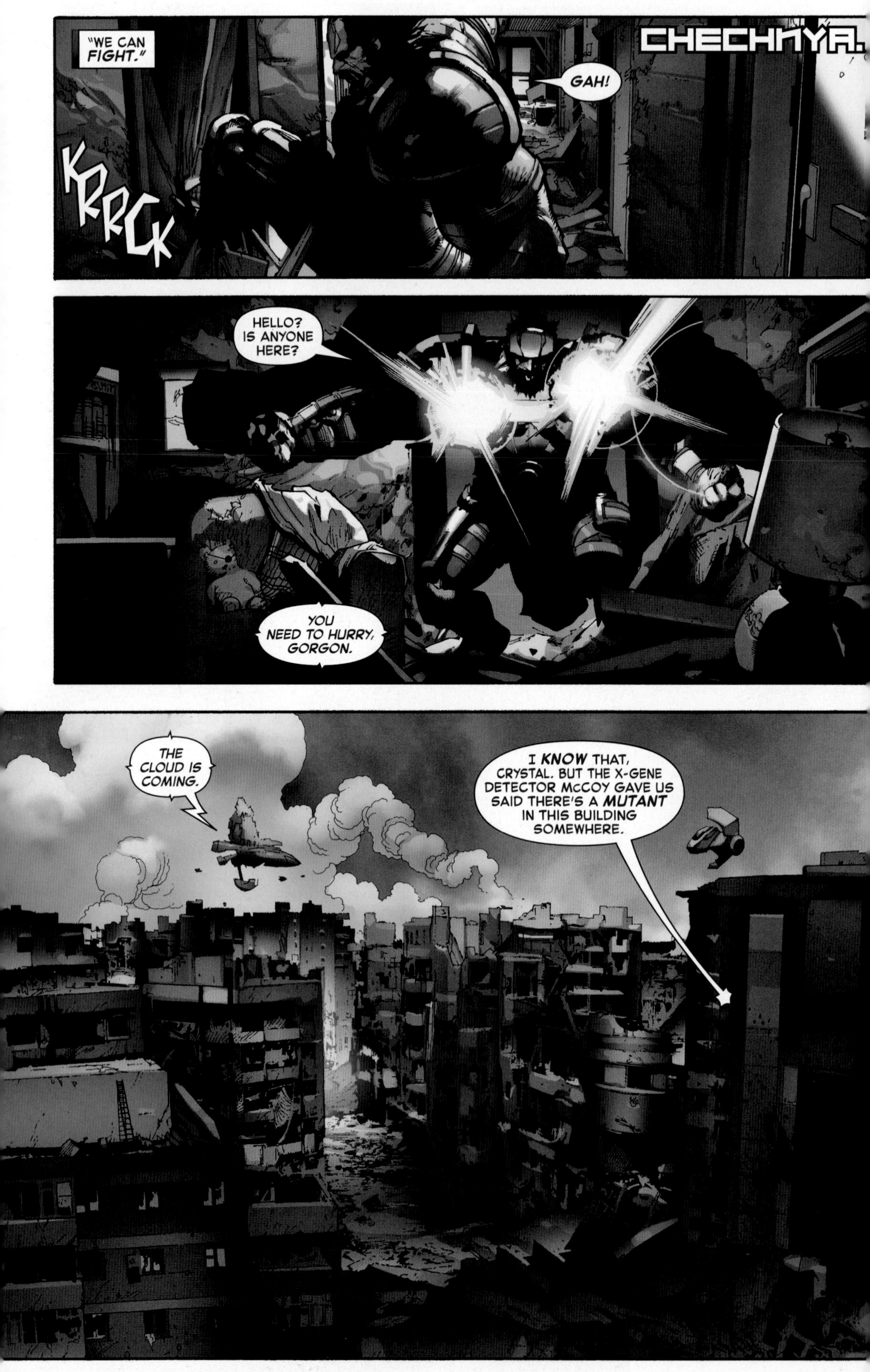

"WE CAN FIGHT."
CHECHNYA.
GAH!
KRRCK
HELLO? IS ANYONE HERE?
YOU NEED TO HURRY, GORGON.
THE CLOUD IS COMING.
I KNOW THAT, CRYSTAL. BUT THE X-GENE DETECTOR McCOY GAVE US SAID THERE'S A MUTANT IN THIS BUILDING SOMEWHERE.

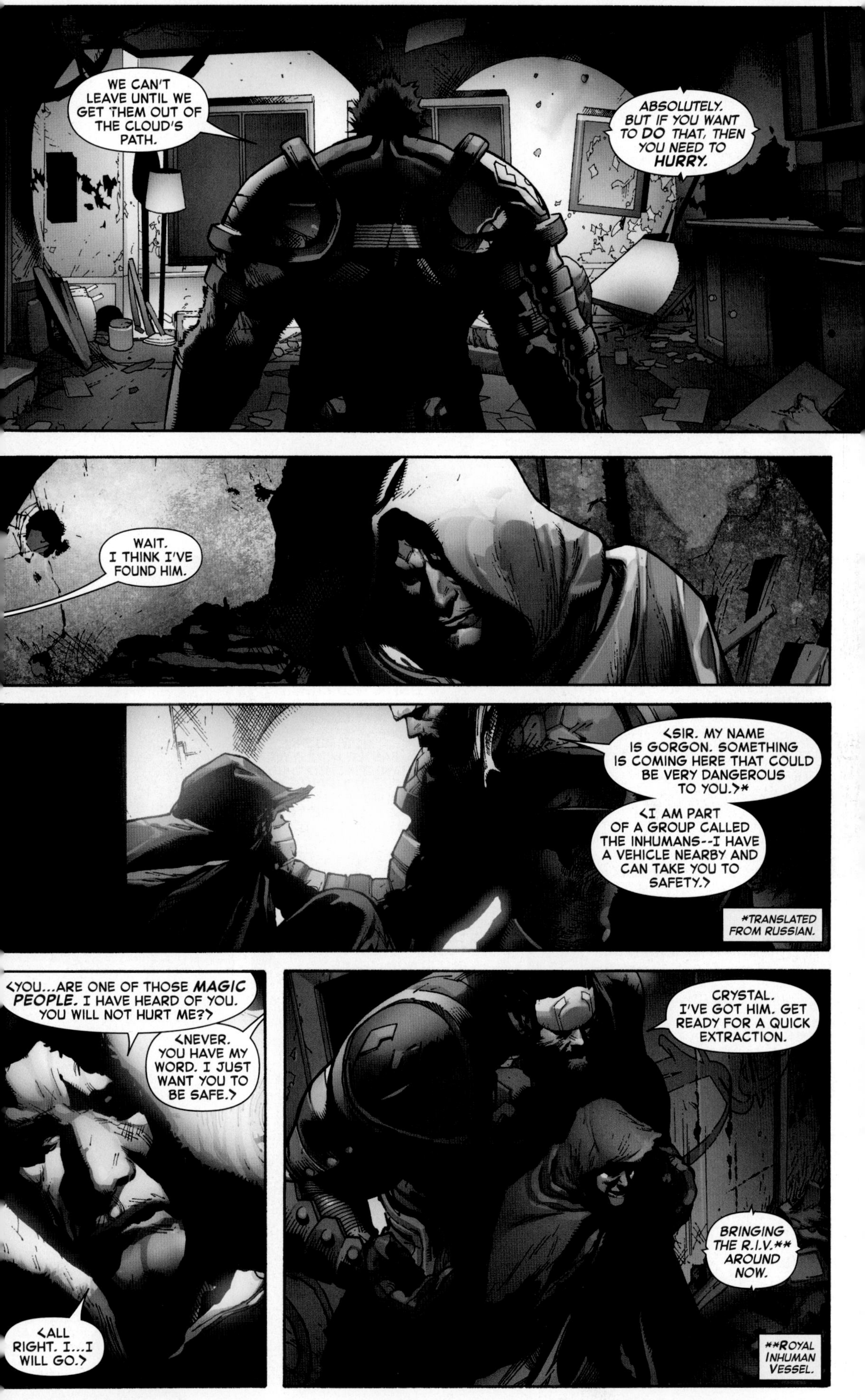
WE CAN'T LEAVE UNTIL WE GET THEM OUT OF THE CLOUD'S PATH.
ABSOLUTELY. BUT IF YOU WANT TO DO THAT, THEN YOU NEED TO HURRY.
WAIT. I THINK I'VE FOUND HIM.
<SIR. MY NAME IS GORGON. SOMETHING IS COMING HERE THAT COULD BE VERY DANGEROUS TO YOU.>*
<I AM PART OF A GROUP CALLED THE INHUMANS--I HAVE A VEHICLE NEARBY AND CAN TAKE YOU TO SAFETY.>
*TRANSLATED FROM RUSSIAN.
<YOU...ARE ONE OF THOSE MAGIC PEOPLE. I HAVE HEARD OF YOU. YOU WILL NOT HURT ME?>
<NEVER. YOU HAVE MY WORD. I JUST WANT YOU TO BE SAFE.>
<ALL RIGHT. I...I WILL GO.>
CRYSTAL. I'VE GOT HIM. GET READY FOR A QUICK EXTRACTION.
BRINGING THE R.I.V.** AROUND NOW.
**ROYAL INHUMAN VESSEL.

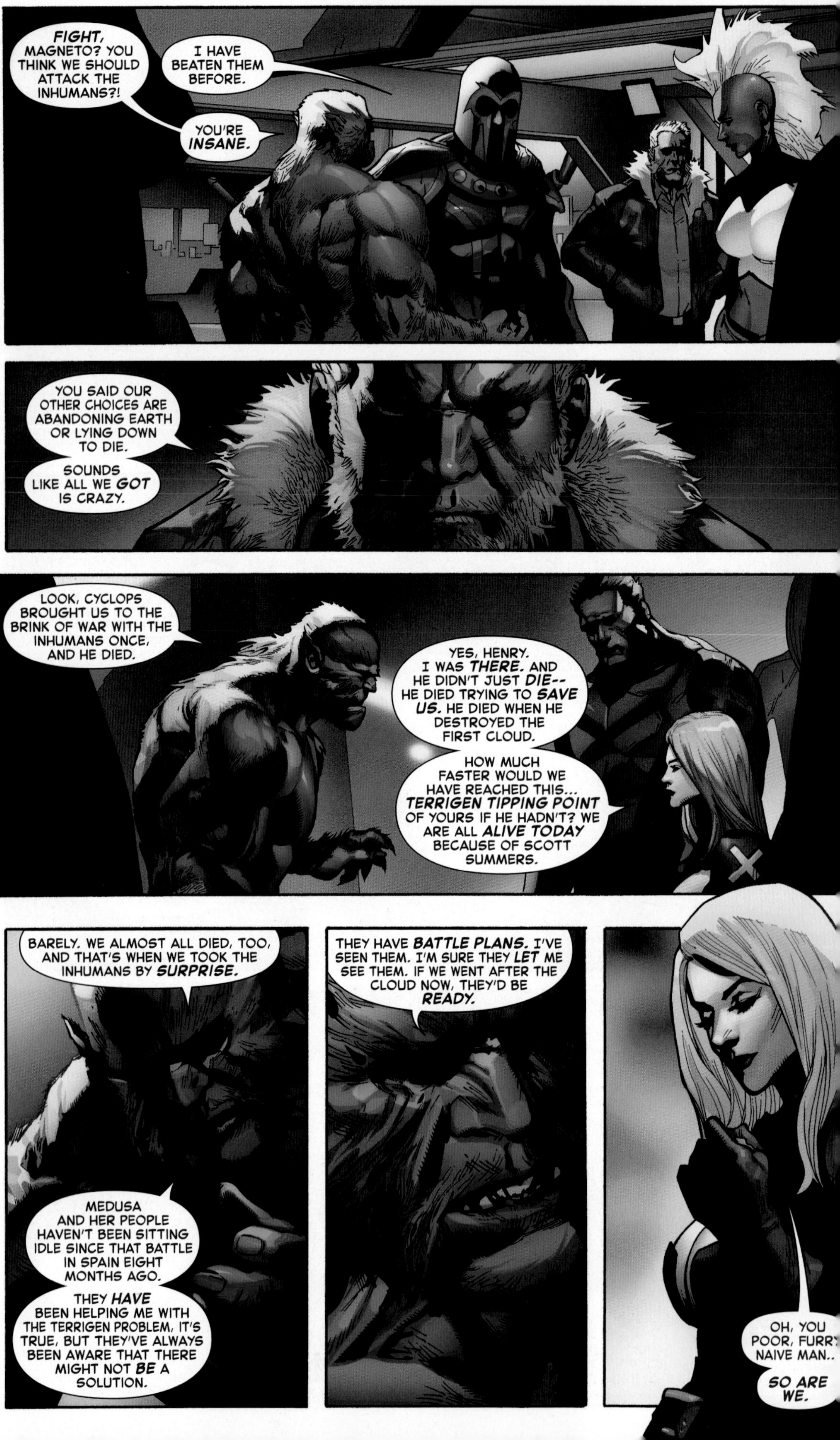

FIGHT, MAGNETO? YOU THINK WE SHOULD ATTACK THE INHUMANS?!
I HAVE BEATEN THEM BEFORE.
YOU'RE INSANE.
YOU SAID OUR OTHER CHOICES ARE ABANDONING EARTH OR LYING DOWN TO DIE.
SOUNDS LIKE ALL WE GOT IS CRAZY.
LOOK, CYCLOPS BROUGHT US TO THE BRINK OF WAR WITH THE INHUMANS ONCE, AND HE DIED.
YES, HENRY. I WAS THERE. AND HE DIDN'T JUST DIE-- HE DIED TRYING TO SAVE US. HE DIED WHEN HE DESTROYED THE FIRST CLOUD.
HOW MUCH FASTER WOULD WE HAVE REACHED THIS... TERRIGEN TIPPING POINT OF YOURS IF HE HADN'T? WE ARE ALL ALIVE TODAY BECAUSE OF SCOTT SUMMERS.
BARELY. WE ALMOST ALL DIED, TOO, AND THAT'S WHEN WE TOOK THE INHUMANS BY SURPRISE.
MEDUSA AND HER PEOPLE HAVEN'T BEEN SITTING IDLE SINCE THAT BATTLE IN SPAIN EIGHT MONTHS AGO.
THEY HAVE BEEN HELPING ME WITH THE TERRIGEN PROBLEM, IT'S TRUE, BUT THEY'VE ALWAYS BEEN AWARE THAT THERE MIGHT NOT BE A SOLUTION.
THEY HAVE BATTLE PLANS. I'VE SEEN THEM. I'M SURE THEY LET ME SEE THEM. IF WE WENT AFTER THE CLOUD NOW, THEY'D BE READY.
OH, YOU POOR, FURRY NAIVE MAN..
SO ARE WE.

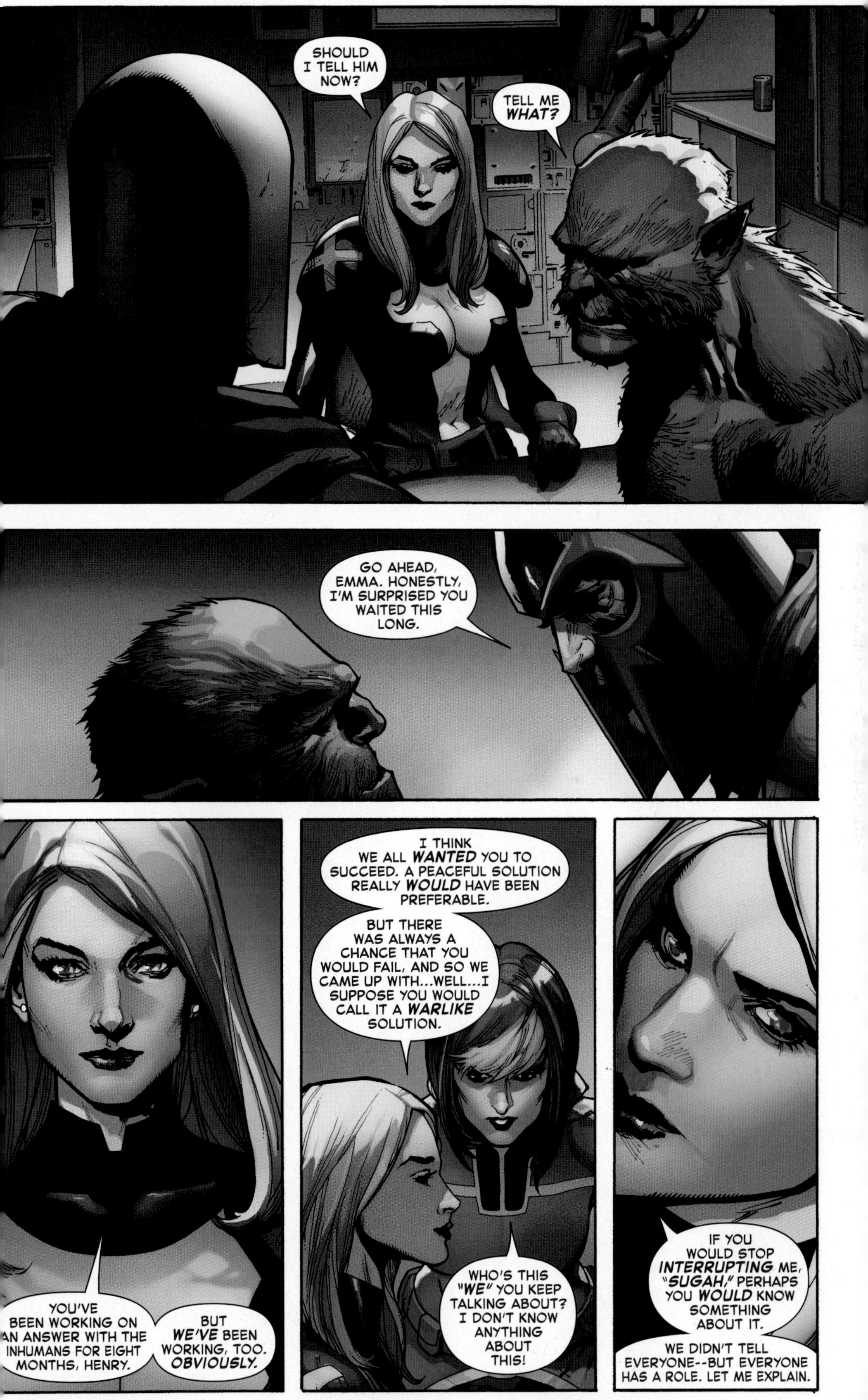
SHOULD I TELL HIM NOW?
TELL ME WHAT?
GO AHEAD, EMMA. HONESTLY, I'M SURPRISED YOU WAITED THIS LONG.
YOU'VE BEEN WORKING ON AN ANSWER WITH THE INHUMANS FOR EIGHT MONTHS, HENRY.
BUT WE'VE BEEN WORKING, TOO. OBVIOUSLY.
I THINK WE ALL WANTED YOU TO SUCCEED. A PEACEFUL SOLUTION REALLY WOULD HAVE BEEN PREFERABLE.
BUT THERE WAS ALWAYS A CHANCE THAT YOU WOULD FAIL, AND SO WE CAME UP WITH...WELL...I SUPPOSE YOU WOULD CALL IT A WARLIKE SOLUTION.
WHO'S THIS "WE" YOU KEEP TALKING ABOUT? I DON'T KNOW ANYTHING ABOUT THIS!
IF YOU WOULD STOP INTERRUPTING ME, "SUGAH," PERHAPS YOU WOULD KNOW SOMETHING ABOUT IT.
WE DIDN'T TELL EVERYONE--BUT EVERYONE HAS A ROLE. LET ME EXPLAIN.

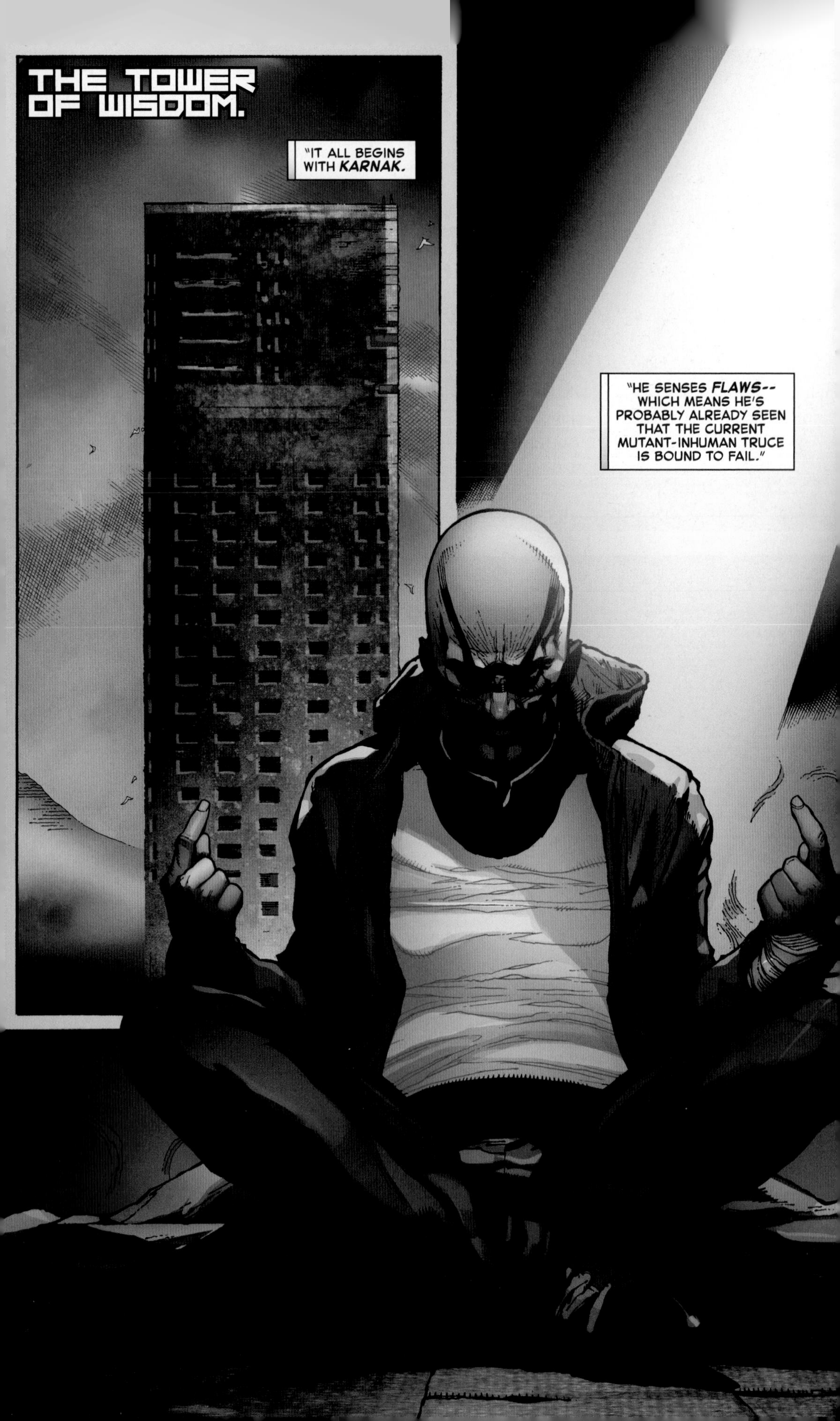
THE TOWER OF WISDOM.
"IT ALL BEGINS WITH KARNAK.
"HE SENSES FLAWS-- WHICH MEANS HE'S PROBABLY ALREADY SEEN THAT THE CURRENT MUTANT-INHUMAN TRUCE IS BOUND TO FAIL."

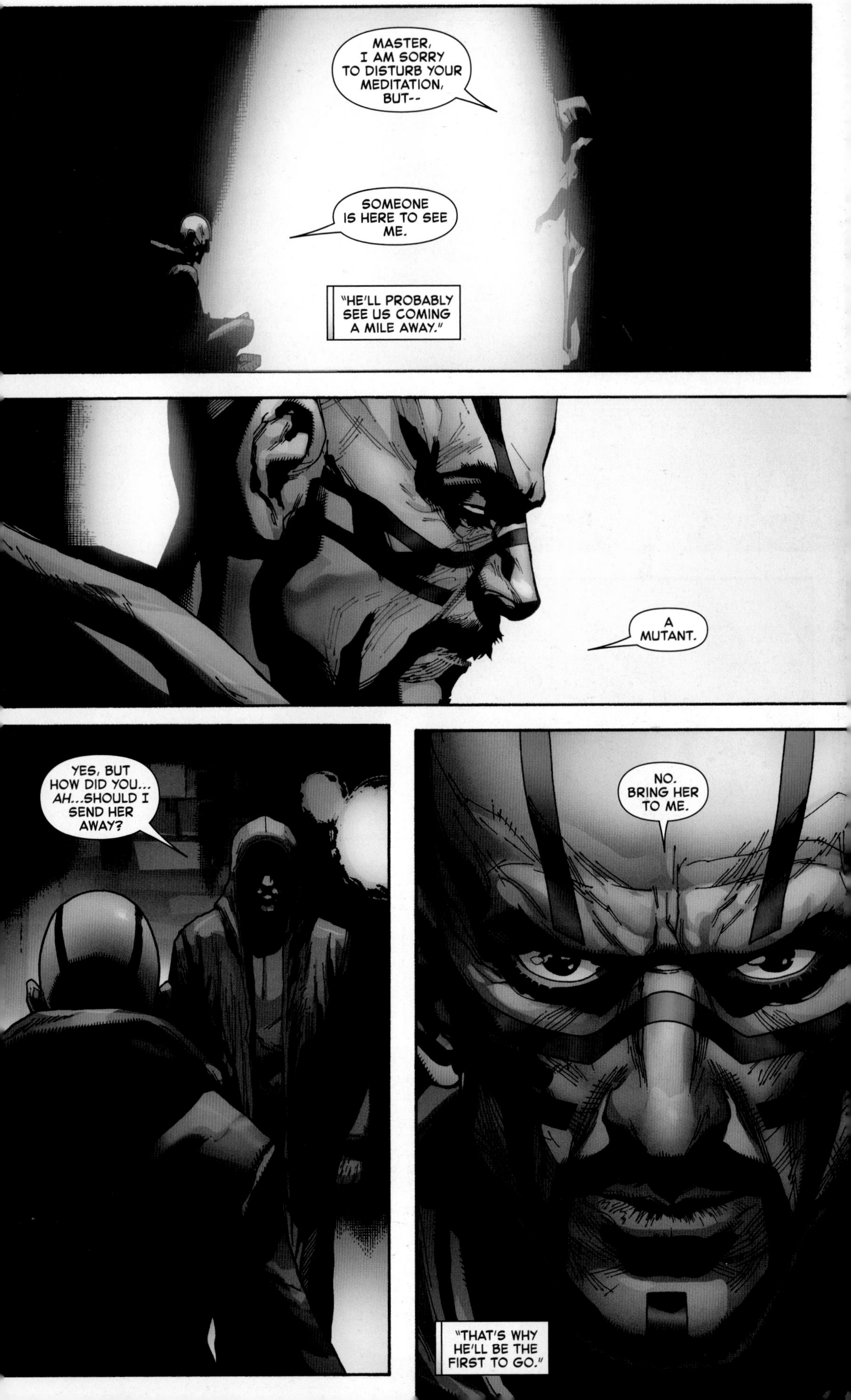
MASTER, I AM SORRY TO DISTURB YOUR MEDITATION, BUT--
SOMEONE IS HERE TO SEE ME.
"HE'LL PROBABLY SEE US COMING A MILE AWAY."
A MUTANT.
YES, BUT HOW DID YOU... AH...SHOULD I SEND HER AWAY?
NO. BRING HER TO ME.
"THAT'S WHY HE'LL BE THE FIRST TO GO."

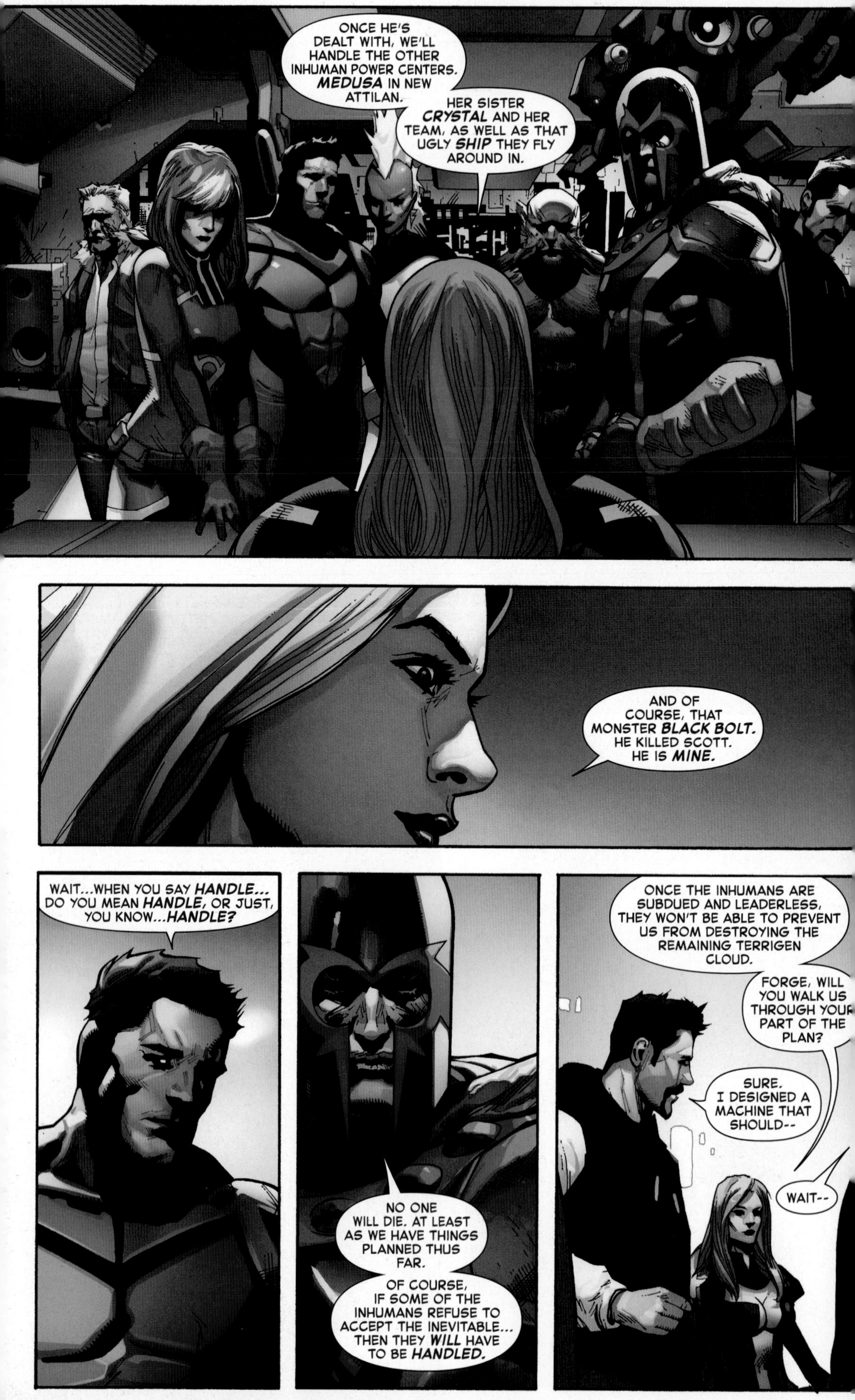
ONCE HE'S DEALT WITH, WE'LL HANDLE THE OTHER INHUMAN POWER CENTERS. MEDUSA IN NEW ATTILAN.
HER SISTER CRYSTAL AND HER TEAM, AS WELL AS THAT UGLY SHIP THEY FLY AROUND IN.
AND OF COURSE, THAT MONSTER BLACK BOLT. HE KILLED SCOTT. HE IS MINE.
WAIT...WHEN YOU SAY HANDLE... DO YOU MEAN HANDLE, OR JUST, YOU KNOW...HANDLE?
NO ONE WILL DIE. AT LEAST AS WE HAVE THINGS PLANNED THUS FAR.
OF COURSE, IF SOME OF THE INHUMANS REFUSE TO ACCEPT THE INEVITABLE... THEN THEY WILL HAVE TO BE HANDLED.
ONCE THE INHUMANS ARE SUBDUED AND LEADERLESS, THEY WON'T BE ABLE TO PREVENT US FROM DESTROYING THE REMAINING TERRIGEN CLOUD.
FORGE, WILL YOU WALK US THROUGH YOUR PART OF THE PLAN?
SURE. I DESIGNED A MACHINE THAT SHOULD--
WAIT--

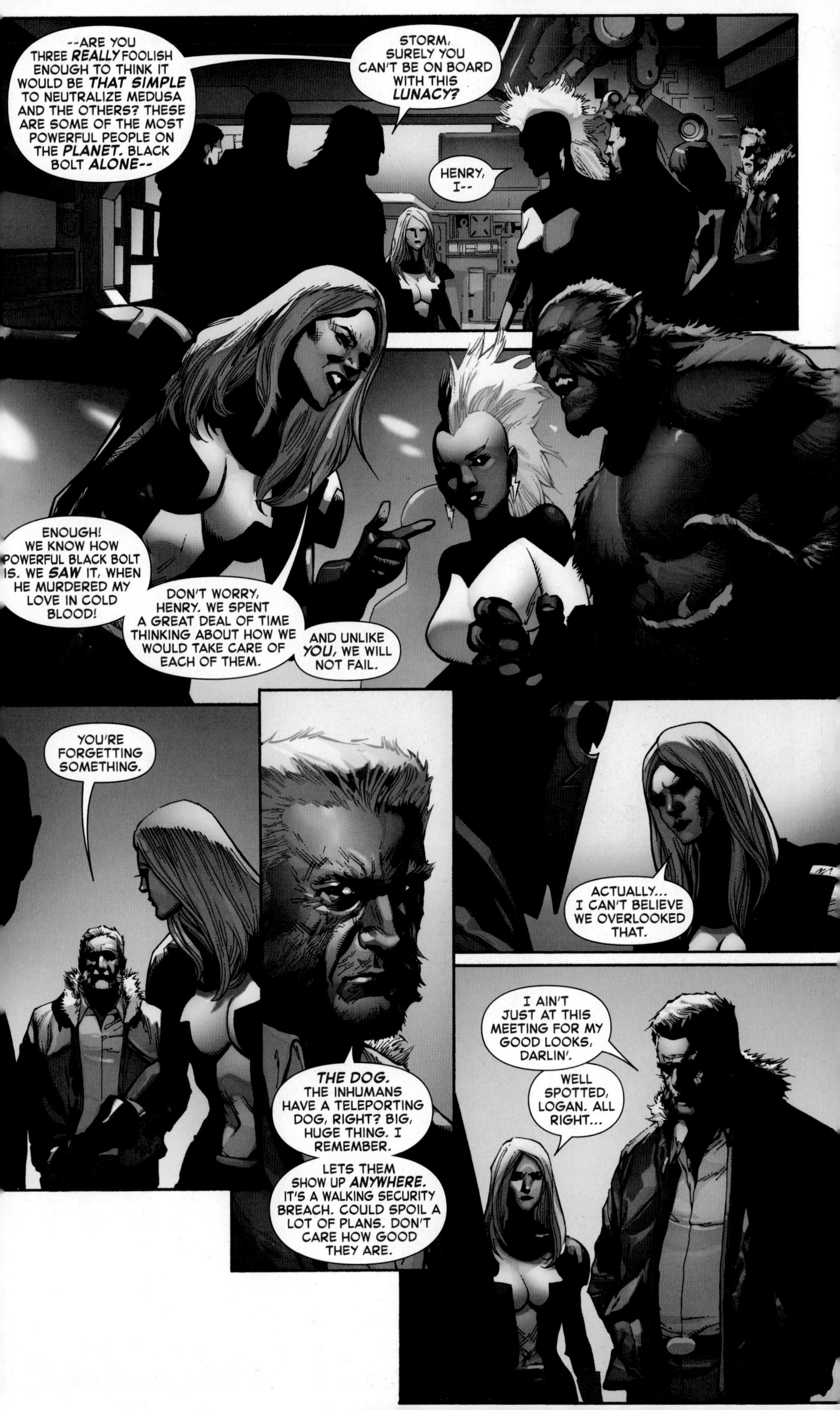
--ARE YOU THREE REALLY FOOLISH ENOUGH TO THINK IT WOULD BE THAT SIMPLE TO NEUTRALIZE MEDUSA AND THE OTHERS? THESE ARE SOME OF THE MOST POWERFUL PEOPLE ON THE PLANET. BLACK BOLT ALONE--
STORM, SURELY YOU CAN'T BE ON BOARD WITH THIS LUNACY?
HENRY, I--
ENOUGH! WE KNOW HOW POWERFUL BLACK BOLT IS. WE SAW IT, WHEN HE MURDERED MY LOVE IN COLD BLOOD!
DON'T WORRY, HENRY. WE SPENT A GREAT DEAL OF TIME THINKING ABOUT HOW WE WOULD TAKE CARE OF EACH OF THEM.
AND UNLIKE YOU, WE WILL NOT FAIL.
YOU'RE FORGETTING SOMETHING.
THE DOG. THE INHUMANS HAVE A TELEPORTING DOG, RIGHT? BIG, HUGE THING. I REMEMBER.
LETS THEM SHOW UP ANYWHERE. IT'S A WALKING SECURITY BREACH. COULD SPOIL A LOT OF PLANS. DON'T CARE HOW GOOD THEY ARE.
ACTUALLY... I CAN'T BELIEVE WE OVERLOOKED THAT.
I AIN'T JUST AT THIS MEETING FOR MY GOOD LOOKS, DARLIN'.
WELL SPOTTED, LOGAN. ALL RIGHT...

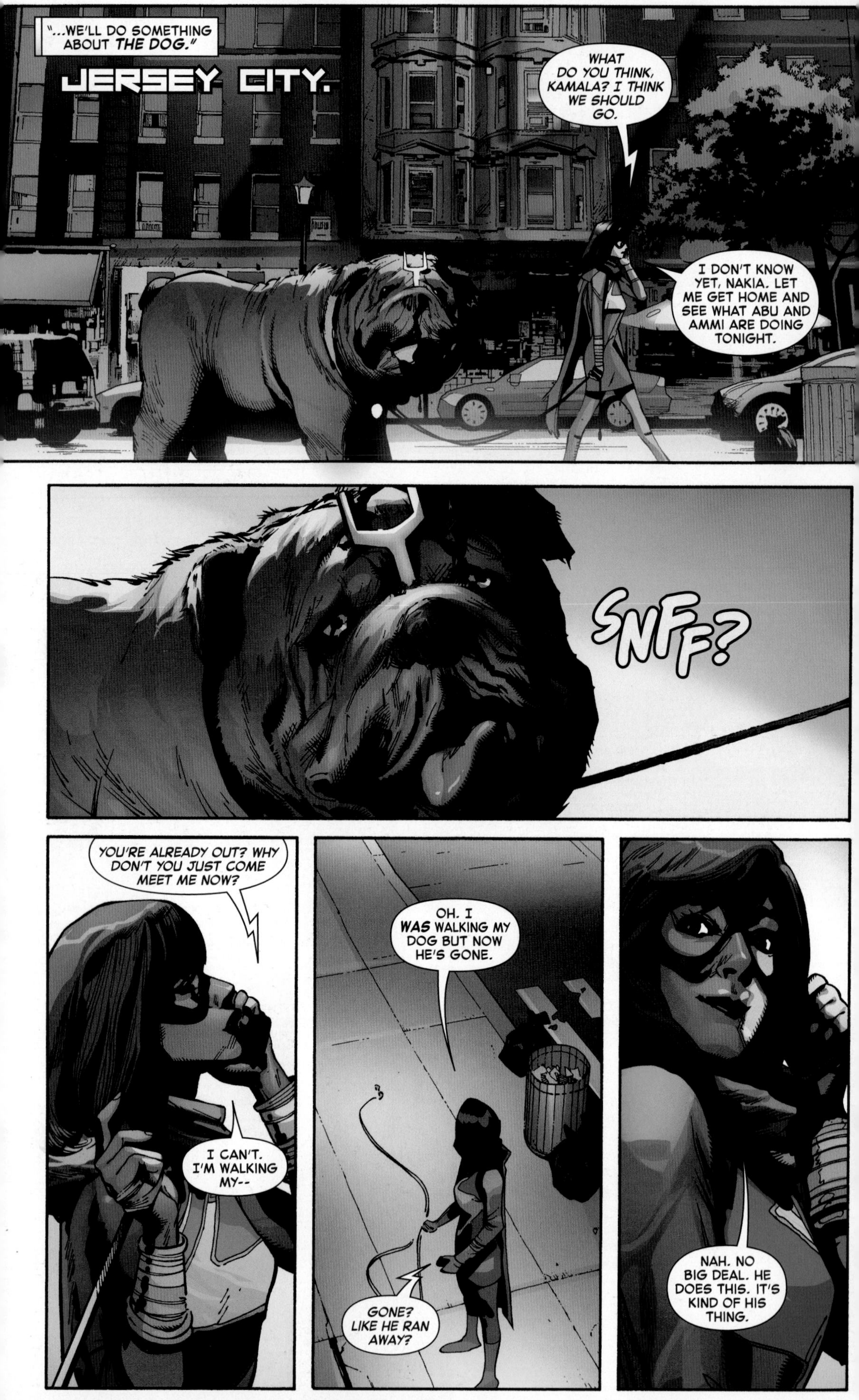

"...WE'LL DO SOMETHING ABOUT *THE DOG.*"
JERSEY CITY.
WHAT DO YOU THINK, KAMALA? I THINK WE SHOULD GO.
I DON'T KNOW YET, NAKIA. LET ME GET HOME AND SEE WHAT ABU AND AMMI ARE DOING TONIGHT.
SNFF?
YOU'RE ALREADY OUT? WHY DON'T YOU JUST COME MEET ME NOW?
I CAN'T. I'M WALKING MY--
OH. I **WAS** WALKING MY DOG BUT NOW HE'S GONE.
GONE? LIKE HE RAN AWAY?
NAH. NO BIG DEAL. HE DOES THIS. IT'S KIND OF HIS THING.

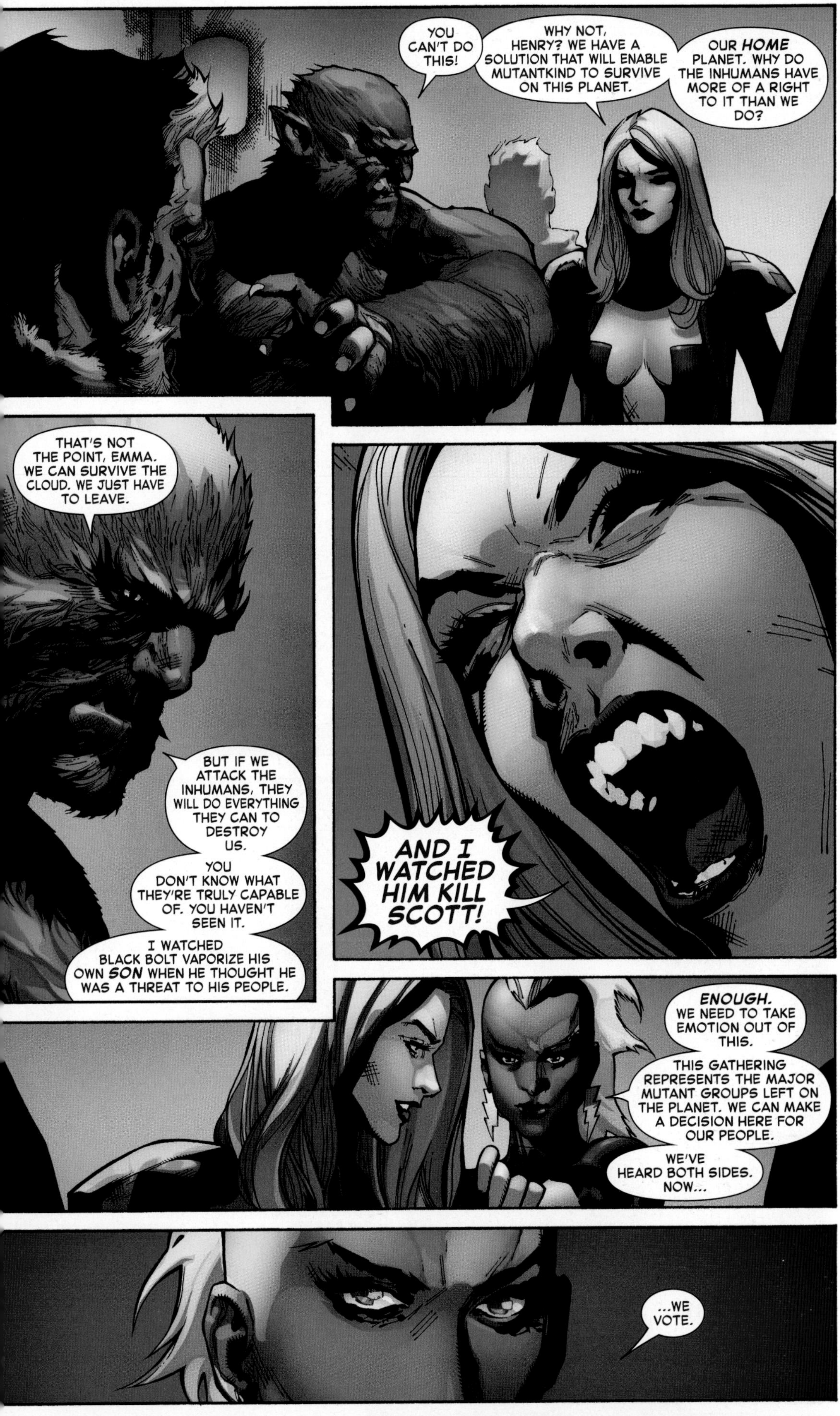
YOU CAN'T DO THIS!
WHY NOT, HENRY? WE HAVE A SOLUTION THAT WILL ENABLE MUTANTKIND TO SURVIVE ON THIS PLANET.
OUR HOME PLANET. WHY DO THE INHUMANS HAVE MORE OF A RIGHT TO IT THAN WE DO?
THAT'S NOT THE POINT, EMMA. WE CAN SURVIVE THE CLOUD. WE JUST HAVE TO LEAVE.
BUT IF WE ATTACK THE INHUMANS, THEY WILL DO EVERYTHING THEY CAN TO DESTROY US.
YOU DON'T KNOW WHAT THEY'RE TRULY CAPABLE OF. YOU HAVEN'T SEEN IT.
I WATCHED BLACK BOLT VAPORIZE HIS OWN SON WHEN HE THOUGHT HE WAS A THREAT TO HIS PEOPLE.
AND I WATCHED HIM KILL SCOTT!
ENOUGH. WE NEED TO TAKE EMOTION OUT OF THIS.
THIS GATHERING REPRESENTS THE MAJOR MUTANT GROUPS LEFT ON THE PLANET. WE CAN MAKE A DECISION HERE FOR OUR PEOPLE.
WE'VE HEARD BOTH SIDES. NOW...
...WE VOTE.

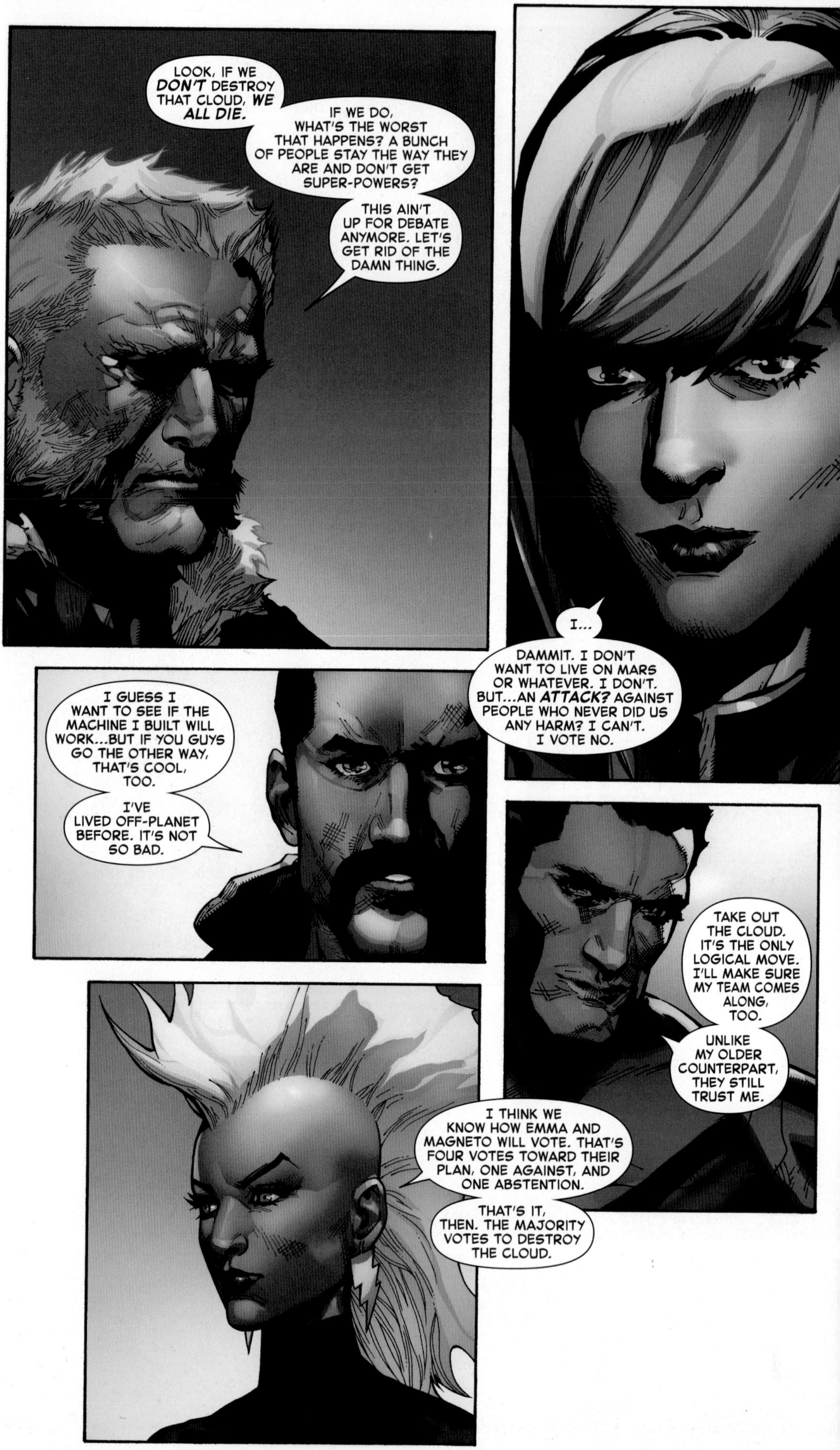
LOOK, IF WE DON'T DESTROY THAT CLOUD, WE ALL DIE.
IF WE DO, WHAT'S THE WORST THAT HAPPENS? A BUNCH OF PEOPLE STAY THE WAY THEY ARE AND DON'T GET SUPER-POWERS?
THIS AIN'T UP FOR DEBATE ANYMORE. LET'S GET RID OF THE DAMN THING.
I...
DAMMIT. I DON'T WANT TO LIVE ON MARS OR WHATEVER. I DON'T. BUT...AN ATTACK? AGAINST PEOPLE WHO NEVER DID US ANY HARM? I CAN'T. I VOTE NO.
I GUESS I WANT TO SEE IF THE MACHINE I BUILT WILL WORK...BUT IF YOU GUYS GO THE OTHER WAY, THAT'S COOL, TOO.
I'VE LIVED OFF-PLANET BEFORE. IT'S NOT SO BAD.
TAKE OUT THE CLOUD. IT'S THE ONLY LOGICAL MOVE. I'LL MAKE SURE MY TEAM COMES ALONG, TOO.
UNLIKE MY OLDER COUNTERPART, THEY STILL TRUST ME.
I THINK WE KNOW HOW EMMA AND MAGNETO WILL VOTE. THAT'S FOUR VOTES TOWARD THEIR PLAN, ONE AGAINST, AND ONE ABSTENTION.
THAT'S IT, THEN. THE MAJORITY VOTES TO DESTROY THE CLOUD.

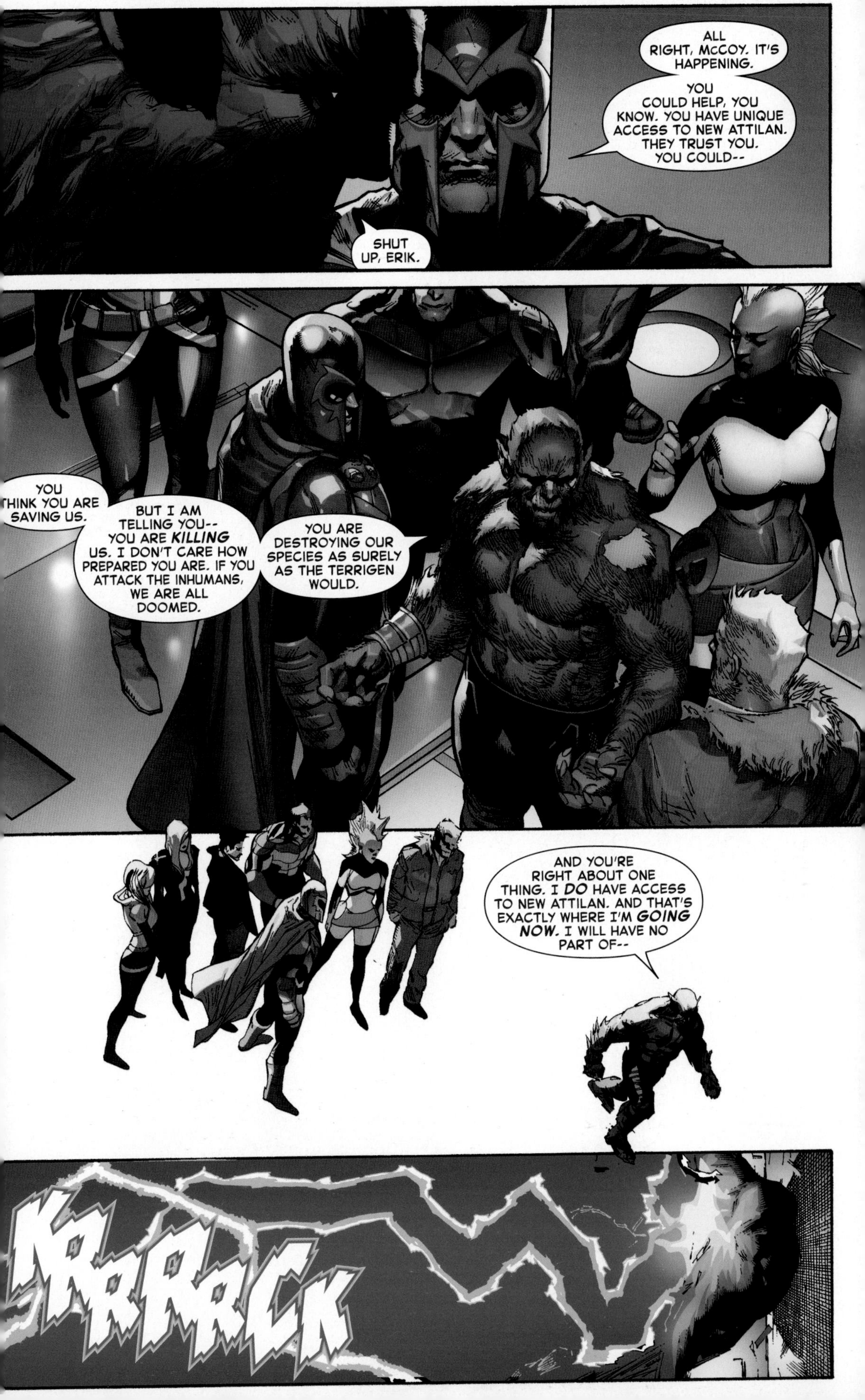
ALL RIGHT, McCOY. IT'S HAPPENING.
YOU COULD HELP, YOU KNOW. YOU HAVE UNIQUE ACCESS TO NEW ATTILAN. THEY TRUST YOU. YOU COULD--
SHUT UP, ERIK.
YOU THINK YOU ARE SAVING US.
BUT I AM TELLING YOU-- YOU ARE KILLING US. I DON'T CARE HOW PREPARED YOU ARE. IF YOU ATTACK THE INHUMANS, WE ARE ALL DOOMED.
YOU ARE DESTROYING OUR SPECIES AS SURELY AS THE TERRIGEN WOULD.
AND YOU'RE RIGHT ABOUT ONE THING. I DO HAVE ACCESS TO NEW ATTILAN. AND THAT'S EXACTLY WHERE I'M GOING NOW. I WILL HAVE NO PART OF--
KRRRRCK

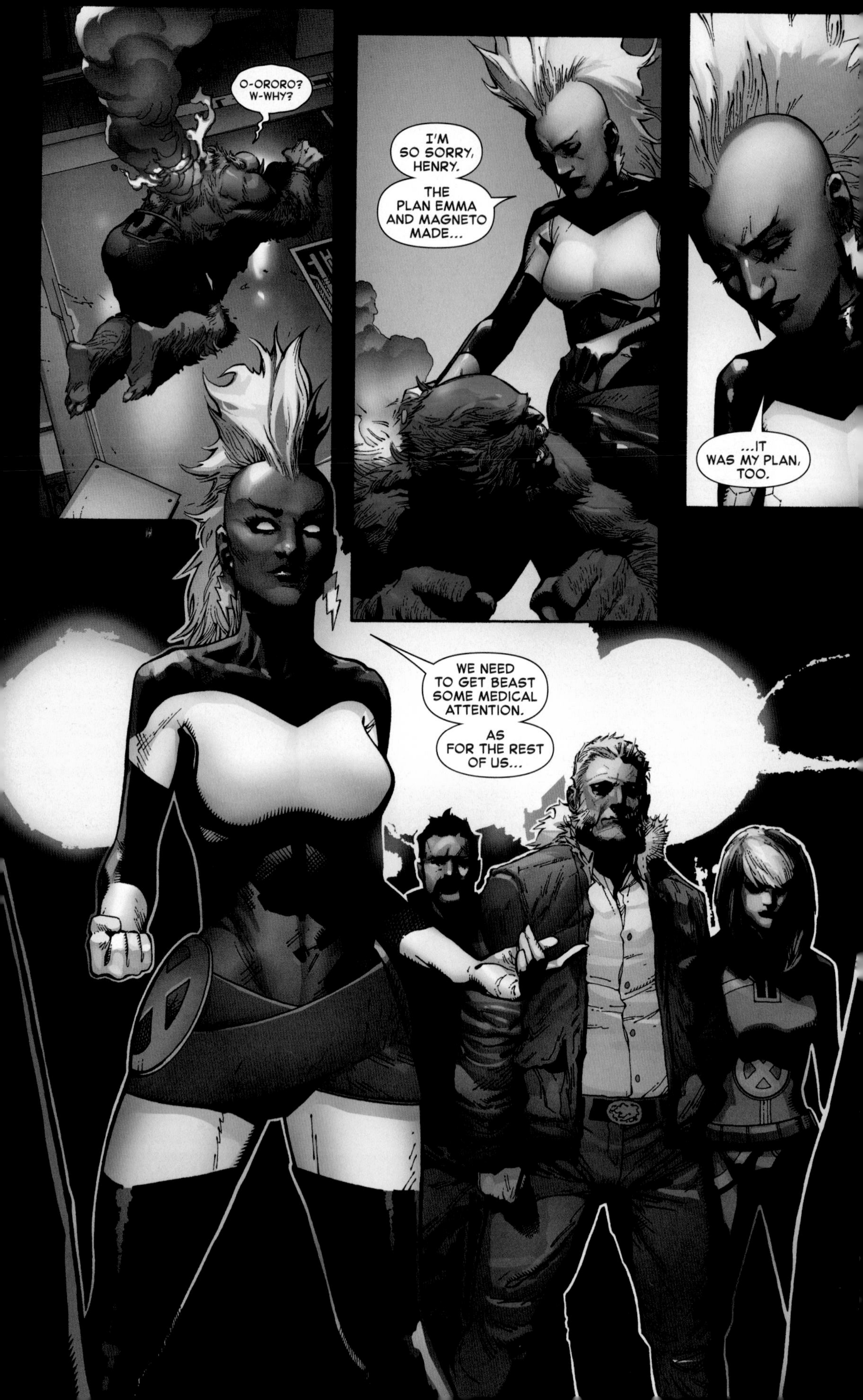
O-ORORO? W-WHY?
I'M SO SORRY, HENRY.
THE PLAN EMMA AND MAGNETO MADE...
...IT WAS MY PLAN, TOO.
WE NEED TO GET BEAST SOME MEDICAL ATTENTION.
AS FOR THE REST OF US...

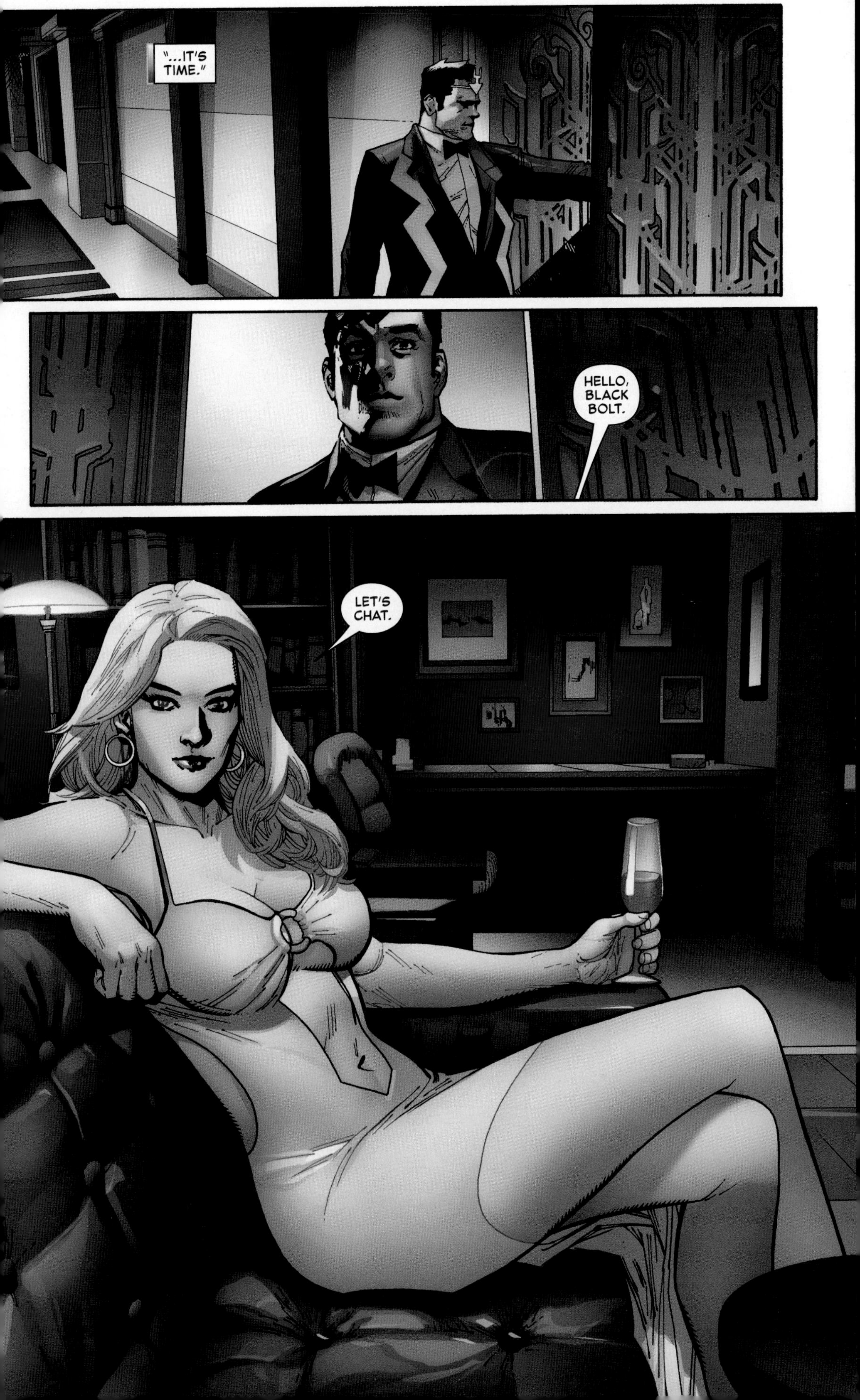
"...IT'S TIME."
HELLO, BLACK BOLT.
LET'S CHAT.

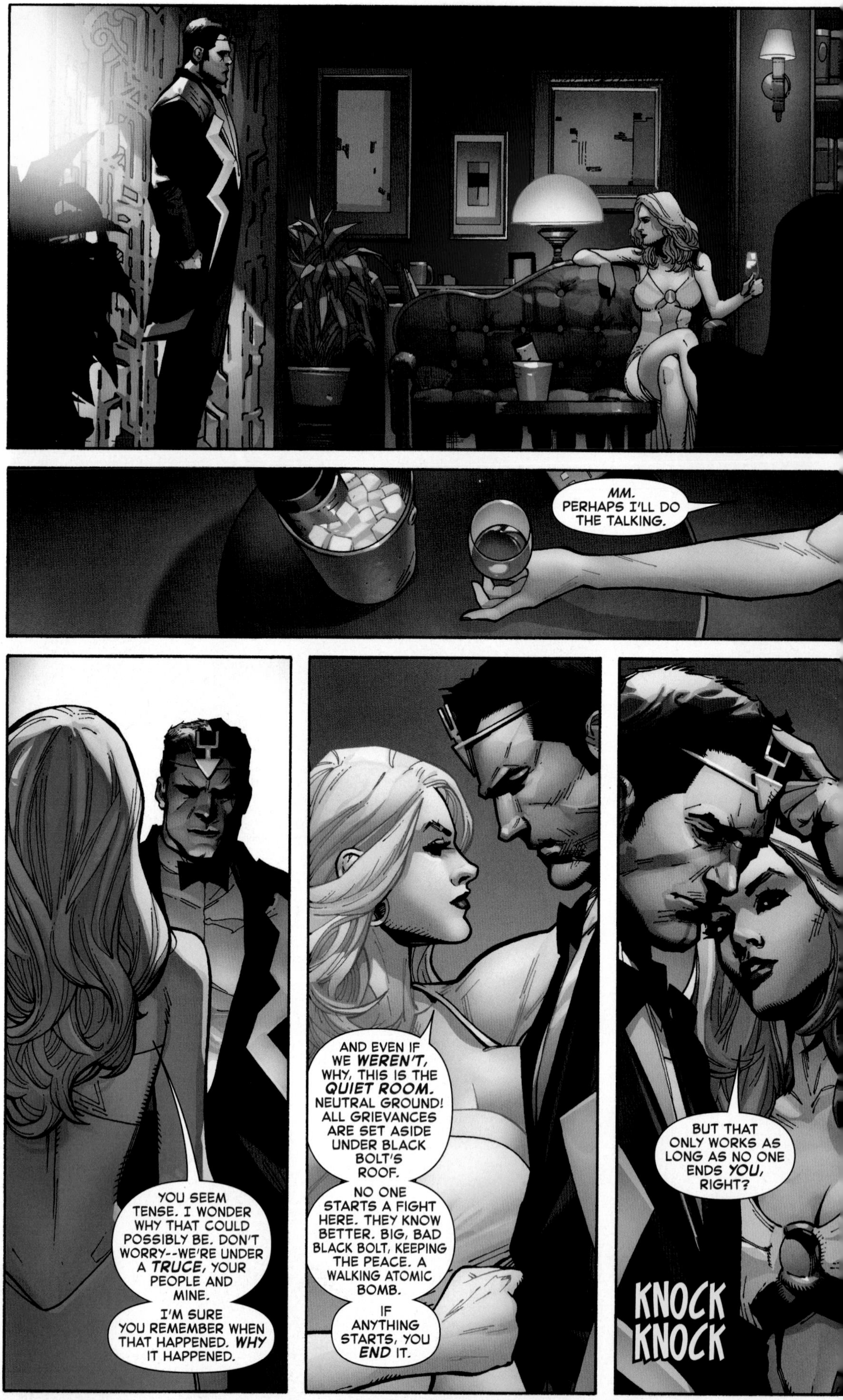
MM. PERHAPS I'LL DO THE TALKING.
YOU SEEM TENSE. I WONDER WHY THAT COULD POSSIBLY BE. DON'T WORRY--WE'RE UNDER A TRUCE, YOUR PEOPLE AND MINE.
I'M SURE YOU REMEMBER WHEN THAT HAPPENED. WHY IT HAPPENED.
AND EVEN IF WE WEREN'T, WHY, THIS IS THE QUIET ROOM. NEUTRAL GROUND! ALL GRIEVANCES ARE SET ASIDE UNDER BLACK BOLT'S ROOF.
NO ONE STARTS A FIGHT HERE. THEY KNOW BETTER. BIG, BAD BLACK BOLT, KEEPING THE PEACE. A WALKING ATOMIC BOMB.
IF ANYTHING STARTS, YOU END IT.
BUT THAT ONLY WORKS AS LONG AS NO ONE ENDS YOU, RIGHT?
KNOCK KNOCK

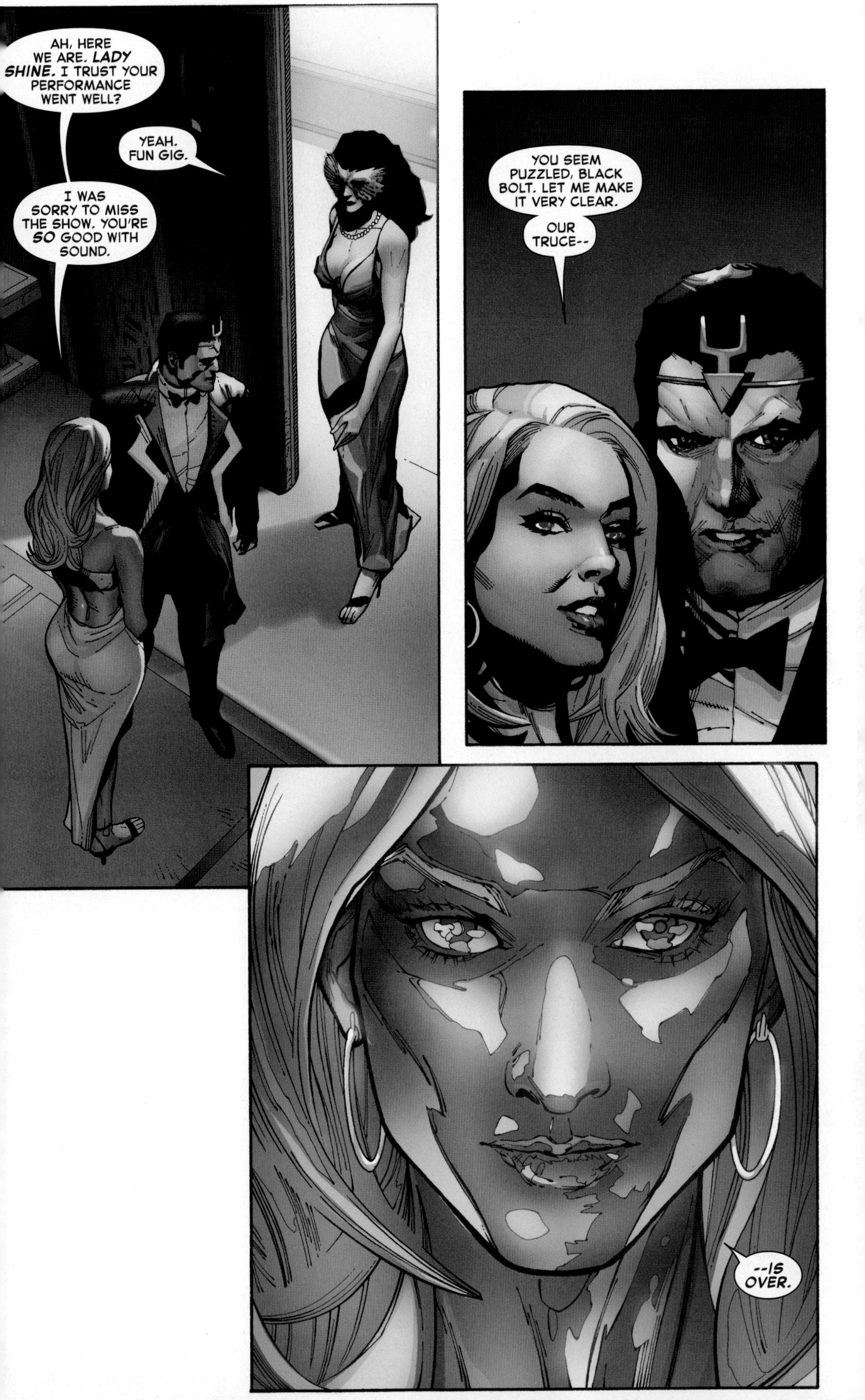
AH, HERE WE ARE. LADY SHINE. I TRUST YOUR PERFORMANCE WENT WELL?
YEAH. FUN GIG.
I WAS SORRY TO MISS THE SHOW. YOU'RE SO GOOD WITH SOUND.
YOU SEEM PUZZLED, BLACK BOLT. LET ME MAKE IT VERY CLEAR.
OUR TRUCE--
--IS OVER.

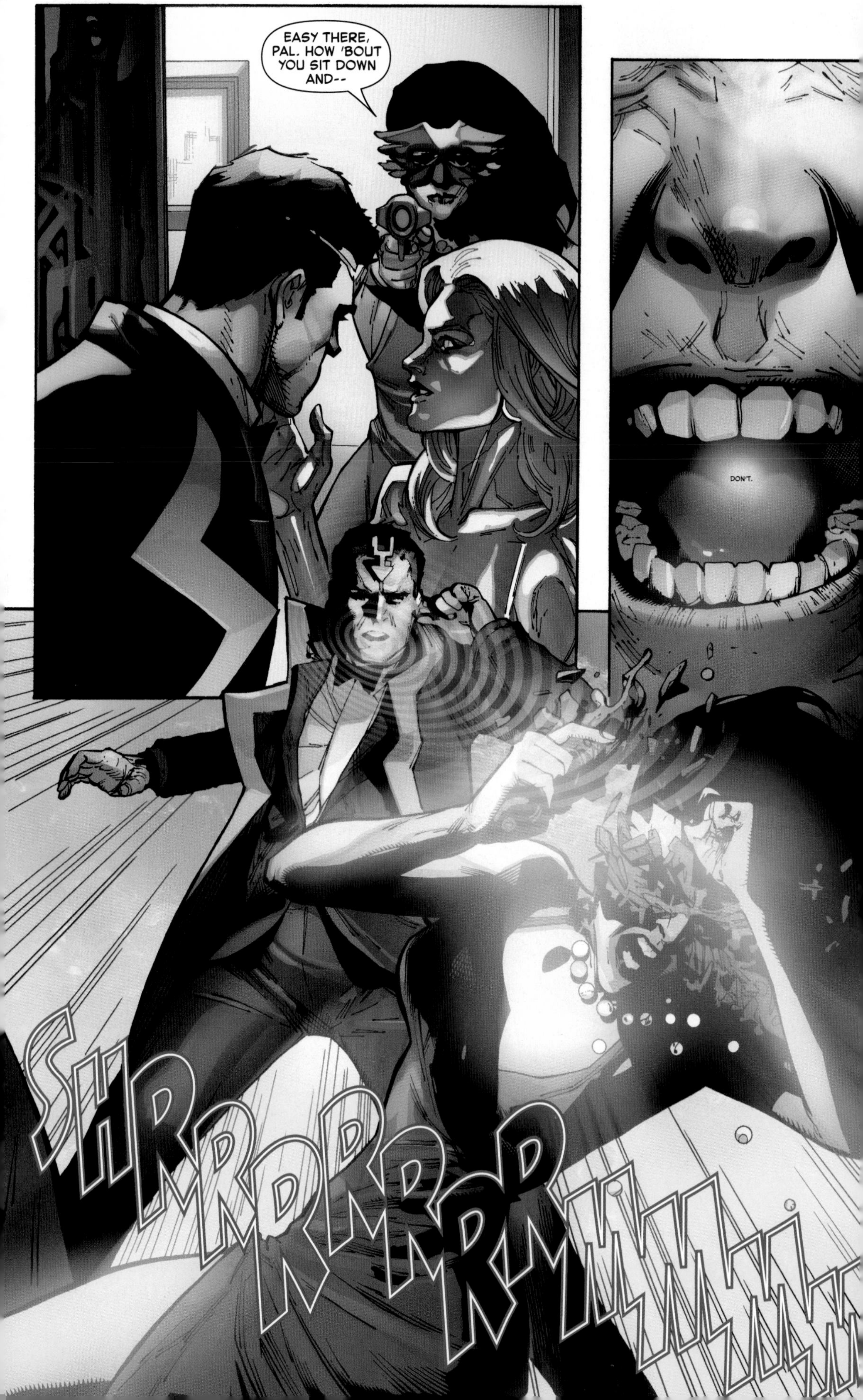
EASY THERE, PAL. HOW 'BOUT YOU SIT DOWN AND--
DON'T.
SHRRRRRRMMMMMM

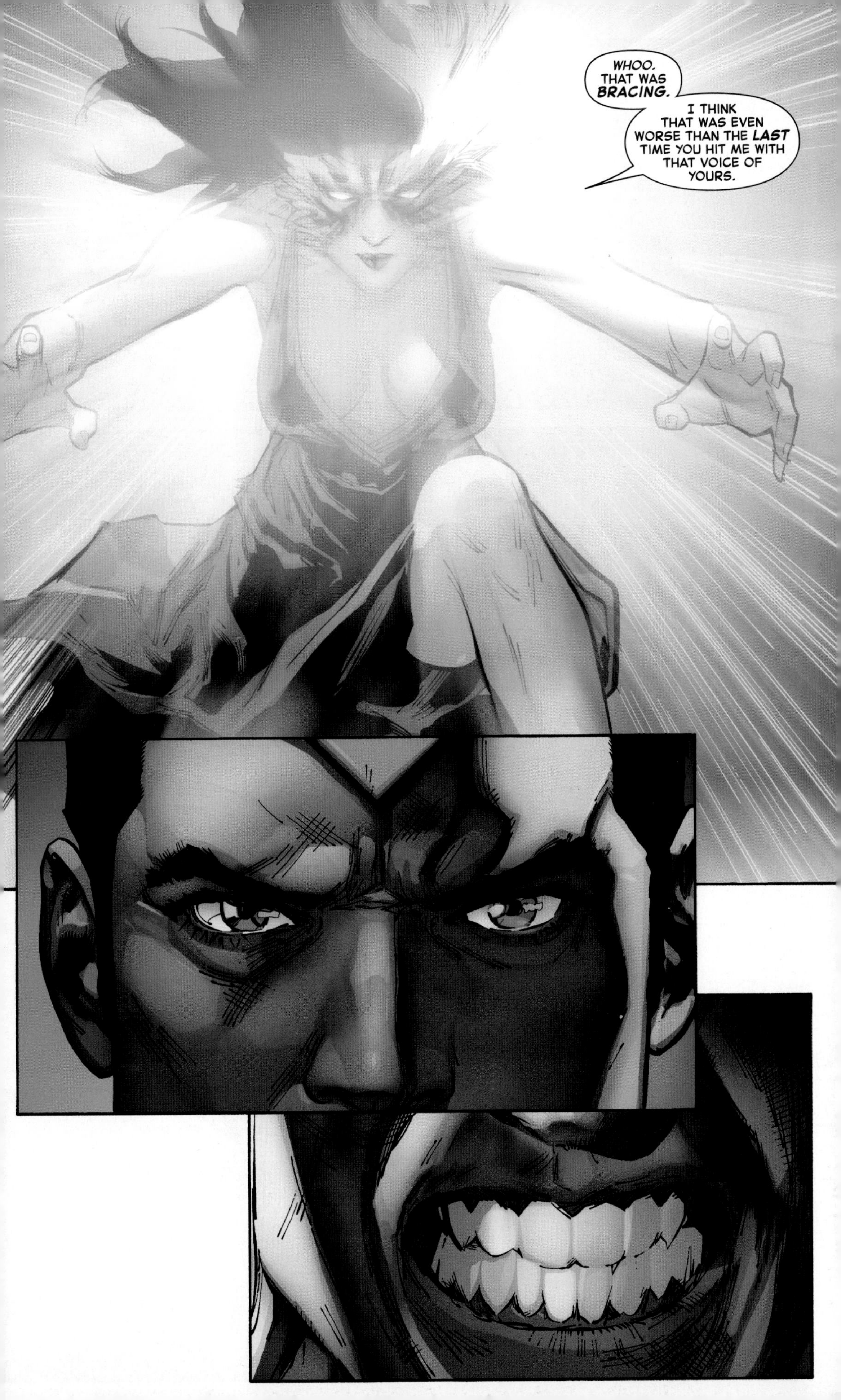
WHOO. THAT WAS BRACING.
I THINK THAT WAS EVEN WORSE THAN THE LAST TIME YOU HIT ME WITH THAT VOICE OF YOURS.

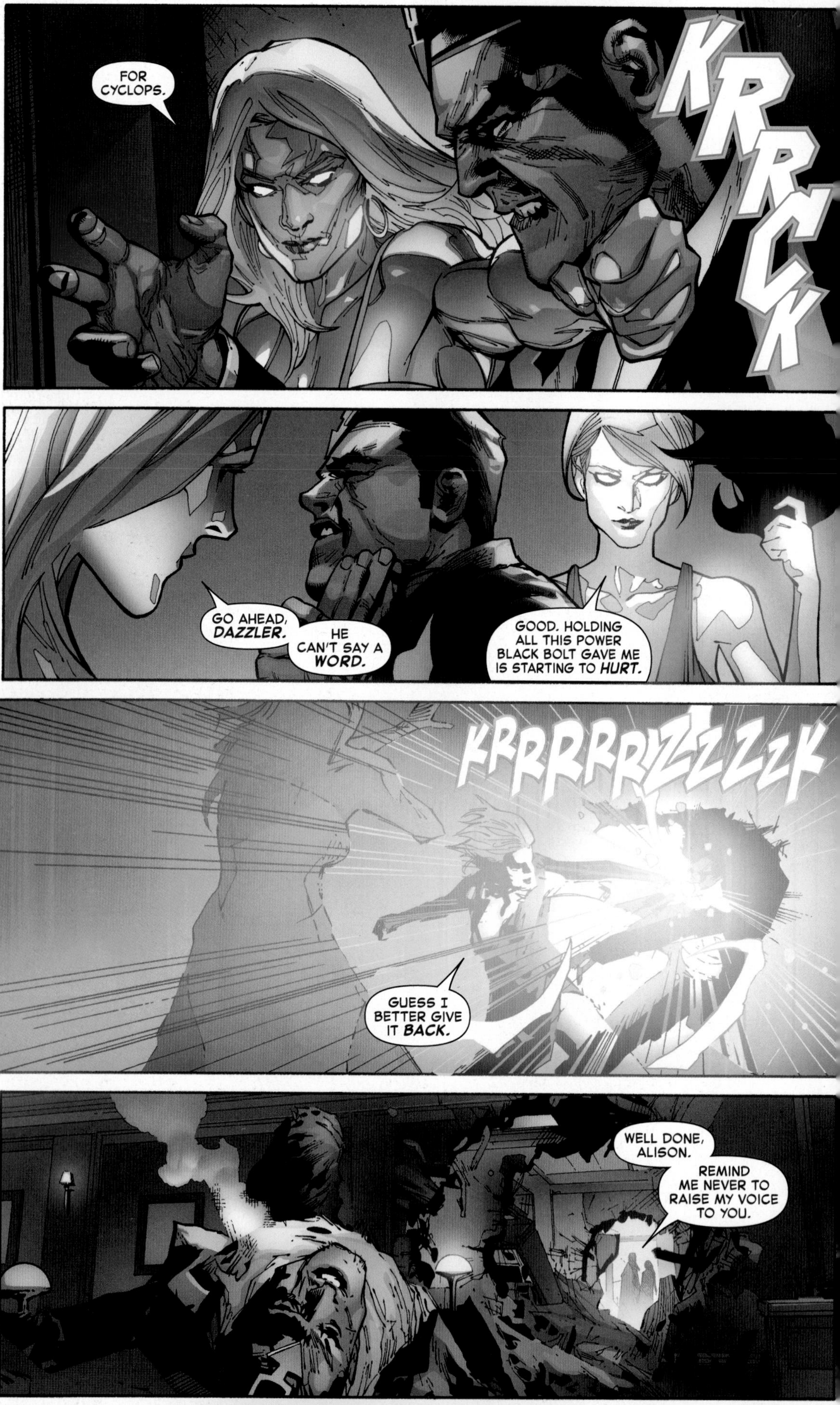
FOR CYCLOPS.
KRRCK
GO AHEAD, DAZZLER.
HE CAN'T SAY A WORD.
GOOD. HOLDING ALL THIS POWER BLACK BOLT GAVE ME IS STARTING TO HURT.
KRRRRRZZZZK
GUESS I BETTER GIVE IT BACK.
WELL DONE, ALISON.
REMIND ME NEVER TO RAISE MY VOICE TO YOU.

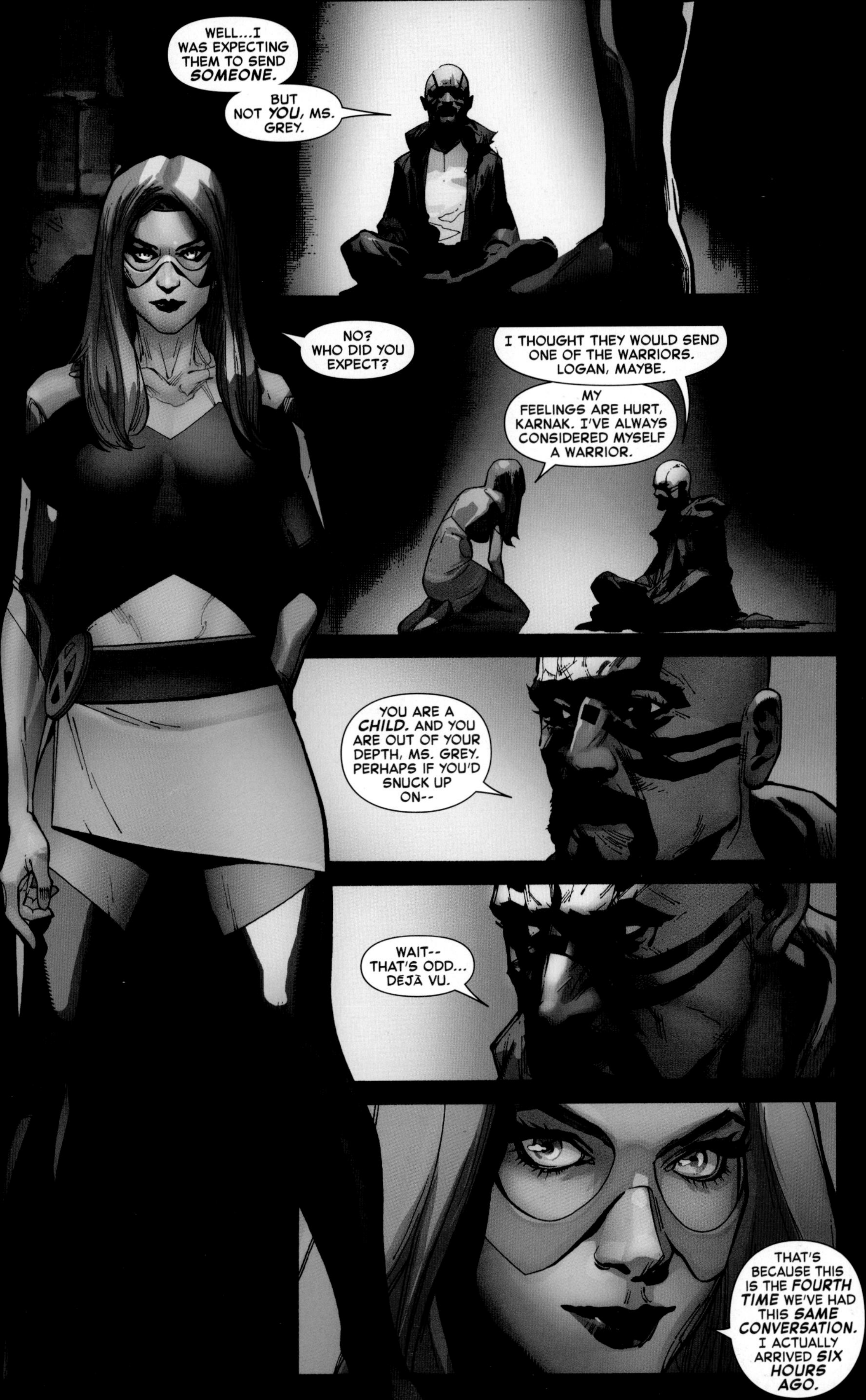

WELL...I WAS EXPECTING THEM TO SEND SOMEONE.
BUT NOT YOU, MS. GREY.
NO? WHO DID YOU EXPECT?
I THOUGHT THEY WOULD SEND ONE OF THE WARRIORS. LOGAN, MAYBE.
MY FEELINGS ARE HURT, KARNAK. I'VE ALWAYS CONSIDERED MYSELF A WARRIOR.
YOU ARE A CHILD. AND YOU ARE OUT OF YOUR DEPTH, MS. GREY. PERHAPS IF YOU'D SNUCK UP ON--
WAIT-- THAT'S ODD... DÉJÀ VU.
THAT'S BECAUSE THIS IS THE FOURTH TIME WE'VE HAD THIS SAME CONVERSATION. I ACTUALLY ARRIVED SIX HOURS AGO.

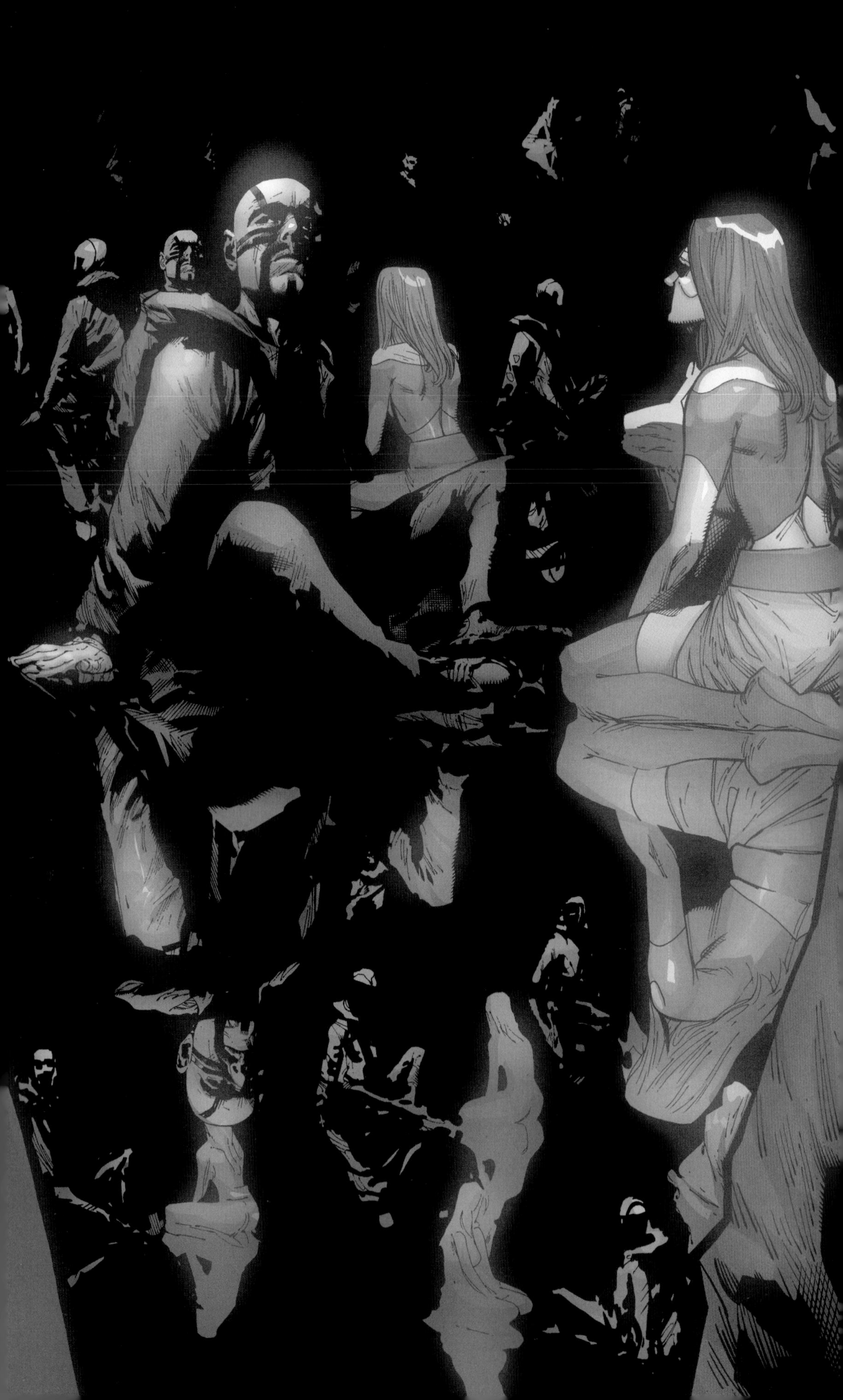

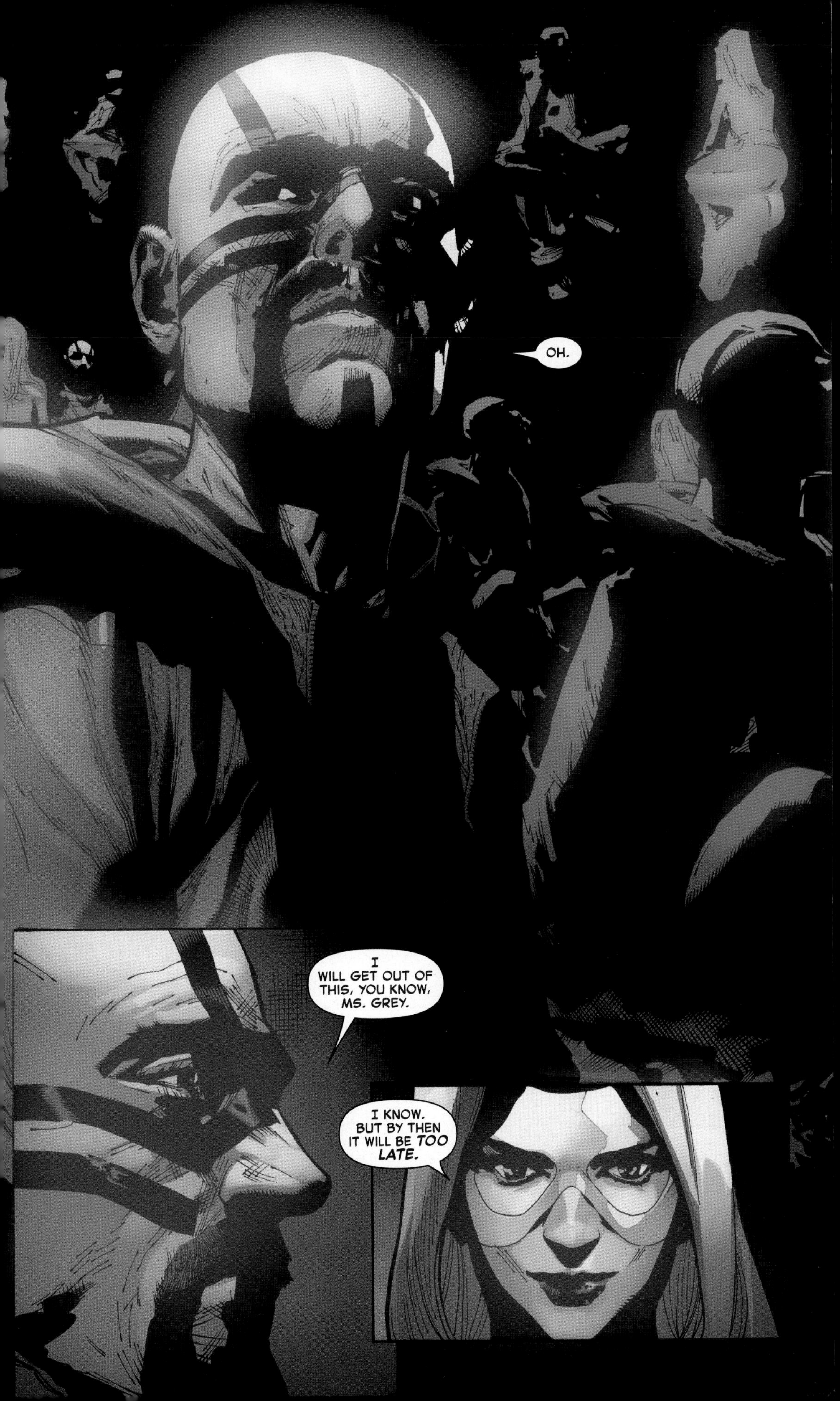
OH.
I WILL GET OUT OF THIS, YOU KNOW, MS. GREY.
I KNOW. BUT BY THEN IT WILL BE *TOO LATE.*

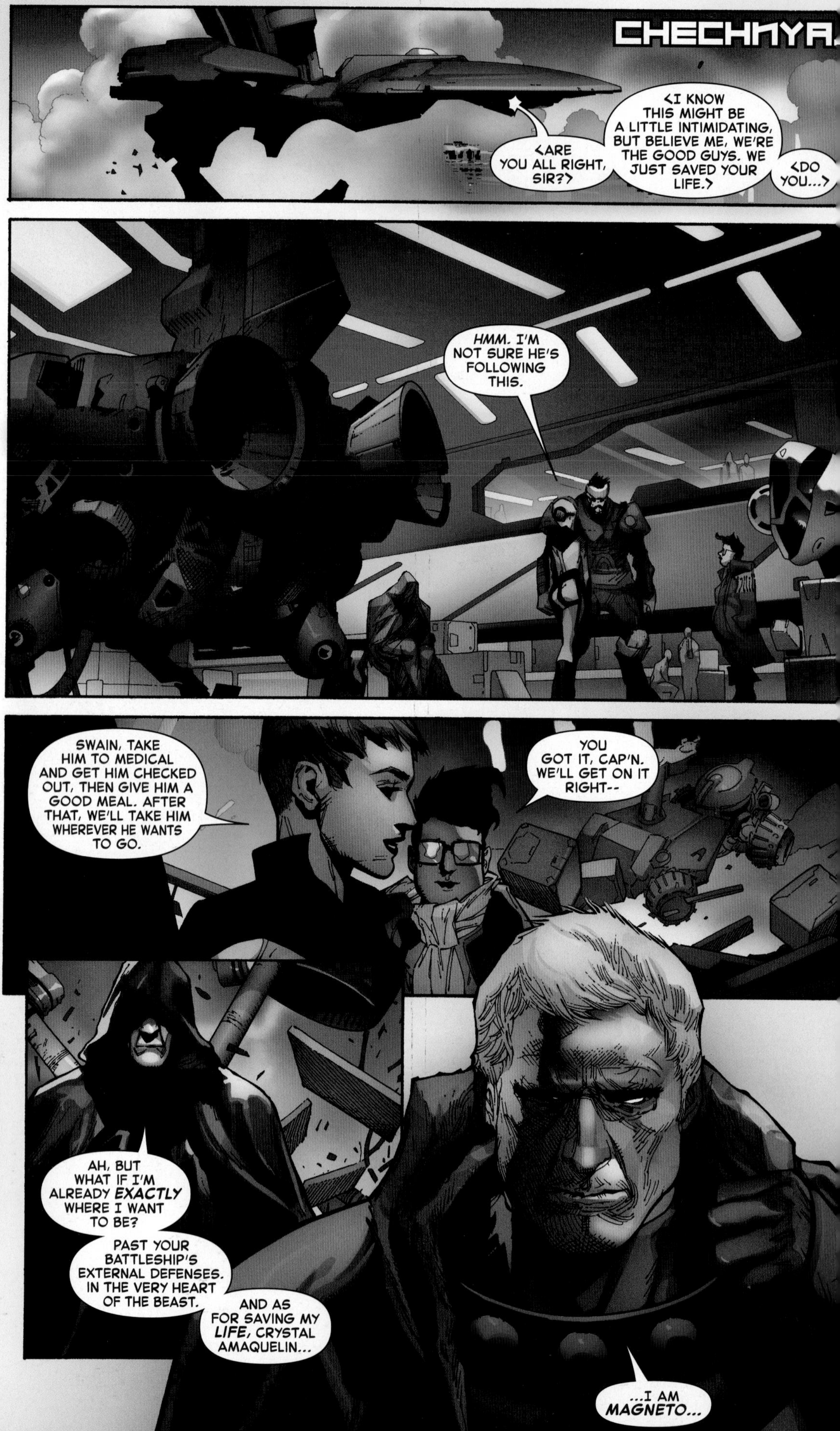
CHECHNYA.
<ARE YOU ALL RIGHT, SIR?>
<I KNOW THIS MIGHT BE A LITTLE INTIMIDATING, BUT BELIEVE ME, WE'RE THE GOOD GUYS. WE JUST SAVED YOUR LIFE.>
<DO YOU...>
HMM. I'M NOT SURE HE'S FOLLOWING THIS.
SWAIN, TAKE HIM TO MEDICAL AND GET HIM CHECKED OUT, THEN GIVE HIM A GOOD MEAL. AFTER THAT, WE'LL TAKE HIM WHEREVER HE WANTS TO GO.
YOU GOT IT, CAP'N. WE'LL GET ON IT RIGHT--
AH, BUT WHAT IF I'M ALREADY EXACTLY WHERE I WANT TO BE?
PAST YOUR BATTLESHIP'S EXTERNAL DEFENSES. IN THE VERY HEART OF THE BEAST.
AND AS FOR SAVING MY LIFE, CRYSTAL AMAQUELIN...
...I AM MAGNETO...

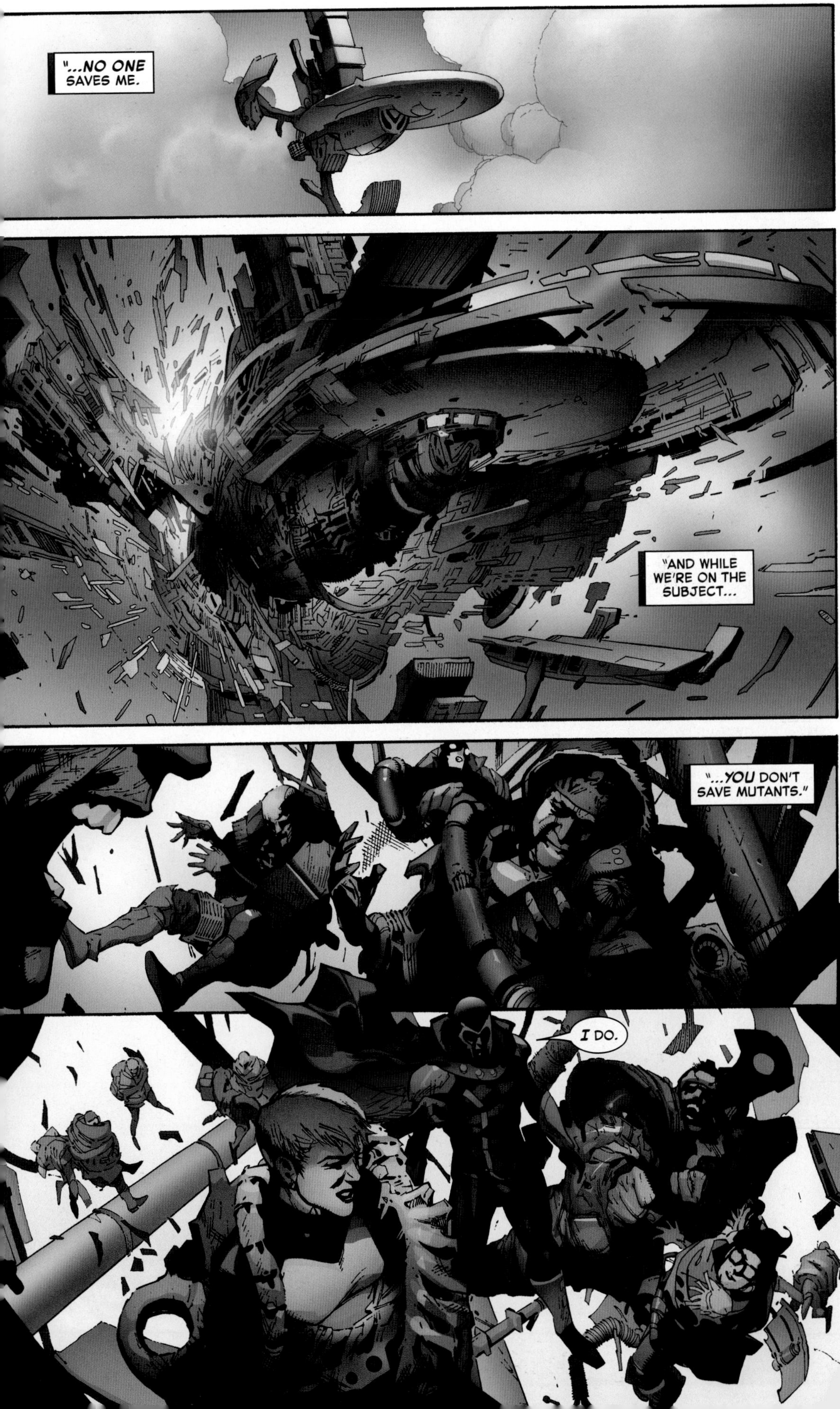
"...NO ONE SAVES ME.
"AND WHILE WE'RE ON THE SUBJECT...
"...YOU DON'T SAVE MUTANTS."
I DO.

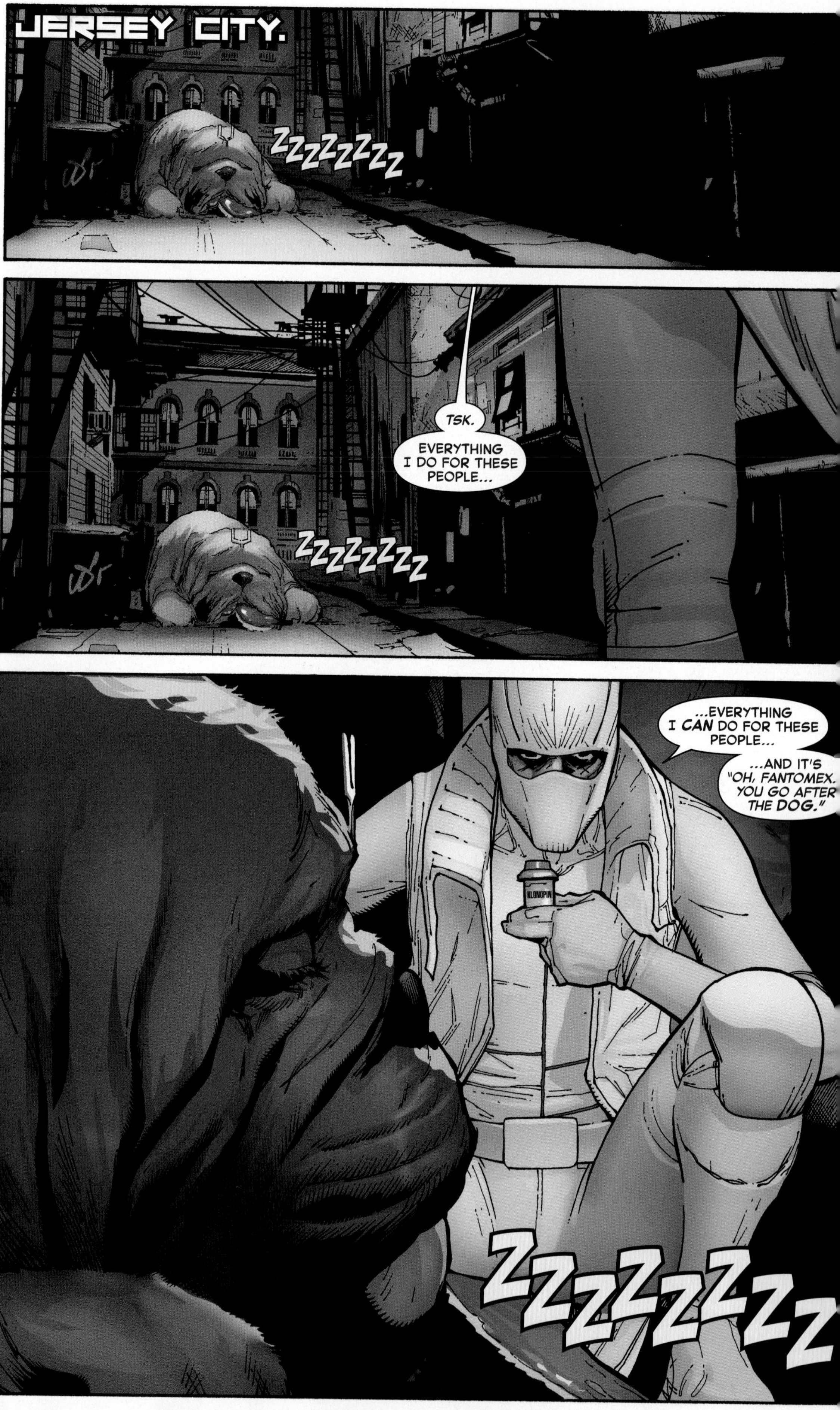
JERSEY CITY.
ZZZZZZZZ
TSK.
EVERYTHING I DO FOR THESE PEOPLE...
ZZZZZZZZ
...EVERYTHING I CAN DO FOR THESE PEOPLE...
...AND IT'S "OH, FANTOMEX. YOU GO AFTER THE DOG."
KLONOPIN
ZZZZZZZZZ

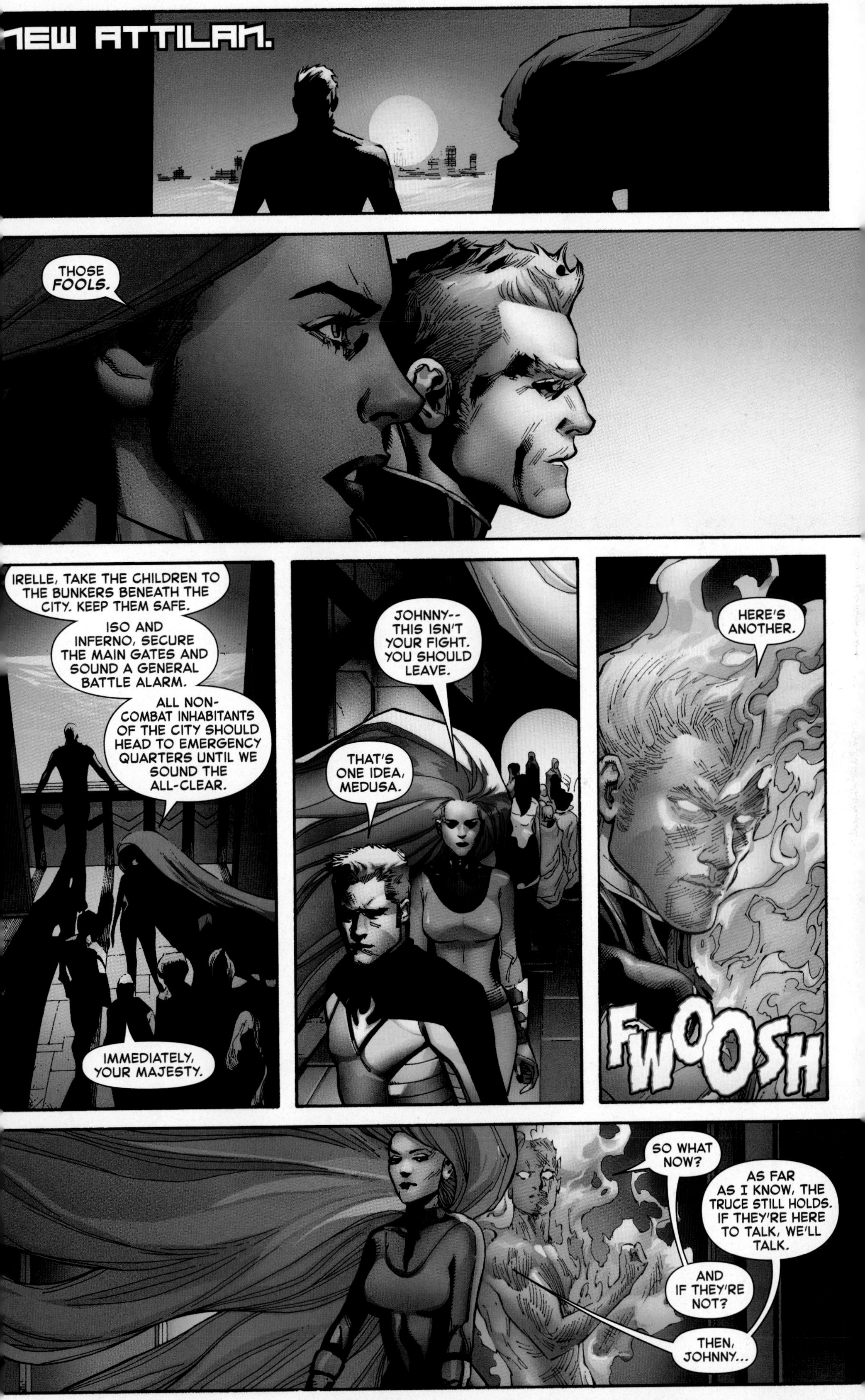
NEW ATTILAN.
THOSE FOOLS.
IRELLE, TAKE THE CHILDREN TO THE BUNKERS BENEATH THE CITY. KEEP THEM SAFE.
ISO AND INFERNO, SECURE THE MAIN GATES AND SOUND A GENERAL BATTLE ALARM.
ALL NON-COMBAT INHABITANTS OF THE CITY SHOULD HEAD TO EMERGENCY QUARTERS UNTIL WE SOUND THE ALL-CLEAR.
IMMEDIATELY, YOUR MAJESTY.
JOHNNY-- THIS ISN'T YOUR FIGHT. YOU SHOULD LEAVE.
THAT'S ONE IDEA, MEDUSA.
HERE'S ANOTHER.
FWOOSH
SO WHAT NOW?
AS FAR AS I KNOW, THE TRUCE STILL HOLDS. IF THEY'RE HERE TO TALK, WE'LL TALK.
AND IF THEY'RE NOT?
THEN, JOHNNY...

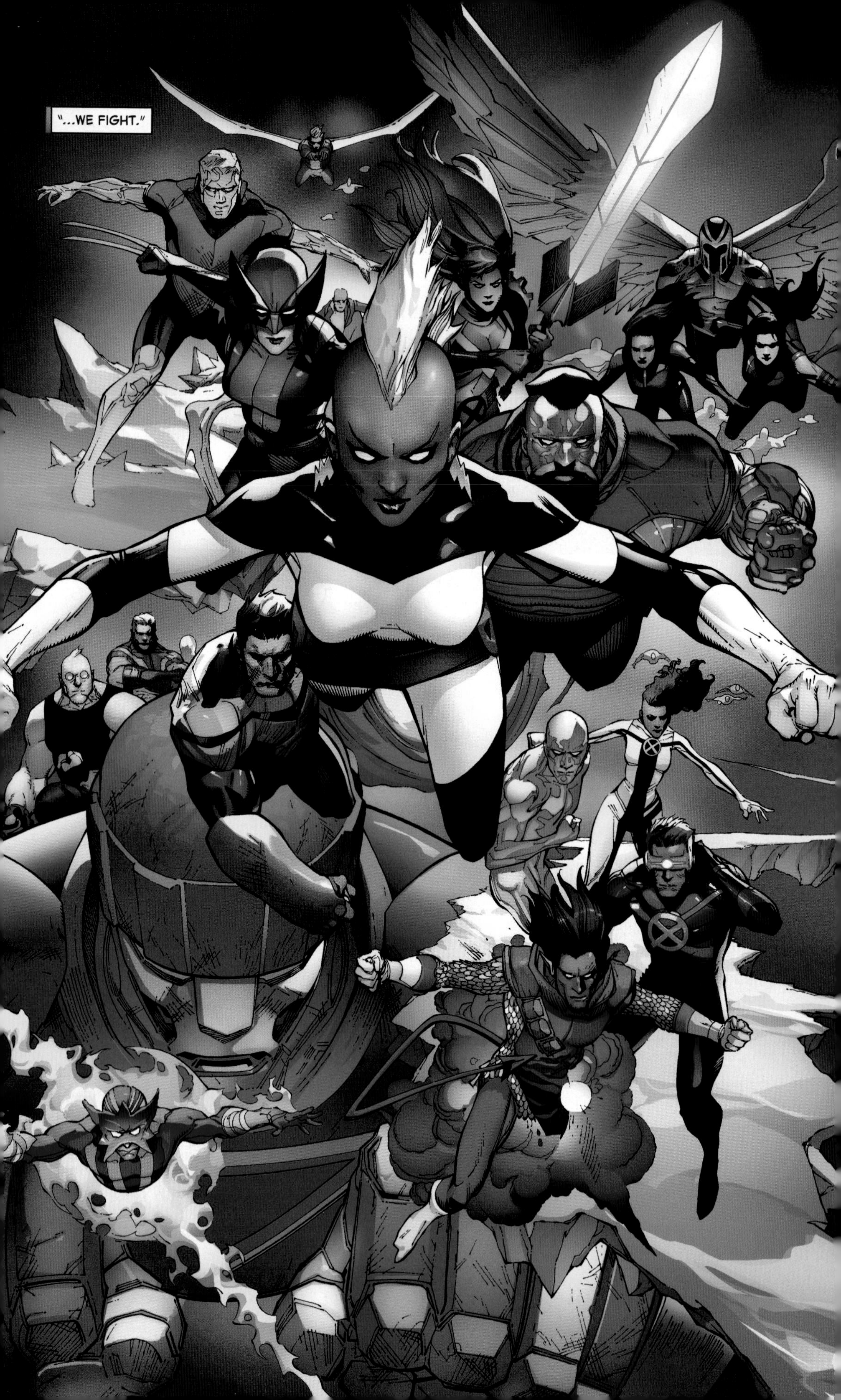
"...WE FIGHT."

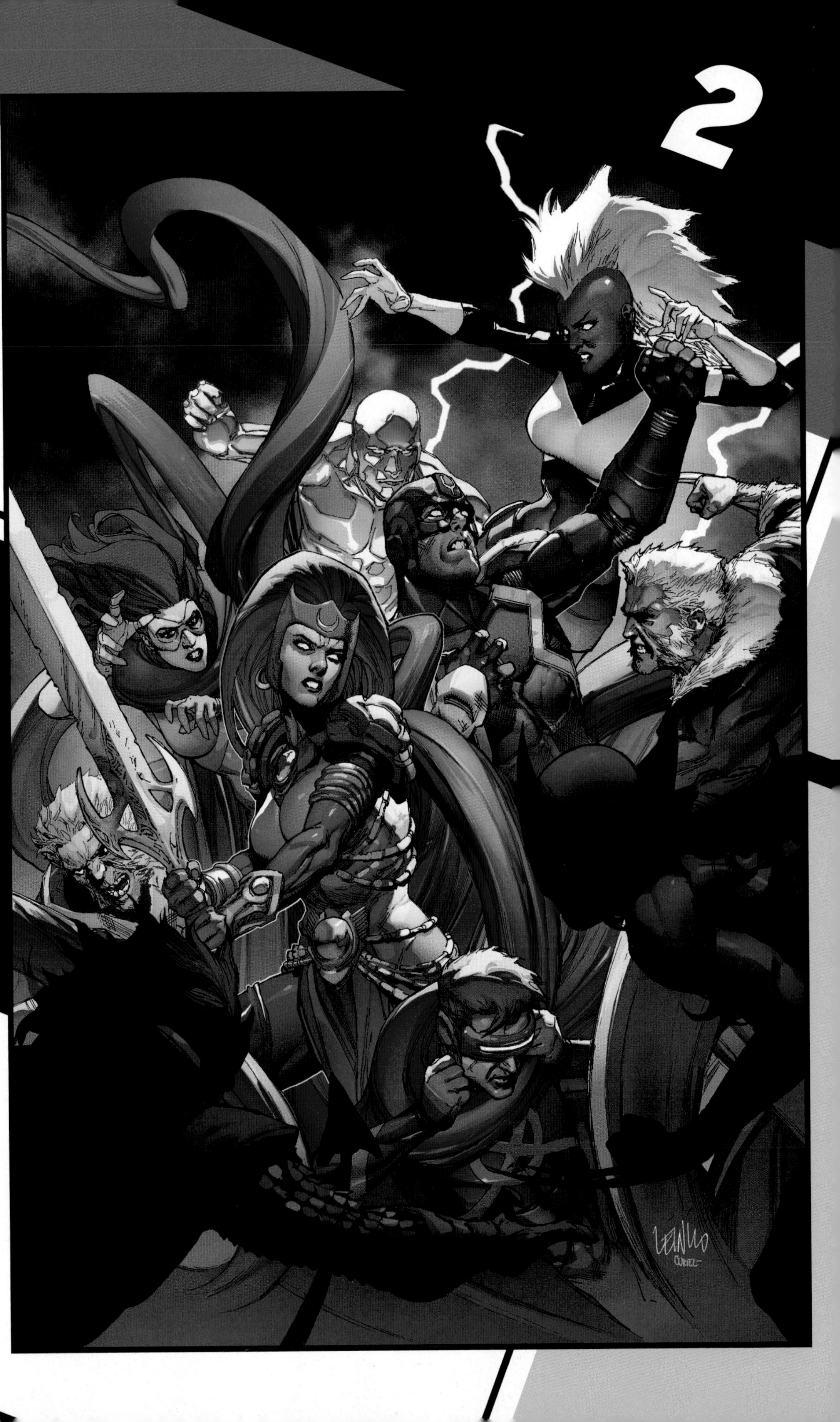
2

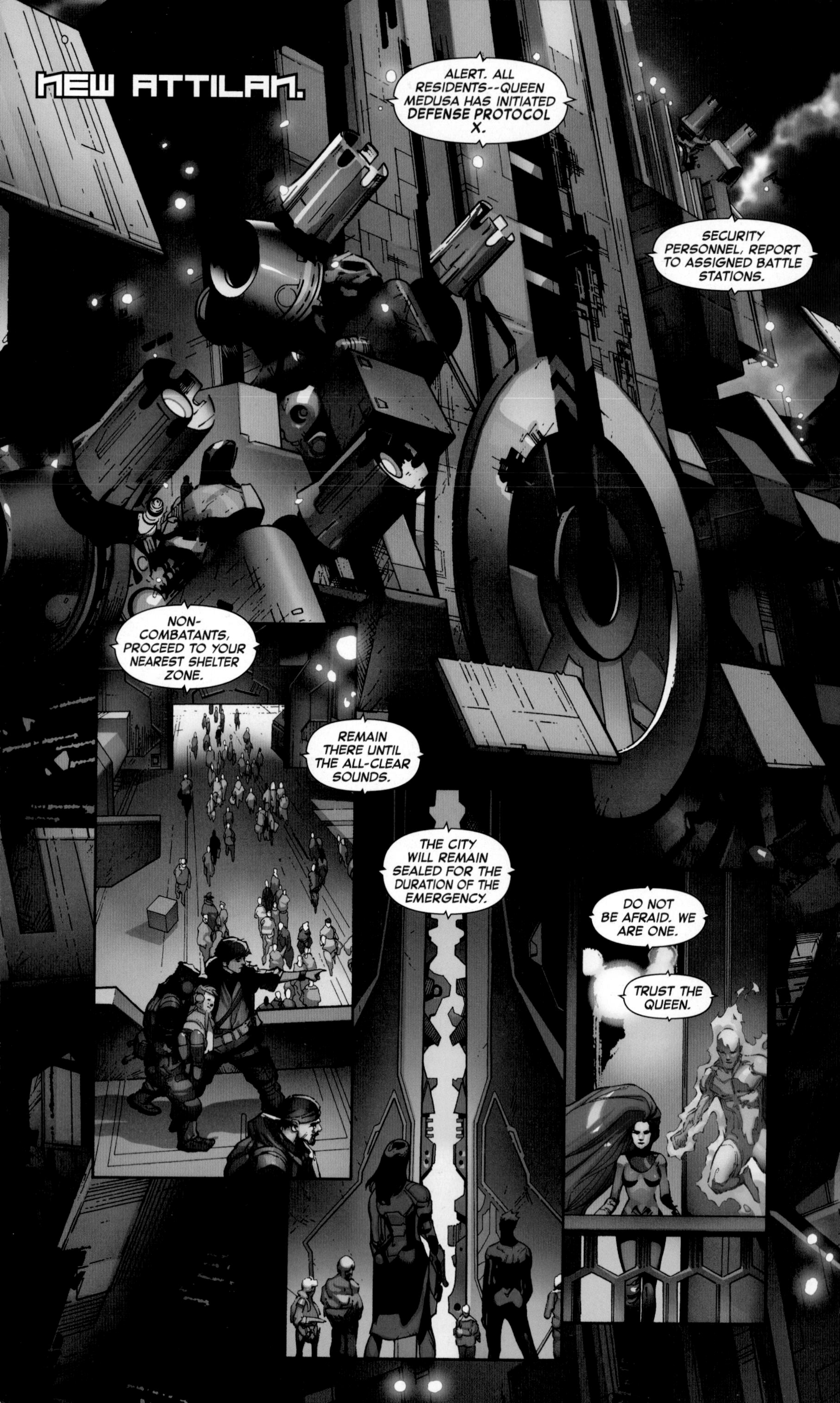
NEW ATTILAN.
ALERT. ALL RESIDENTS--QUEEN MEDUSA HAS INITIATED DEFENSE PROTOCOL X.
SECURITY PERSONNEL, REPORT TO ASSIGNED BATTLE STATIONS.
NON-COMBATANTS, PROCEED TO YOUR NEAREST SHELTER ZONE.
REMAIN THERE UNTIL THE ALL-CLEAR SOUNDS.
THE CITY WILL REMAIN SEALED FOR THE DURATION OF THE EMERGENCY.
DO NOT BE AFRAID. WE ARE ONE.
TRUST THE QUEEN.

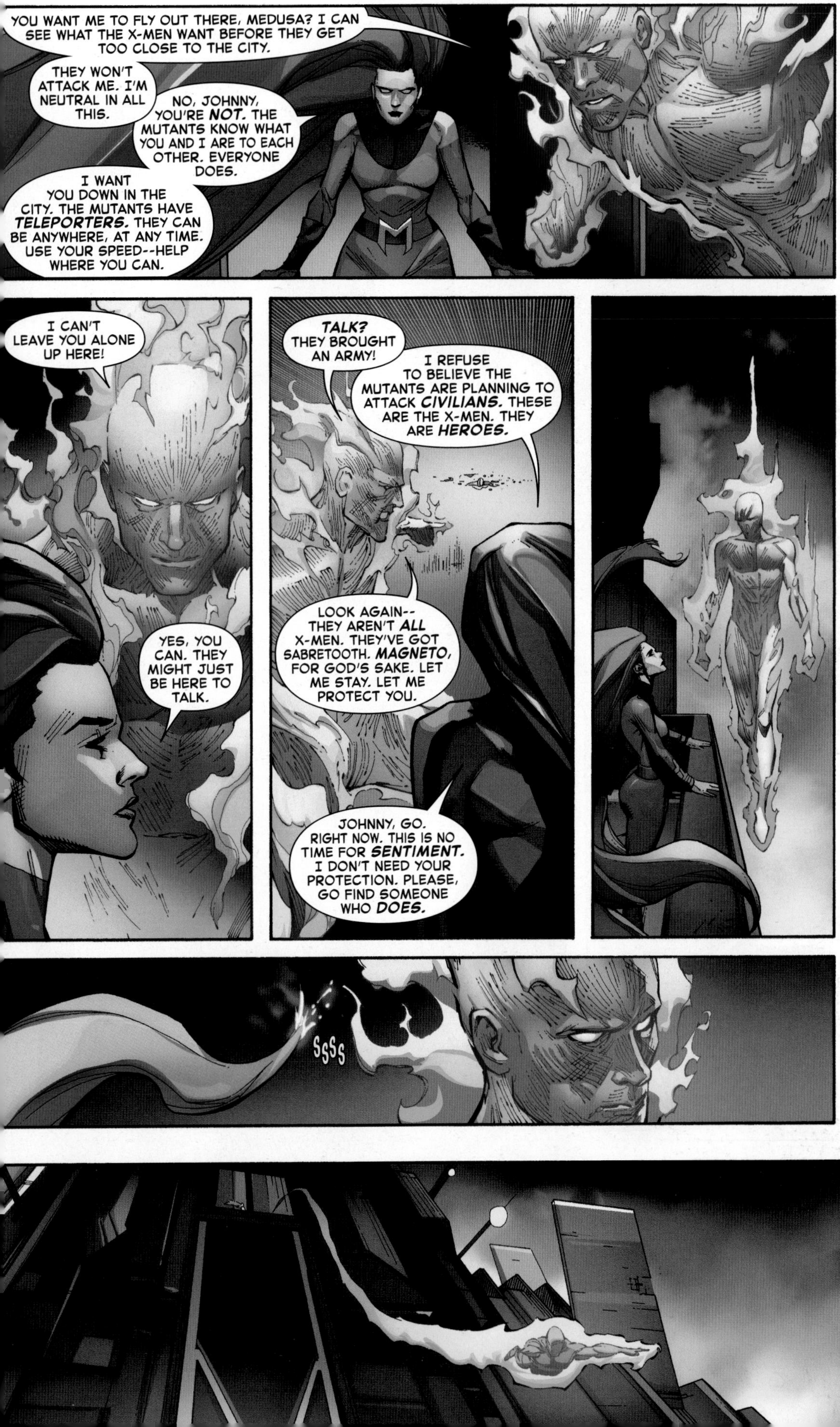

YOU WANT ME TO FLY OUT THERE, MEDUSA? I CAN SEE WHAT THE X-MEN WANT BEFORE THEY GET TOO CLOSE TO THE CITY.
THEY WON'T ATTACK ME. I'M NEUTRAL IN ALL THIS.
NO, JOHNNY, YOU'RE NOT. THE MUTANTS KNOW WHAT YOU AND I ARE TO EACH OTHER. EVERYONE DOES.
I WANT YOU DOWN IN THE CITY. THE MUTANTS HAVE TELEPORTERS. THEY CAN BE ANYWHERE, AT ANY TIME. USE YOUR SPEED--HELP WHERE YOU CAN.
I CAN'T LEAVE YOU ALONE UP HERE!
YES, YOU CAN. THEY MIGHT JUST BE HERE TO TALK.
TALK? THEY BROUGHT AN ARMY!
I REFUSE TO BELIEVE THE MUTANTS ARE PLANNING TO ATTACK CIVILIANS. THESE ARE THE X-MEN. THEY ARE HEROES.
LOOK AGAIN-- THEY AREN'T ALL X-MEN. THEY'VE GOT SABRETOOTH. MAGNETO, FOR GOD'S SAKE. LET ME STAY. LET ME PROTECT YOU.
JOHNNY, GO. RIGHT NOW. THIS IS NO TIME FOR SENTIMENT. I DON'T NEED YOUR PROTECTION. PLEASE, GO FIND SOMEONE WHO DOES.
SSSS

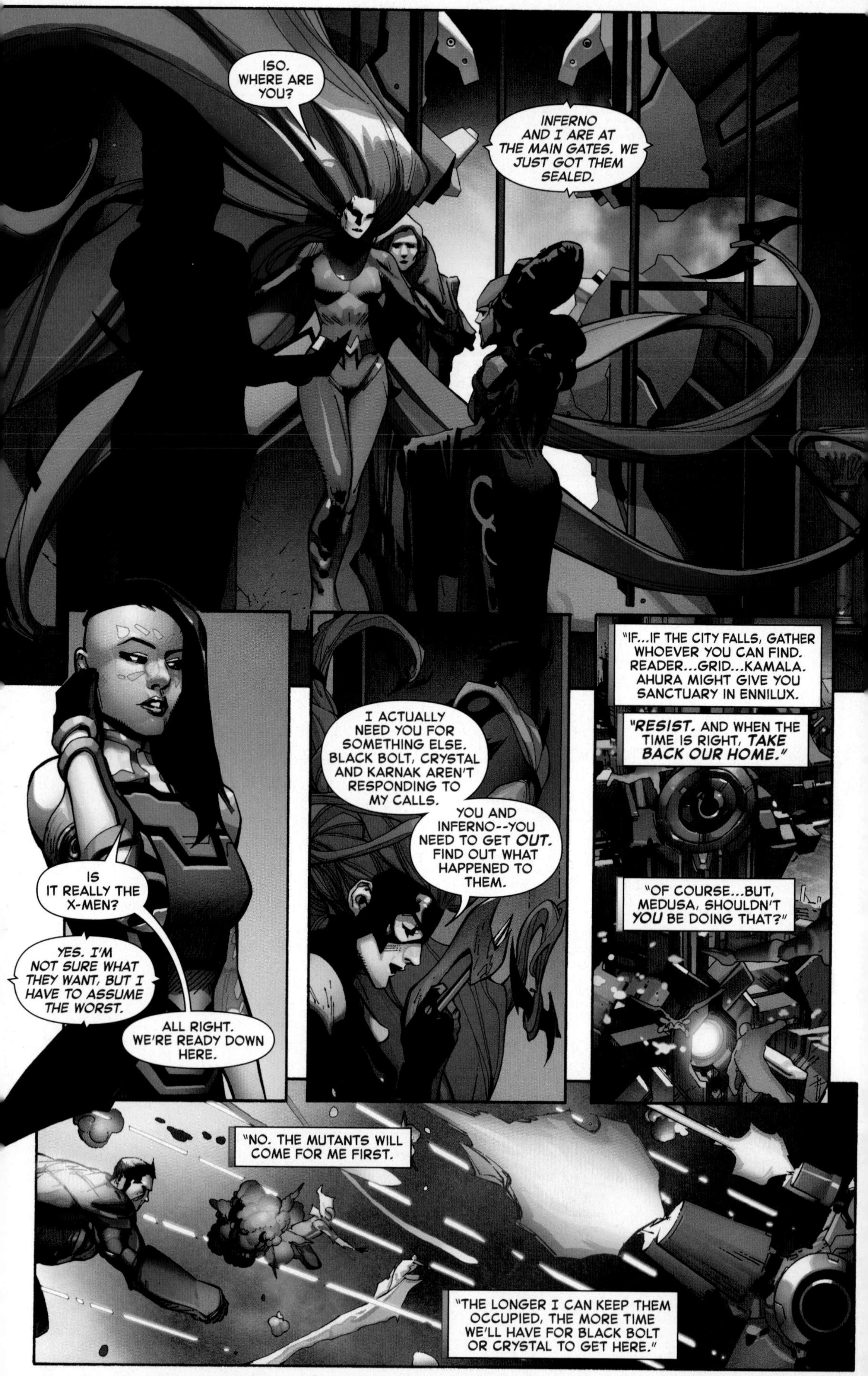
ISO. WHERE ARE YOU?
INFERNO AND I ARE AT THE MAIN GATES. WE JUST GOT THEM SEALED.
IS IT REALLY THE X-MEN?
YES. I'M NOT SURE WHAT THEY WANT, BUT I HAVE TO ASSUME THE WORST.
ALL RIGHT. WE'RE READY DOWN HERE.
I ACTUALLY NEED YOU FOR SOMETHING ELSE. BLACK BOLT, CRYSTAL AND KARNAK AREN'T RESPONDING TO MY CALLS.
YOU AND INFERNO--YOU NEED TO GET OUT. FIND OUT WHAT HAPPENED TO THEM.
"IF...IF THE CITY FALLS, GATHER WHOEVER YOU CAN FIND. READER...GRID...KAMALA. AHURA MIGHT GIVE YOU SANCTUARY IN ENNILUX.
"RESIST. AND WHEN THE TIME IS RIGHT, TAKE BACK OUR HOME."
"OF COURSE...BUT, MEDUSA, SHOULDN'T YOU BE DOING THAT?"
"NO. THE MUTANTS WILL COME FOR ME FIRST.
"THE LONGER I CAN KEEP THEM OCCUPIED, THE MORE TIME WE'LL HAVE FOR BLACK BOLT OR CRYSTAL TO GET HERE."

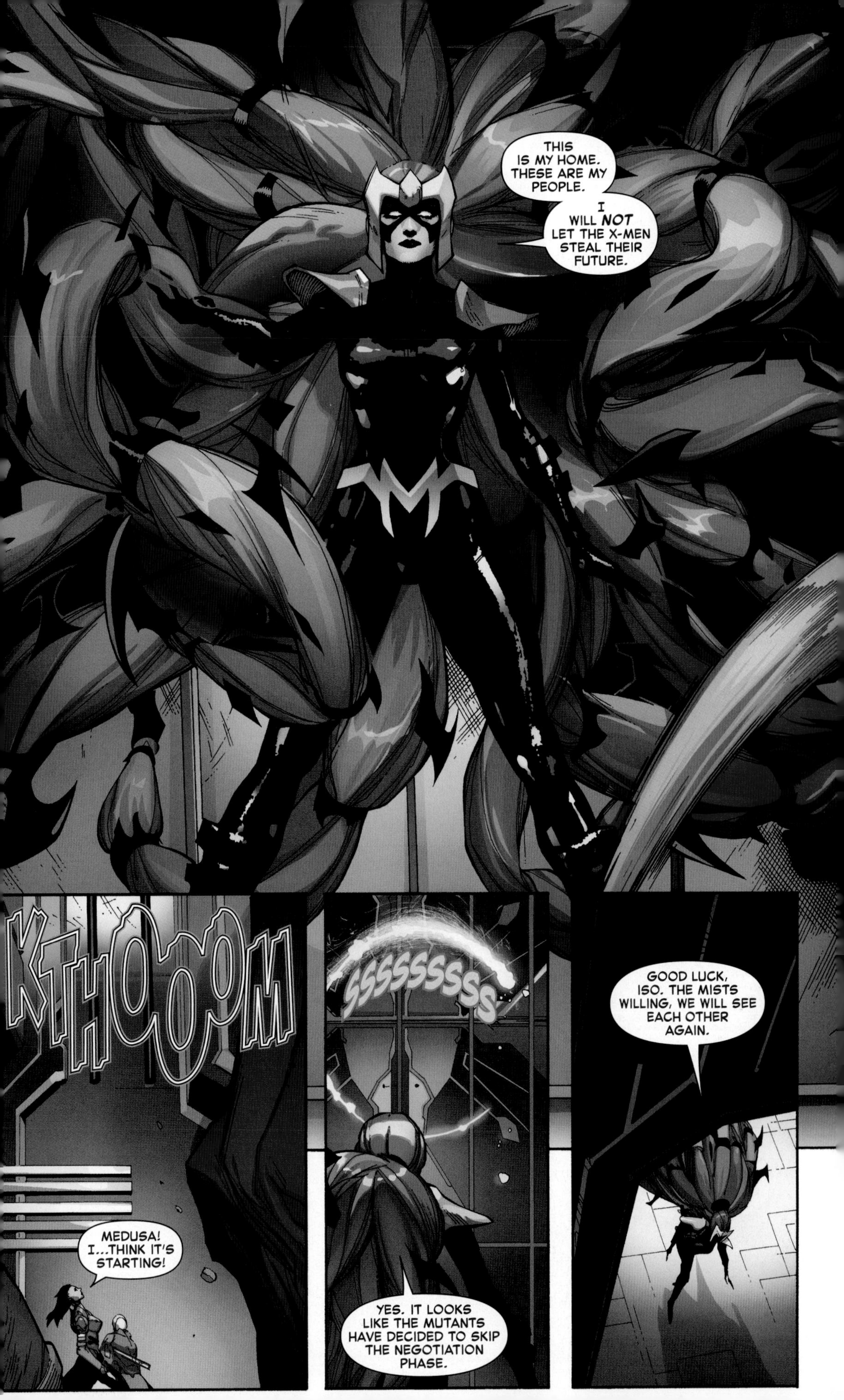
THIS IS MY HOME. THESE ARE MY PEOPLE.
I WILL **NOT** LET THE X-MEN STEAL THEIR FUTURE.
KTHOOOOM
MEDUSA! I...THINK IT'S STARTING!
SSSSSSSSS
YES. IT LOOKS LIKE THE MUTANTS HAVE DECIDED TO SKIP THE NEGOTIATION PHASE.
GOOD LUCK, ISO. THE MISTS WILLING, WE WILL SEE EACH OTHER AGAIN.

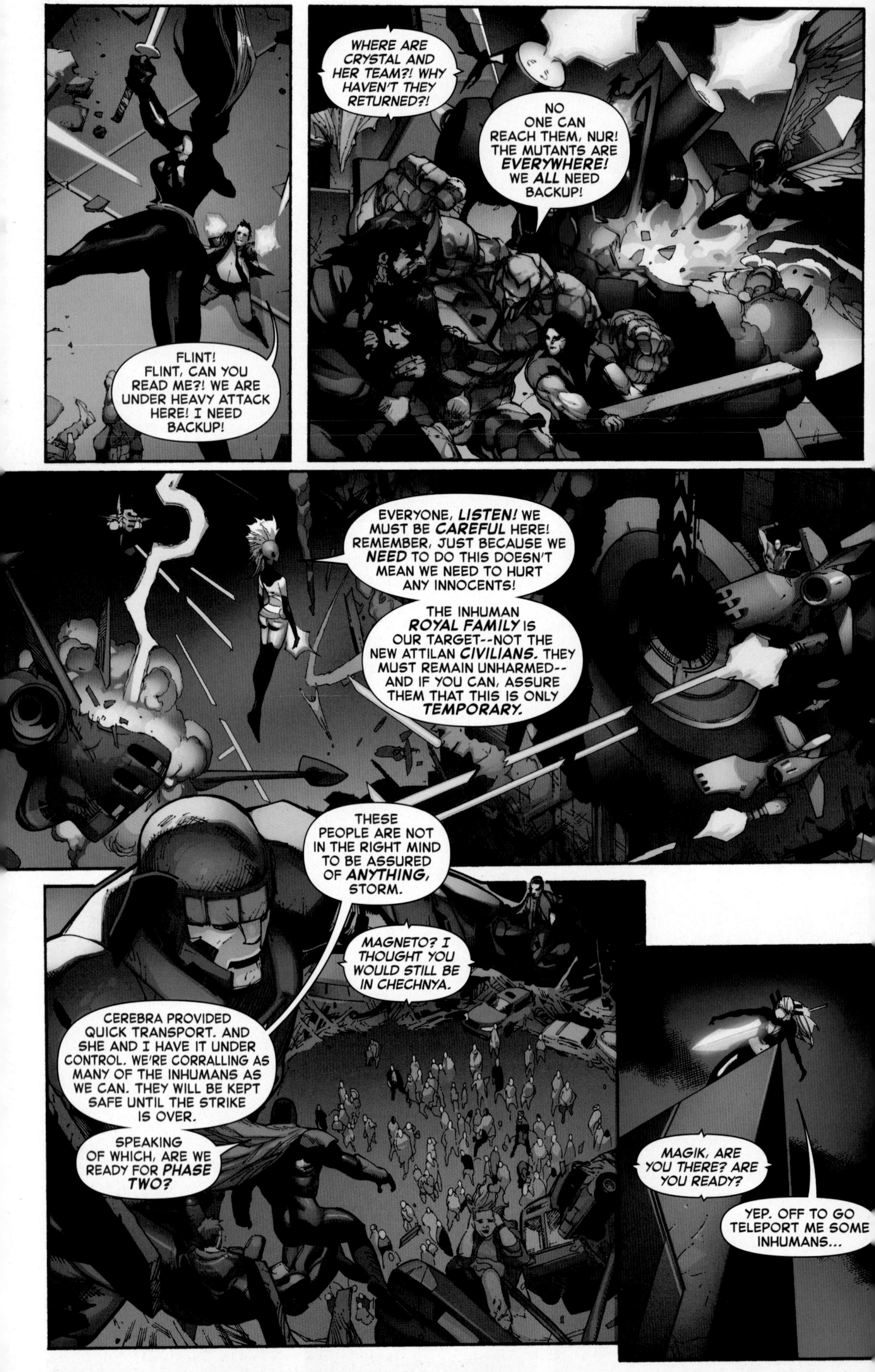
WHERE ARE CRYSTAL AND HER TEAM?! WHY HAVEN'T THEY RETURNED?!
NO ONE CAN REACH THEM, NUR! THE MUTANTS ARE EVERYWHERE! WE ALL NEED BACKUP!
FLINT! FLINT, CAN YOU READ ME?! WE ARE UNDER HEAVY ATTACK HERE! I NEED BACKUP!
EVERYONE, LISTEN! WE MUST BE CAREFUL HERE! REMEMBER, JUST BECAUSE WE NEED TO DO THIS DOESN'T MEAN WE NEED TO HURT ANY INNOCENTS!
THE INHUMAN ROYAL FAMILY IS OUR TARGET--NOT THE NEW ATTILAN CIVILIANS. THEY MUST REMAIN UNHARMED--AND IF YOU CAN, ASSURE THEM THAT THIS IS ONLY TEMPORARY.
THESE PEOPLE ARE NOT IN THE RIGHT MIND TO BE ASSURED OF ANYTHING, STORM.
MAGNETO? I THOUGHT YOU WOULD STILL BE IN CHECHNYA.
CEREBRA PROVIDED QUICK TRANSPORT. AND SHE AND I HAVE IT UNDER CONTROL. WE'RE CORRALLING AS MANY OF THE INHUMANS AS WE CAN. THEY WILL BE KEPT SAFE UNTIL THE STRIKE IS OVER.
SPEAKING OF WHICH, ARE WE READY FOR PHASE TWO?
MAGIK, ARE YOU THERE? ARE YOU READY?
YEP. OFF TO GO TELEPORT ME SOME INHUMANS...

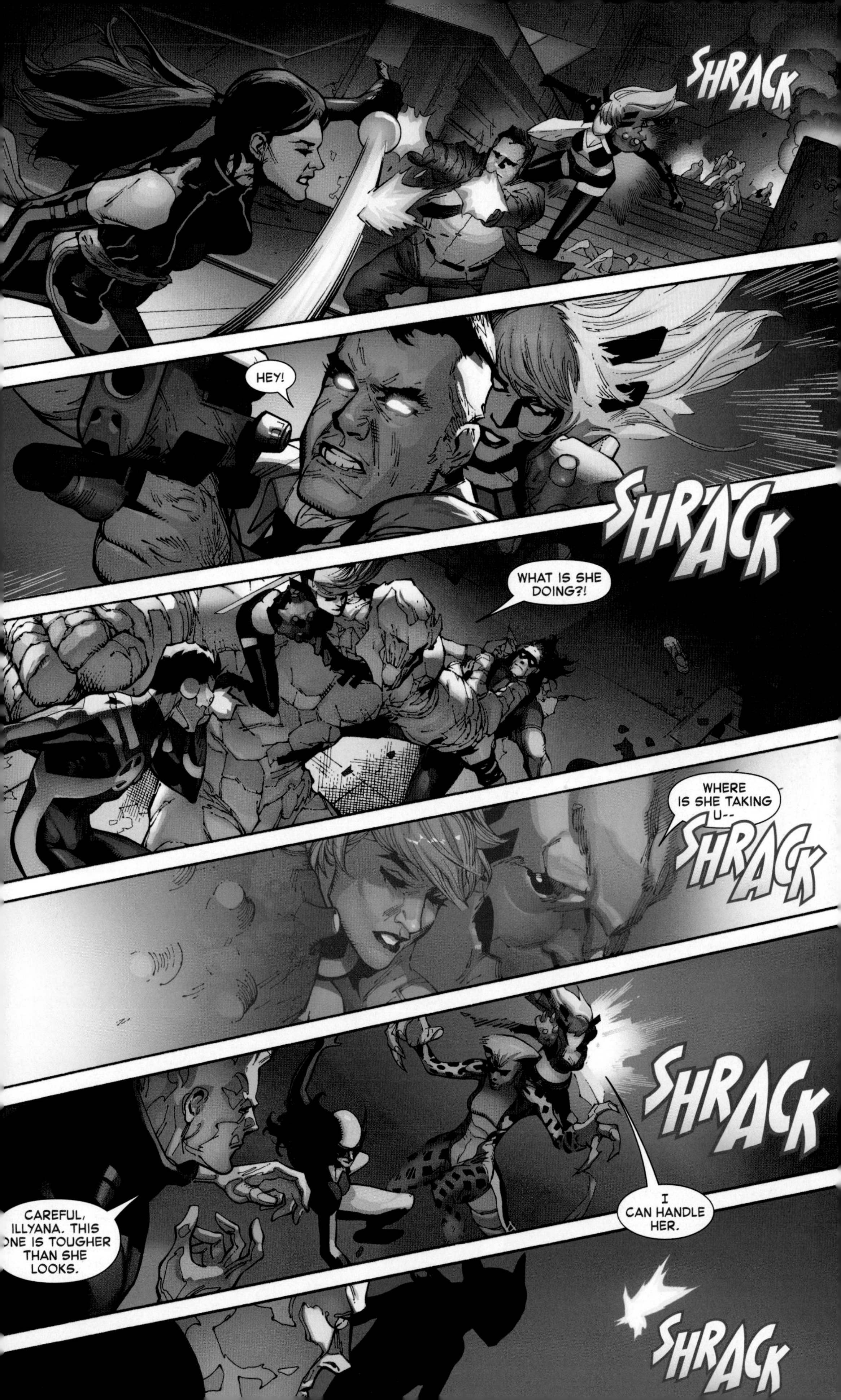
SHRACK
HEY!
SHRACK
WHAT IS SHE DOING?!
WHERE IS SHE TAKING U--
SHRACK
SHRACK
CAREFUL, ILLYANA. THIS ONE IS TOUGHER THAN SHE LOOKS.
I CAN HANDLE HER.
SHRACK

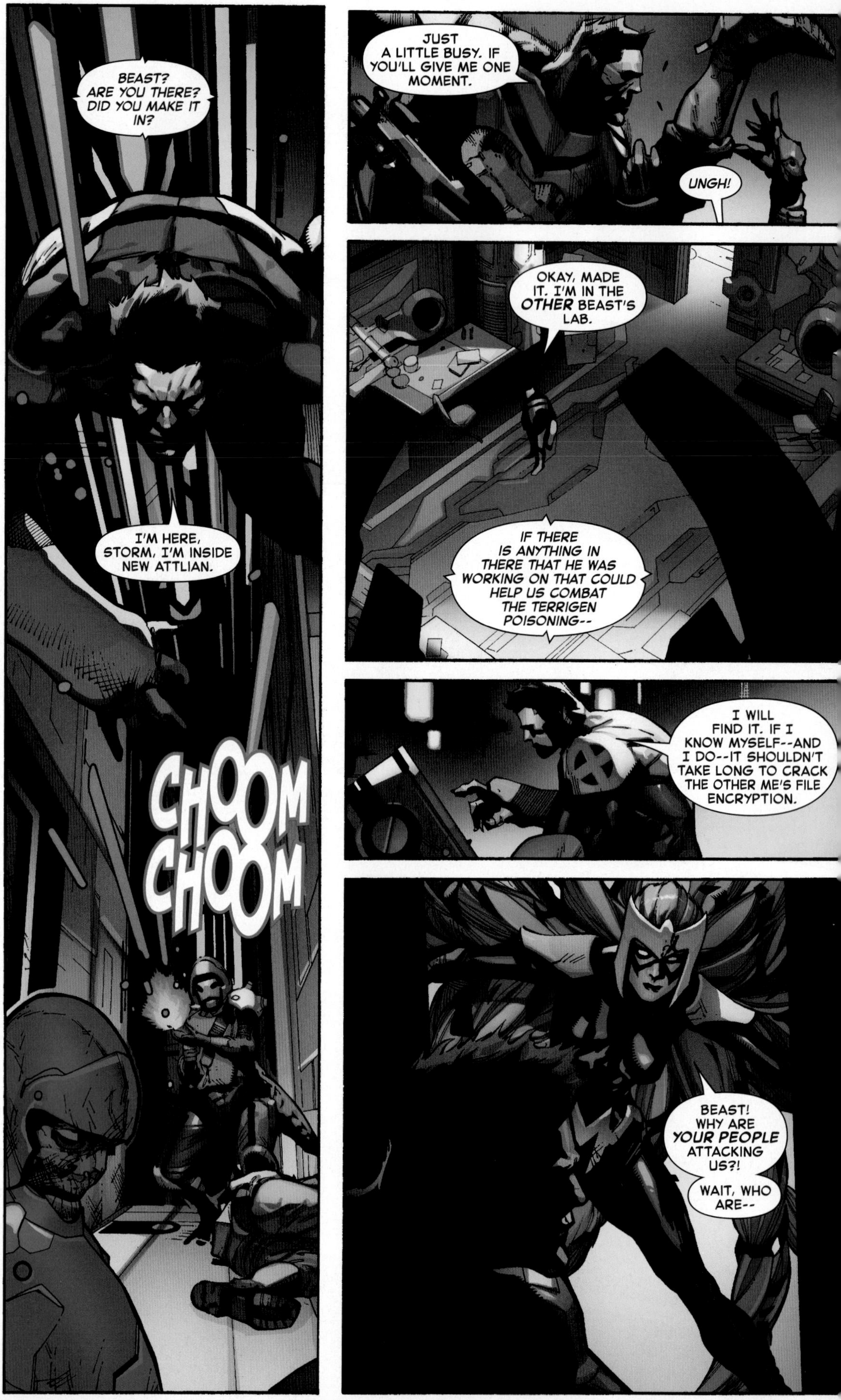

BEAST? ARE YOU THERE? DID YOU MAKE IT IN?
I'M HERE, STORM, I'M INSIDE NEW ATTLIAN.
CHOOM CHOOM
JUST A LITTLE BUSY. IF YOU'LL GIVE ME ONE MOMENT.
UNGH!
OKAY, MADE IT. I'M IN THE OTHER BEAST'S LAB.
IF THERE IS ANYTHING IN THERE THAT HE WAS WORKING ON THAT COULD HELP US COMBAT THE TERRIGEN POISONING--
I WILL FIND IT. IF I KNOW MYSELF--AND I DO--IT SHOULDN'T TAKE LONG TO CRACK THE OTHER ME'S FILE ENCRYPTION.
BEAST! WHY ARE YOUR PEOPLE ATTACKING US?!
WAIT, WHO ARE--

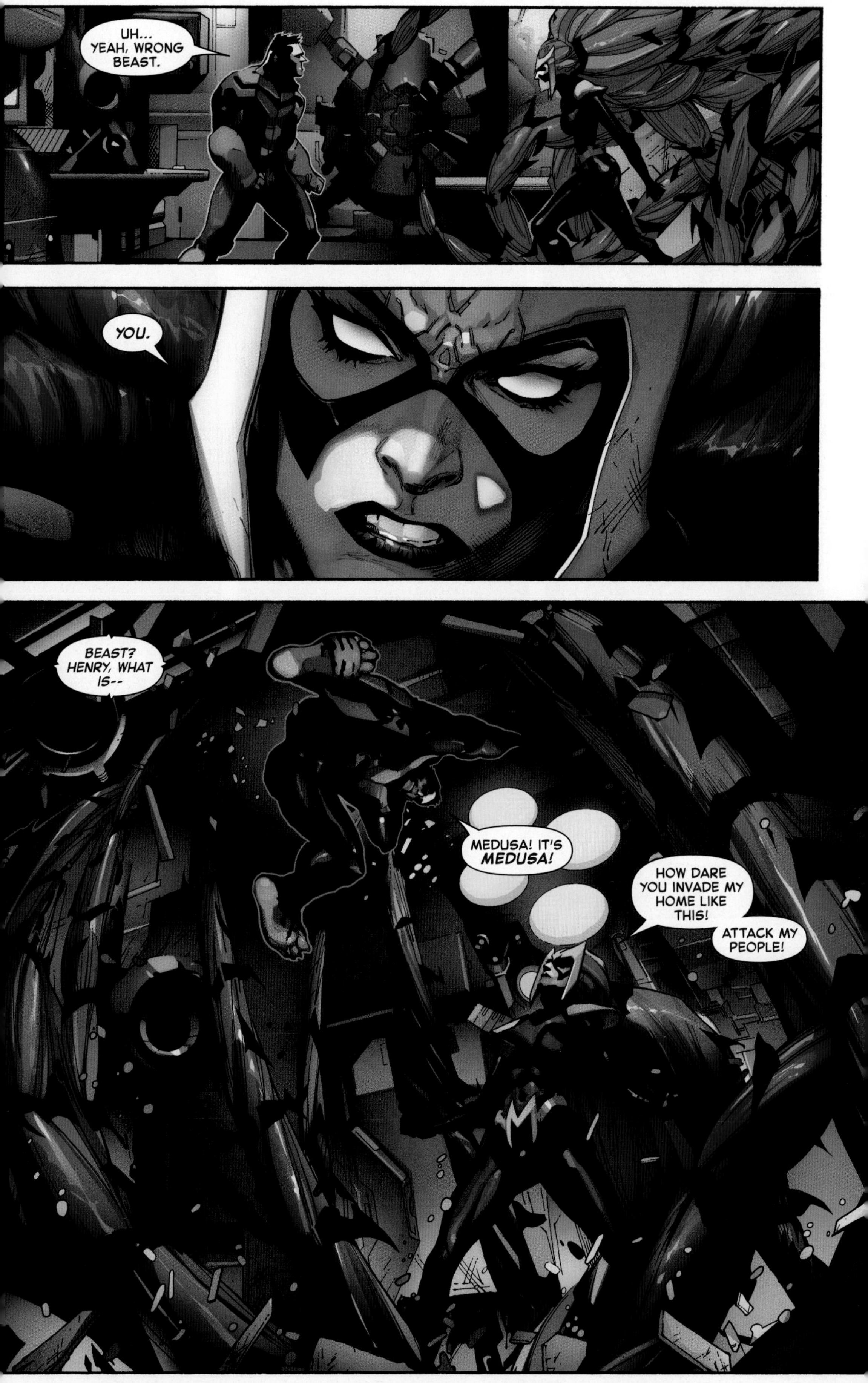
UH... YEAH, WRONG BEAST.
YOU.
BEAST? HENRY, WHAT IS--
MEDUSA! IT'S MEDUSA!
HOW DARE YOU INVADE MY HOME LIKE THIS!
ATTACK MY PEOPLE!

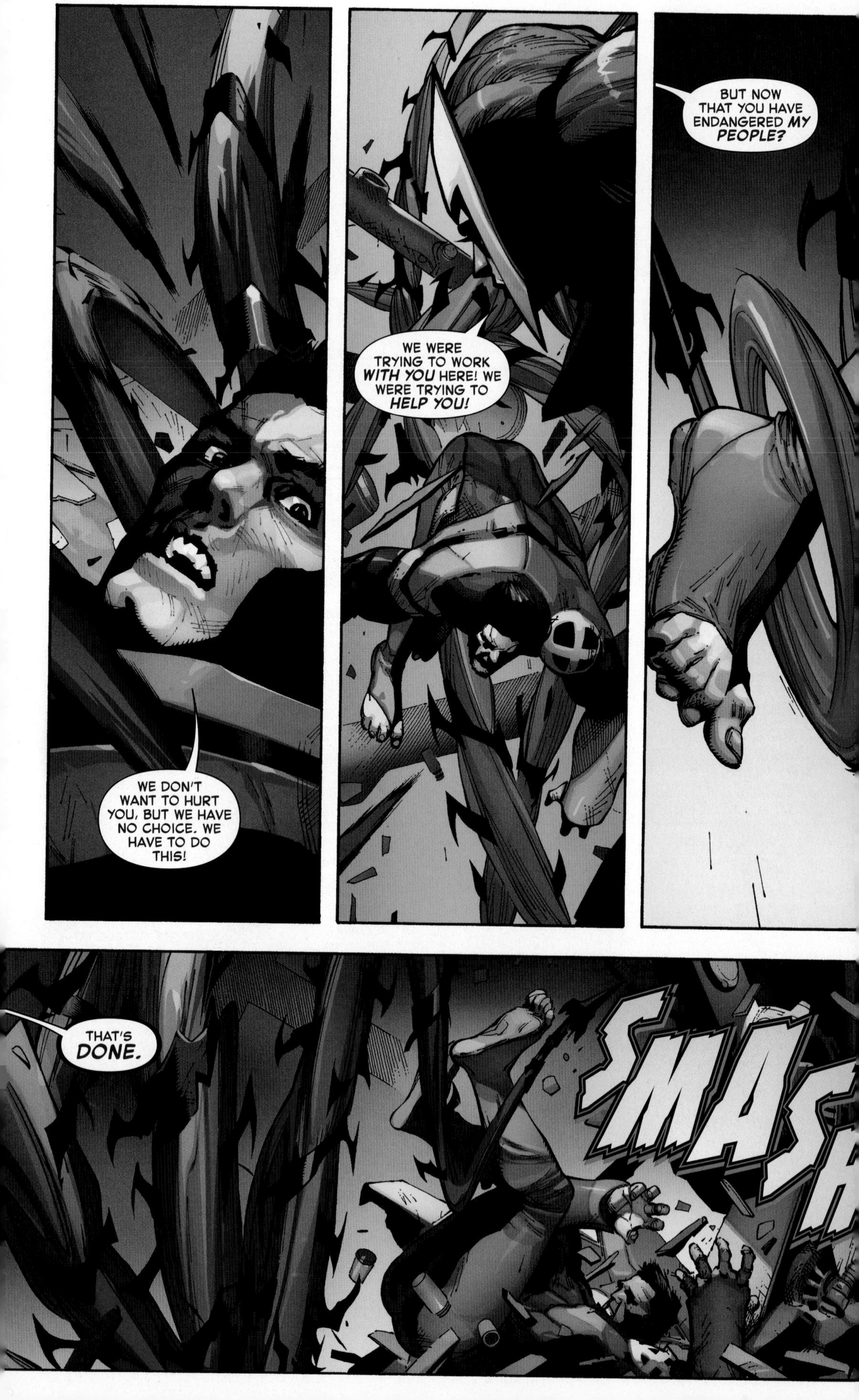

WE DON'T WANT TO HURT YOU, BUT WE HAVE NO CHOICE. WE HAVE TO DO THIS!
WE WERE TRYING TO WORK *WITH YOU* HERE! WE WERE TRYING TO *HELP YOU!*
BUT NOW THAT YOU HAVE ENDANGERED *MY PEOPLE?*
THAT'S *DONE.*
SMASH

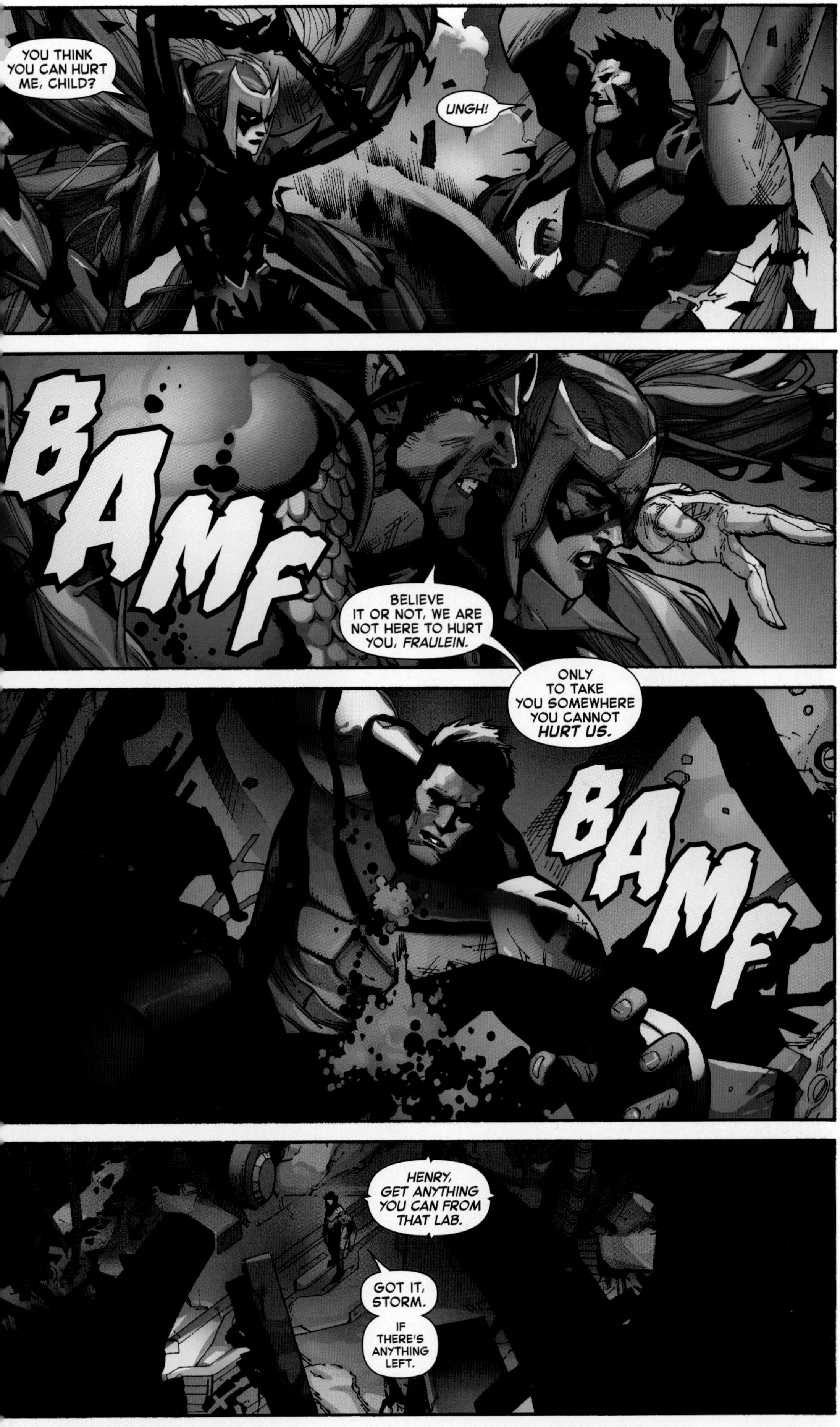
YOU THINK YOU CAN HURT ME, CHILD?
UNGH!
BAMF
BELIEVE IT OR NOT, WE ARE NOT HERE TO HURT YOU, *FRAULEIN.*
ONLY TO TAKE YOU SOMEWHERE YOU CANNOT *HURT US.*
BAMF
HENRY, GET ANYTHING YOU CAN FROM THAT LAB.
GOT IT, STORM.
IF THERE'S ANYTHING LEFT.

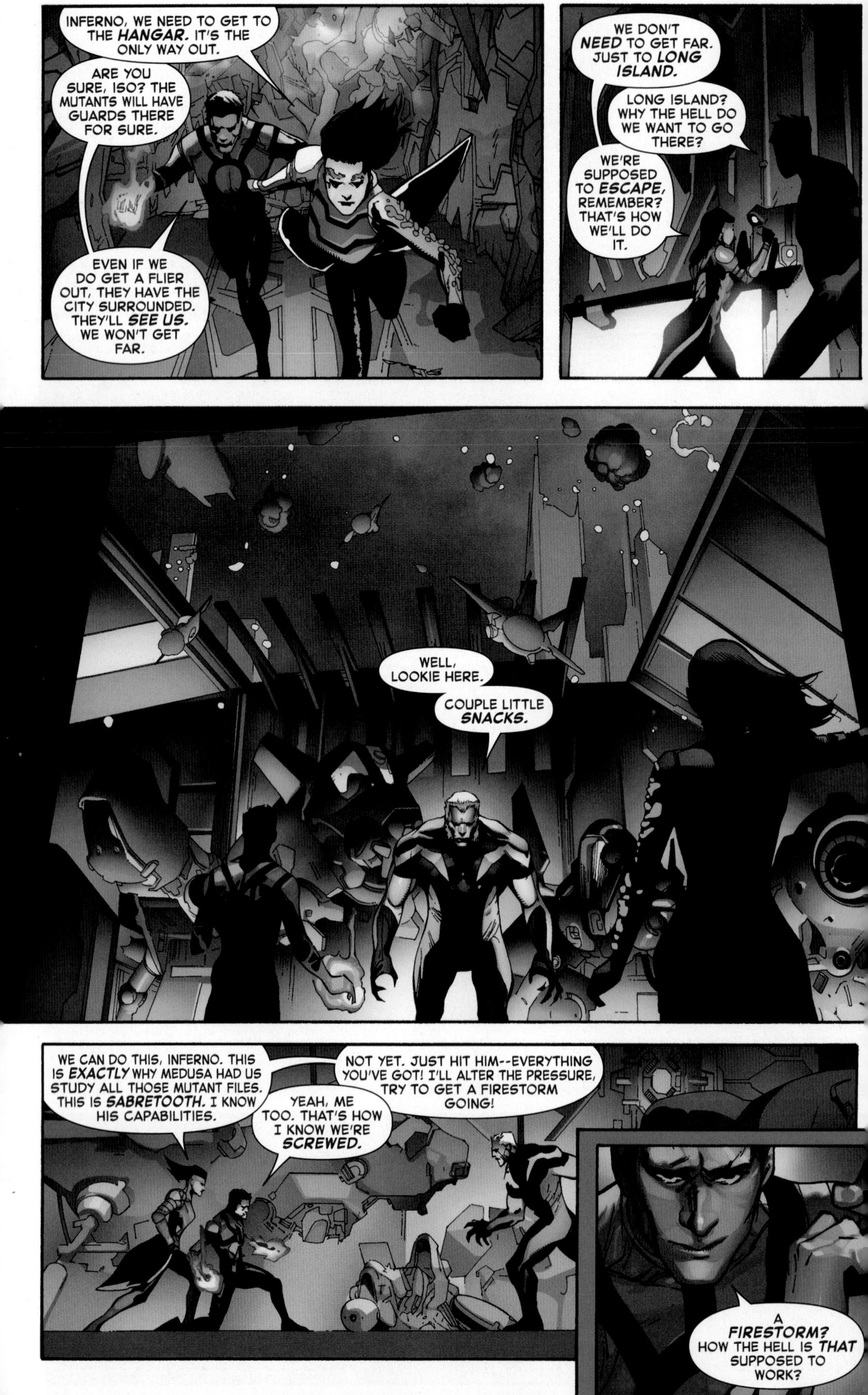

INFERNO, WE NEED TO GET TO THE *HANGAR.* IT'S THE ONLY WAY OUT.
ARE YOU SURE, ISO? THE MUTANTS WILL HAVE GUARDS THERE FOR SURE.
EVEN IF WE DO GET A FLIER OUT, THEY HAVE THE CITY SURROUNDED. THEY'LL *SEE US.* WE WON'T GET FAR.
WE DON'T *NEED* TO GET FAR. JUST TO *LONG ISLAND.*
LONG ISLAND? WHY THE HELL DO WE WANT TO GO THERE?
WE'RE SUPPOSED TO *ESCAPE,* REMEMBER? THAT'S HOW WE'LL DO IT.
WELL, LOOKIE HERE.
COUPLE LITTLE *SNACKS.*
WE CAN DO THIS, INFERNO. THIS IS *EXACTLY* WHY MEDUSA HAD US STUDY ALL THOSE MUTANT FILES. THIS IS *SABRETOOTH.* I KNOW HIS CAPABILITIES.
YEAH, ME TOO. THAT'S HOW I KNOW WE'RE *SCREWED.*
NOT YET. JUST HIT HIM--EVERYTHING YOU'VE GOT! I'LL ALTER THE PRESSURE, TRY TO GET A FIRESTORM GOING!
A *FIRESTORM?* HOW THE HELL IS *THAT* SUPPOSED TO WORK?

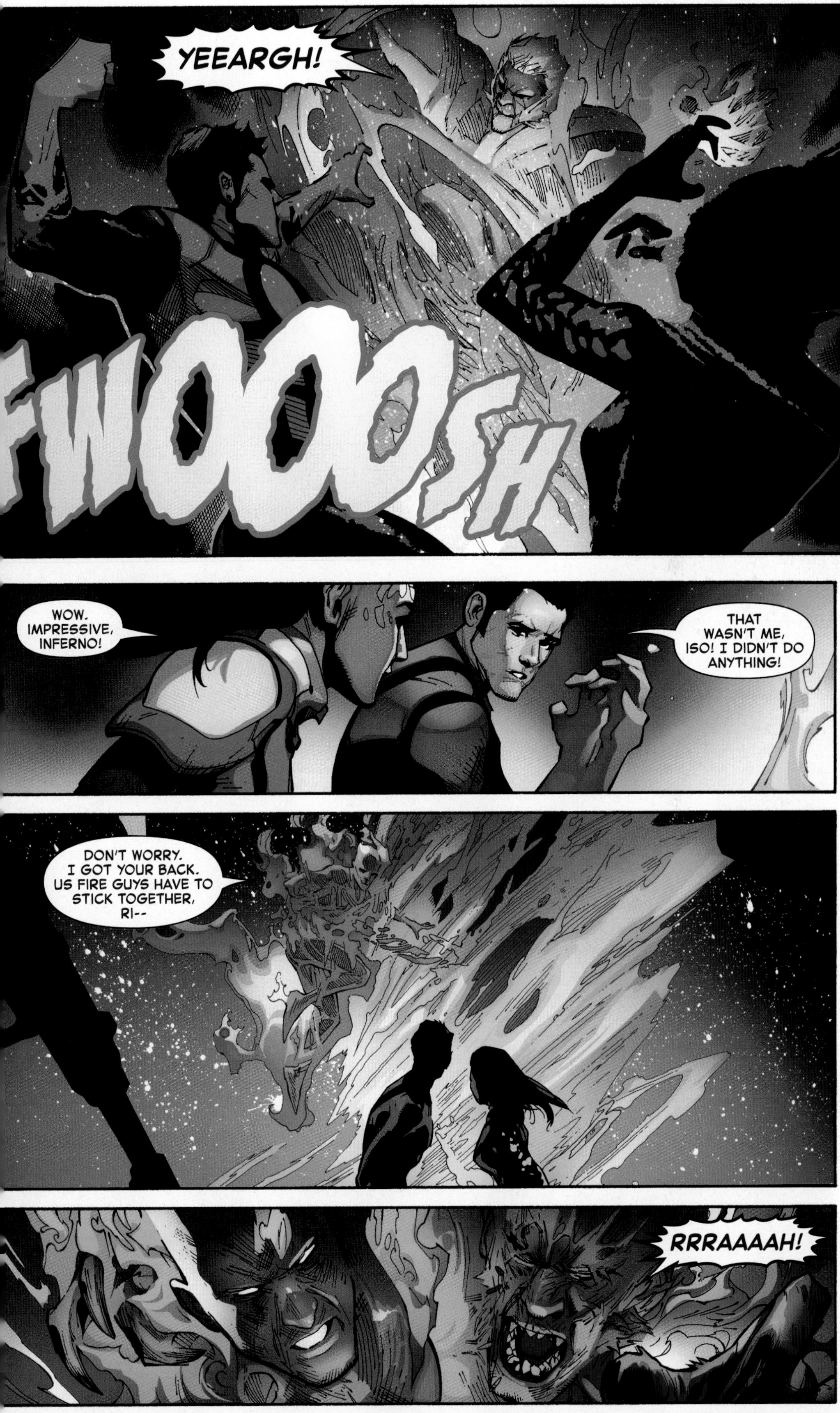
YEEARGH!
FWOOSH
WOW. IMPRESSIVE, INFERNO!
THAT WASN'T ME, ISO! I DIDN'T DO ANYTHING!
DON'T WORRY. I GOT YOUR BACK. US FIRE GUYS HAVE TO STICK TOGETHER, RI--
RRRAAAAH!

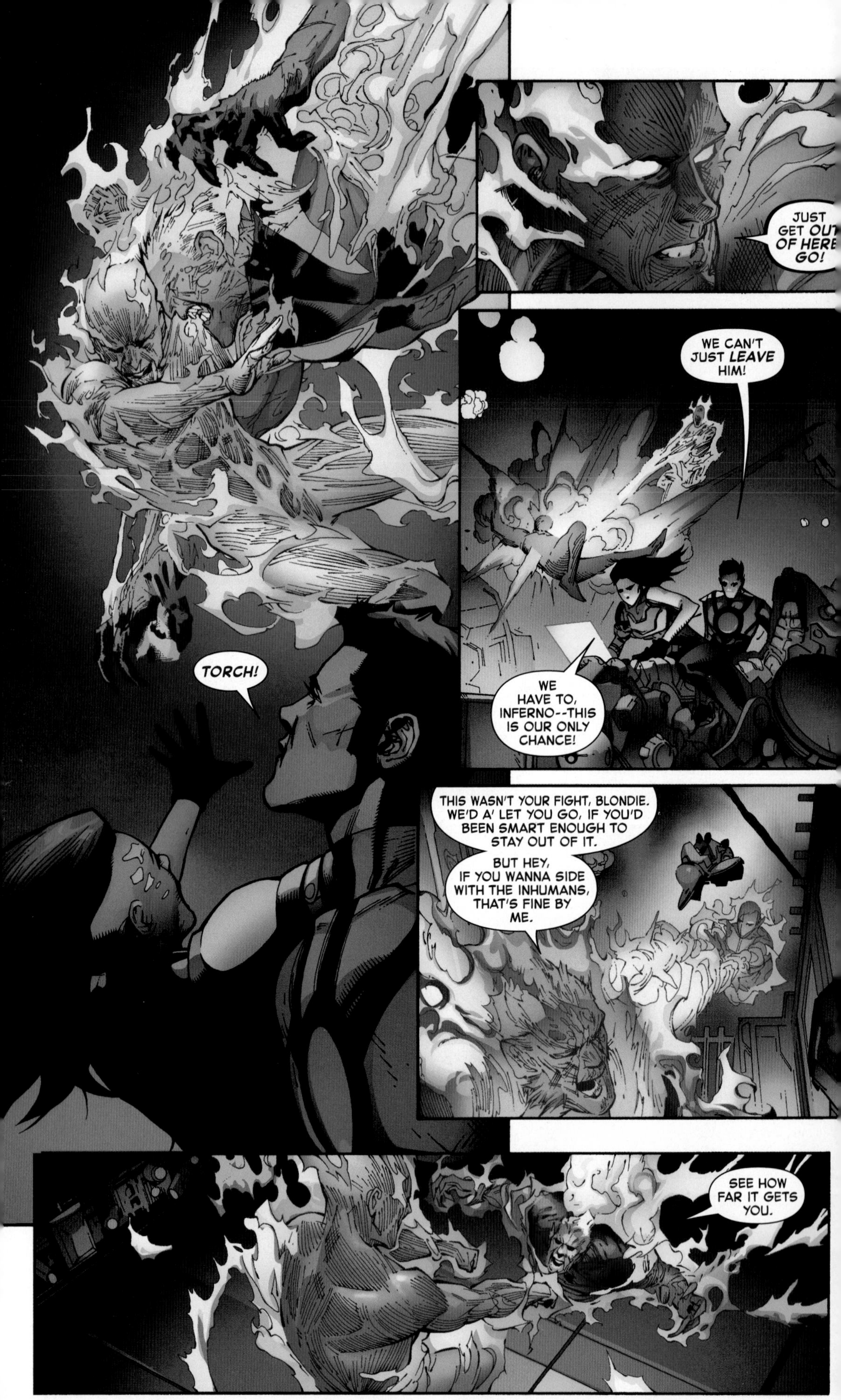
JUST GET OUT OF HERE GO!
WE CAN'T JUST LEAVE HIM!
WE HAVE TO, INFERNO--THIS IS OUR ONLY CHANCE!
TORCH!
THIS WASN'T YOUR FIGHT, BLONDIE. WE'D A' LET YOU GO, IF YOU'D BEEN SMART ENOUGH TO STAY OUT OF IT.
BUT HEY, IF YOU WANNA SIDE WITH THE INHUMANS, THAT'S FINE BY ME.
SEE HOW FAR IT GETS YOU.

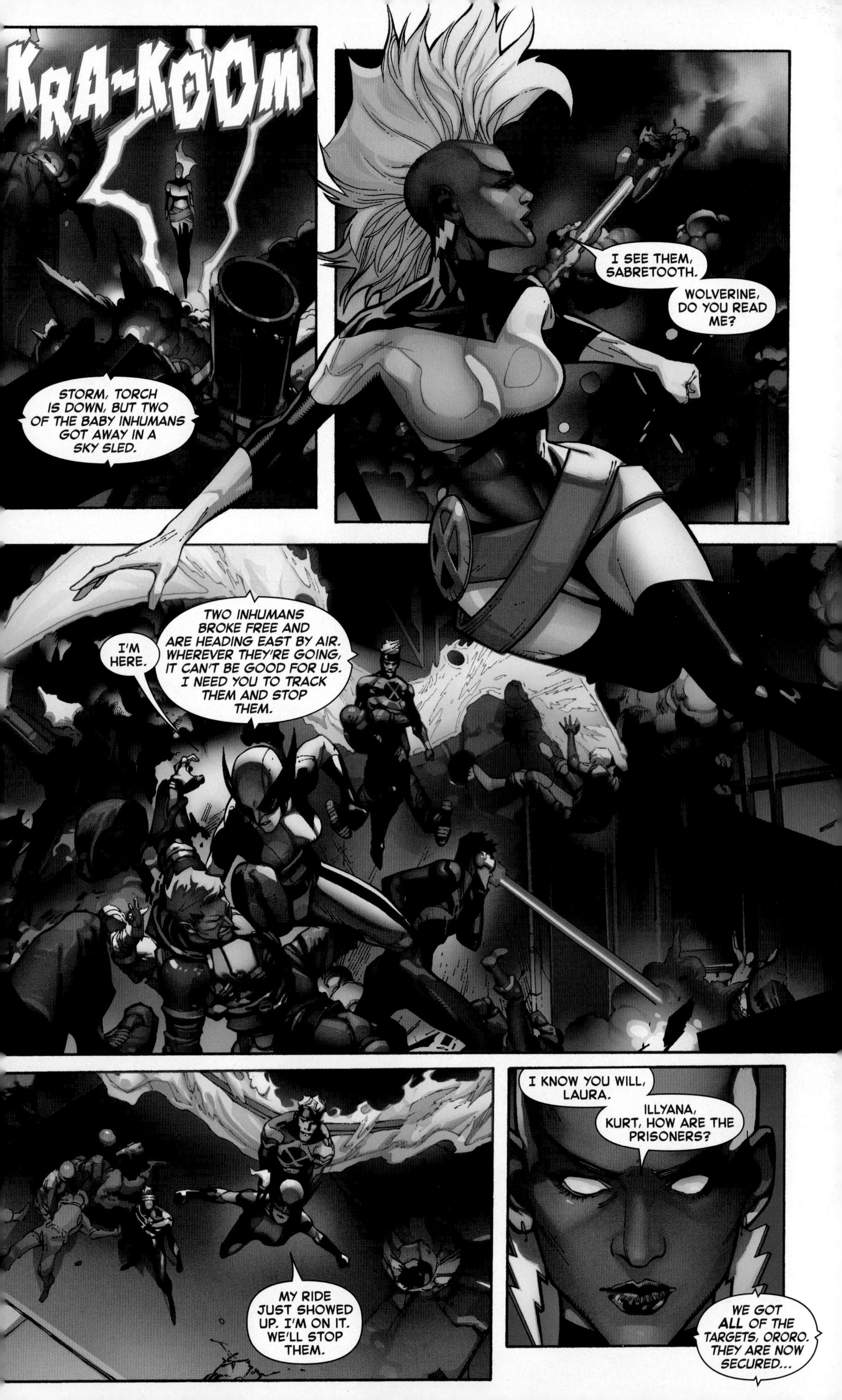
KRA-KOOM
STORM, TORCH IS DOWN, BUT TWO OF THE BABY INHUMANS GOT AWAY IN A SKY SLED.
I SEE THEM, SABRETOOTH.
WOLVERINE, DO YOU READ ME?
I'M HERE.
TWO INHUMANS BROKE FREE AND ARE HEADING EAST BY AIR. WHEREVER THEY'RE GOING, IT CAN'T BE GOOD FOR US. I NEED YOU TO TRACK THEM AND STOP THEM.
MY RIDE JUST SHOWED UP. I'M ON IT. WE'LL STOP THEM.
I KNOW YOU WILL, LAURA.
ILLYANA, KURT, HOW ARE THE PRISONERS?
WE GOT ALL OF THE TARGETS, ORORO. THEY ARE NOW SECURED...

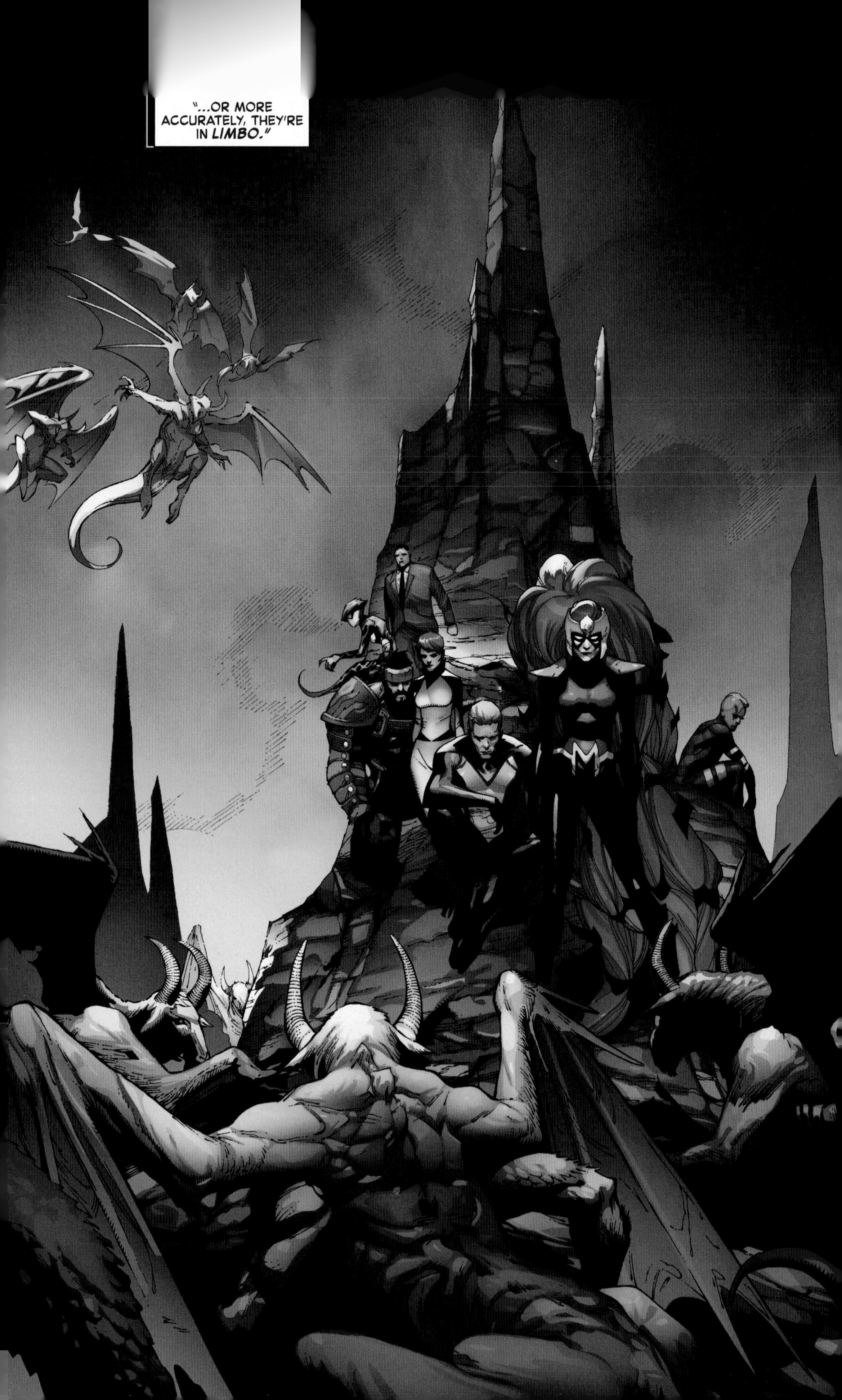
"...OR MORE ACCURATELY, THEY'RE IN LIMBO."

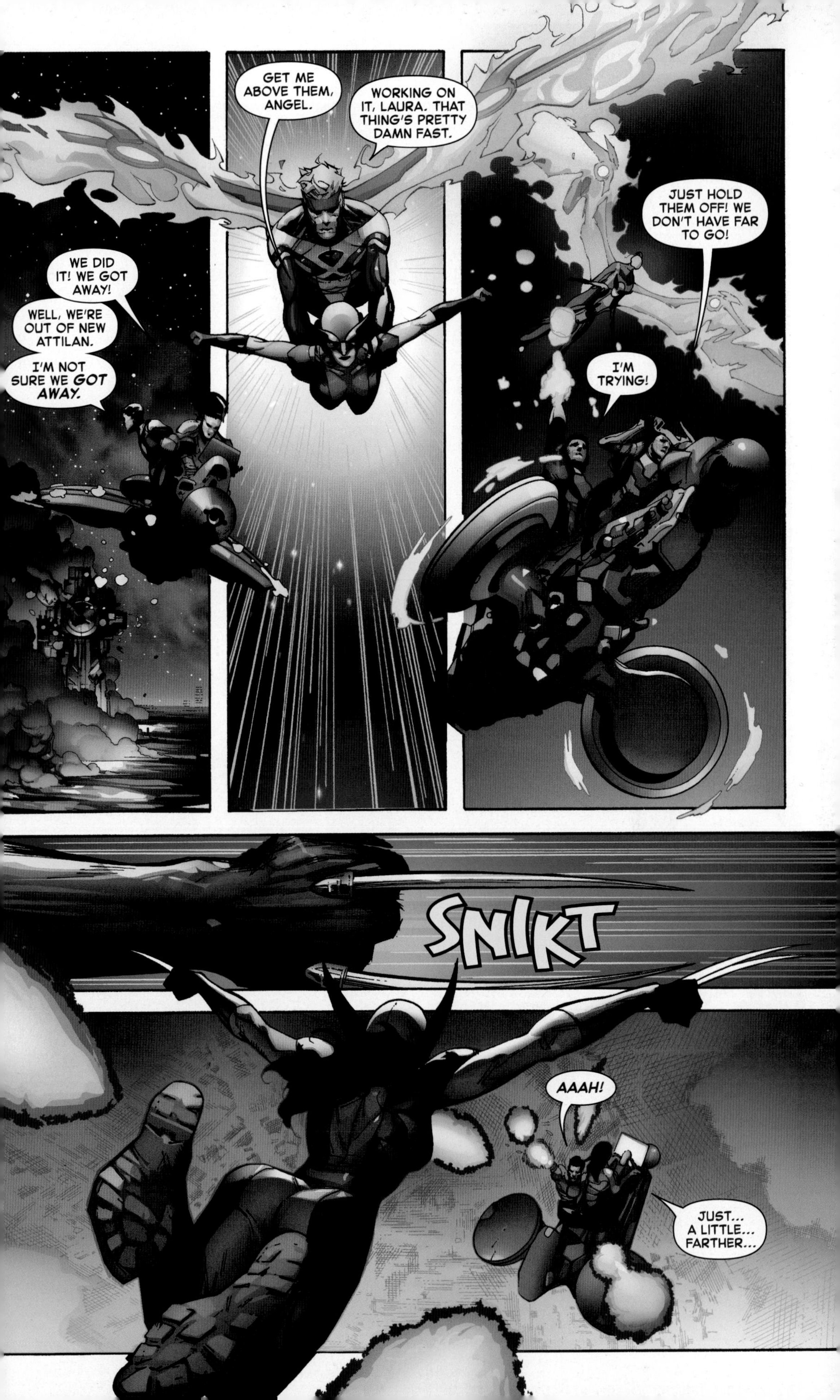

WE DID IT! WE GOT AWAY!
WELL, WE'RE OUT OF NEW ATTILAN.
I'M NOT SURE WE *GOT AWAY.*
GET ME ABOVE THEM, ANGEL.
WORKING ON IT, LAURA. THAT THING'S PRETTY DAMN FAST.
JUST HOLD THEM OFF! WE DON'T HAVE FAR TO GO!
I'M TRYING!
SNIKT
AAAH!
JUST... A LITTLE... FARTHER...

SLSH

NNNGH... HOW...ARE WE *ALIVE?*

I... CUSHIONED THE FALL...WITH MY POWERS.

NOT FOR *HER*, THOUGH. SHE HAS...A HEALING FACTOR. SHE CAN TAKE IT.

YEAH, BUT THAT MEANS SHE'LL *WAKE UP* SOON. ANGEL'S STILL UP THERE, TOO!

DON'T WORRY. WE MA IT. THIS IS TH SPOT.

THE SPOT FO *WHAT?*

NOT *WHAT--*

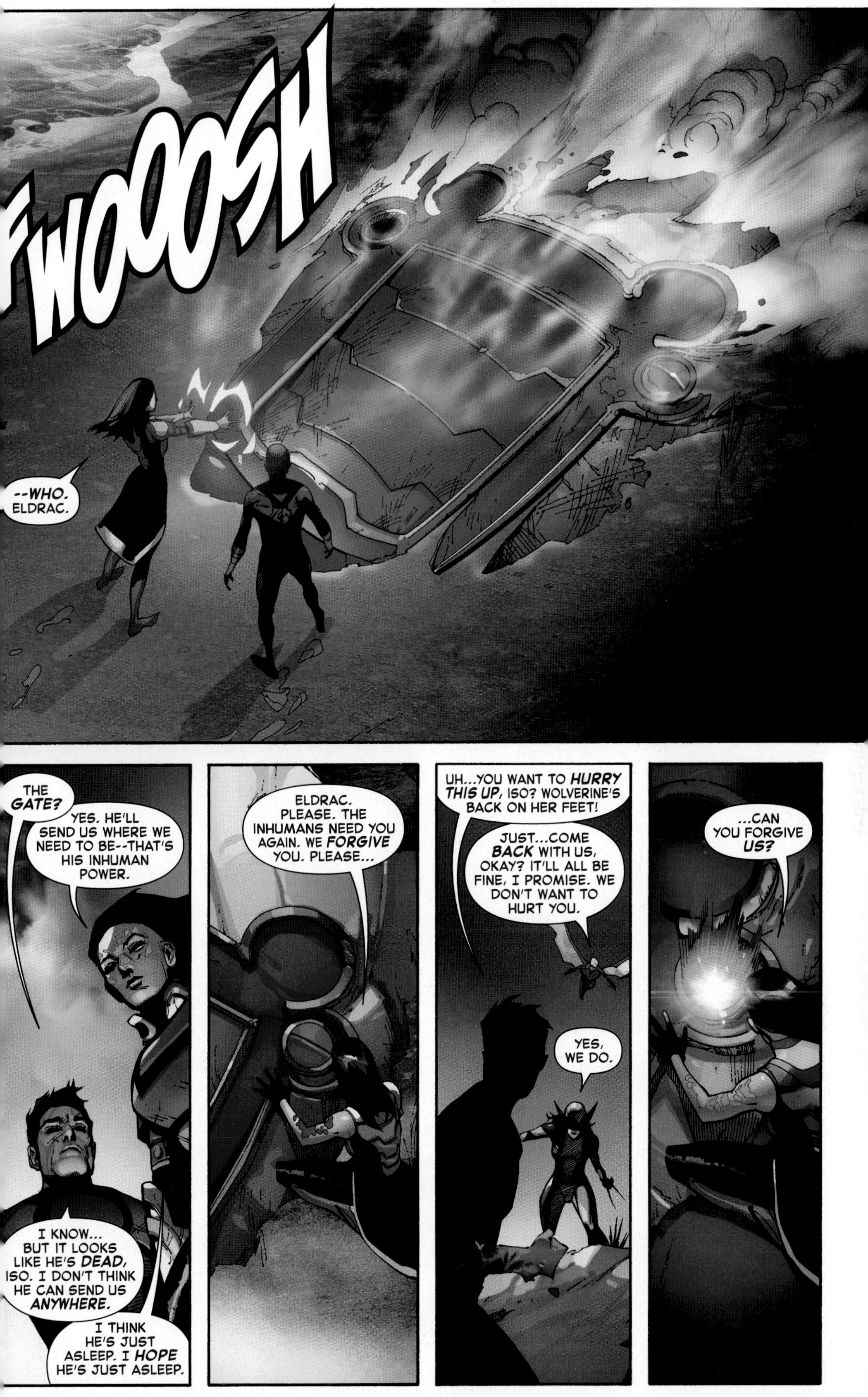
FWOOOSH
--WHO. ELDRAC.
THE GATE?
YES. HE'LL SEND US WHERE WE NEED TO BE--THAT'S HIS INHUMAN POWER.
I KNOW... BUT IT LOOKS LIKE HE'S DEAD, ISO. I DON'T THINK HE CAN SEND US ANYWHERE.
I THINK HE'S JUST ASLEEP. I HOPE HE'S JUST ASLEEP.
ELDRAC. PLEASE. THE INHUMANS NEED YOU AGAIN. WE FORGIVE YOU. PLEASE...
UH...YOU WANT TO HURRY THIS UP, ISO? WOLVERINE'S BACK ON HER FEET!
JUST...COME BACK WITH US, OKAY? IT'LL ALL BE FINE, I PROMISE. WE DON'T WANT TO HURT YOU.
YES, WE DO.
...CAN YOU FORGIVE US?

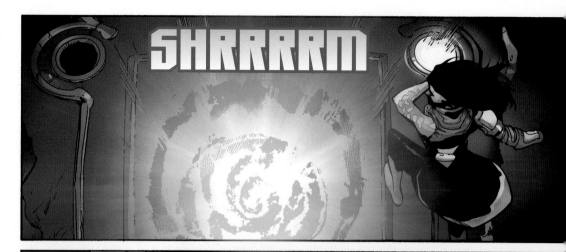

SHRRRRM

SHHK

YOU KNOW, I'M ALMOST GLAD THEY GOT AWAY. I KNOW HOW IMPORTANT IT IS THAT WE WIN THIS FIGHT, BUT...SHOULD WE REALLY BE TRYING TO *KILL* EACH OTHER?

AREN'T WE TRYING TO *KEEP* PEOPLE FROM DYING?

HNH.

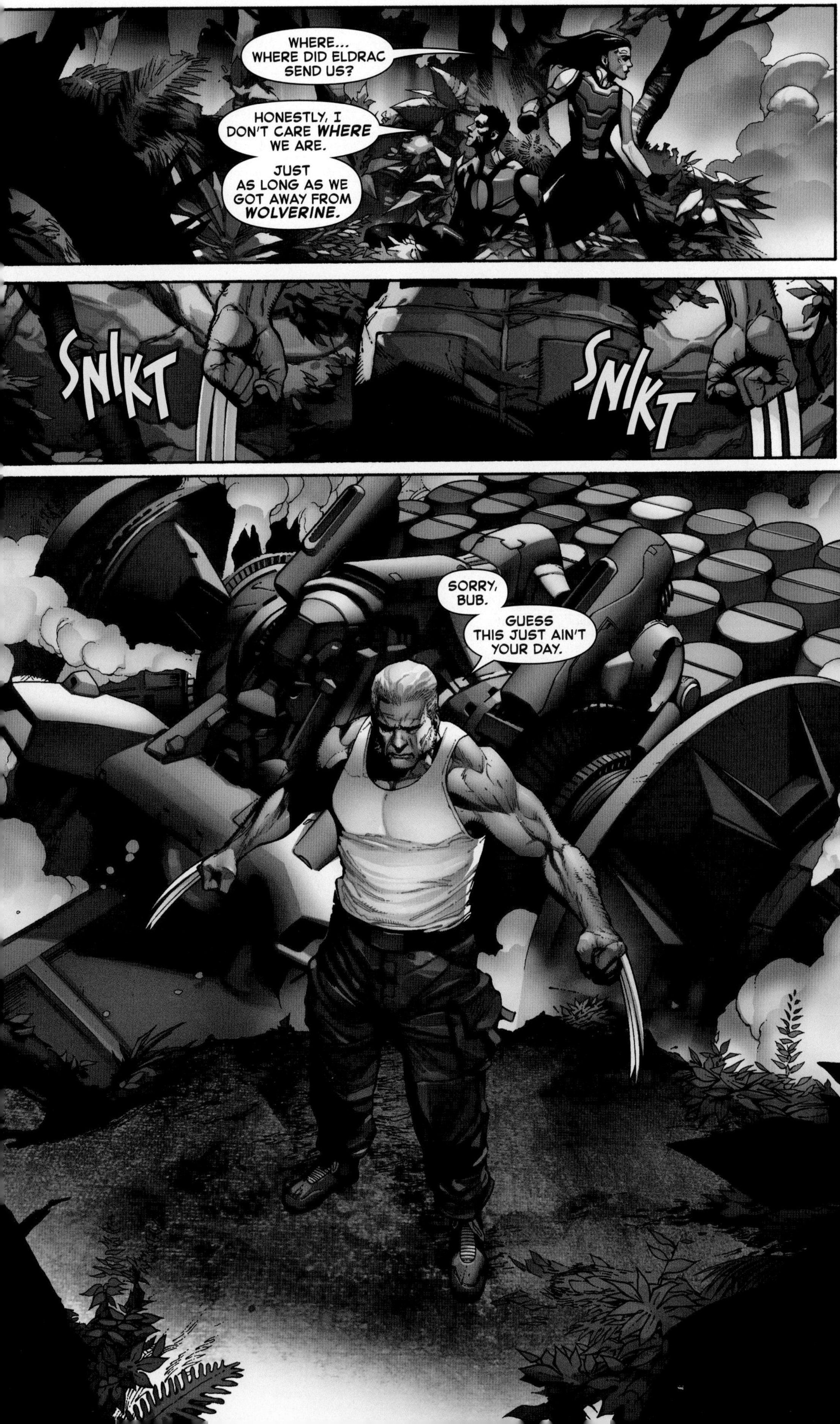
WHERE... WHERE DID ELDRAC SEND US?
HONESTLY, I DON'T CARE WHERE WE ARE.
JUST AS LONG AS WE GOT AWAY FROM WOLVERINE.
SNIKT
SNIKT
SORRY, BUB.
GUESS THIS JUST AIN'T YOUR DAY.

3

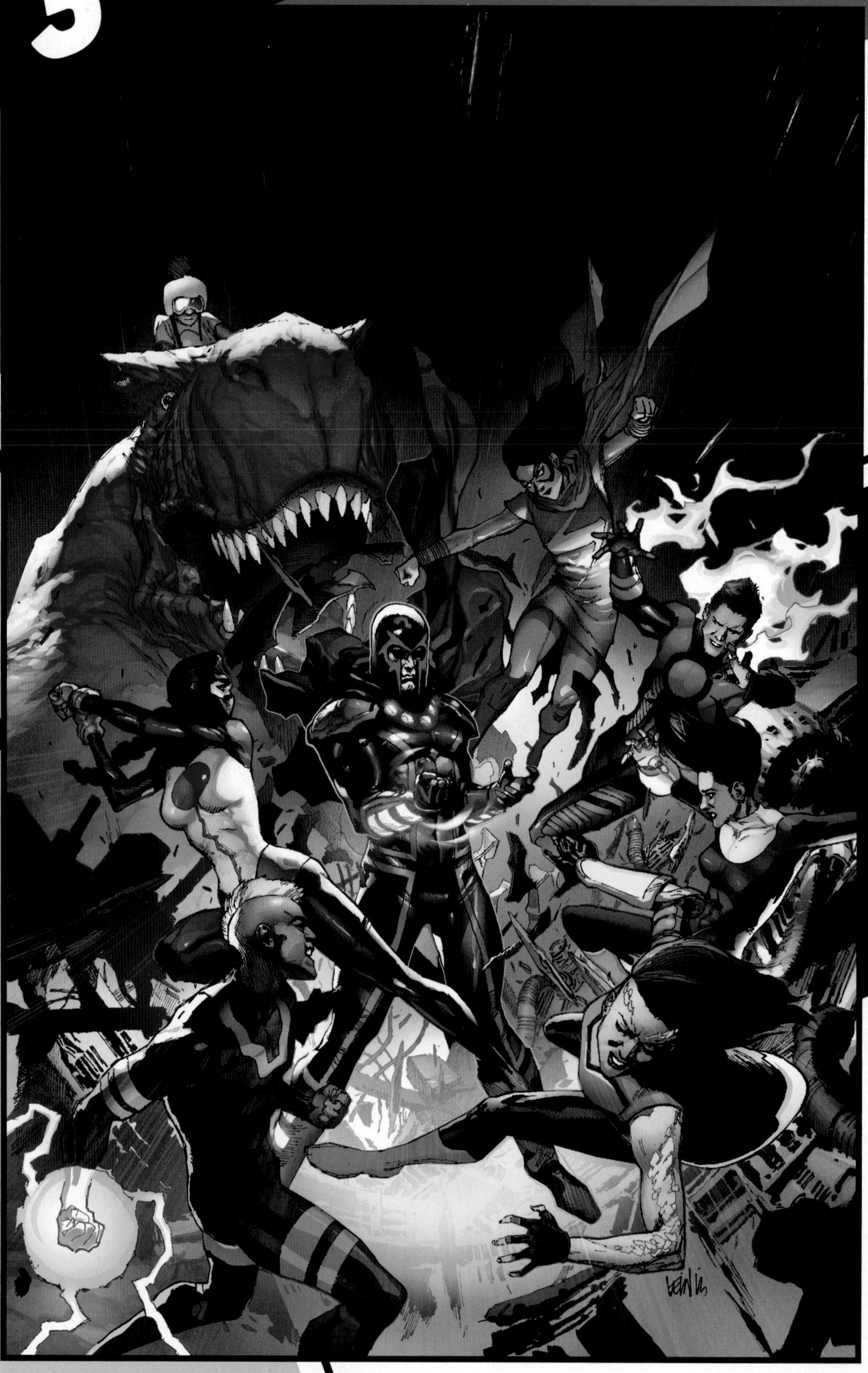

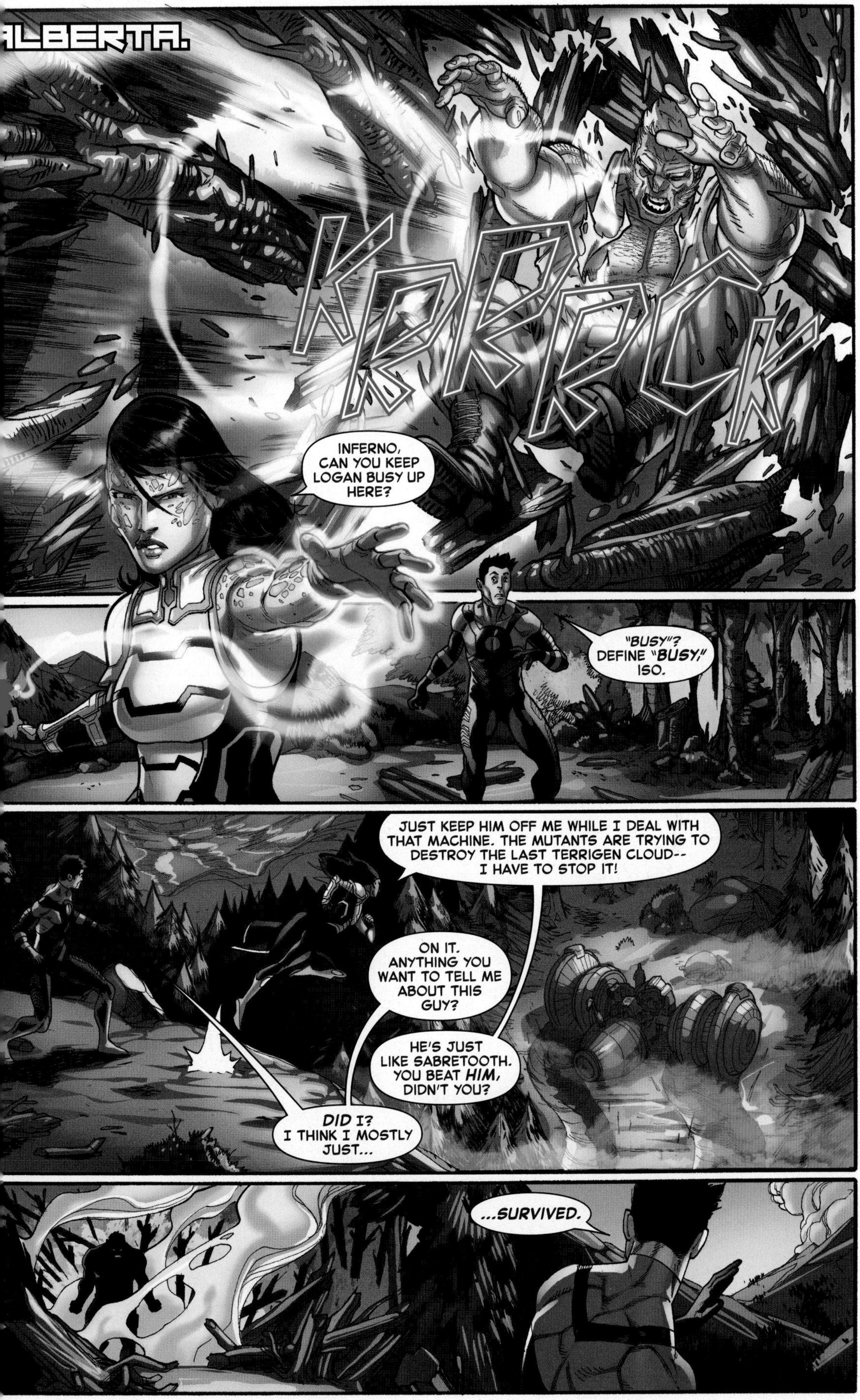
ALBERTA.
KRRRACK
INFERNO, CAN YOU KEEP LOGAN BUSY UP HERE?
"BUSY"? DEFINE "BUSY," ISO.
JUST KEEP HIM OFF ME WHILE I DEAL WITH THAT MACHINE. THE MUTANTS ARE TRYING TO DESTROY THE LAST TERRIGEN CLOUD-- I HAVE TO STOP IT!
ON IT. ANYTHING YOU WANT TO TELL ME ABOUT THIS GUY?
HE'S JUST LIKE SABRETOOTH. YOU BEAT HIM, DIDN'T YOU?
DID I? I THINK I MOSTLY JUST...
...SURVIVED.

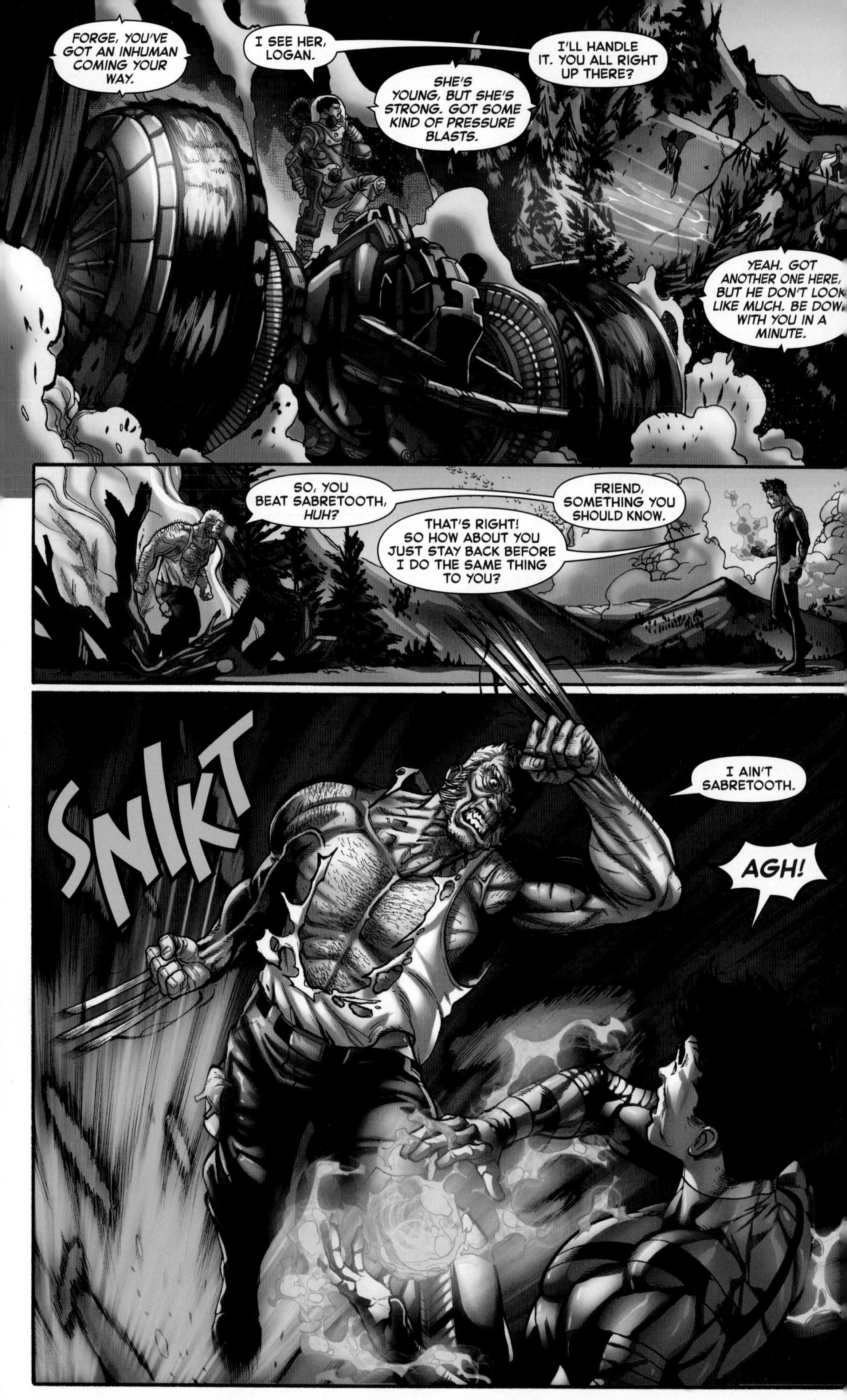

FORGE, YOU'VE GOT AN INHUMAN COMING YOUR WAY.
I SEE HER, LOGAN.
I'LL HANDLE IT. YOU ALL RIGHT UP THERE?
SHE'S YOUNG, BUT SHE'S STRONG. GOT SOME KIND OF PRESSURE BLASTS.
YEAH. GOT ANOTHER ONE HERE, BUT HE DON'T LOOK LIKE MUCH. BE DOW WITH YOU IN A MINUTE.
SO, YOU BEAT SABRETOOTH, HUH?
FRIEND, SOMETHING YOU SHOULD KNOW.
THAT'S RIGHT! SO HOW ABOUT YOU JUST STAY BACK BEFORE I DO THE SAME THING TO YOU?
SNIKT
I AIN'T SABRETOOTH.
AGH!

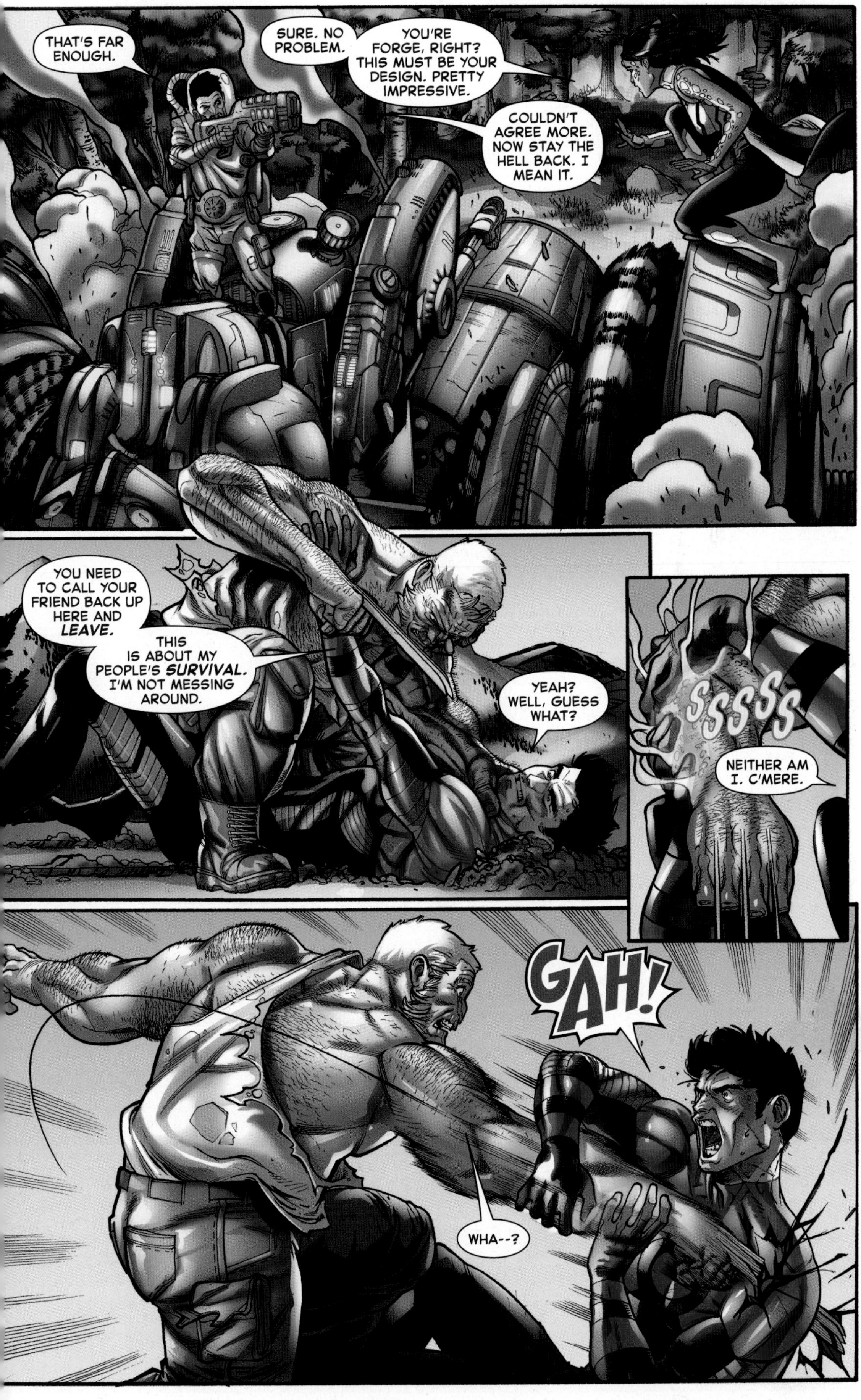
THAT'S FAR ENOUGH.
SURE. NO PROBLEM.
YOU'RE FORGE, RIGHT? THIS MUST BE YOUR DESIGN. PRETTY IMPRESSIVE.
COULDN'T AGREE MORE. NOW STAY THE HELL BACK. I MEAN IT.
YOU NEED TO CALL YOUR FRIEND BACK UP HERE AND *LEAVE.*
THIS IS ABOUT MY PEOPLE'S *SURVIVAL.* I'M NOT MESSING AROUND.
YEAH? WELL, GUESS WHAT?
SSSSS
NEITHER AM I. C'MERE.
GAH!
WHA--?

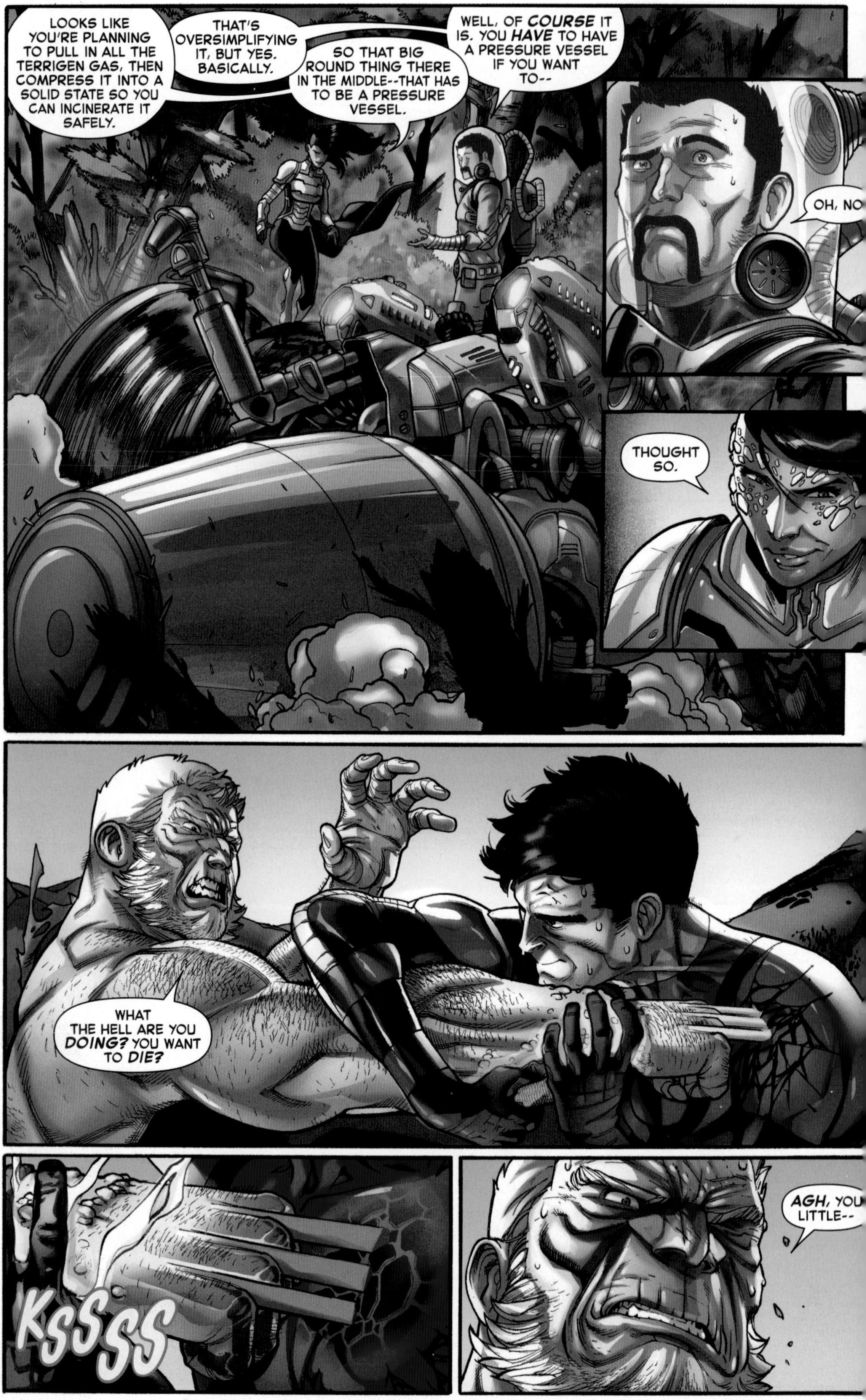
LOOKS LIKE YOU'RE PLANNING TO PULL IN ALL THE TERRIGEN GAS, THEN COMPRESS IT INTO A SOLID STATE SO YOU CAN INCINERATE IT SAFELY.
THAT'S OVERSIMPLIFYING IT, BUT YES. BASICALLY.
SO THAT BIG ROUND THING THERE IN THE MIDDLE--THAT HAS TO BE A PRESSURE VESSEL.
WELL, OF COURSE IT IS. YOU HAVE TO HAVE A PRESSURE VESSEL IF YOU WANT TO--
OH, NO
THOUGHT SO.
WHAT THE HELL ARE YOU DOING? YOU WANT TO DIE?
KSSSS
AGH, YOU LITTLE--

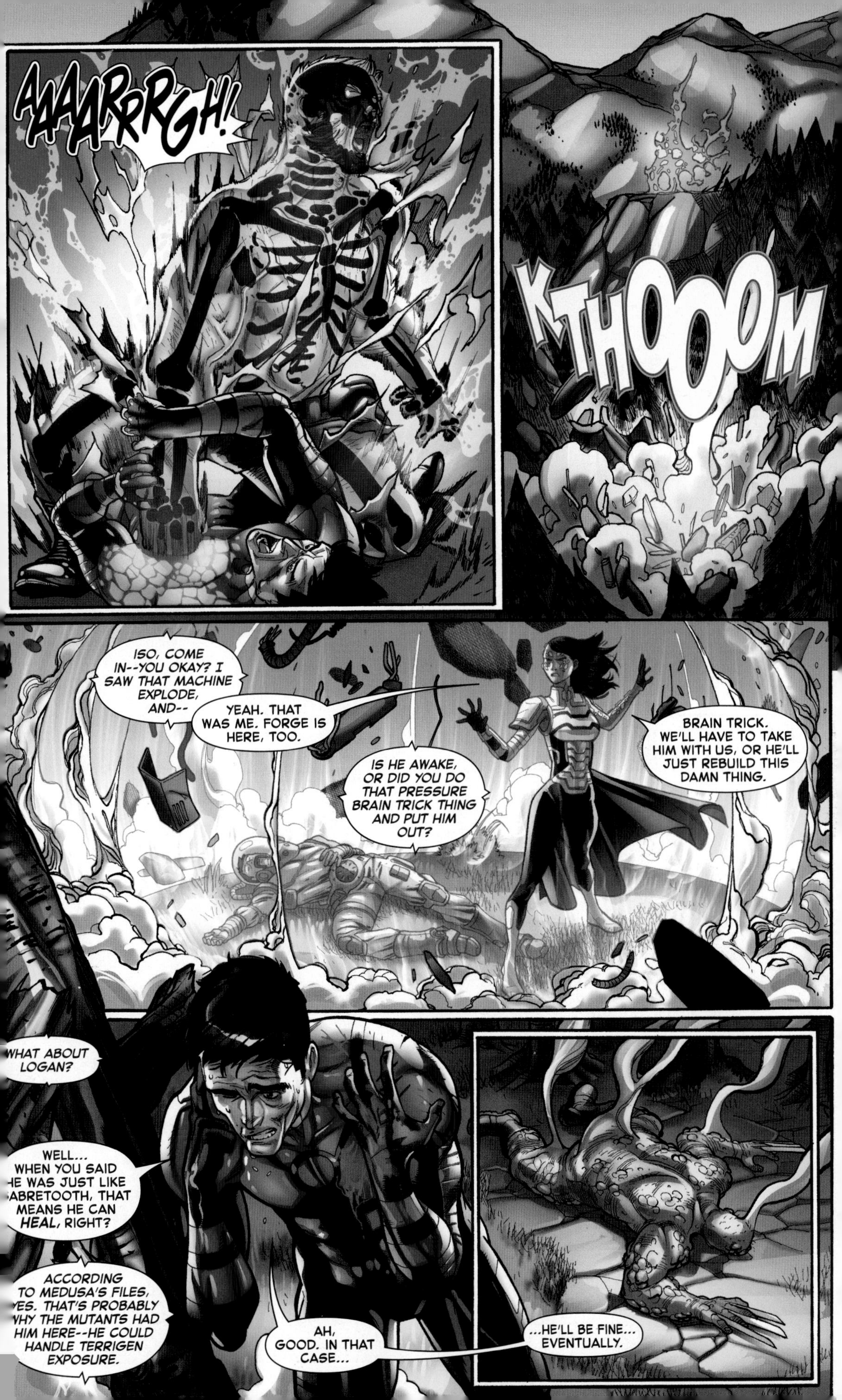
AAAARRRGH!!
KTHOOOM
ISO, COME IN--YOU OKAY? I SAW THAT MACHINE EXPLODE, AND--
YEAH. THAT WAS ME. FORGE IS HERE, TOO.
IS HE AWAKE, OR DID YOU DO THAT PRESSURE BRAIN TRICK THING AND PUT HIM OUT?
BRAIN TRICK. WE'LL HAVE TO TAKE HIM WITH US, OR HE'LL JUST REBUILD THIS DAMN THING.
WHAT ABOUT LOGAN?
WELL... WHEN YOU SAID HE WAS JUST LIKE SABRETOOTH, THAT MEANS HE CAN HEAL, RIGHT?
ACCORDING TO MEDUSA'S FILES, YES. THAT'S PROBABLY WHY THE MUTANTS HAD HIM HERE--HE COULD HANDLE TERRIGEN EXPOSURE.
AH, GOOD. IN THAT CASE...
...HE'LL BE FINE... EVENTUALLY.

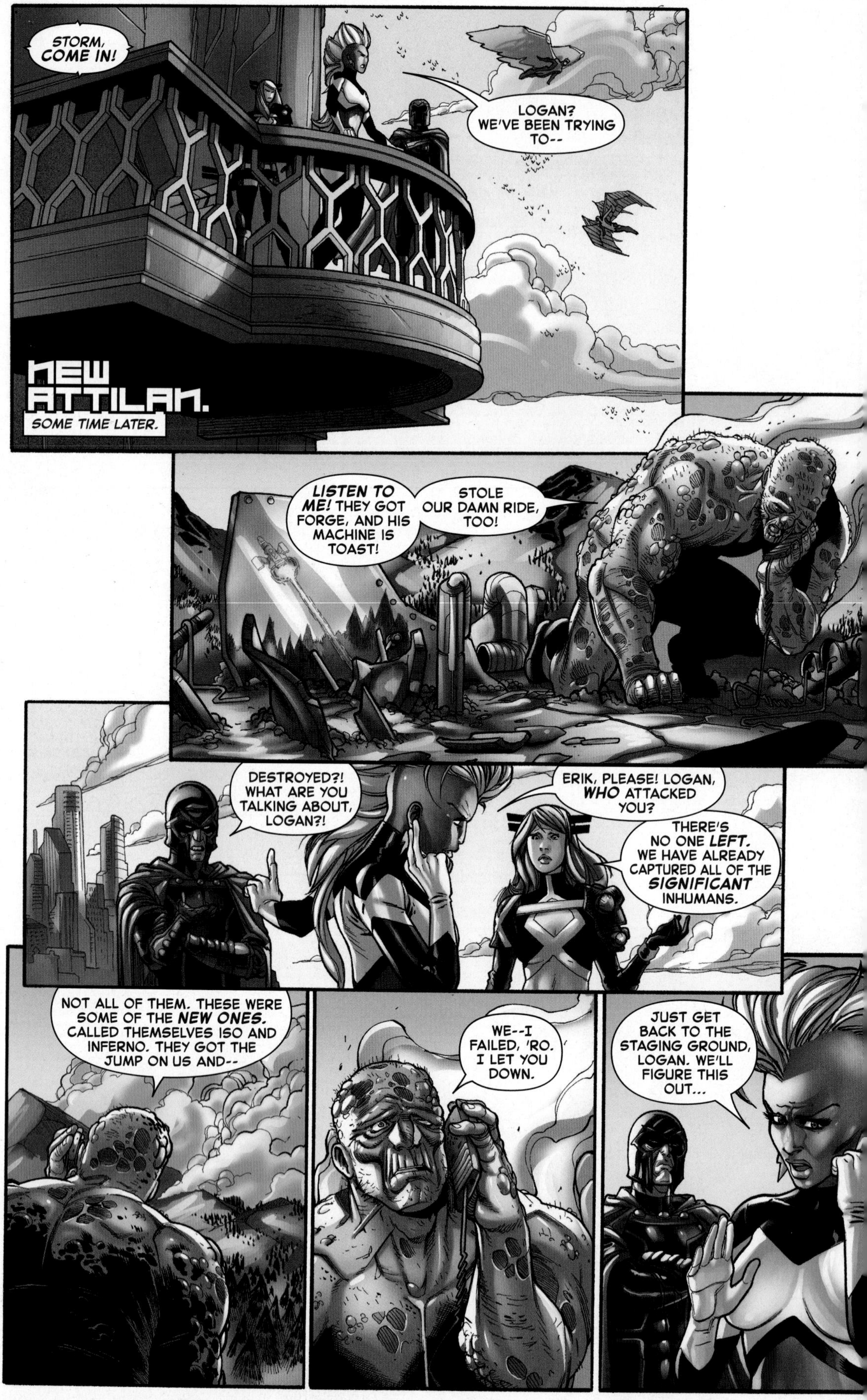

STORM, COME IN!
LOGAN? WE'VE BEEN TRYING TO--
NEW ATTILAN.
SOME TIME LATER.
LISTEN TO ME! THEY GOT FORGE, AND HIS MACHINE IS TOAST!
STOLE OUR DAMN RIDE, TOO!
DESTROYED?! WHAT ARE YOU TALKING ABOUT, LOGAN?!
ERIK, PLEASE! LOGAN, WHO ATTACKED YOU?
THERE'S NO ONE LEFT. WE HAVE ALREADY CAPTURED ALL OF THE SIGNIFICANT INHUMANS.
NOT ALL OF THEM. THESE WERE SOME OF THE NEW ONES. CALLED THEMSELVES ISO AND INFERNO. THEY GOT THE JUMP ON US AND--
WE--I FAILED, 'RO. I LET YOU DOWN.
JUST GET BACK TO THE STAGING GROUND, LOGAN. WE'LL FIGURE THIS OUT...

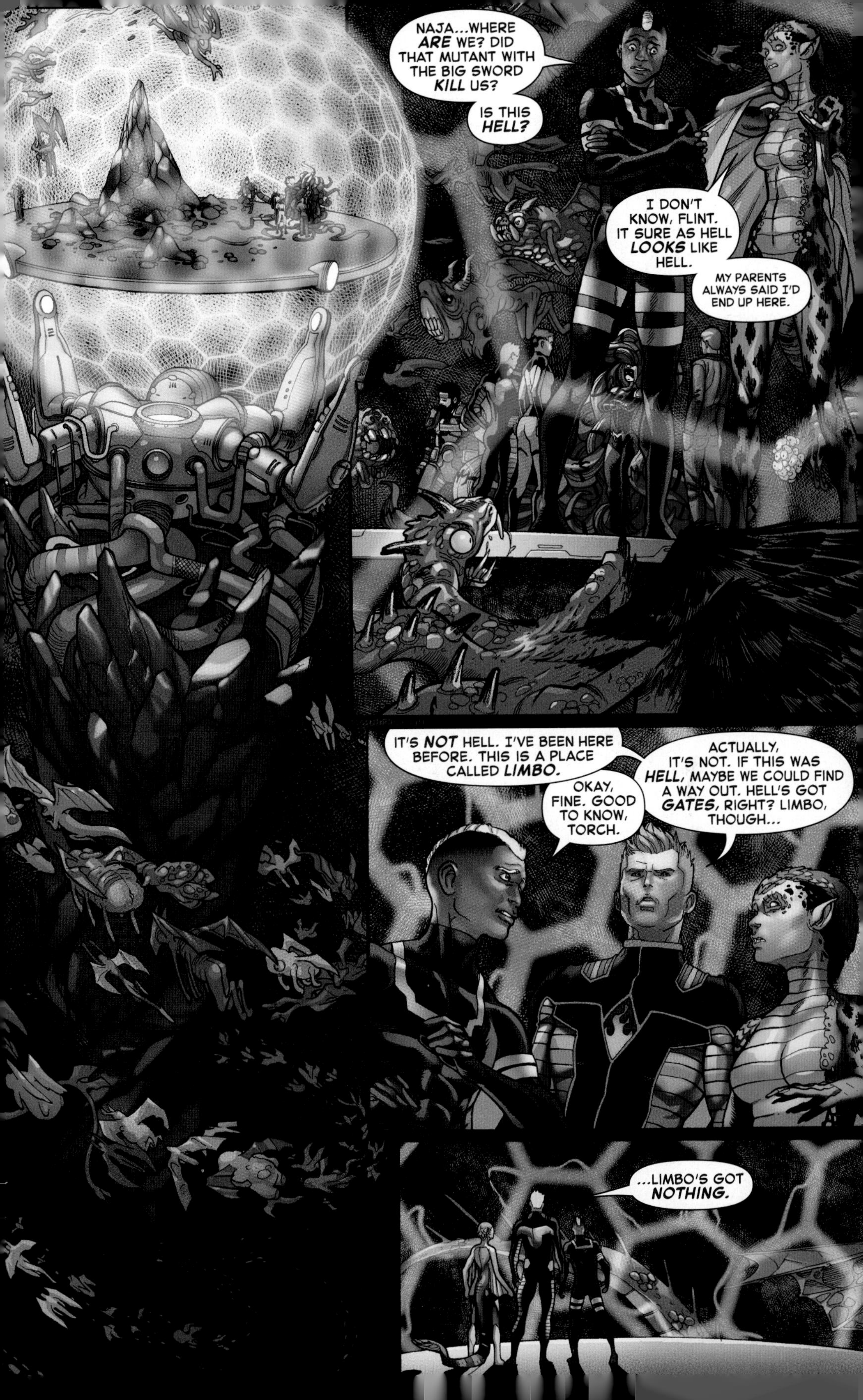
NAJA...WHERE ARE WE? DID THAT MUTANT WITH THE BIG SWORD KILL US?
IS THIS HELL?
I DON'T KNOW, FLINT. IT SURE AS HELL LOOKS LIKE HELL.
MY PARENTS ALWAYS SAID I'D END UP HERE.
IT'S NOT HELL. I'VE BEEN HERE BEFORE. THIS IS A PLACE CALLED LIMBO.
OKAY, FINE. GOOD TO KNOW, TORCH.
ACTUALLY, IT'S NOT. IF THIS WAS HELL, MAYBE WE COULD FIND A WAY OUT. HELL'S GOT GATES, RIGHT? LIMBO, THOUGH...
...LIMBO'S GOT NOTHING.

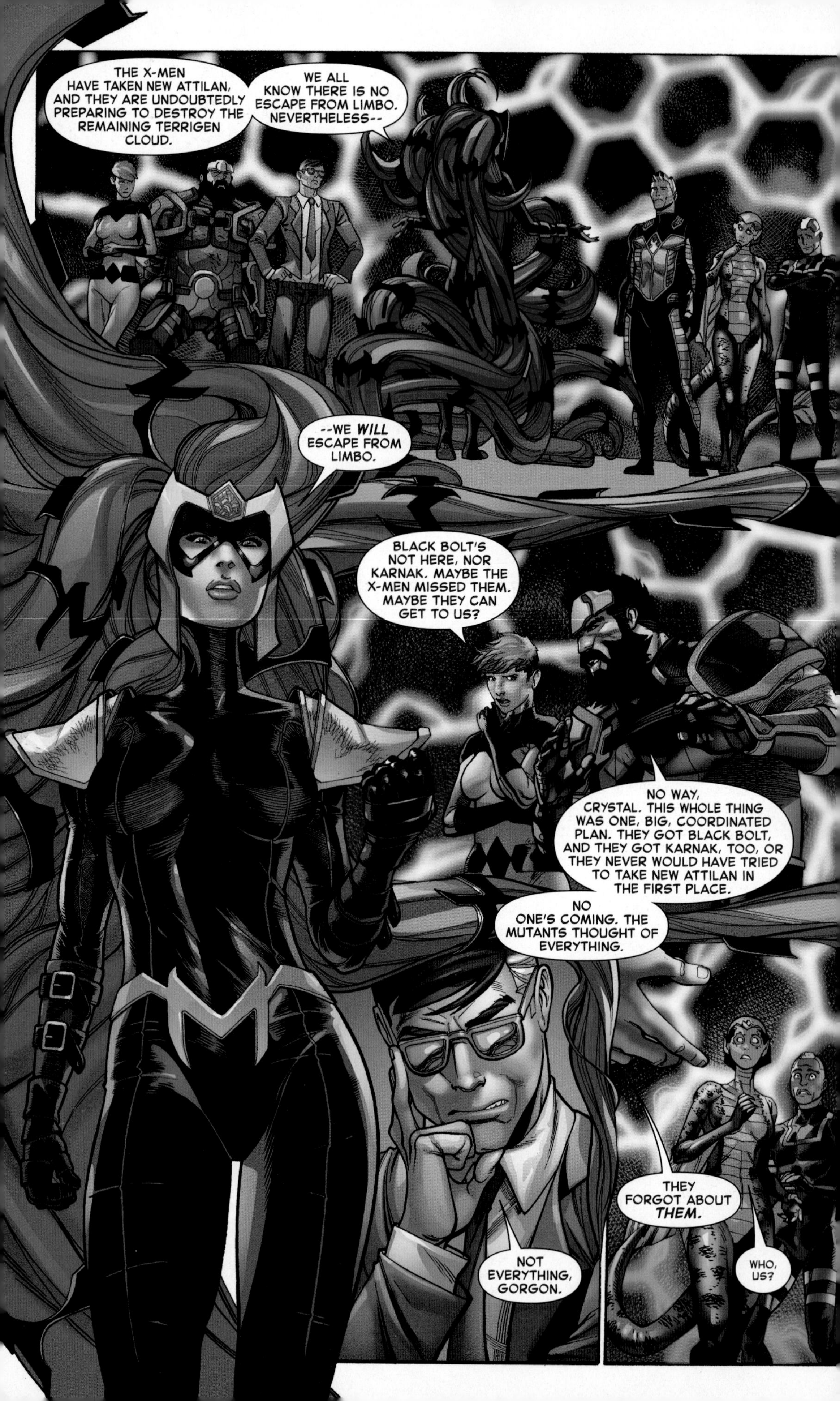

THE X-MEN HAVE TAKEN NEW ATTILAN, AND THEY ARE UNDOUBTEDLY PREPARING TO DESTROY THE REMAINING TERRIGEN CLOUD.
WE ALL KNOW THERE IS NO ESCAPE FROM LIMBO. NEVERTHELESS--
--WE *WILL* ESCAPE FROM LIMBO.
BLACK BOLT'S NOT HERE, NOR KARNAK. MAYBE THE X-MEN MISSED THEM. MAYBE THEY CAN GET TO US?
NO WAY, CRYSTAL. THIS WHOLE THING WAS ONE, BIG, COORDINATED PLAN. THEY GOT BLACK BOLT, AND THEY GOT KARNAK, TOO, OR THEY NEVER WOULD HAVE TRIED TO TAKE NEW ATTILAN IN THE FIRST PLACE.
NO ONE'S COMING. THE MUTANTS THOUGHT OF EVERYTHING.
NOT EVERYTHING, GORGON.
THEY FORGOT ABOUT *THEM.*
WHO, US?

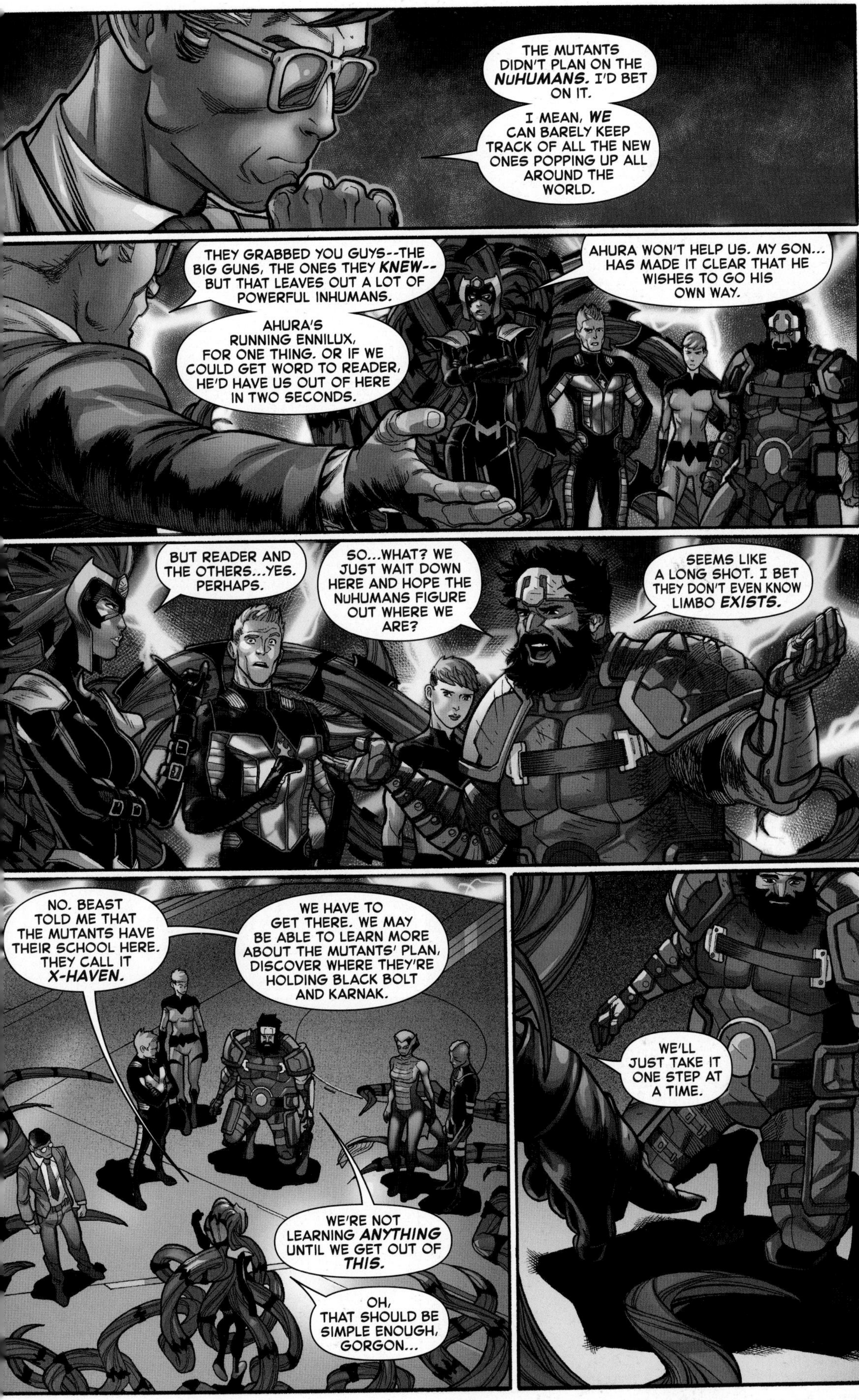
THE MUTANTS DIDN'T PLAN ON THE NUHUMANS. I'D BET ON IT.
I MEAN, WE CAN BARELY KEEP TRACK OF ALL THE NEW ONES POPPING UP ALL AROUND THE WORLD.
THEY GRABBED YOU GUYS--THE BIG GUNS, THE ONES THEY KNEW--BUT THAT LEAVES OUT A LOT OF POWERFUL INHUMANS.
AHURA'S RUNNING ENNILUX, FOR ONE THING. OR IF WE COULD GET WORD TO READER, HE'D HAVE US OUT OF HERE IN TWO SECONDS.
AHURA WON'T HELP US. MY SON... HAS MADE IT CLEAR THAT HE WISHES TO GO HIS OWN WAY.
BUT READER AND THE OTHERS...YES. PERHAPS.
SO...WHAT? WE JUST WAIT DOWN HERE AND HOPE THE NUHUMANS FIGURE OUT WHERE WE ARE?
SEEMS LIKE A LONG SHOT. I BET THEY DON'T EVEN KNOW LIMBO EXISTS.
NO. BEAST TOLD ME THAT THE MUTANTS HAVE THEIR SCHOOL HERE. THEY CALL IT X-HAVEN.
WE HAVE TO GET THERE. WE MAY BE ABLE TO LEARN MORE ABOUT THE MUTANTS' PLAN, DISCOVER WHERE THEY'RE HOLDING BLACK BOLT AND KARNAK.
WE'RE NOT LEARNING ANYTHING UNTIL WE GET OUT OF THIS.
OH, THAT SHOULD BE SIMPLE ENOUGH, GORGON...
WE'LL JUST TAKE IT ONE STEP AT A TIME.

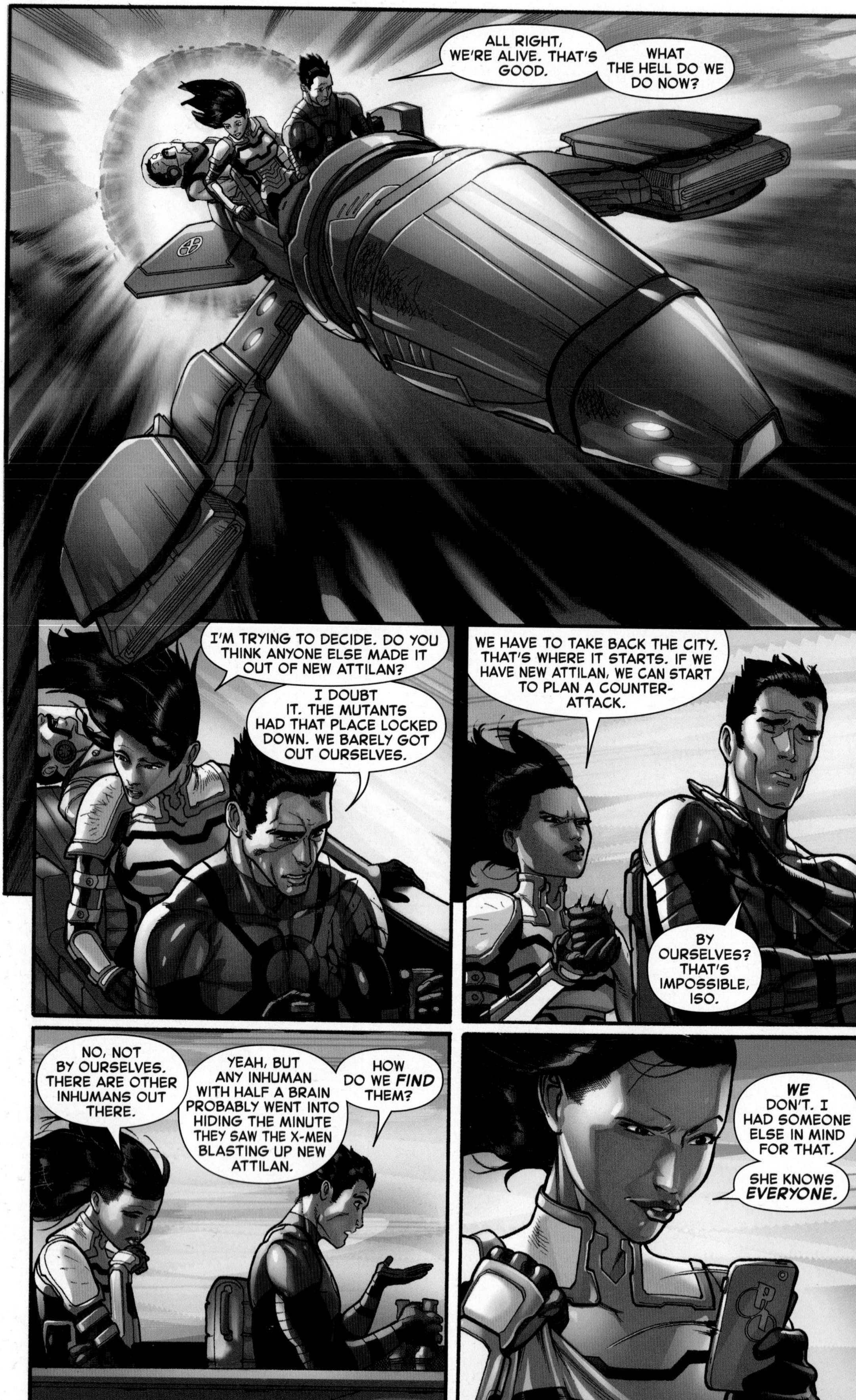

ALL RIGHT, WE'RE ALIVE. THAT'S GOOD.
WHAT THE HELL DO WE DO NOW?
I'M TRYING TO DECIDE. DO YOU THINK ANYONE ELSE MADE IT OUT OF NEW ATTILAN?
I DOUBT IT. THE MUTANTS HAD THAT PLACE LOCKED DOWN. WE BARELY GOT OUT OURSELVES.
WE HAVE TO TAKE BACK THE CITY. THAT'S WHERE IT STARTS. IF WE HAVE NEW ATTILAN, WE CAN START TO PLAN A COUNTER-ATTACK.
BY OURSELVES? THAT'S IMPOSSIBLE, ISO.
NO, NOT BY OURSELVES. THERE ARE OTHER INHUMANS OUT THERE.
YEAH, BUT ANY INHUMAN WITH HALF A BRAIN PROBABLY WENT INTO HIDING THE MINUTE THEY SAW THE X-MEN BLASTING UP NEW ATTILAN.
HOW DO WE *FIND* THEM?
WE DON'T. I HAD SOMEONE ELSE IN MIND FOR THAT.
SHE KNOWS *EVERYONE.*

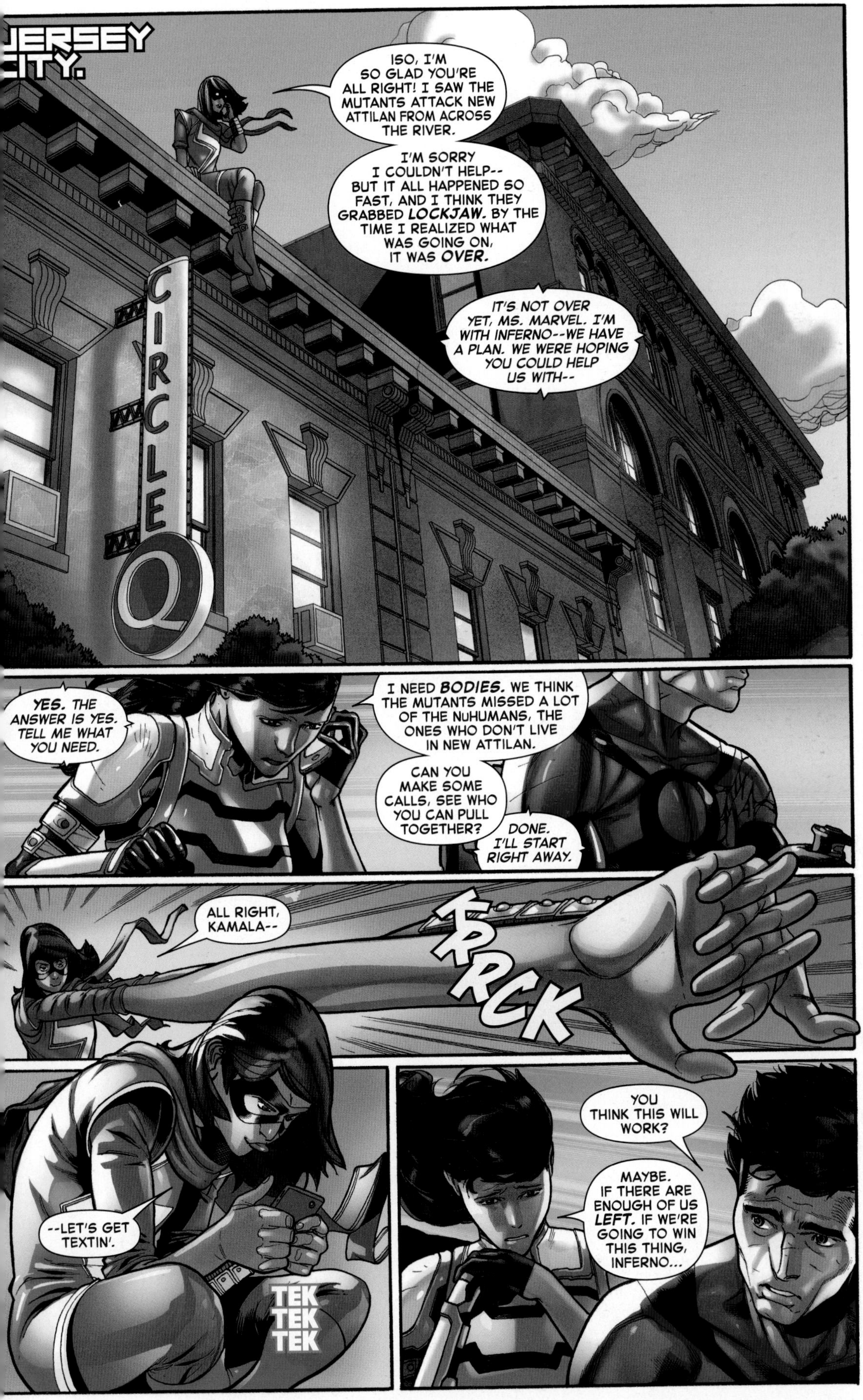
JERSEY CITY.
ISO, I'M SO GLAD YOU'RE ALL RIGHT! I SAW THE MUTANTS ATTACK NEW ATTILAN FROM ACROSS THE RIVER.
I'M SORRY I COULDN'T HELP-- BUT IT ALL HAPPENED SO FAST, AND I THINK THEY GRABBED LOCKJAW. BY THE TIME I REALIZED WHAT WAS GOING ON, IT WAS OVER.
CIRCLE Q
IT'S NOT OVER YET, MS. MARVEL. I'M WITH INFERNO--WE HAVE A PLAN. WE WERE HOPING YOU COULD HELP US WITH--
YES. THE ANSWER IS YES. TELL ME WHAT YOU NEED.
I NEED BODIES. WE THINK THE MUTANTS MISSED A LOT OF THE NUHUMANS, THE ONES WHO DON'T LIVE IN NEW ATTILAN.
CAN YOU MAKE SOME CALLS, SEE WHO YOU CAN PULL TOGETHER?
DONE. I'LL START RIGHT AWAY.
ALL RIGHT, KAMALA--
KRRCK
--LET'S GET TEXTIN'.
TEK TEK TEK
YOU THINK THIS WILL WORK?
MAYBE. IF THERE ARE ENOUGH OF US LEFT. IF WE'RE GOING TO WIN THIS THING, INFERNO...

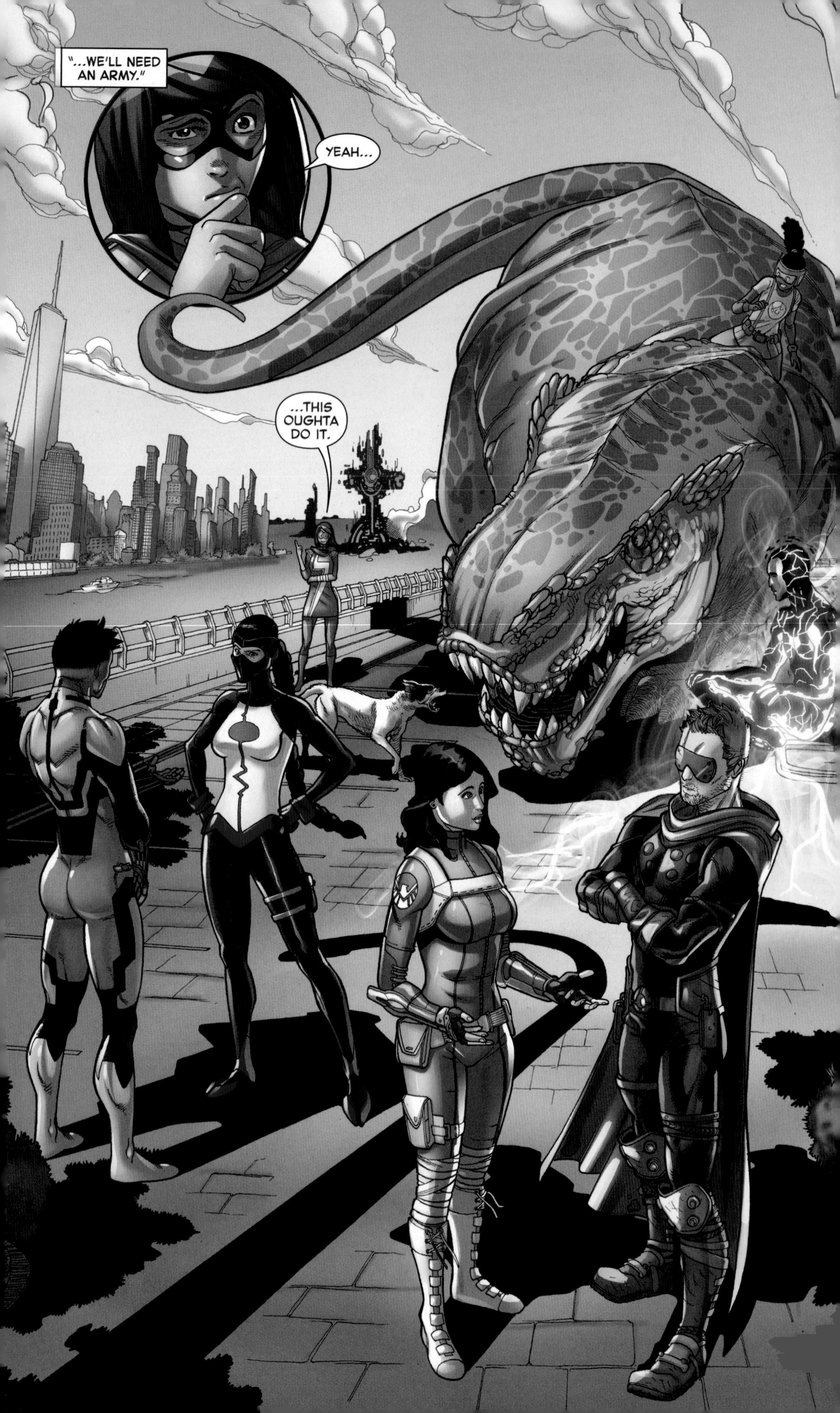
"...WE'LL NEED AN ARMY."
YEAH...
...THIS OUGHTA DO IT.

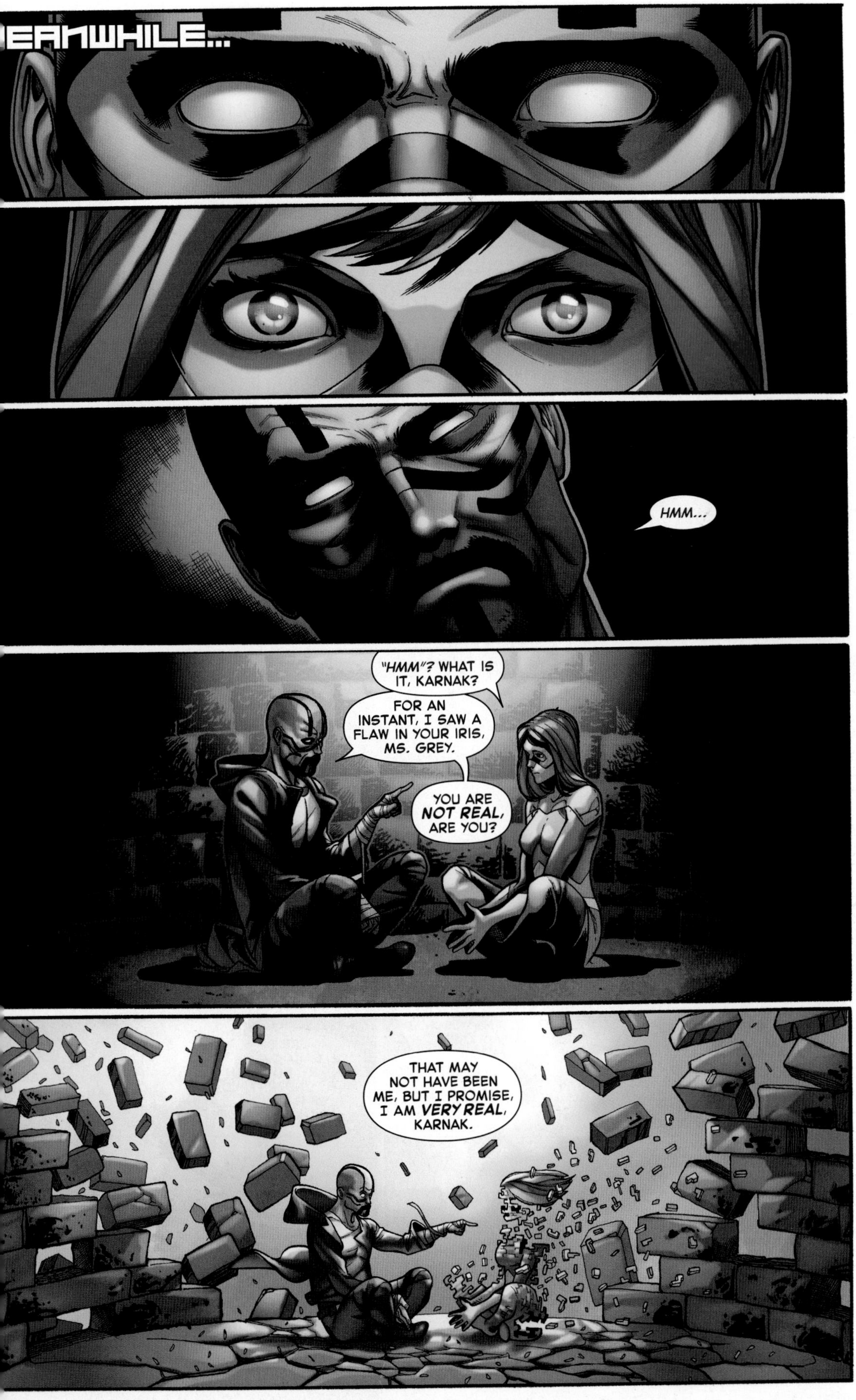
EANWHILE...
HMM...
"HMM"? WHAT IS IT, KARNAK?
FOR AN INSTANT, I SAW A FLAW IN YOUR IRIS, MS. GREY.
YOU ARE NOT REAL, ARE YOU?
THAT MAY NOT HAVE BEEN ME, BUT I PROMISE, I AM VERY REAL, KARNAK.

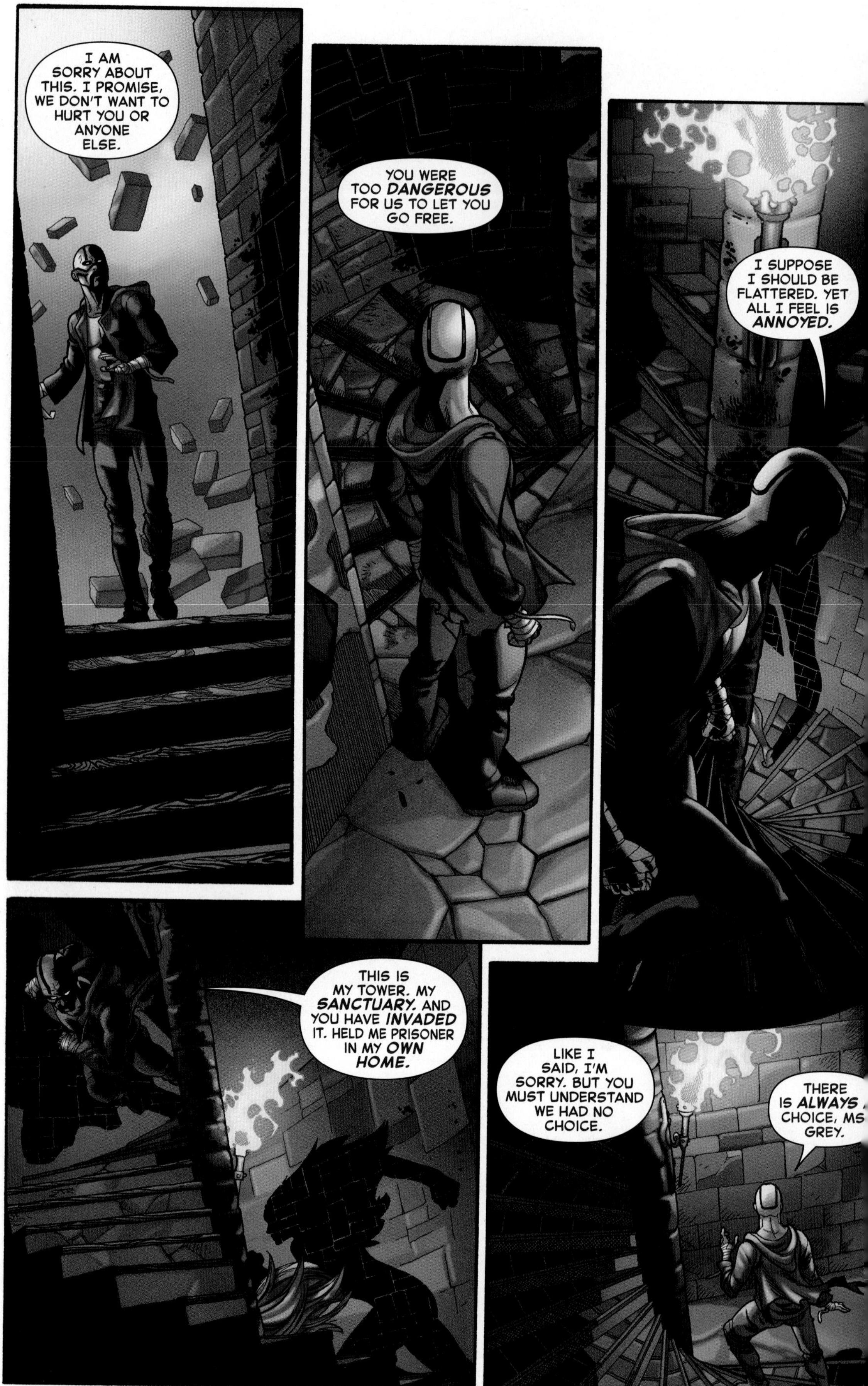
I AM SORRY ABOUT THIS. I PROMISE, WE DON'T WANT TO HURT YOU OR ANYONE ELSE.
YOU WERE TOO DANGEROUS FOR US TO LET YOU GO FREE.
I SUPPOSE I SHOULD BE FLATTERED. YET ALL I FEEL IS ANNOYED.
THIS IS MY TOWER. MY SANCTUARY. AND YOU HAVE INVADED IT. HELD ME PRISONER IN MY OWN HOME.
LIKE I SAID, I'M SORRY. BUT YOU MUST UNDERSTAND WE HAD NO CHOICE.
THERE IS ALWAYS CHOICE, MS GREY.

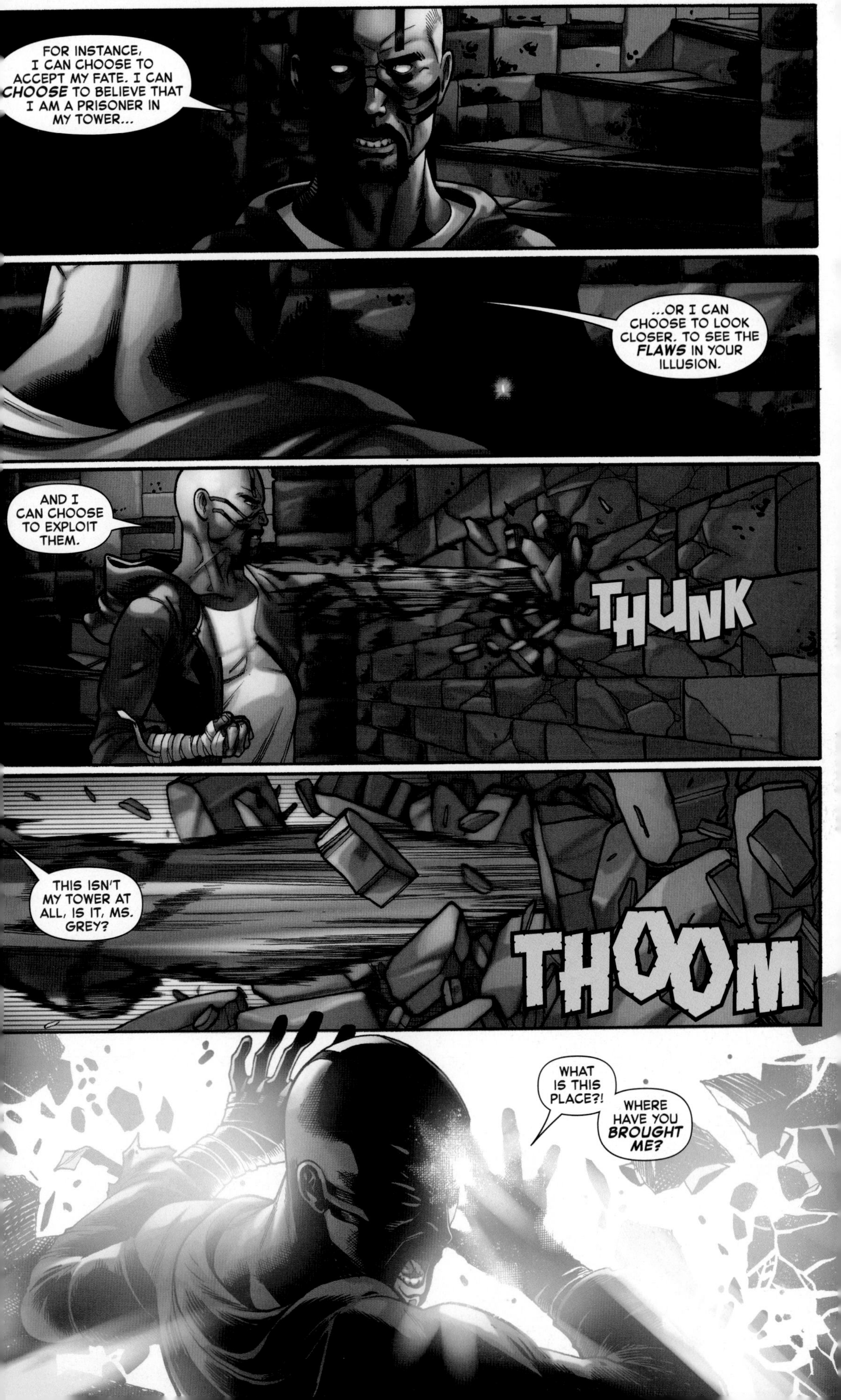
FOR INSTANCE, I CAN CHOOSE TO ACCEPT MY FATE. I CAN CHOOSE TO BELIEVE THAT I AM A PRISONER IN MY TOWER...
...OR I CAN CHOOSE TO LOOK CLOSER. TO SEE THE FLAWS IN YOUR ILLUSION.
AND I CAN CHOOSE TO EXPLOIT THEM.
THUNK
THIS ISN'T MY TOWER AT ALL, IS IT, MS. GREY?
THOOM
WHAT IS THIS PLACE?!
WHERE HAVE YOU BROUGHT ME?

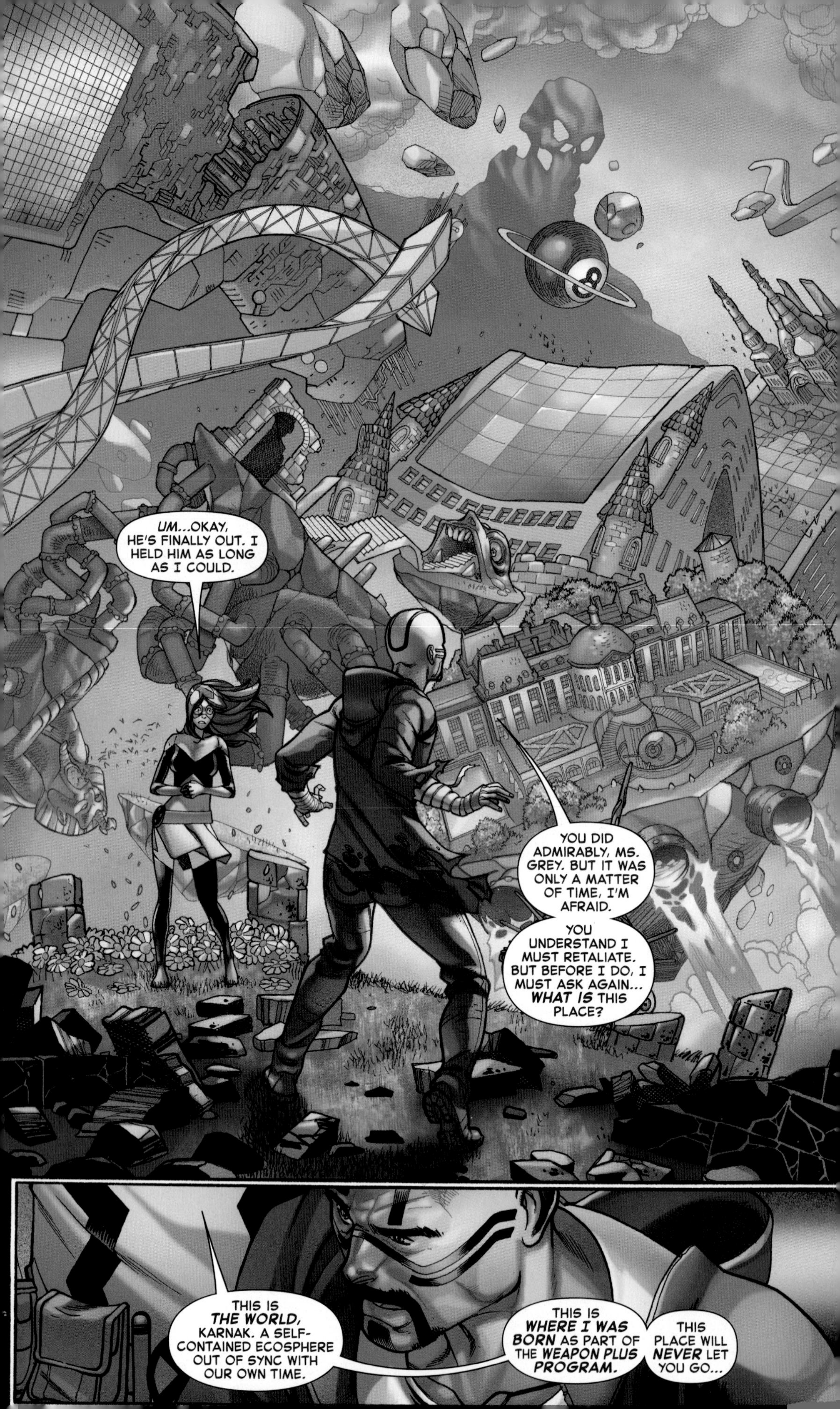
UM...OKAY, HE'S FINALLY OUT. I HELD HIM AS LONG AS I COULD.
YOU DID ADMIRABLY, MS. GREY. BUT IT WAS ONLY A MATTER OF TIME, I'M AFRAID.
YOU UNDERSTAND I MUST RETALIATE. BUT BEFORE I DO, I MUST ASK AGAIN... WHAT IS THIS... PLACE?
THIS IS THE WORLD, KARNAK. A SELF-CONTAINED ECOSPHERE OUT OF SYNC WITH OUR OWN TIME.
THIS IS WHERE I WAS BORN AS PART OF THE WEAPON PLUS PROGRAM.
THIS PLACE WILL NEVER LET YOU GO...

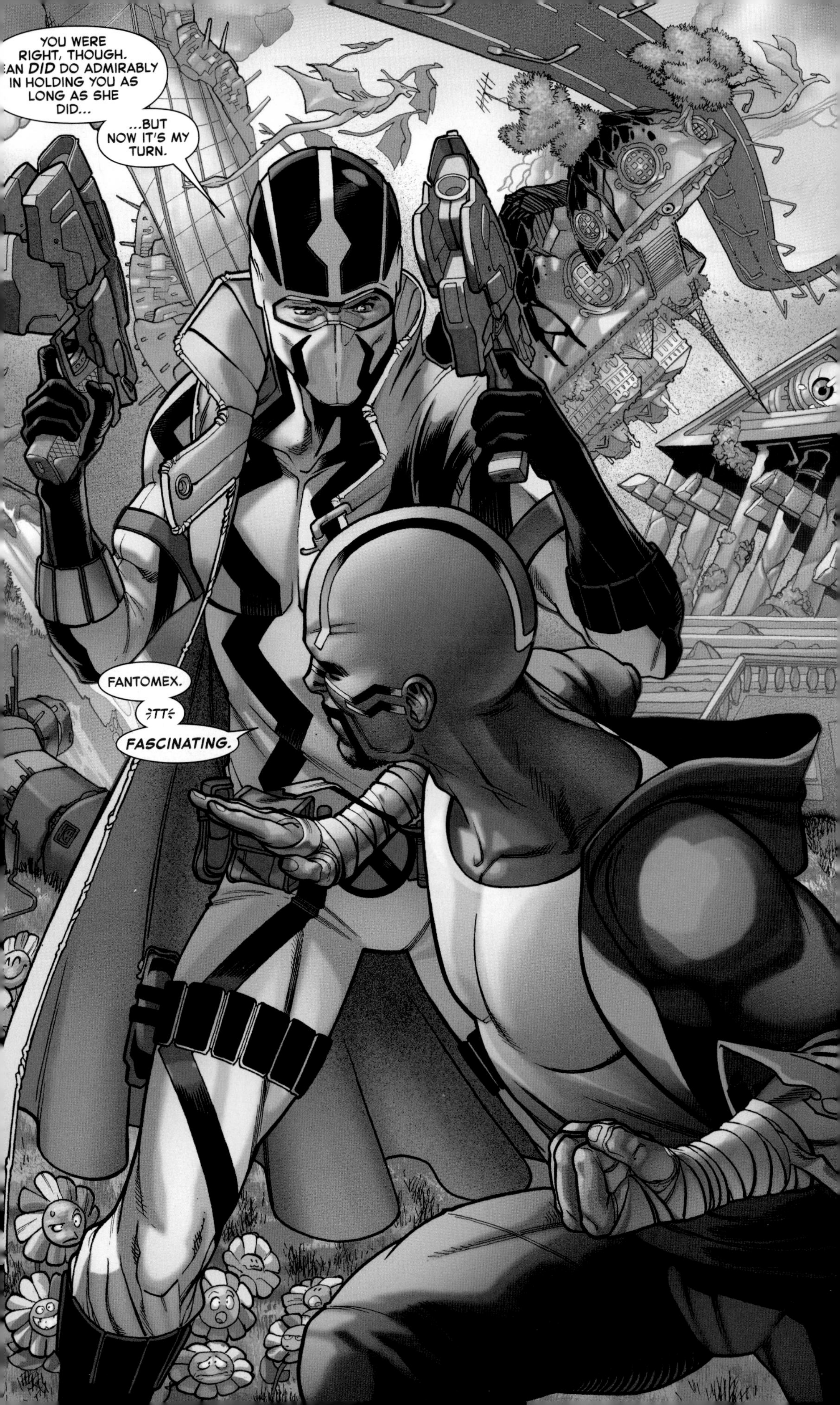

YOU WERE RIGHT, THOUGH. JEAN DID DO ADMIRABLY IN HOLDING YOU AS LONG AS SHE DID...
...BUT NOW IT'S MY TURN.
FANTOMEX.
TT
FASCINATING.

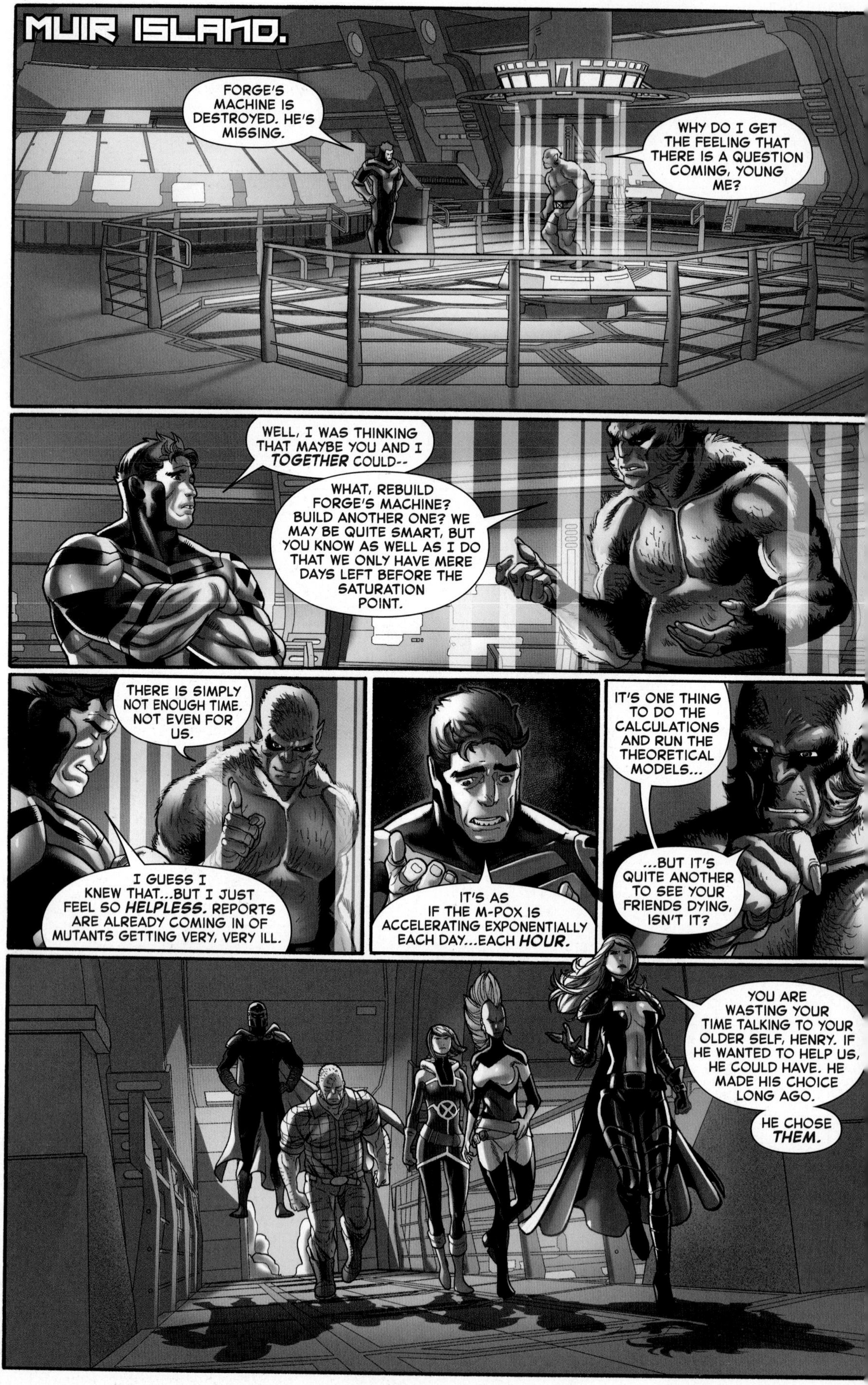
MUIR ISLAND.
FORGE'S MACHINE IS DESTROYED. HE'S MISSING.
WHY DO I GET THE FEELING THAT THERE IS A QUESTION COMING, YOUNG ME?
WELL, I WAS THINKING THAT MAYBE YOU AND I *TOGETHER* COULD--
WHAT, REBUILD FORGE'S MACHINE? BUILD ANOTHER ONE? WE MAY BE QUITE SMART, BUT YOU KNOW AS WELL AS I DO THAT WE ONLY HAVE MERE DAYS LEFT BEFORE THE SATURATION POINT.
THERE IS SIMPLY NOT ENOUGH TIME. NOT EVEN FOR US.
I GUESS I KNEW THAT...BUT I JUST FEEL SO ***HELPLESS.*** REPORTS ARE ALREADY COMING IN OF MUTANTS GETTING VERY, VERY ILL.
IT'S AS IF THE M-POX IS ACCELERATING EXPONENTIALLY EACH DAY...EACH ***HOUR.***
IT'S ONE THING TO DO THE CALCULATIONS AND RUN THE THEORETICAL MODELS...
...BUT IT'S QUITE ANOTHER TO SEE YOUR FRIENDS DYING, ISN'T IT?
YOU ARE WASTING YOUR TIME TALKING TO YOUR OLDER SELF, HENRY. IF HE WANTED TO HELP US, HE COULD HAVE. HE MADE HIS CHOICE LONG AGO.
HE CHOSE ***THEM.***

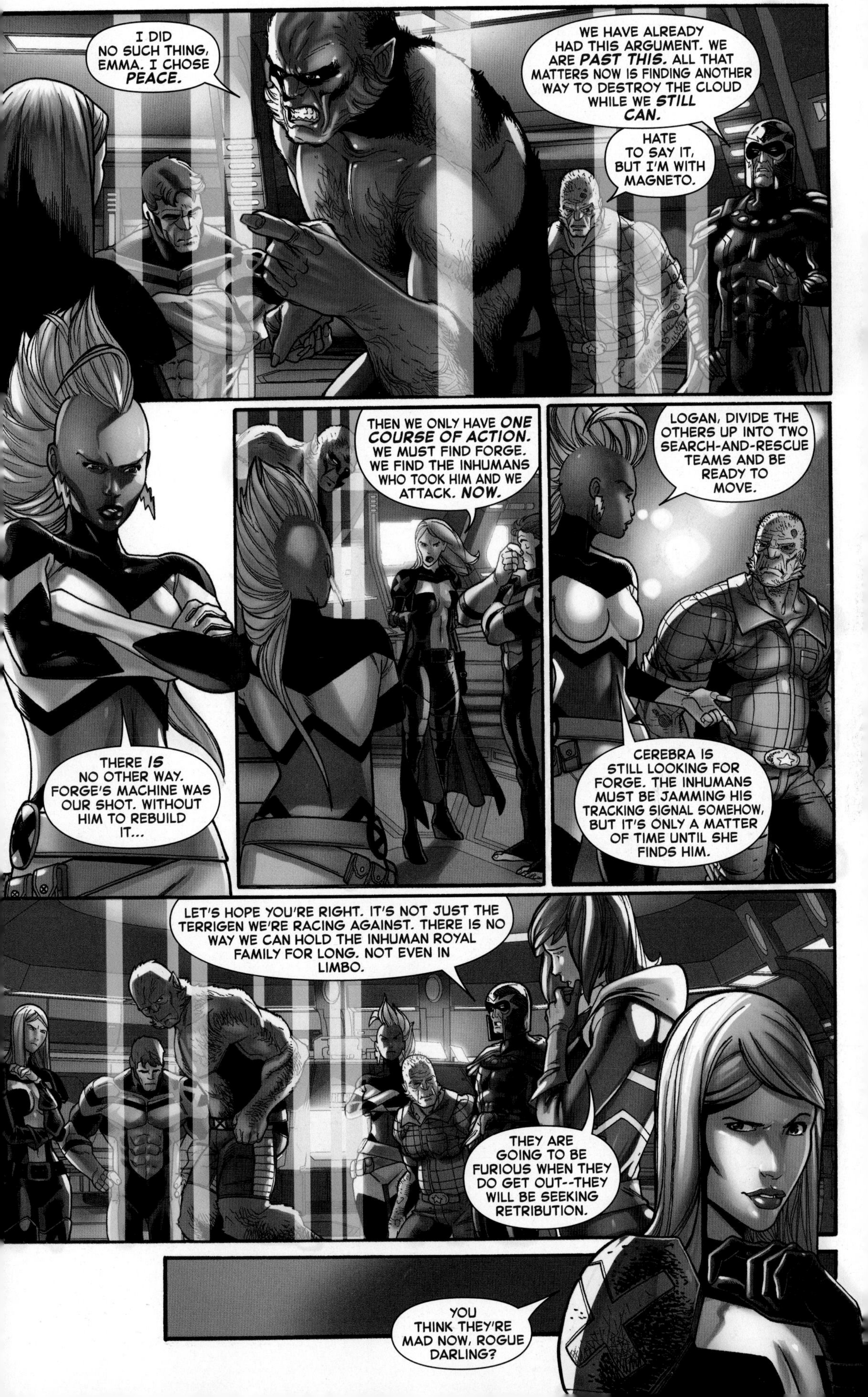
I DID NO SUCH THING, EMMA. I CHOSE PEACE.
WE HAVE ALREADY HAD THIS ARGUMENT. WE ARE PAST THIS. ALL THAT MATTERS NOW IS FINDING ANOTHER WAY TO DESTROY THE CLOUD WHILE WE STILL CAN.
HATE TO SAY IT, BUT I'M WITH MAGNETO.
THERE IS NO OTHER WAY. FORGE'S MACHINE WAS OUR SHOT. WITHOUT HIM TO REBUILD IT...
THEN WE ONLY HAVE ONE COURSE OF ACTION. WE MUST FIND FORGE. WE FIND THE INHUMANS WHO TOOK HIM AND WE ATTACK. NOW.
LOGAN, DIVIDE THE OTHERS UP INTO TWO SEARCH-AND-RESCUE TEAMS AND BE READY TO MOVE.
CEREBRA IS STILL LOOKING FOR FORGE. THE INHUMANS MUST BE JAMMING HIS TRACKING SIGNAL SOMEHOW, BUT IT'S ONLY A MATTER OF TIME UNTIL SHE FINDS HIM.
LET'S HOPE YOU'RE RIGHT. IT'S NOT JUST THE TERRIGEN WE'RE RACING AGAINST. THERE IS NO WAY WE CAN HOLD THE INHUMAN ROYAL FAMILY FOR LONG. NOT EVEN IN LIMBO.
THEY ARE GOING TO BE FURIOUS WHEN THEY DO GET OUT--THEY WILL BE SEEKING RETRIBUTION.
YOU THINK THEY'RE MAD NOW, ROGUE DARLING?

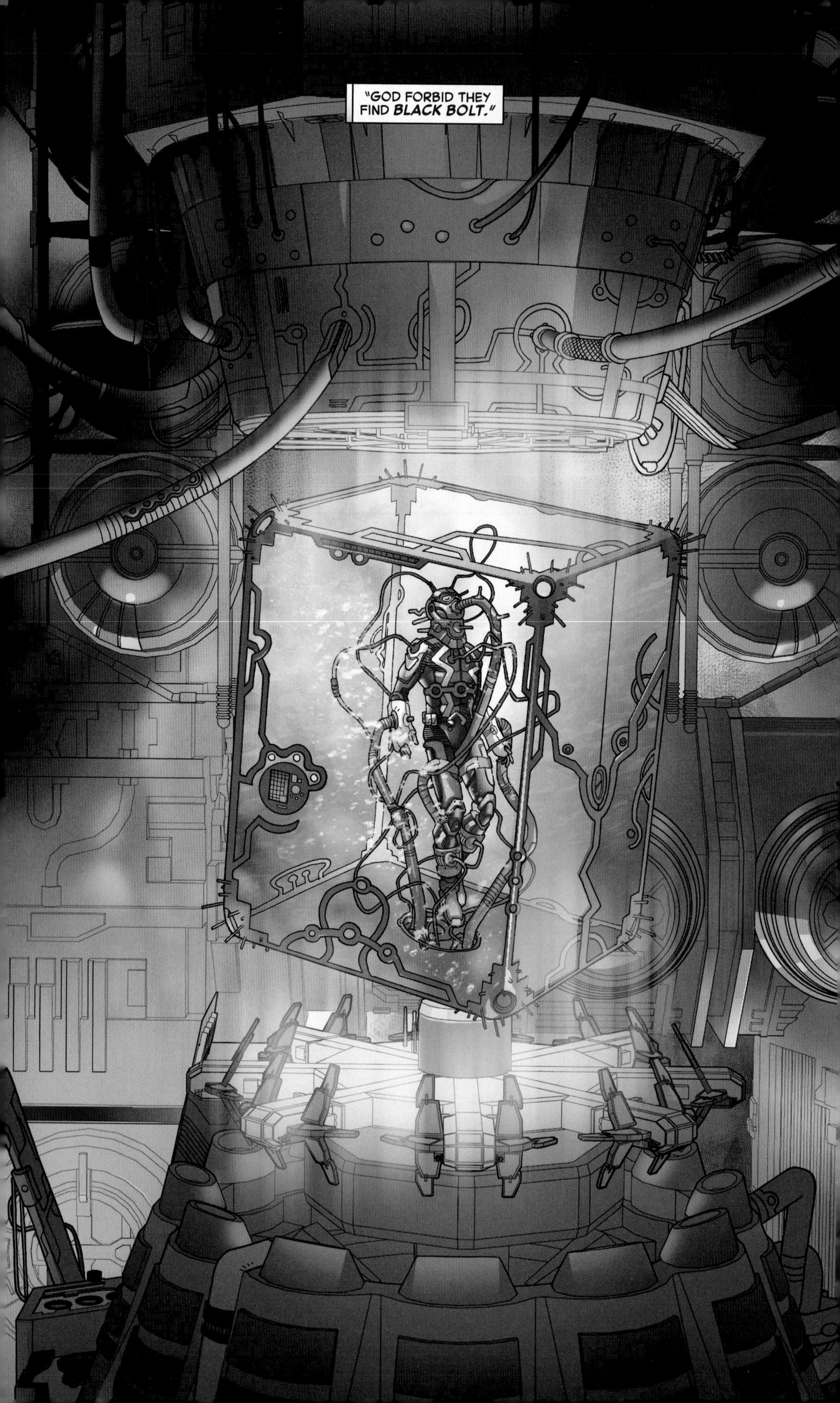
"GOD FORBID THEY FIND BLACK BOLT."

#4 Variant
by Ryan Sook

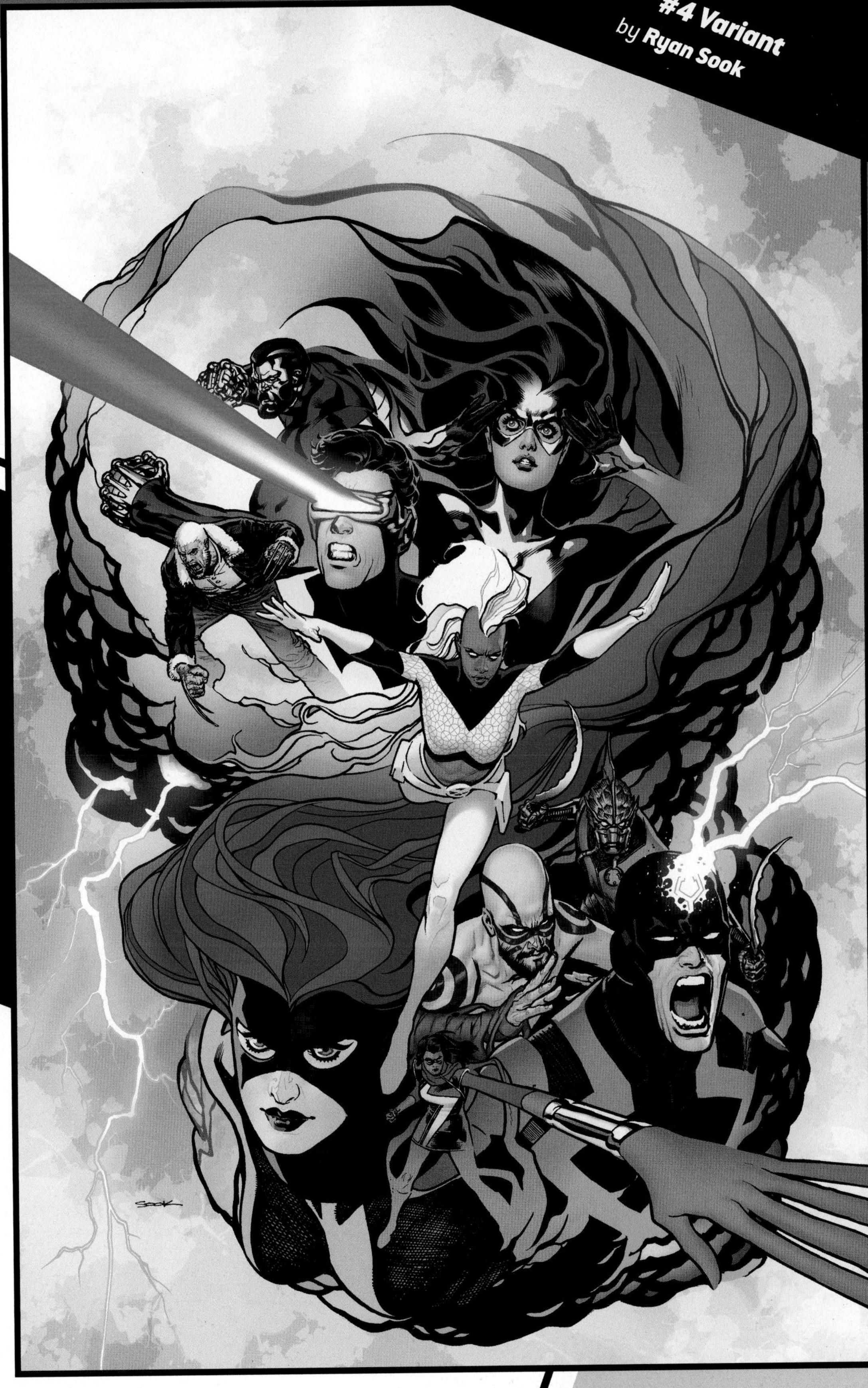

4

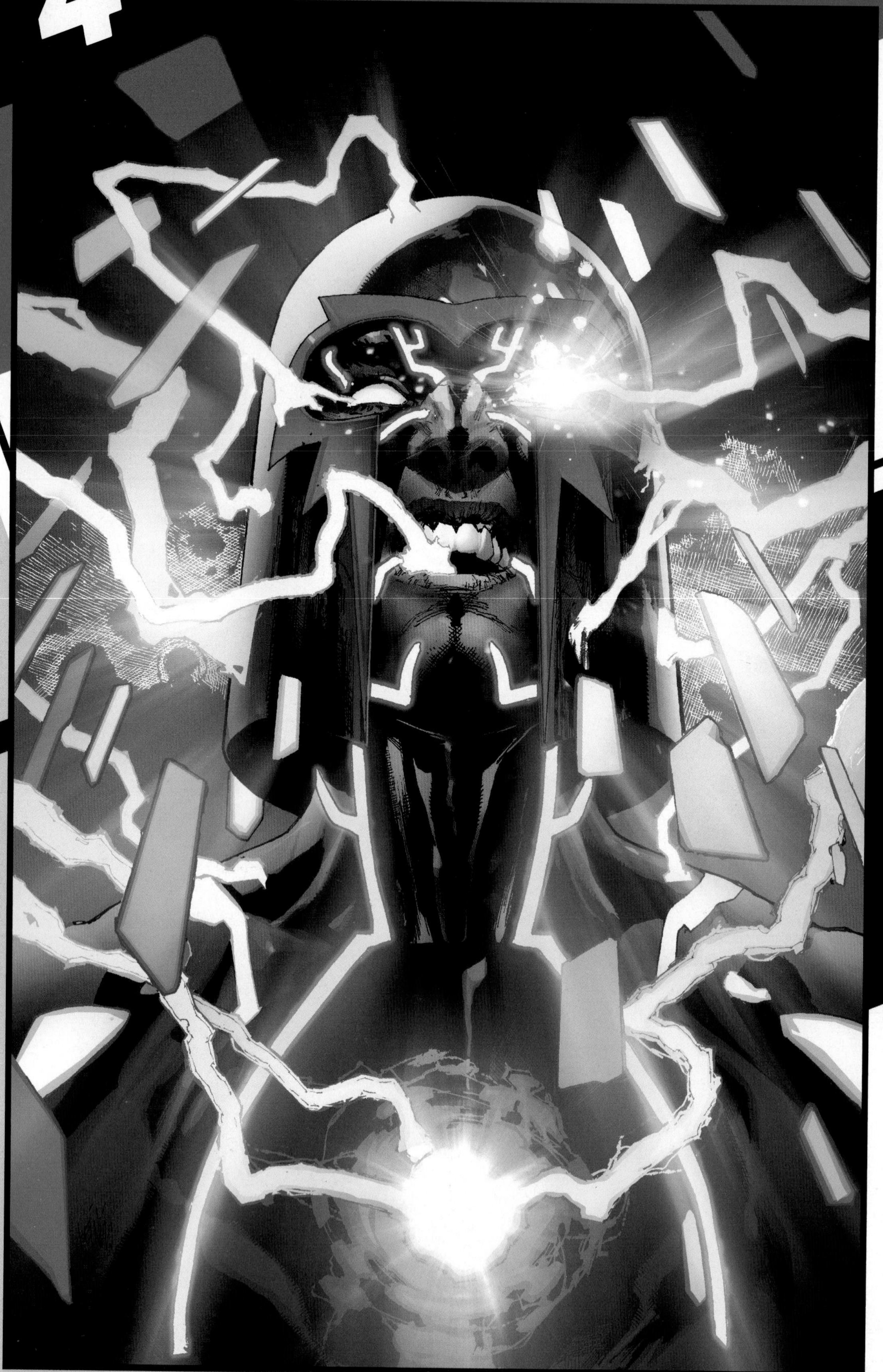

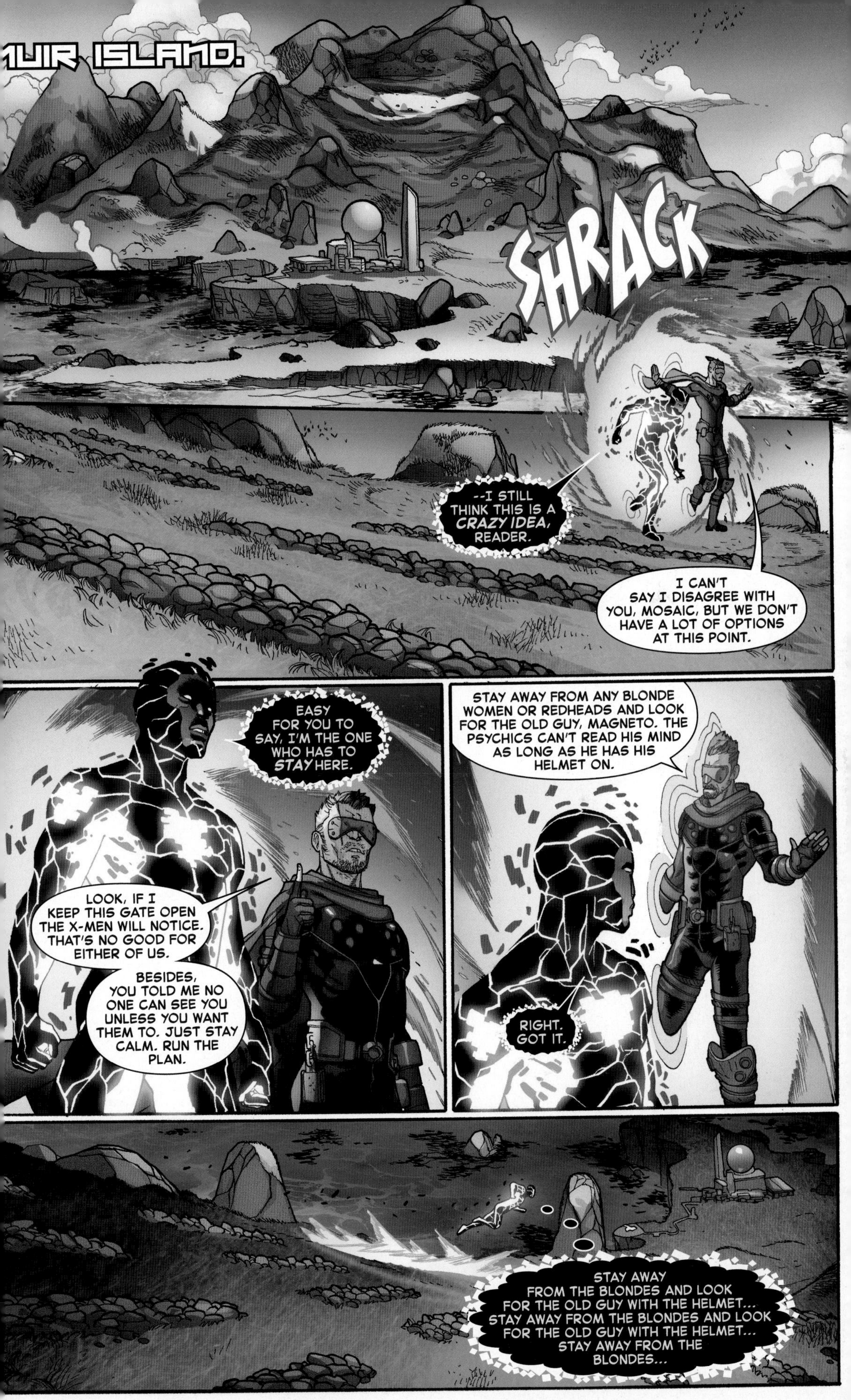
MUIR ISLAND.
SHRACK
--I STILL THINK THIS IS A CRAZY IDEA, READER.
I CAN'T SAY I DISAGREE WITH YOU, MOSAIC, BUT WE DON'T HAVE A LOT OF OPTIONS AT THIS POINT.
EASY FOR YOU TO SAY, I'M THE ONE WHO HAS TO STAY HERE.
LOOK, IF I KEEP THIS GATE OPEN THE X-MEN WILL NOTICE. THAT'S NO GOOD FOR EITHER OF US.
BESIDES, YOU TOLD ME NO ONE CAN SEE YOU UNLESS YOU WANT THEM TO. JUST STAY CALM. RUN THE PLAN.
STAY AWAY FROM ANY BLONDE WOMEN OR REDHEADS AND LOOK FOR THE OLD GUY, MAGNETO. THE PSYCHICS CAN'T READ HIS MIND AS LONG AS HE HAS HIS HELMET ON.
RIGHT. GOT IT.
STAY AWAY FROM THE BLONDES AND LOOK FOR THE OLD GUY WITH THE HELMET... STAY AWAY FROM THE BLONDES AND LOOK FOR THE OLD GUY WITH THE HELMET... STAY AWAY FROM THE BLONDES...

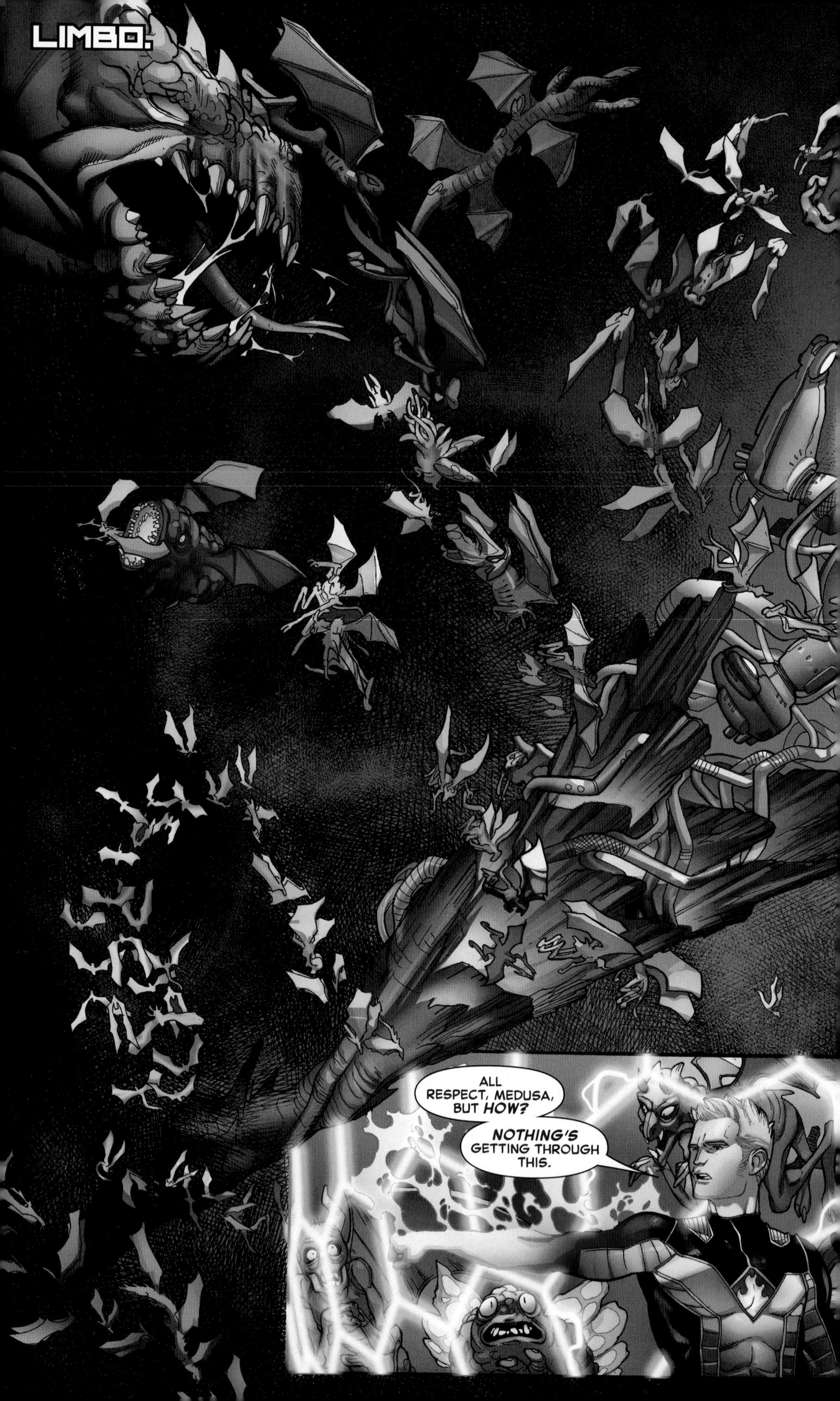
LIMBO.
ALL RESPECT, MEDUSA, BUT HOW?
NOTHING'S GETTING THROUGH THIS.

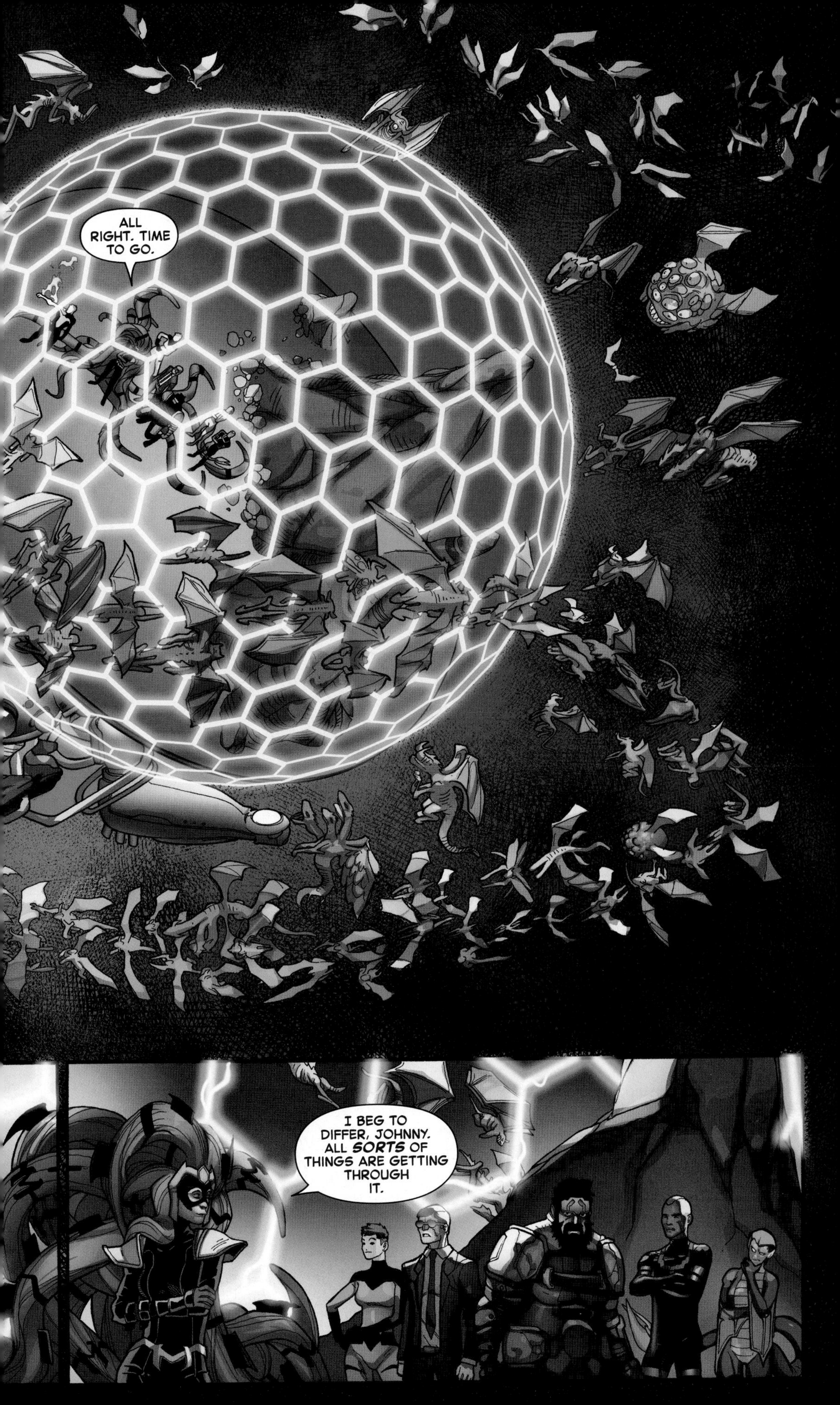
ALL RIGHT. TIME TO GO.
I BEG TO DIFFER, JOHNNY. ALL SORTS OF THINGS ARE GETTING THROUGH IT.

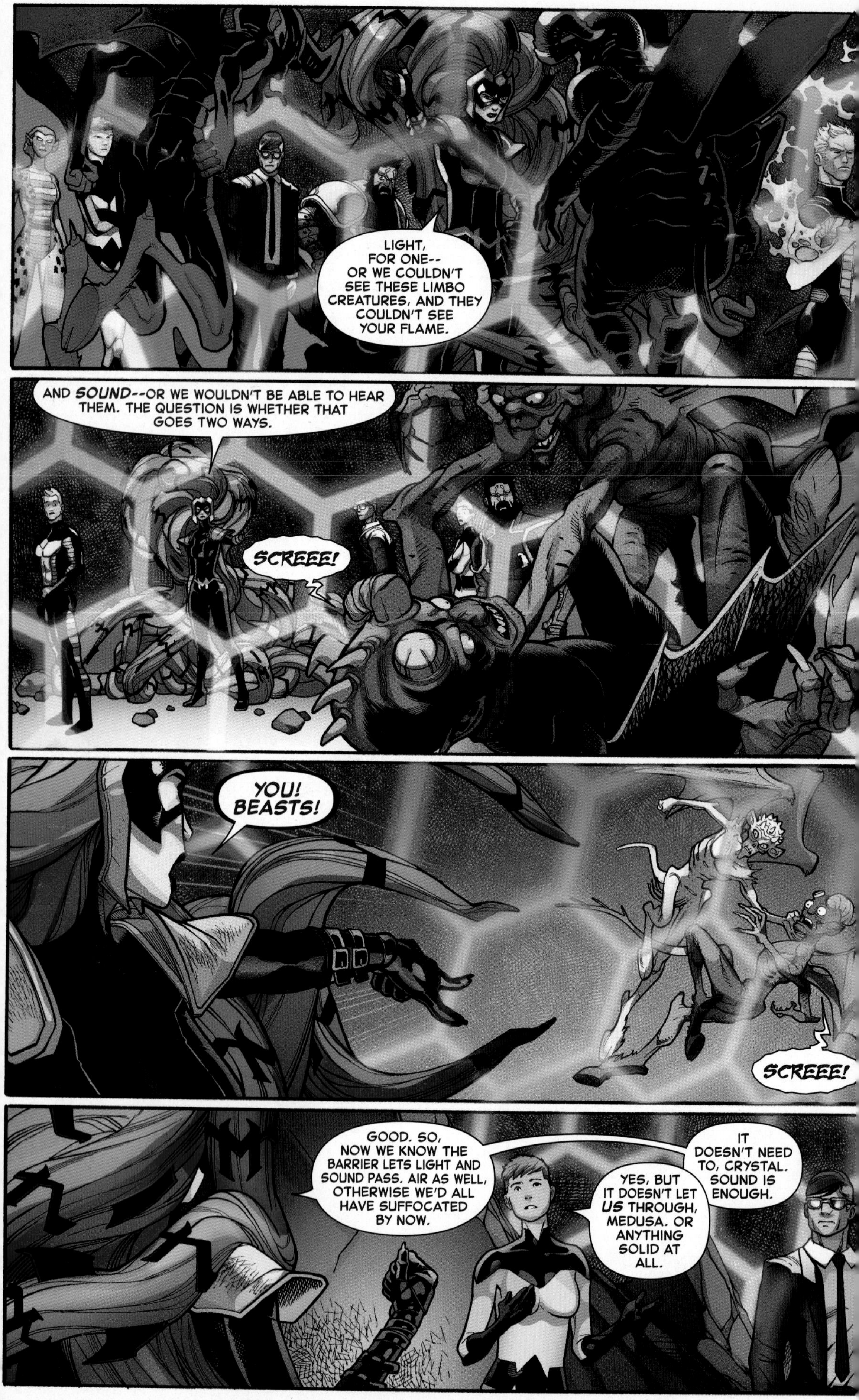
LIGHT, FOR ONE-- OR WE COULDN'T SEE THESE LIMBO CREATURES, AND THEY COULDN'T SEE YOUR FLAME.
AND SOUND--OR WE WOULDN'T BE ABLE TO HEAR THEM. THE QUESTION IS WHETHER THAT GOES TWO WAYS.
SCREEE!
YOU! BEASTS!
SCREEE!
GOOD. SO, NOW WE KNOW THE BARRIER LETS LIGHT AND SOUND PASS. AIR AS WELL, OTHERWISE WE'D ALL HAVE SUFFOCATED BY NOW.
YES, BUT IT DOESN'T LET US THROUGH, MEDUSA. OR ANYTHING SOLID AT ALL.
IT DOESN'T NEED TO, CRYSTAL. SOUND IS ENOUGH.

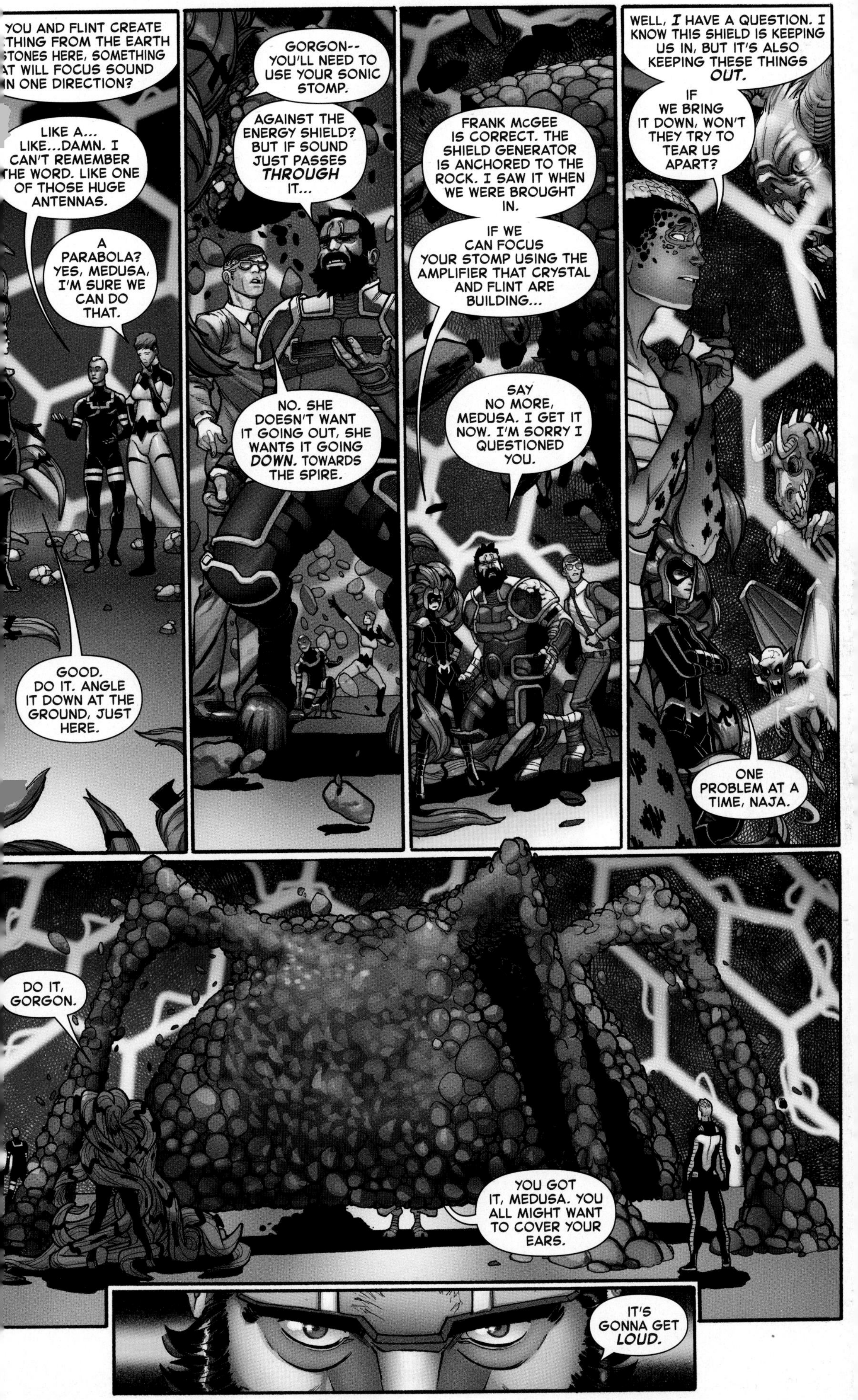

YOU AND FLINT CREATE
THING FROM THE EARTH
STONES HERE, SOMETHING
AT WILL FOCUS SOUND
N ONE DIRECTION?
LIKE A... LIKE...DAMN. I CAN'T REMEMBER THE WORD. LIKE ONE OF THOSE HUGE ANTENNAS.
A PARABOLA? YES, MEDUSA, I'M SURE WE CAN DO THAT.
GOOD. DO IT. ANGLE IT DOWN AT THE GROUND, JUST HERE.
GORGON-- YOU'LL NEED TO USE YOUR SONIC STOMP.
AGAINST THE ENERGY SHIELD? BUT IF SOUND JUST PASSES THROUGH IT...
NO. SHE DOESN'T WANT IT GOING OUT, SHE WANTS IT GOING DOWN. TOWARDS THE SPIRE.
FRANK McGEE IS CORRECT. THE SHIELD GENERATOR IS ANCHORED TO THE ROCK. I SAW IT WHEN WE WERE BROUGHT IN.
IF WE CAN FOCUS YOUR STOMP USING THE AMPLIFIER THAT CRYSTAL AND FLINT ARE BUILDING...
SAY NO MORE, MEDUSA. I GET IT NOW. I'M SORRY I QUESTIONED YOU.
WELL, I HAVE A QUESTION. I KNOW THIS SHIELD IS KEEPING US IN, BUT IT'S ALSO KEEPING THESE THINGS OUT.
IF WE BRING IT DOWN, WON'T THEY TRY TO TEAR US APART?
ONE PROBLEM AT A TIME, NAJA.
DO IT, GORGON.
YOU GOT IT, MEDUSA. YOU ALL MIGHT WANT TO COVER YOUR EARS.
IT'S GONNA GET LOUD.

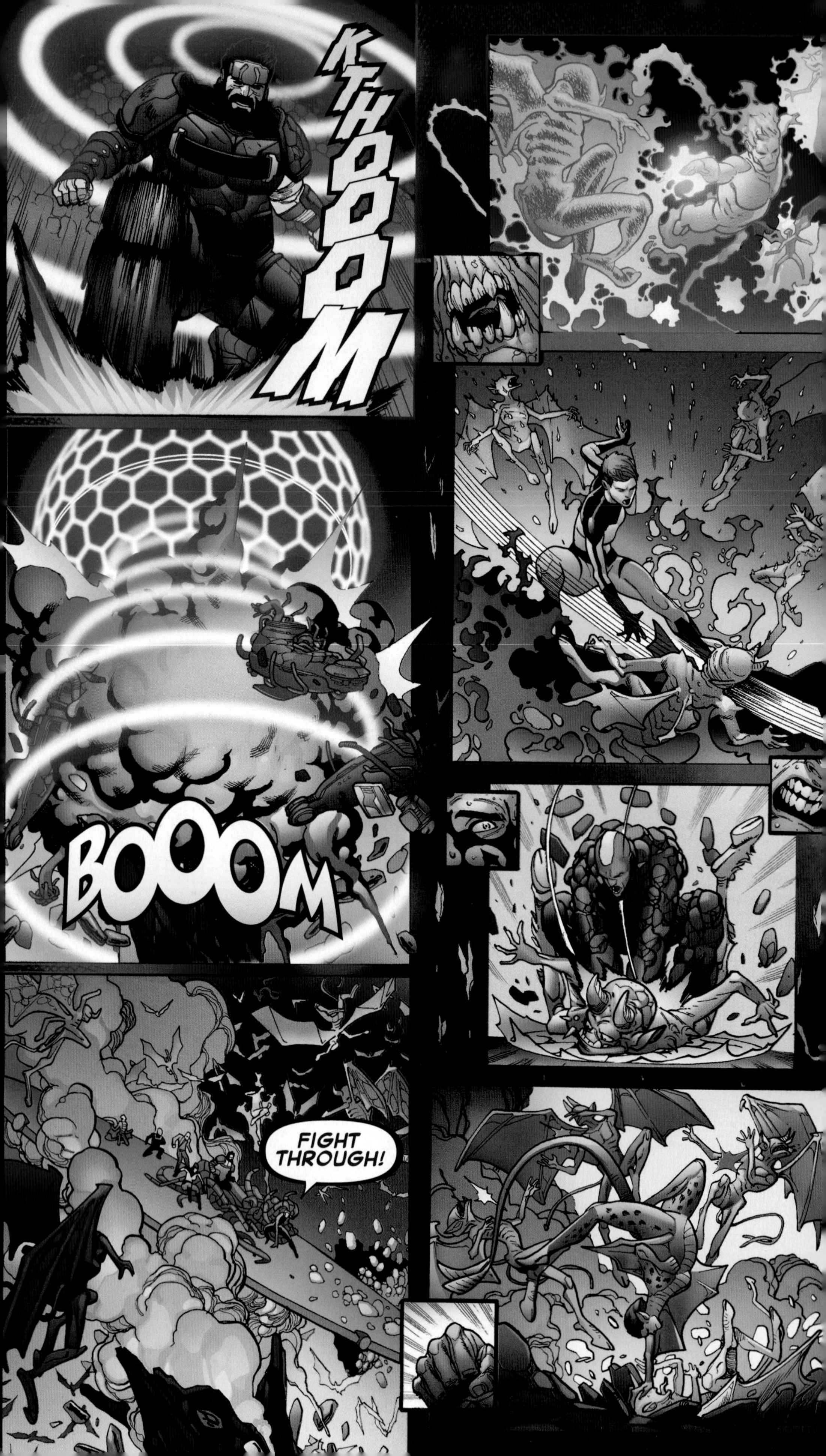
KTHOOOM
BOOOM
FIGHT THROUGH!

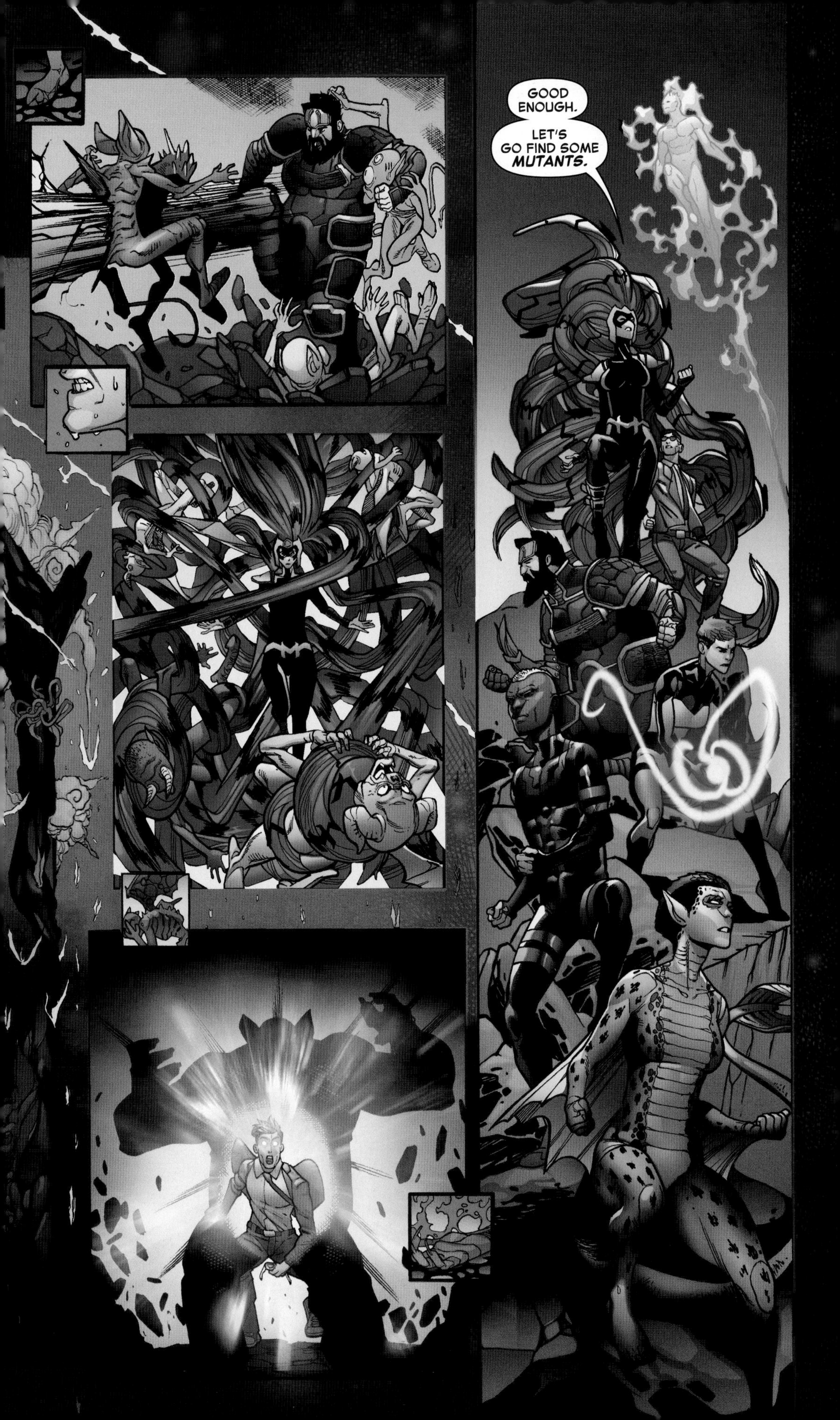
GOOD ENOUGH.
LET'S GO FIND SOME *MUTANTS.*

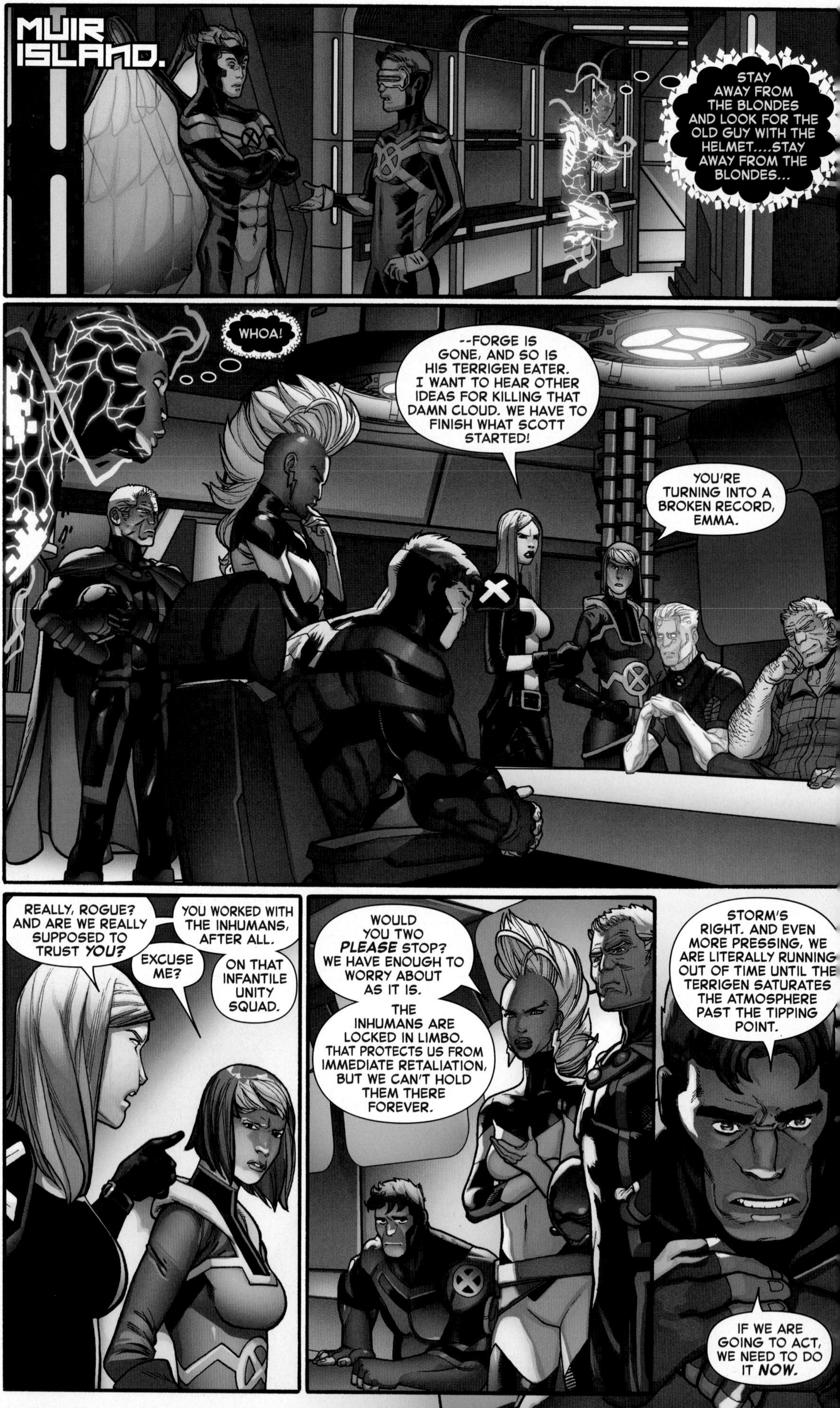
MUIR ISLAND.
STAY AWAY FROM THE BLONDES AND LOOK FOR THE OLD GUY WITH THE HELMET....STAY AWAY FROM THE BLONDES...
WHOA!
--FORGE IS GONE, AND SO IS HIS TERRIGEN EATER. I WANT TO HEAR OTHER IDEAS FOR KILLING THAT DAMN CLOUD. WE HAVE TO FINISH WHAT SCOTT STARTED!
YOU'RE TURNING INTO A BROKEN RECORD, EMMA.
REALLY, ROGUE? AND ARE WE REALLY SUPPOSED TO TRUST YOU?
YOU WORKED WITH THE INHUMANS, AFTER ALL.
EXCUSE ME?
ON THAT INFANTILE UNITY SQUAD.
WOULD YOU TWO PLEASE STOP? WE HAVE ENOUGH TO WORRY ABOUT AS IT IS.
THE INHUMANS ARE LOCKED IN LIMBO. THAT PROTECTS US FROM IMMEDIATE RETALIATION, BUT WE CAN'T HOLD THEM THERE FOREVER.
STORM'S RIGHT. AND EVEN MORE PRESSING, WE ARE LITERALLY RUNNING OUT OF TIME UNTIL THE TERRIGEN SATURATES THE ATMOSPHERE PAST THE TIPPING POINT.
IF WE ARE GOING TO ACT, WE NEED TO DO IT NOW.

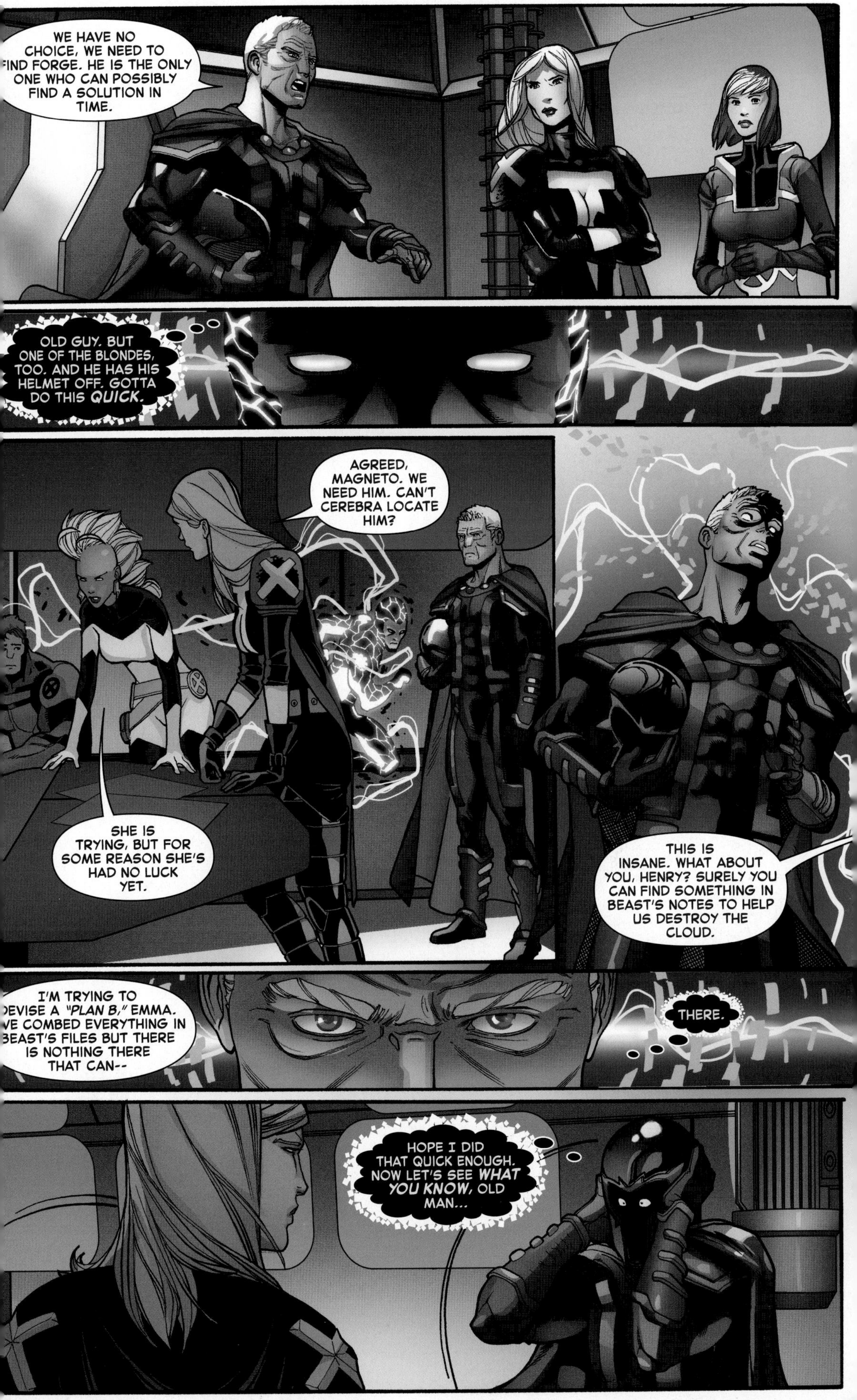
WE HAVE NO CHOICE, WE NEED TO FIND FORGE. HE IS THE ONLY ONE WHO CAN POSSIBLY FIND A SOLUTION IN TIME.
OLD GUY. BUT ONE OF THE BLONDES, TOO. AND HE HAS HIS HELMET OFF. GOTTA DO THIS QUICK.
AGREED, MAGNETO. WE NEED HIM. CAN'T CEREBRA LOCATE HIM?
SHE IS TRYING, BUT FOR SOME REASON SHE'S HAD NO LUCK YET.
THIS IS INSANE. WHAT ABOUT YOU, HENRY? SURELY YOU CAN FIND SOMETHING IN BEAST'S NOTES TO HELP US DESTROY THE CLOUD.
I'M TRYING TO DEVISE A "PLAN B," EMMA. WE COMBED EVERYTHING IN BEAST'S FILES BUT THERE IS NOTHING THERE THAT CAN--
THERE.
HOPE I DID THAT QUICK ENOUGH. NOW LET'S SEE WHAT YOU KNOW, OLD MAN...

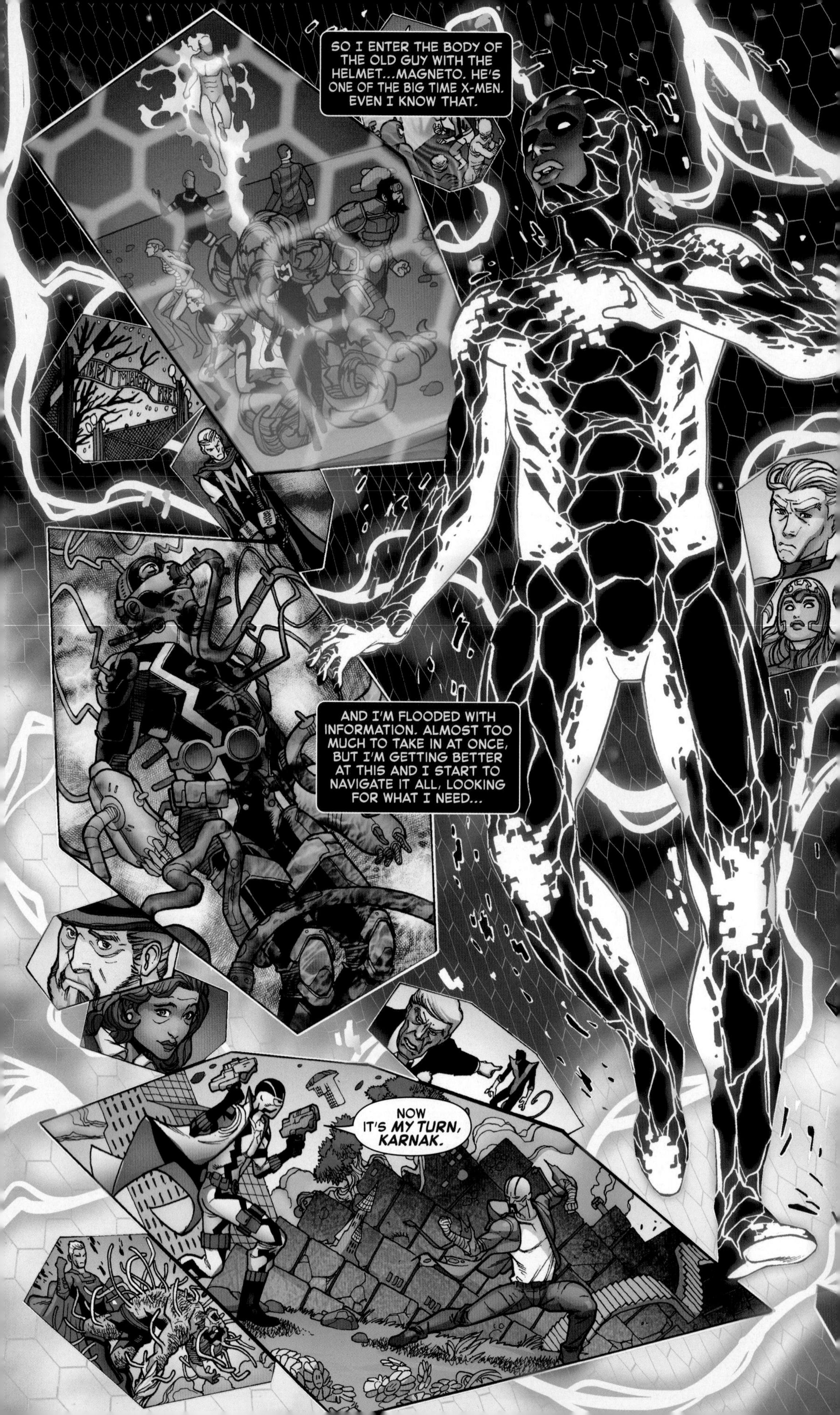
SO I ENTER THE BODY OF THE OLD GUY WITH THE HELMET...MAGNETO. HE'S ONE OF THE BIG TIME X-MEN. EVEN I KNOW THAT.
AND I'M FLOODED WITH INFORMATION. ALMOST TOO MUCH TO TAKE IN AT ONCE, BUT I'M GETTING BETTER AT THIS AND I START TO NAVIGATE IT ALL, LOOKING FOR WHAT I NEED...
NOW IT'S *MY TURN, KARNAK.*

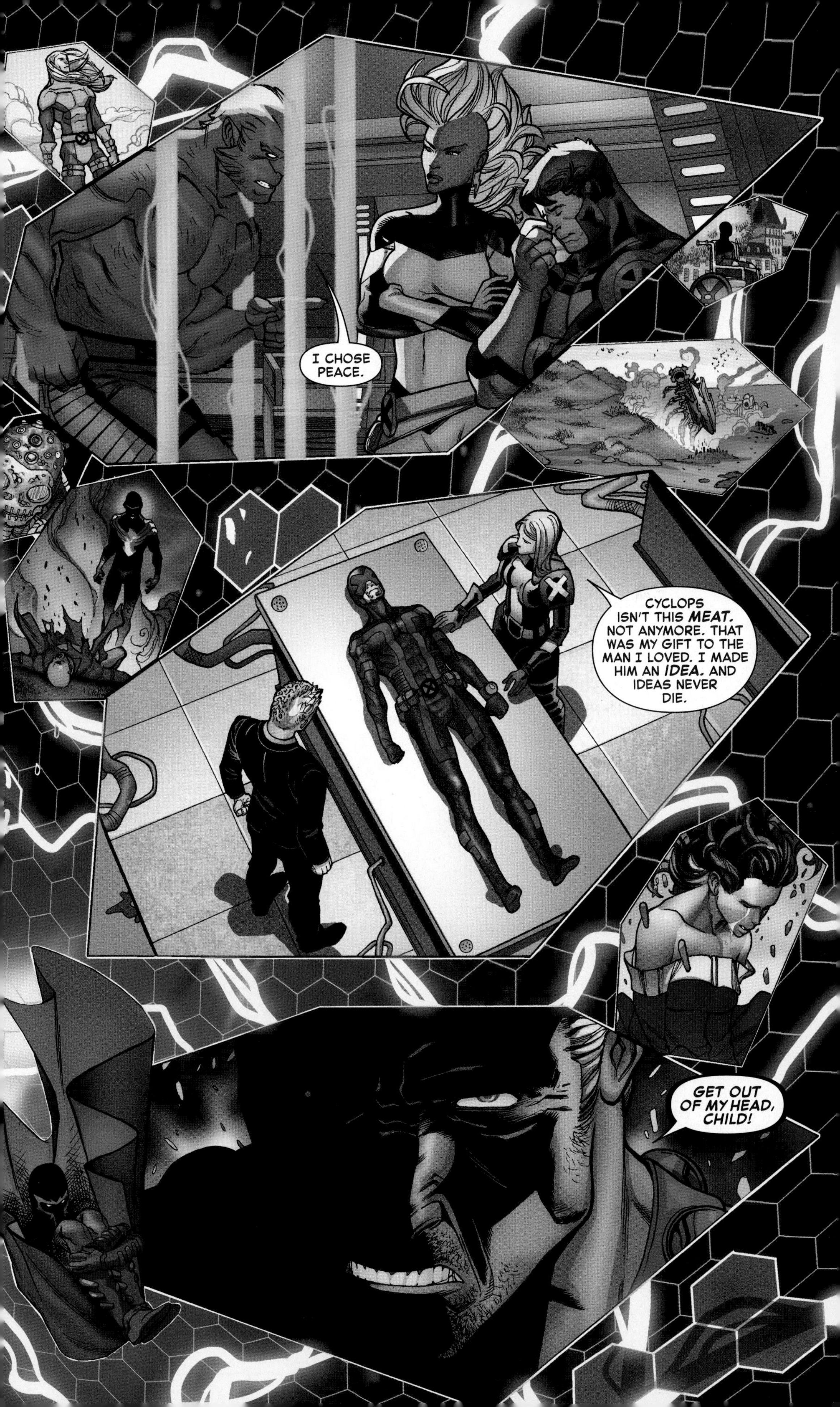
I CHOSE PEACE.
CYCLOPS ISN'T THIS MEAT. NOT ANYMORE. THAT WAS MY GIFT TO THE MAN I LOVED. I MADE HIM AN IDEA. AND IDEAS NEVER DIE.
GET OUT OF MY HEAD, CHILD!

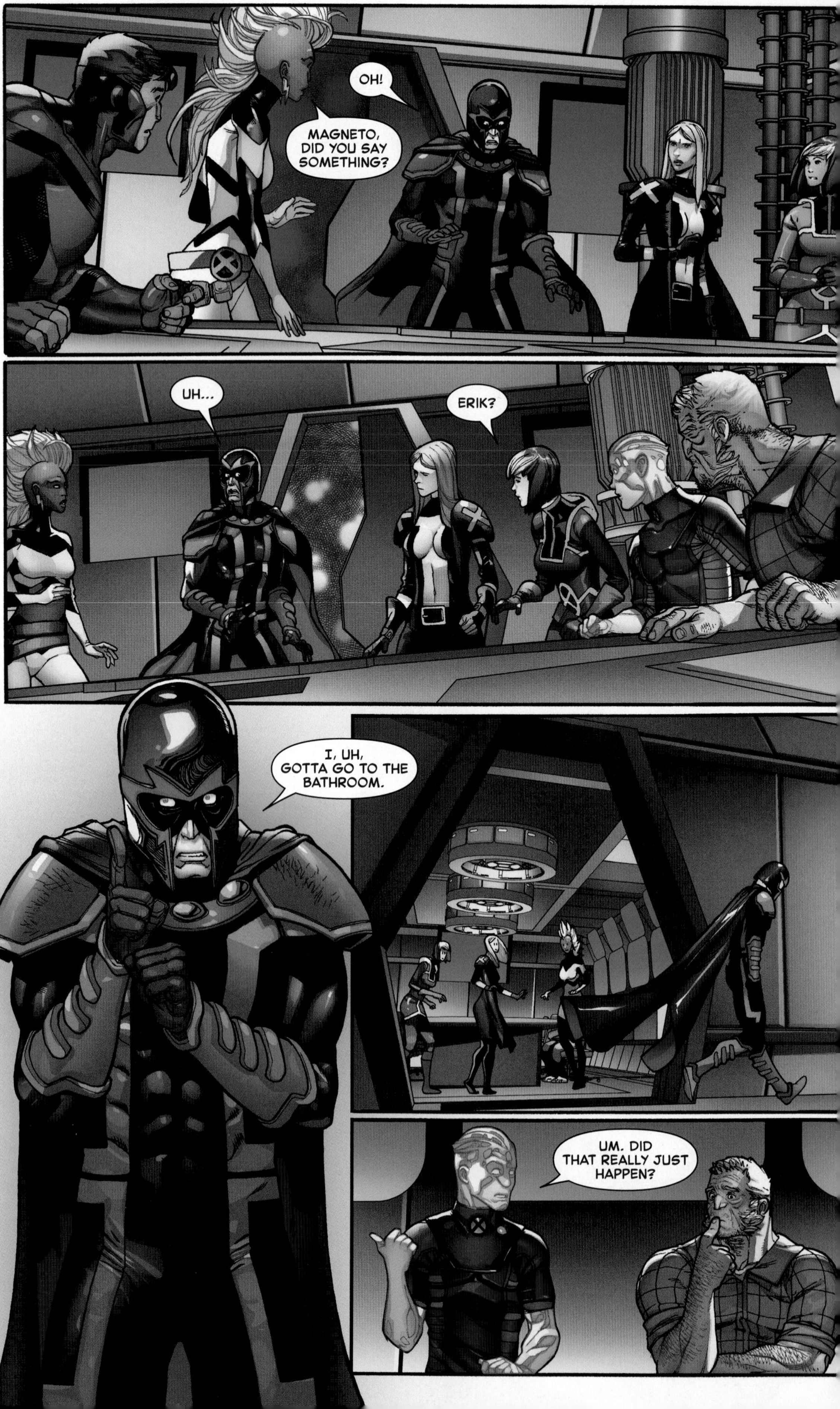
OH!
MAGNETO, DID YOU SAY SOMETHING?
UH...
ERIK?
I, UH, GOTTA GO TO THE BATHROOM.
UM. DID THAT REALLY JUST HAPPEN?

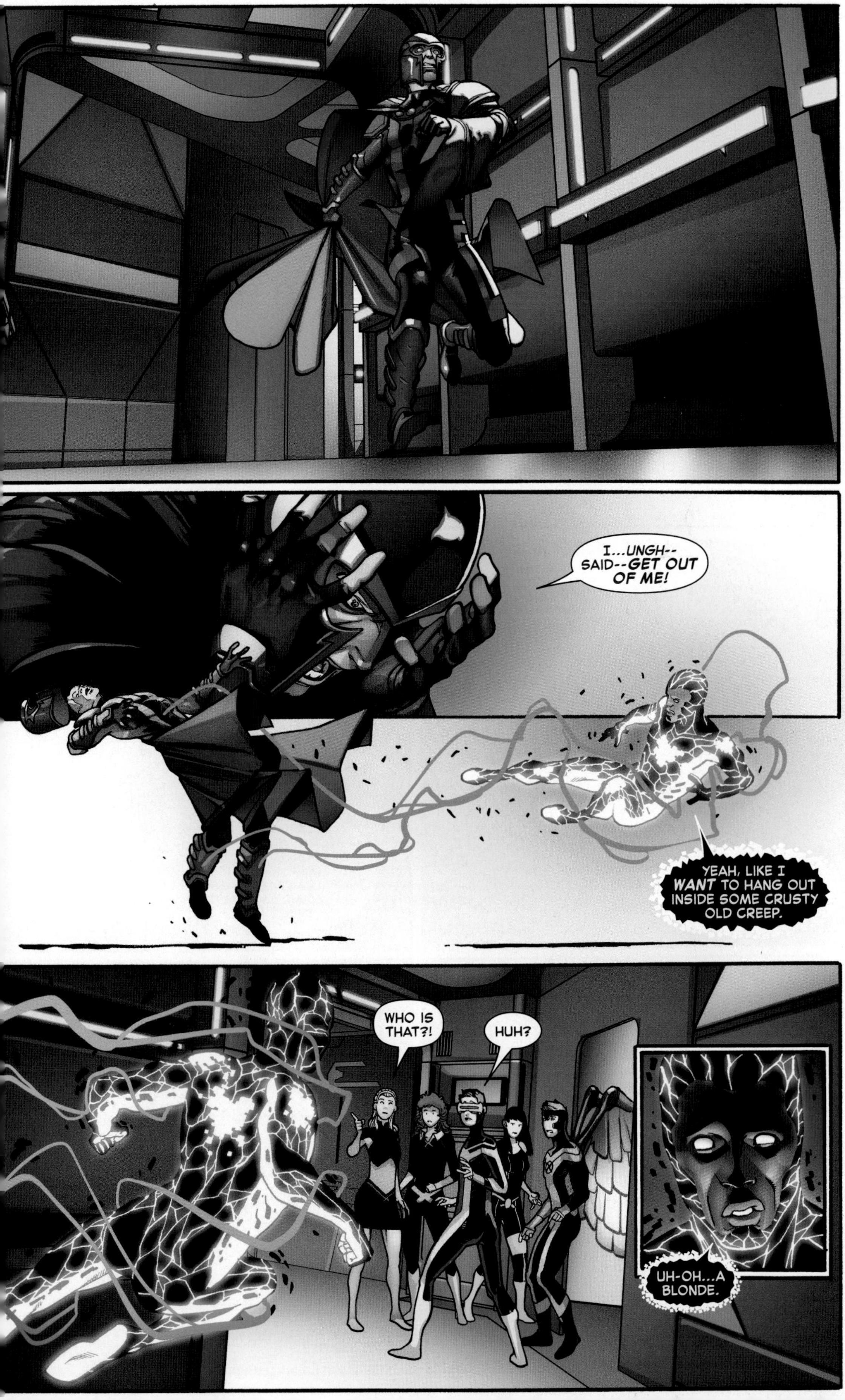
I...UNGH--
SAID--GET OUT OF ME!
YEAH, LIKE I WANT TO HANG OUT INSIDE SOME CRUSTY OLD CREEP.
WHO IS THAT?!
HUH?
UH-OH...A BLONDE.

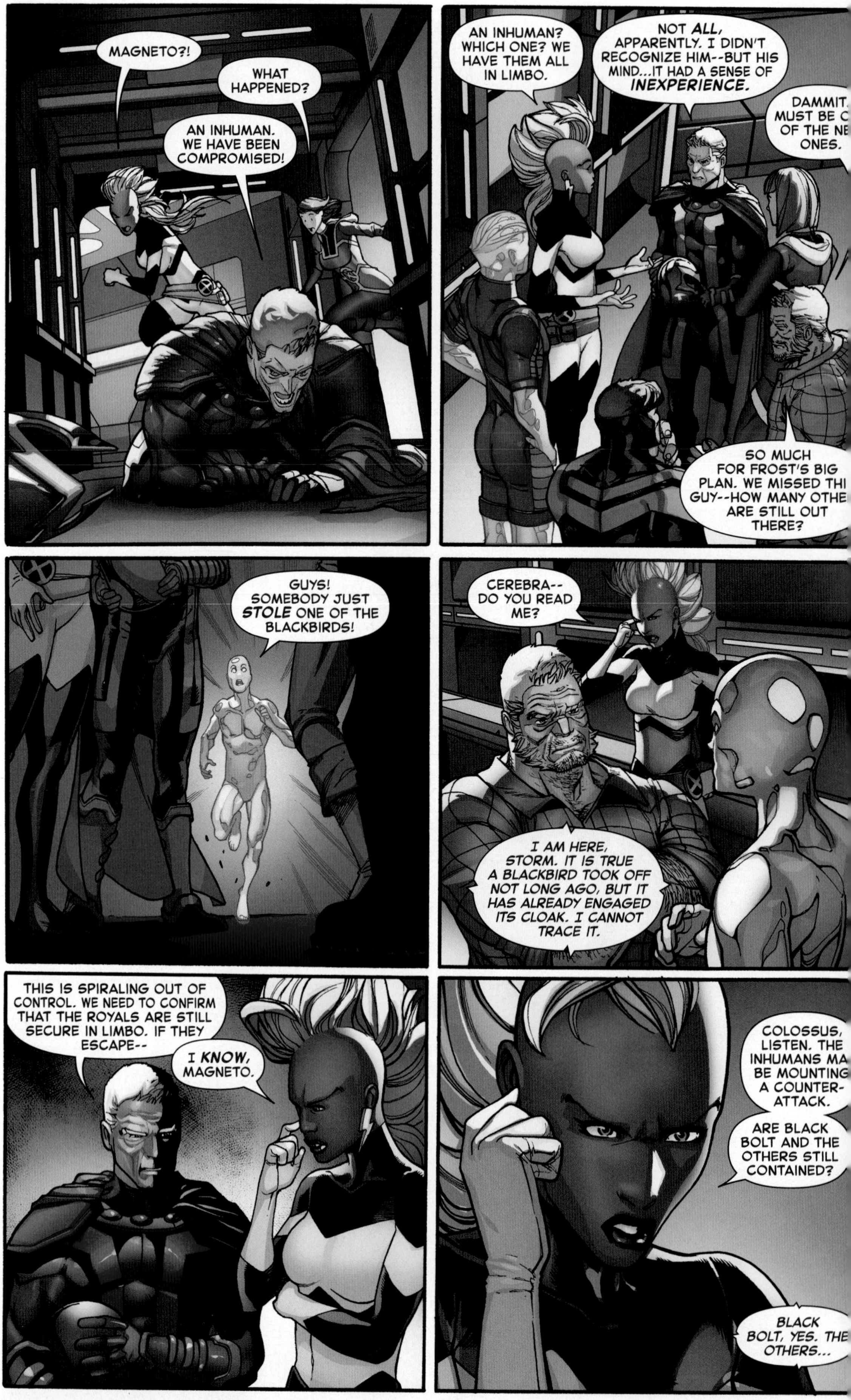
MAGNETO?!
WHAT HAPPENED?
AN INHUMAN. WE HAVE BEEN COMPROMISED!
AN INHUMAN? WHICH ONE? WE HAVE THEM ALL IN LIMBO.
NOT ALL, APPARENTLY. I DIDN'T RECOGNIZE HIM--BUT HIS MIND...IT HAD A SENSE OF INEXPERIENCE.
DAMMIT. MUST BE OF THE NE ONES.
SO MUCH FOR FROST'S BIG PLAN. WE MISSED THI GUY--HOW MANY OTHE ARE STILL OUT THERE?
GUYS! SOMEBODY JUST STOLE ONE OF THE BLACKBIRDS!
CEREBRA-- DO YOU READ ME?
I AM HERE, STORM. IT IS TRUE A BLACKBIRD TOOK OFF NOT LONG AGO, BUT IT HAS ALREADY ENGAGED ITS CLOAK. I CANNOT TRACE IT.
THIS IS SPIRALING OUT OF CONTROL. WE NEED TO CONFIRM THAT THE ROYALS ARE STILL SECURE IN LIMBO. IF THEY ESCAPE--
I KNOW, MAGNETO.
COLOSSUS, LISTEN. THE INHUMANS MA BE MOUNTING A COUNTER-ATTACK.
ARE BLACK BOLT AND THE OTHERS STILL CONTAINED?
BLACK BOLT, YES. THE OTHERS...

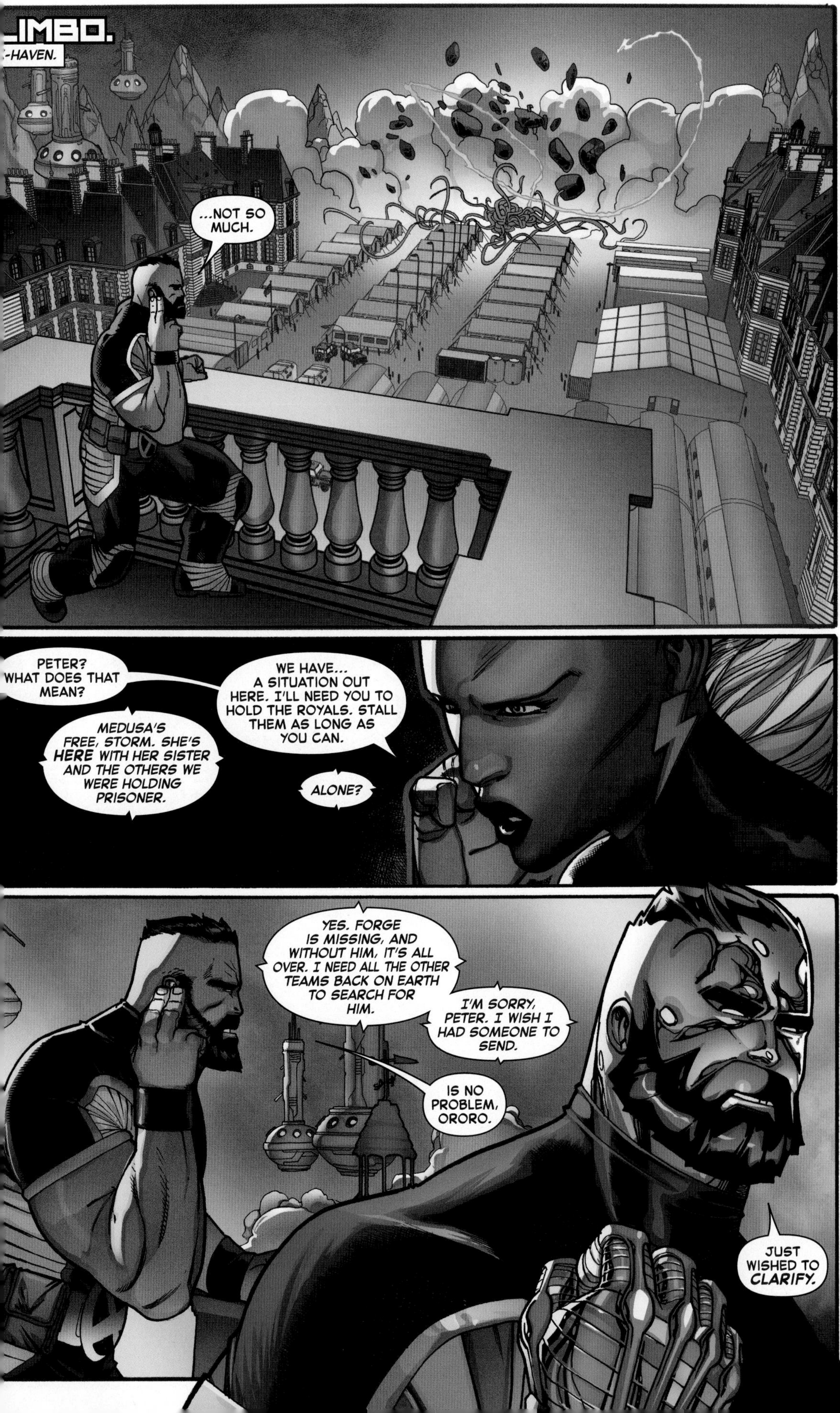
LIMBO.
-HAVEN.
...NOT SO MUCH.
PETER? WHAT DOES THAT MEAN?
WE HAVE... A SITUATION OUT HERE. I'LL NEED YOU TO HOLD THE ROYALS. STALL THEM AS LONG AS YOU CAN.
MEDUSA'S FREE, STORM. SHE'S HERE WITH HER SISTER AND THE OTHERS WE WERE HOLDING PRISONER.
ALONE?
YES. FORGE IS MISSING, AND WITHOUT HIM, IT'S ALL OVER. I NEED ALL THE OTHER TEAMS BACK ON EARTH TO SEARCH FOR HIM.
I'M SORRY, PETER. I WISH I HAD SOMEONE TO SEND.
IS NO PROBLEM, ORORO.
JUST WISHED TO CLARIFY.

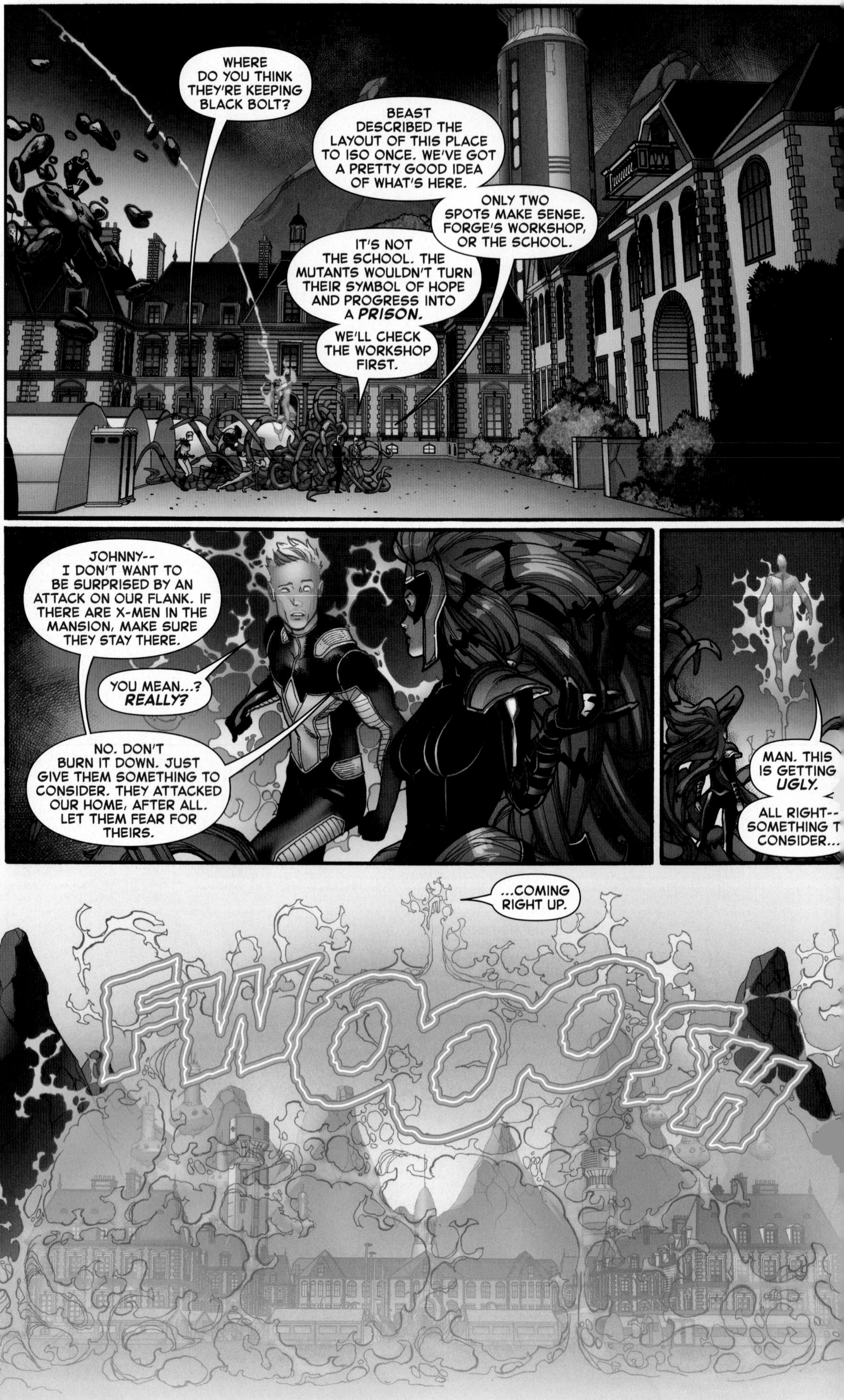
WHERE DO YOU THINK THEY'RE KEEPING BLACK BOLT?
BEAST DESCRIBED THE LAYOUT OF THIS PLACE TO ISO ONCE. WE'VE GOT A PRETTY GOOD IDEA OF WHAT'S HERE.
ONLY TWO SPOTS MAKE SENSE. FORGE'S WORKSHOP, OR THE SCHOOL.
IT'S NOT THE SCHOOL. THE MUTANTS WOULDN'T TURN THEIR SYMBOL OF HOPE AND PROGRESS INTO A PRISON.
WE'LL CHECK THE WORKSHOP FIRST.
JOHNNY-- I DON'T WANT TO BE SURPRISED BY AN ATTACK ON OUR FLANK. IF THERE ARE X-MEN IN THE MANSION, MAKE SURE THEY STAY THERE.
YOU MEAN...? REALLY?
NO. DON'T BURN IT DOWN. JUST GIVE THEM SOMETHING TO CONSIDER. THEY ATTACKED OUR HOME, AFTER ALL. LET THEM FEAR FOR THEIRS.
MAN. THIS IS GETTING UGLY.
ALL RIGHT-- SOMETHING T CONSIDER...
...COMING RIGHT UP.
FWOOOSH

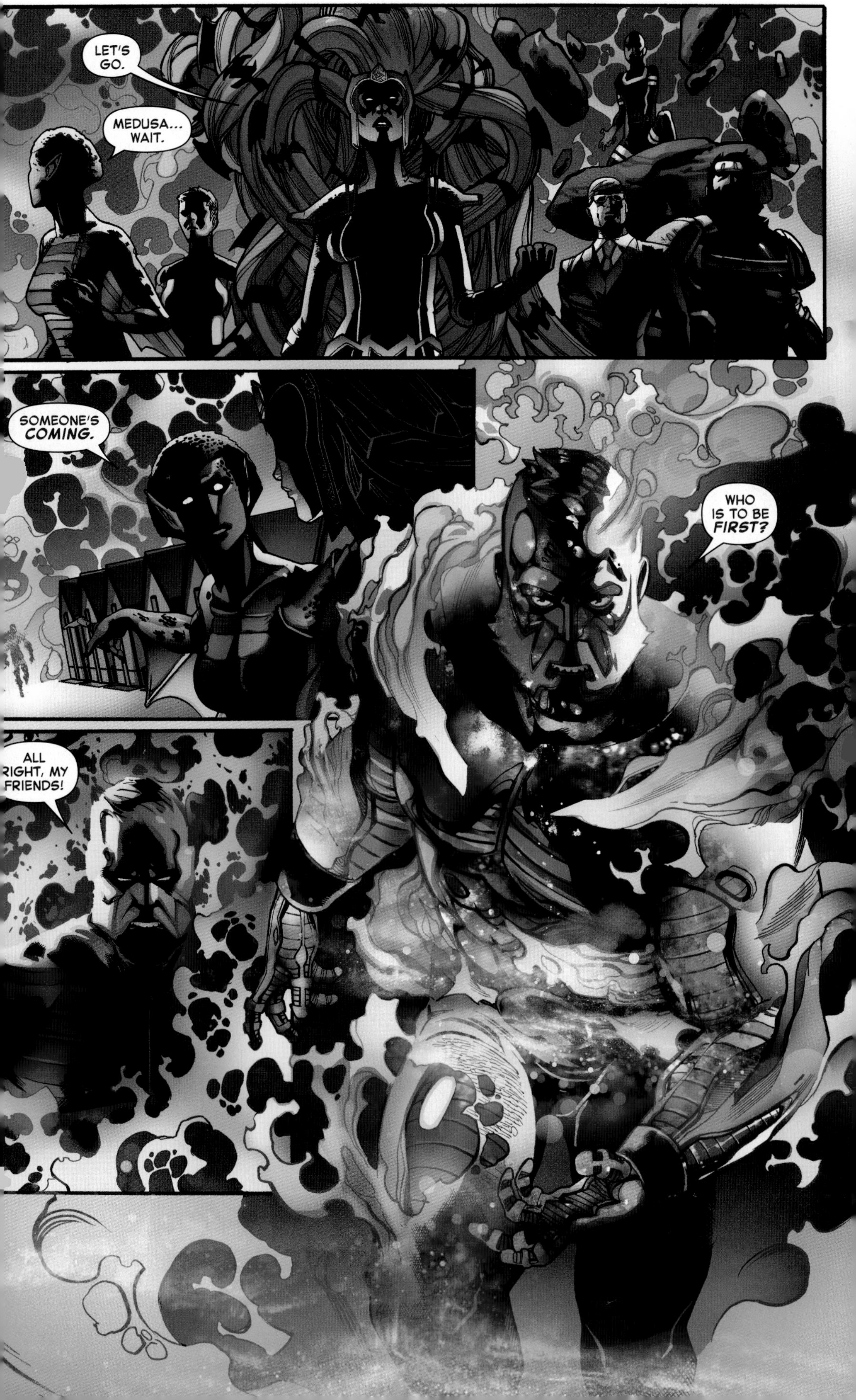
LET'S GO.
MEDUSA... WAIT.
SOMEONE'S COMING.
WHO IS TO BE FIRST?
ALL RIGHT, MY FRIENDS!

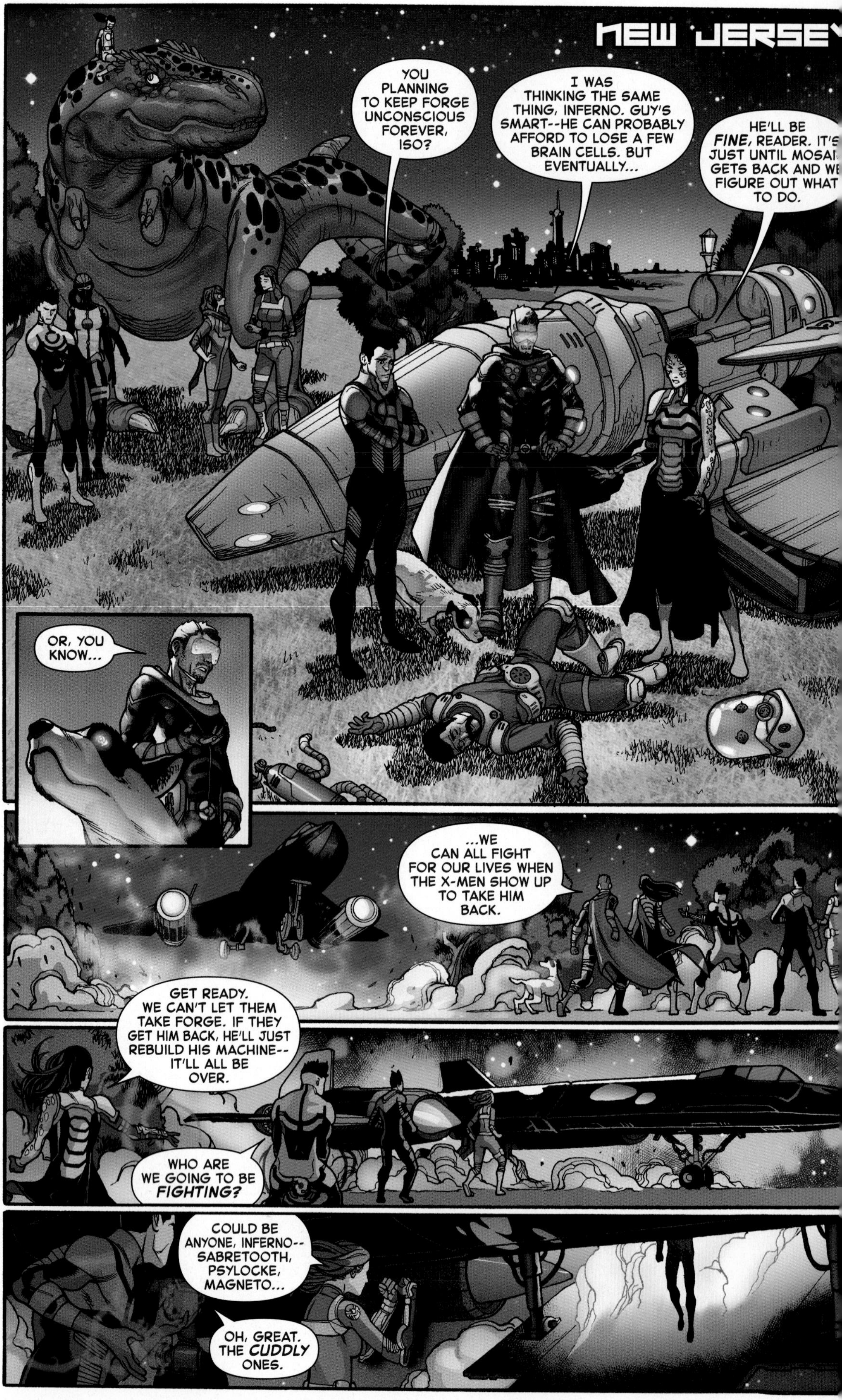
NEW JERSEY
YOU PLANNING TO KEEP FORGE UNCONSCIOUS FOREVER, ISO?
I WAS THINKING THE SAME THING, INFERNO. GUY'S SMART--HE CAN PROBABLY AFFORD TO LOSE A FEW BRAIN CELLS. BUT EVENTUALLY...
HE'LL BE FINE, READER. IT'S JUST UNTIL MOSAIC GETS BACK AND WE FIGURE OUT WHAT TO DO.
OR, YOU KNOW...
...WE CAN ALL FIGHT FOR OUR LIVES WHEN THE X-MEN SHOW UP TO TAKE HIM BACK.
GET READY. WE CAN'T LET THEM TAKE FORGE. IF THEY GET HIM BACK, HE'LL JUST REBUILD HIS MACHINE-- IT'LL ALL BE OVER.
WHO ARE WE GOING TO BE FIGHTING?
COULD BE ANYONE, INFERNO-- SABRETOOTH, PSYLOCKE, MAGNETO...
OH, GREAT. THE CUDDLY ONES.

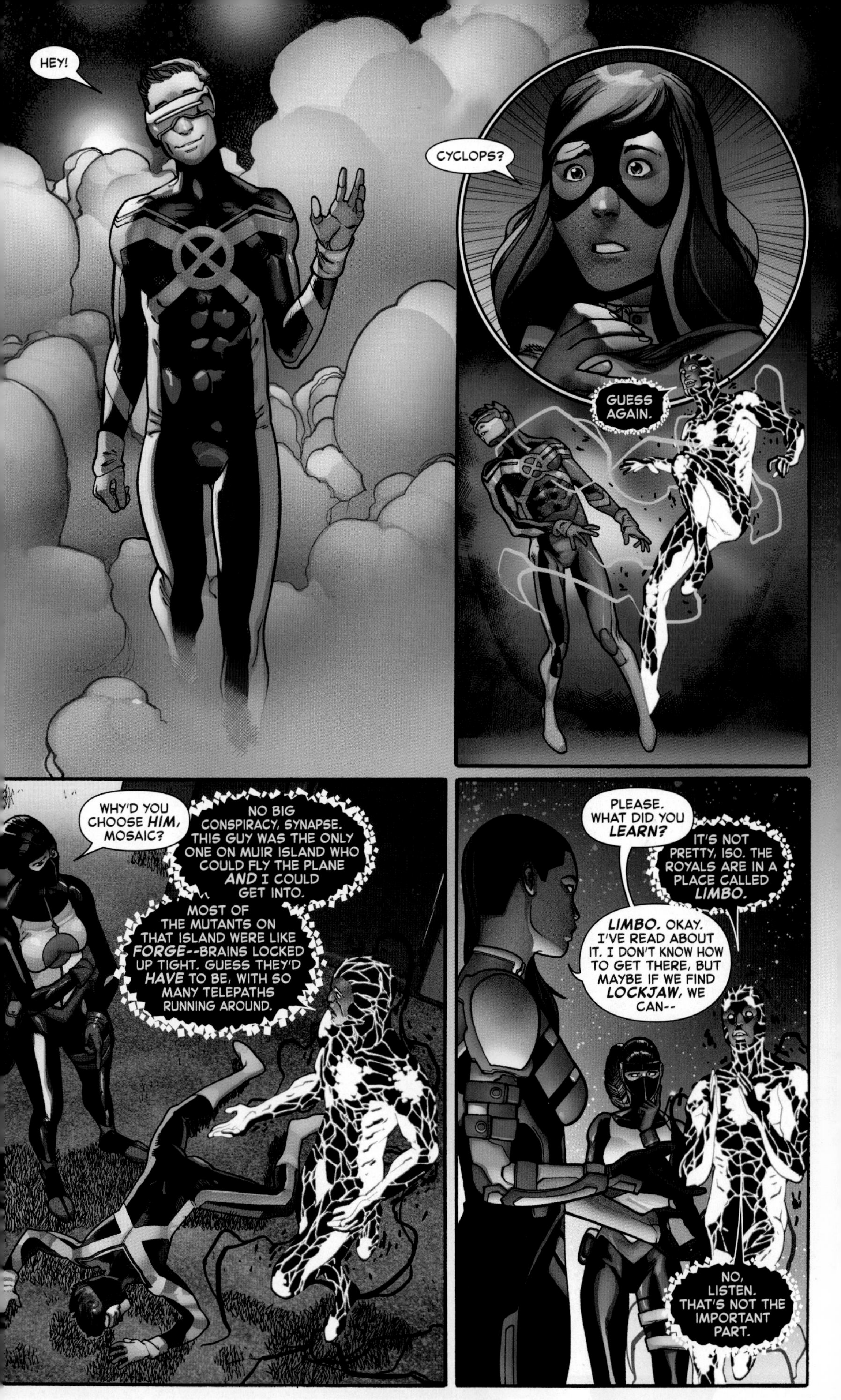
HEY!
CYCLOPS?
GUESS AGAIN.
WHY'D YOU CHOOSE HIM, MOSAIC?
NO BIG CONSPIRACY, SYNAPSE. THIS GUY WAS THE ONLY ONE ON MUIR ISLAND WHO COULD FLY THE PLANE AND I COULD GET INTO.
MOST OF THE MUTANTS ON THAT ISLAND WERE LIKE FORGE--BRAINS LOCKED UP TIGHT. GUESS THEY'D HAVE TO BE, WITH SO MANY TELEPATHS RUNNING AROUND.
PLEASE. WHAT DID YOU LEARN?
IT'S NOT PRETTY, ISO. THE ROYALS ARE IN A PLACE CALLED LIMBO.
LIMBO. OKAY. I'VE READ ABOUT IT. I DON'T KNOW HOW TO GET THERE, BUT MAYBE IF WE FIND LOCKJAW, WE CAN--
NO, LISTEN. THAT'S NOT THE IMPORTANT PART.

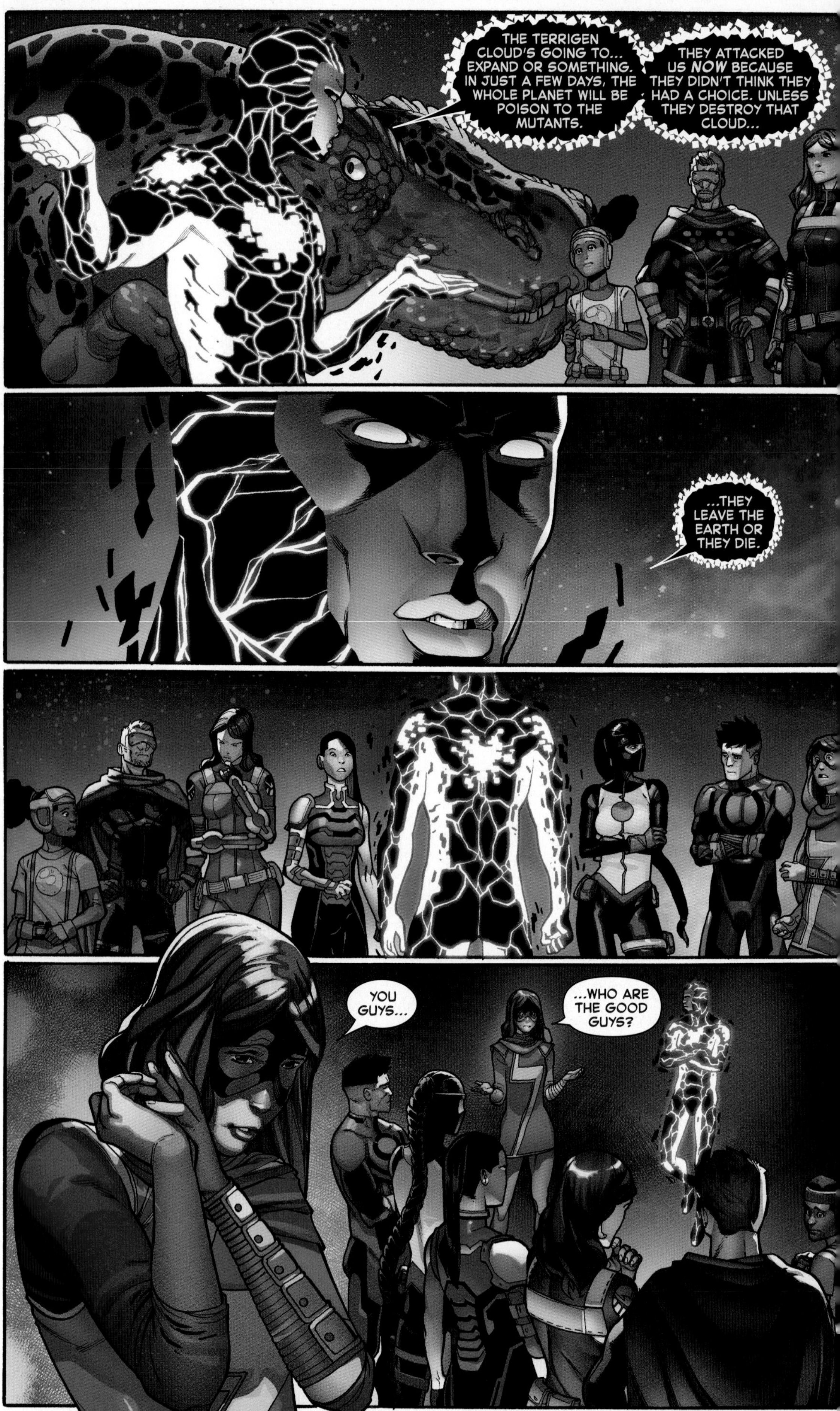
THE TERRIGEN CLOUD'S GOING TO... EXPAND OR SOMETHING. IN JUST A FEW DAYS, THE WHOLE PLANET WILL BE POISON TO THE MUTANTS.
THEY ATTACKED US NOW BECAUSE THEY DIDN'T THINK THEY HAD A CHOICE. UNLESS THEY DESTROY THAT CLOUD...
...THEY LEAVE THE EARTH OR THEY DIE.
YOU GUYS...
...WHO ARE THE GOOD GUYS?

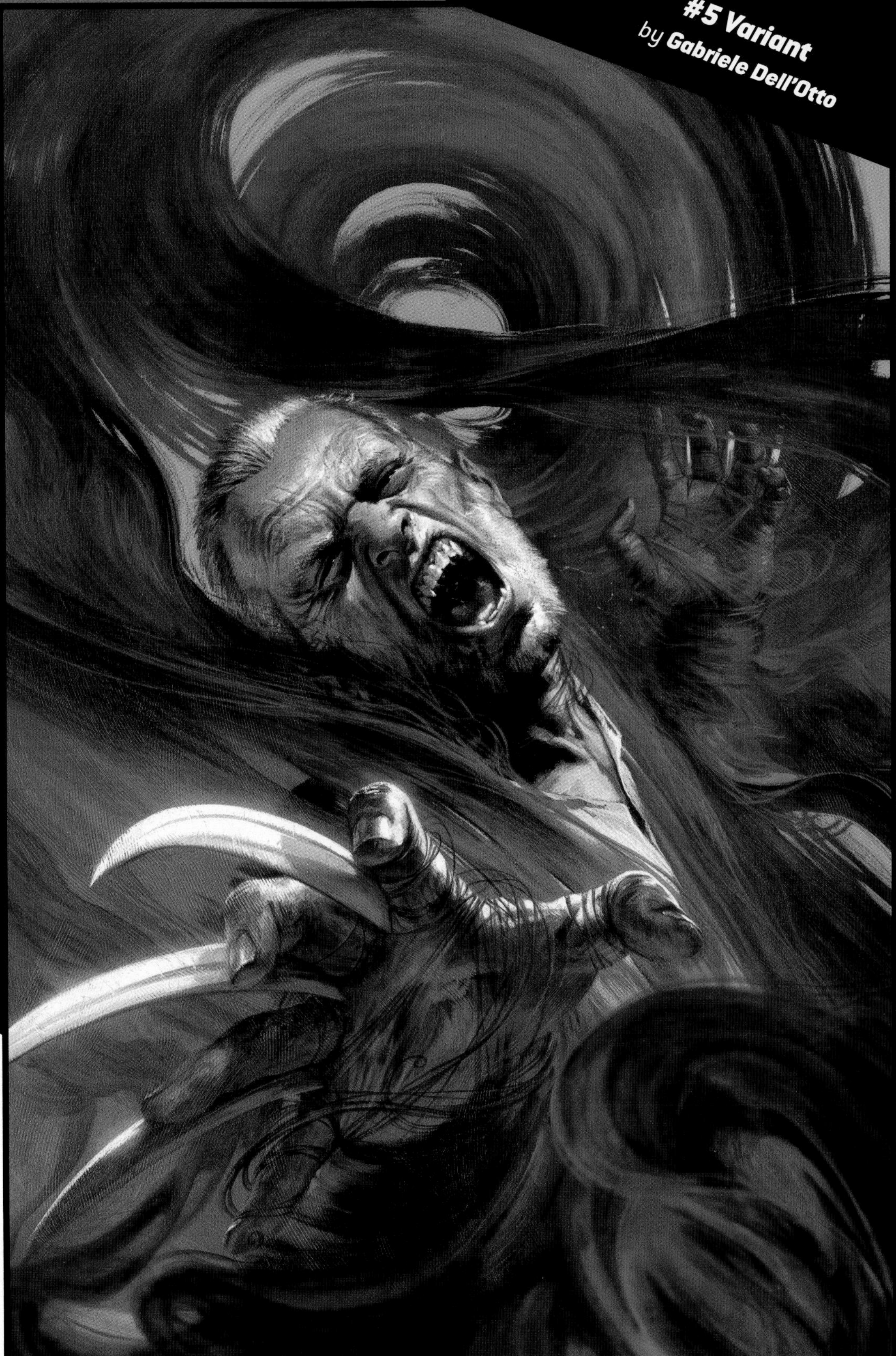

#5 Variant
by **Gabriele Dell'Otto**

5

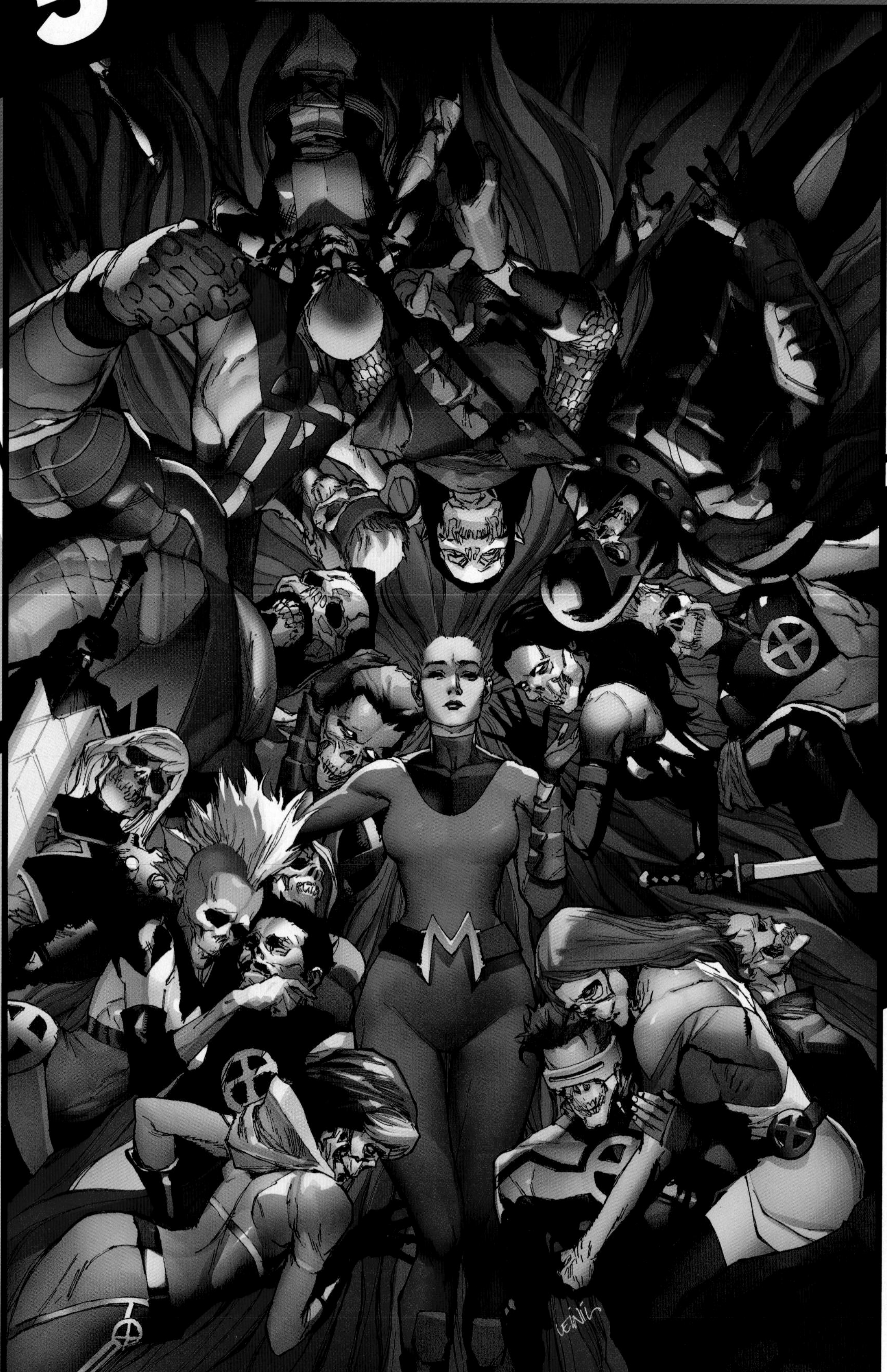

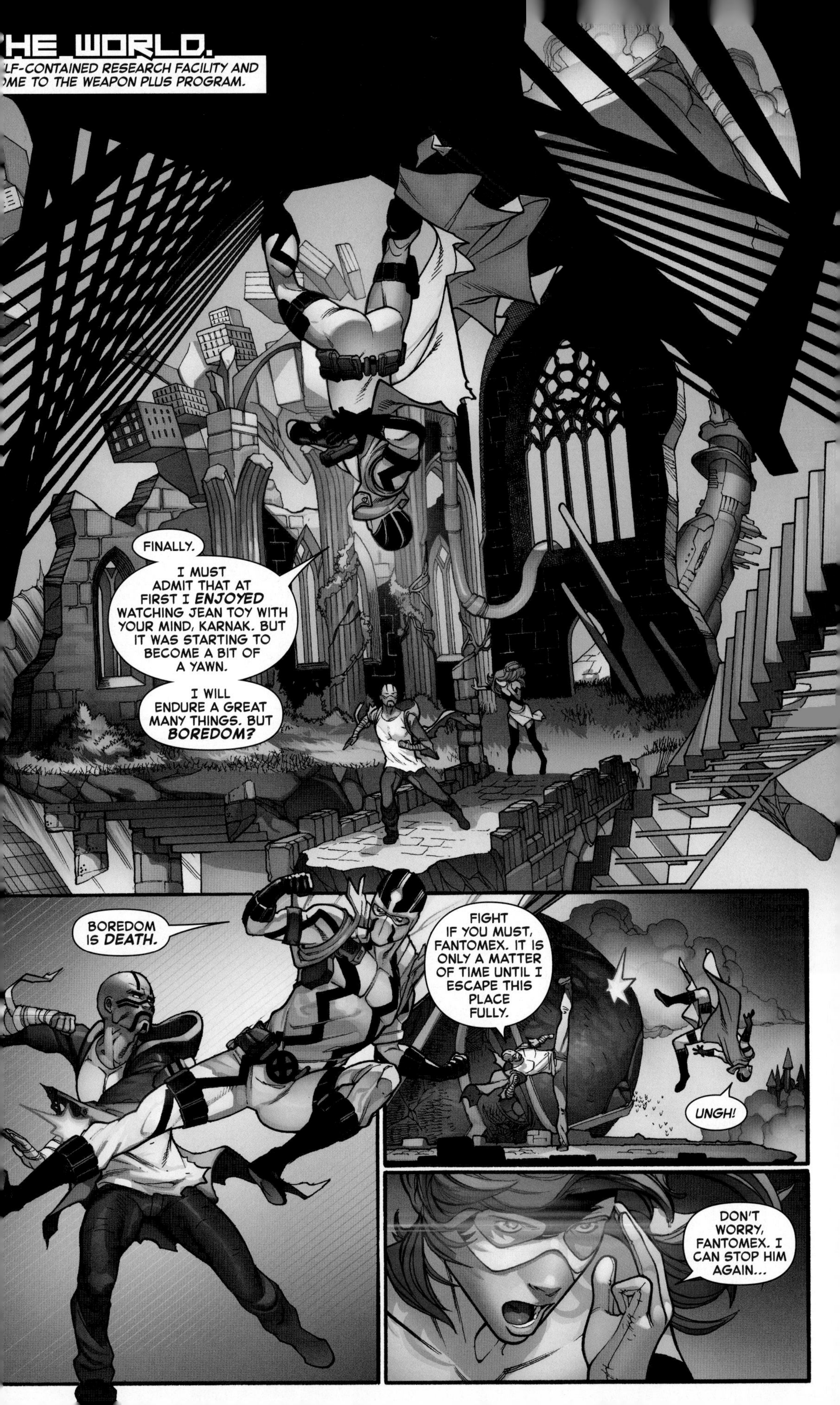
HE WORLD.
LF-CONTAINED RESEARCH FACILITY AND
ME TO THE WEAPON PLUS PROGRAM.
FINALLY.
I MUST ADMIT THAT AT FIRST I ENJOYED WATCHING JEAN TOY WITH YOUR MIND, KARNAK. BUT IT WAS STARTING TO BECOME A BIT OF A YAWN.
I WILL ENDURE A GREAT MANY THINGS. BUT BOREDOM?
BOREDOM IS DEATH.
FIGHT IF YOU MUST, FANTOMEX. IT IS ONLY A MATTER OF TIME UNTIL I ESCAPE THIS PLACE FULLY.
UNGH!
DON'T WORRY, FANTOMEX. I CAN STOP HIM AGAIN...

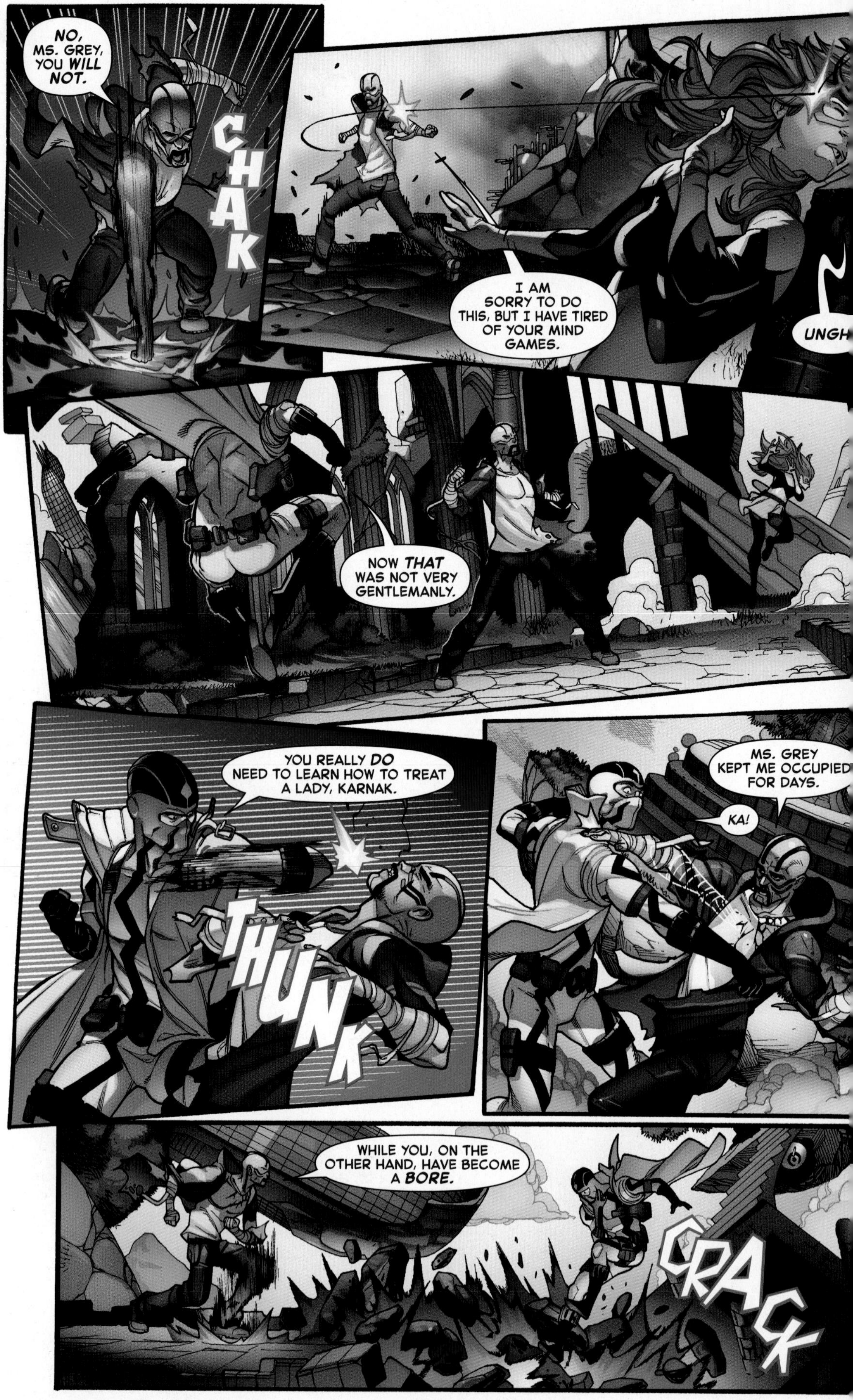
NO, MS. GREY, YOU WILL NOT.
CHAK
I AM SORRY TO DO THIS, BUT I HAVE TIRED OF YOUR MIND GAMES.
UNGH
NOW THAT WAS NOT VERY GENTLEMANLY.
YOU REALLY DO NEED TO LEARN HOW TO TREAT A LADY, KARNAK.
THUNK
MS. GREY KEPT ME OCCUPIED FOR DAYS.
KA!
WHILE YOU, ON THE OTHER HAND, HAVE BECOME A BORE.
CRACK

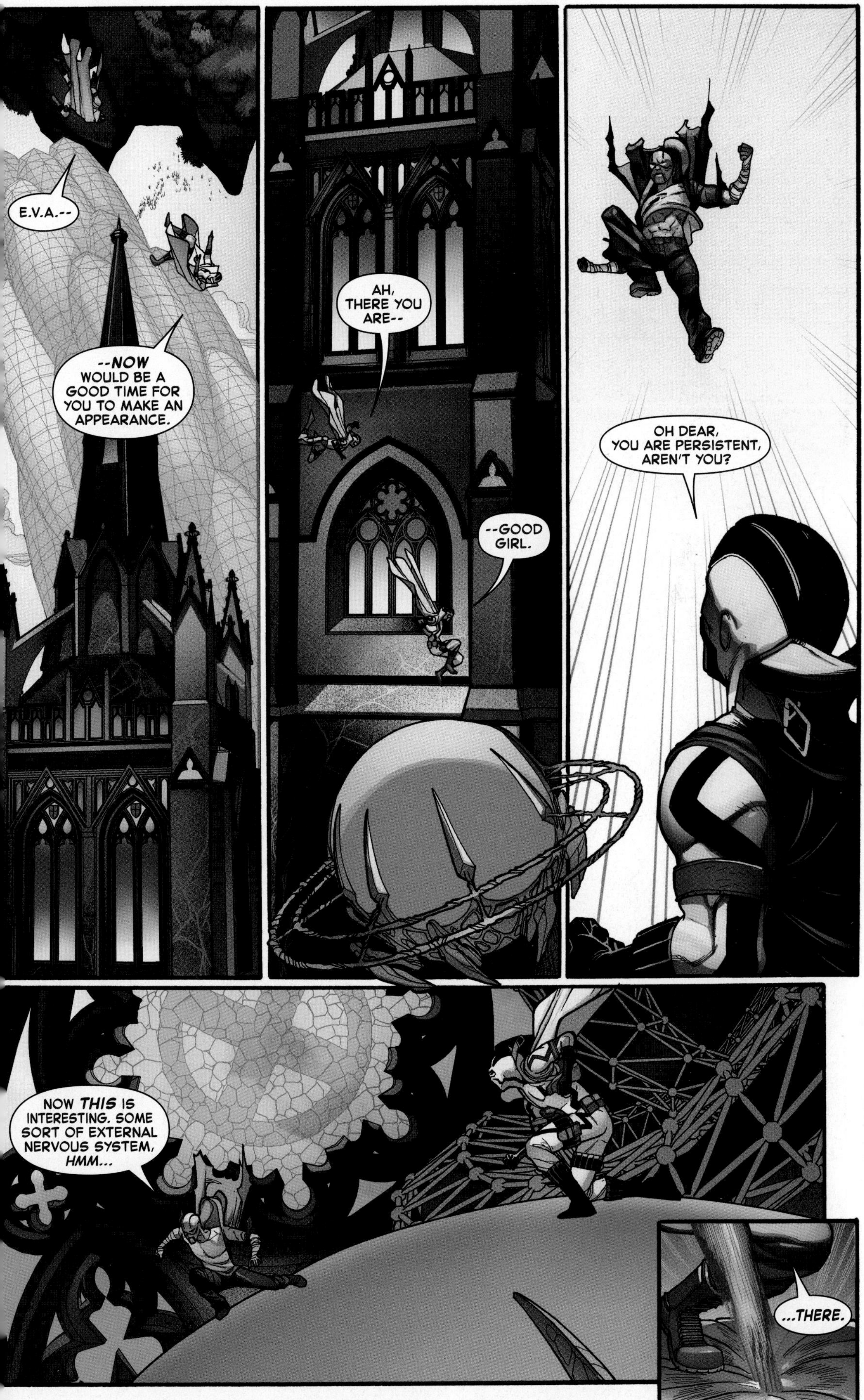
E.V.A.--
--*NOW* WOULD BE A GOOD TIME FOR YOU TO MAKE AN APPEARANCE.
AH, THERE YOU ARE--
--GOOD GIRL.
OH DEAR, YOU ARE PERSISTENT, AREN'T YOU?
NOW *THIS* IS INTERESTING. SOME SORT OF EXTERNAL NERVOUS SYSTEM, *HMM...*
...THERE.

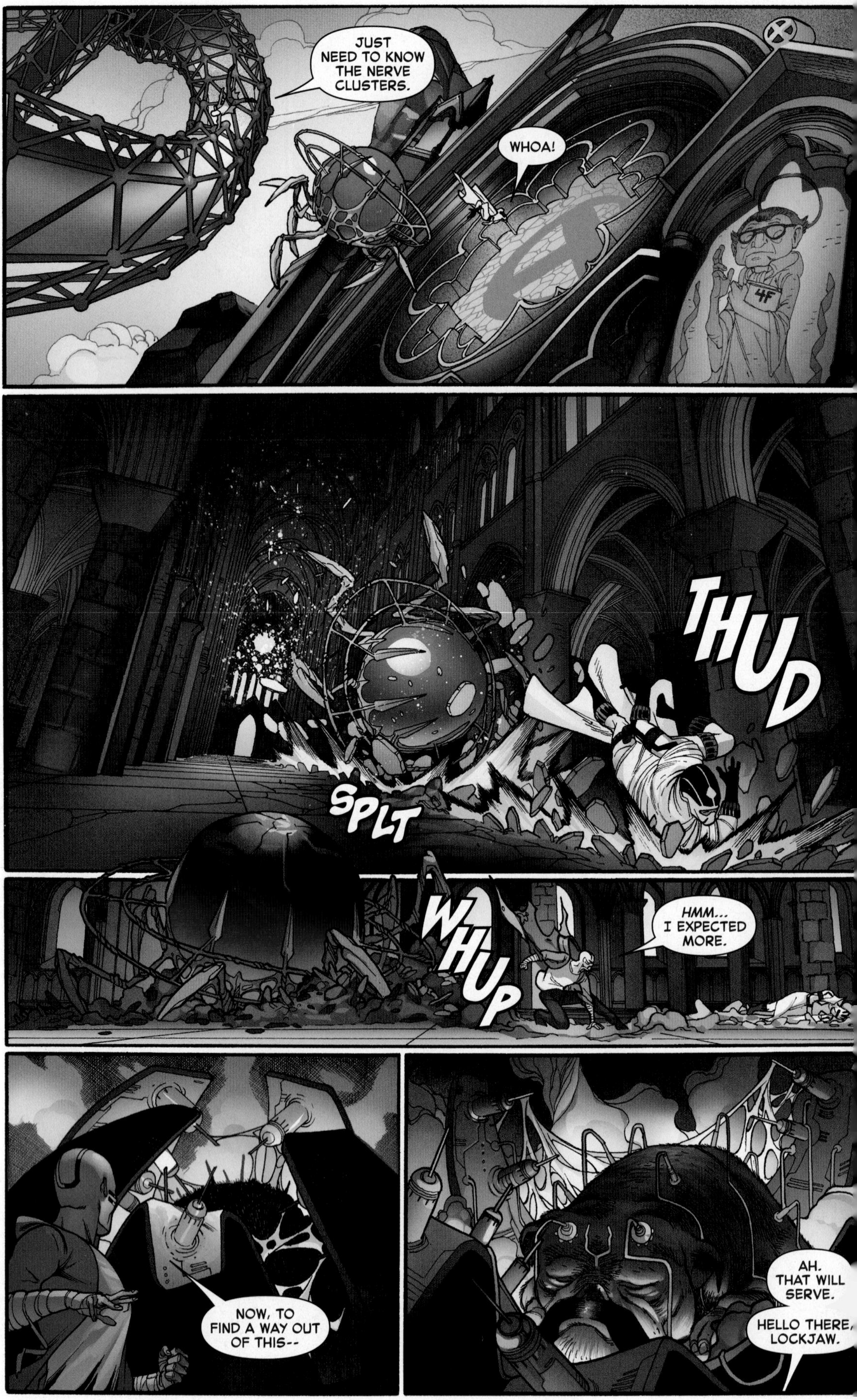
JUST NEED TO KNOW THE NERVE CLUSTERS.
WHOA!
4F
THUD
SPLT
WHUP
HMM... I EXPECTED MORE.
NOW, TO FIND A WAY OUT OF THIS--
AH. THAT WILL SERVE.
HELLO THERE, LOCKJAW.

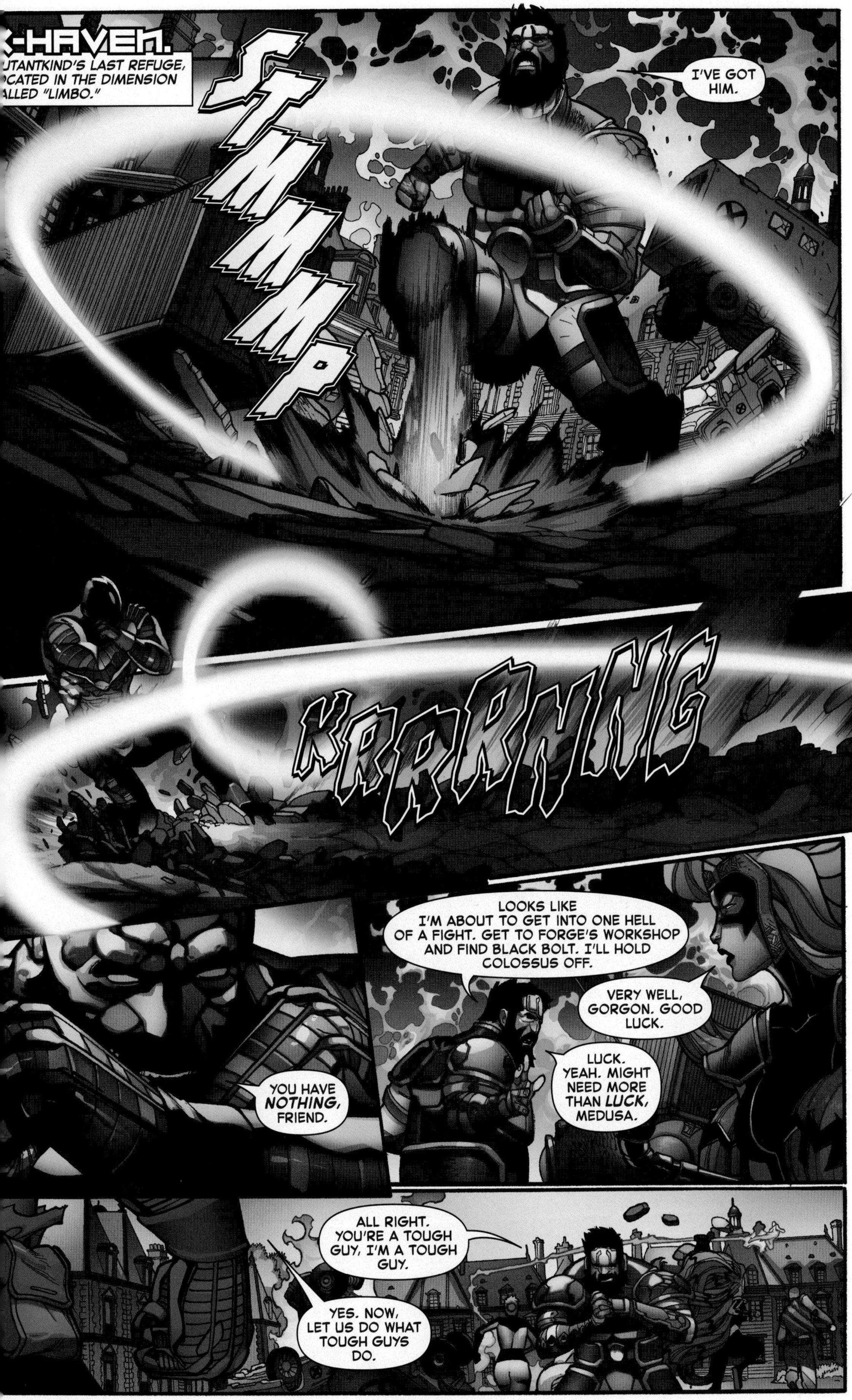

X-HAVEN.
MUTANTKIND'S LAST REFUGE, LOCATED IN THE DIMENSION CALLED "LIMBO."
I'VE GOT HIM.
STMMMP
KRRRNNG
LOOKS LIKE I'M ABOUT TO GET INTO ONE HELL OF A FIGHT. GET TO FORGE'S WORKSHOP AND FIND BLACK BOLT. I'LL HOLD COLOSSUS OFF.
VERY WELL, GORGON. GOOD LUCK.
LUCK. YEAH. MIGHT NEED MORE THAN *LUCK*, MEDUSA.
YOU HAVE *NOTHING*, FRIEND.
ALL RIGHT. YOU'RE A TOUGH GUY, I'M A TOUGH GUY.
YES. NOW, LET US DO WHAT TOUGH GUYS DO.

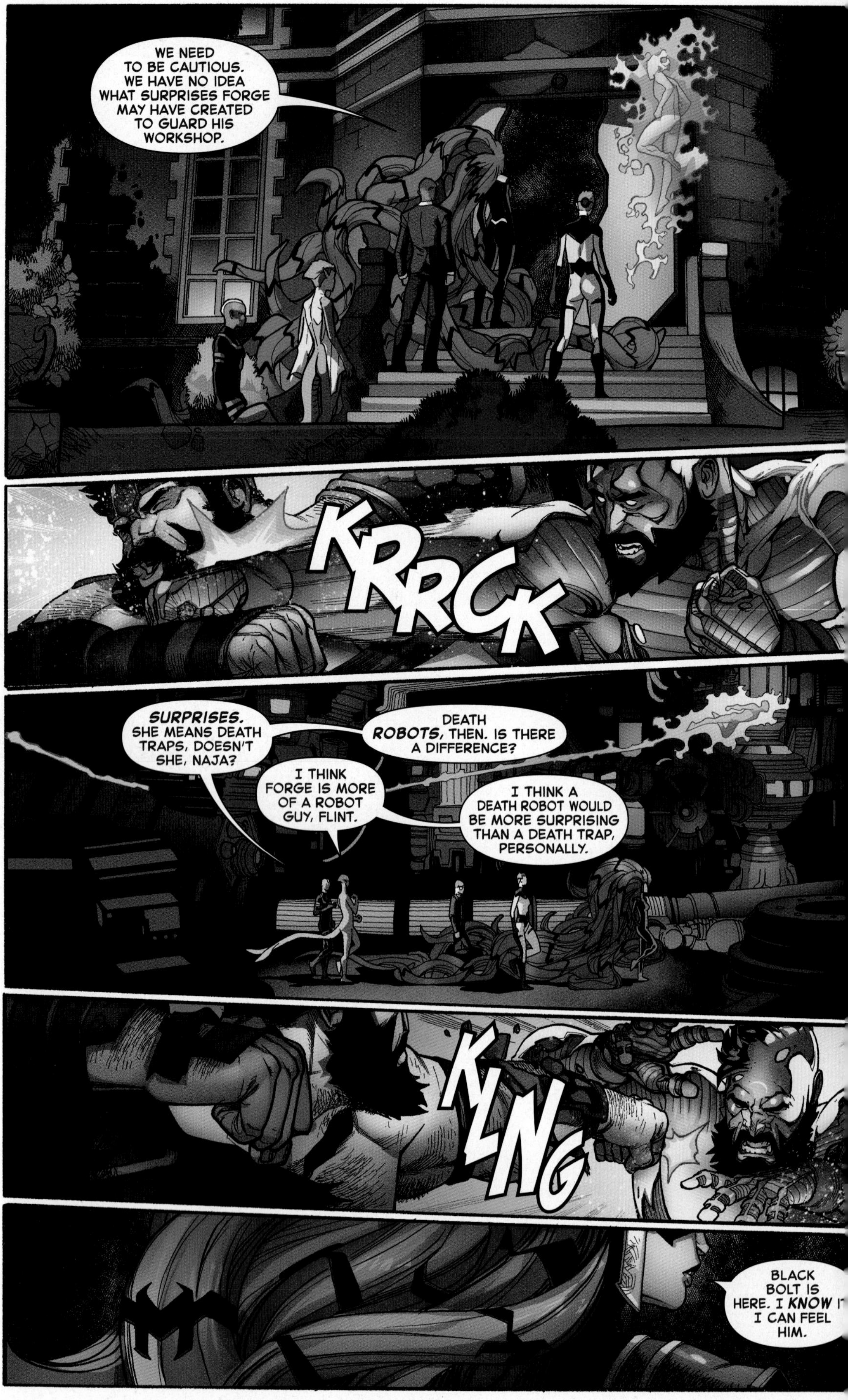
WE NEED TO BE CAUTIOUS. WE HAVE NO IDEA WHAT SURPRISES FORGE MAY HAVE CREATED TO GUARD HIS WORKSHOP.
KRRCK
SURPRISES. SHE MEANS DEATH TRAPS, DOESN'T SHE, NAJA?
DEATH ROBOTS, THEN. IS THERE A DIFFERENCE?
I THINK FORGE IS MORE OF A ROBOT GUY, FLINT.
I THINK A DEATH ROBOT WOULD BE MORE SURPRISING THAN A DEATH TRAP, PERSONALLY.
KLNG
BLACK BOLT IS HERE. I KNOW I CAN FEEL HIM.

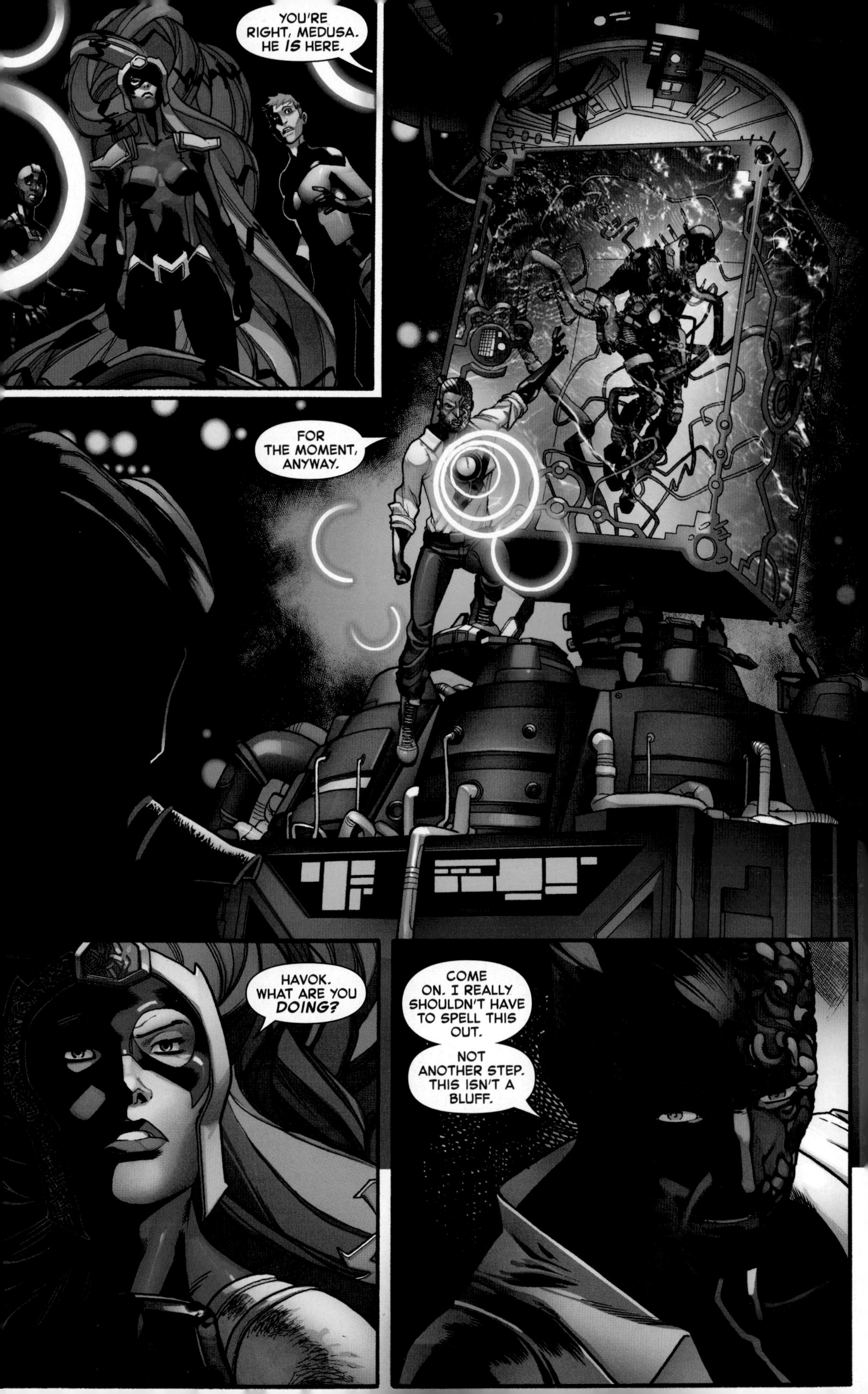
YOU'RE RIGHT, MEDUSA. HE IS HERE.
FOR THE MOMENT, ANYWAY.
HAVOK. WHAT ARE YOU DOING?
COME ON. I REALLY SHOULDN'T HAVE TO SPELL THIS OUT.
NOT ANOTHER STEP. THIS ISN'T A BLUFF.

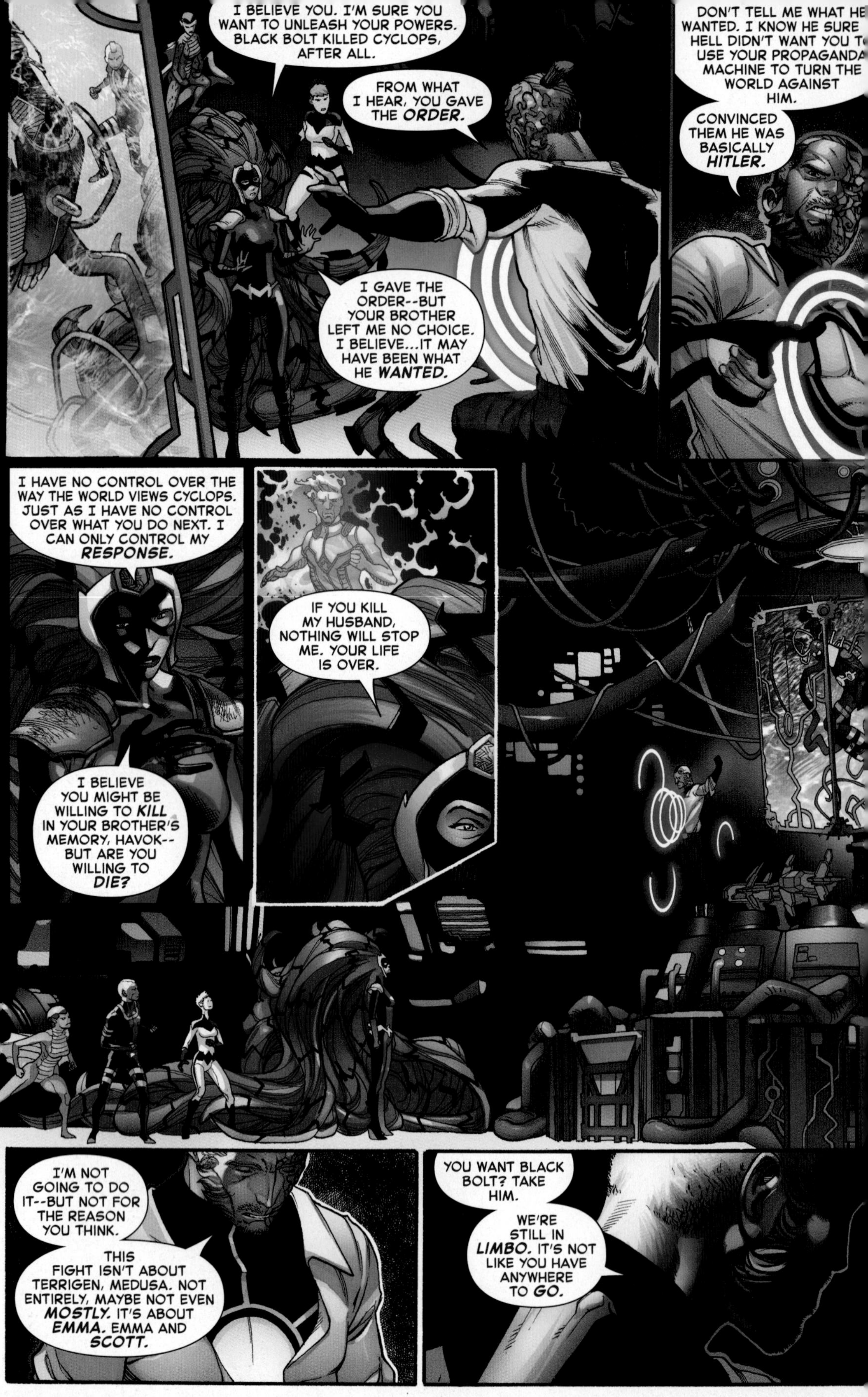
I BELIEVE YOU. I'M SURE YOU WANT TO UNLEASH YOUR POWERS. BLACK BOLT KILLED CYCLOPS, AFTER ALL.
FROM WHAT I HEAR, YOU GAVE THE ORDER.
I GAVE THE ORDER--BUT YOUR BROTHER LEFT ME NO CHOICE. I BELIEVE...IT MAY HAVE BEEN WHAT HE WANTED.
DON'T TELL ME WHAT HE WANTED. I KNOW HE SURE HELL DIDN'T WANT YOU TO USE YOUR PROPAGANDA MACHINE TO TURN THE WORLD AGAINST HIM.
CONVINCED THEM HE WAS BASICALLY HITLER.
I HAVE NO CONTROL OVER THE WAY THE WORLD VIEWS CYCLOPS. JUST AS I HAVE NO CONTROL OVER WHAT YOU DO NEXT. I CAN ONLY CONTROL MY RESPONSE.
I BELIEVE YOU MIGHT BE WILLING TO KILL IN YOUR BROTHER'S MEMORY, HAVOK--BUT ARE YOU WILLING TO DIE?
IF YOU KILL MY HUSBAND, NOTHING WILL STOP ME. YOUR LIFE IS OVER.
I'M NOT GOING TO DO IT--BUT NOT FOR THE REASON YOU THINK.
THIS FIGHT ISN'T ABOUT TERRIGEN, MEDUSA. NOT ENTIRELY, MAYBE NOT EVEN MOSTLY. IT'S ABOUT EMMA. EMMA AND SCOTT.
YOU WANT BLACK BOLT? TAKE HIM.
WE'RE STILL IN LIMBO. IT'S NOT LIKE YOU HAVE ANYWHERE TO GO.

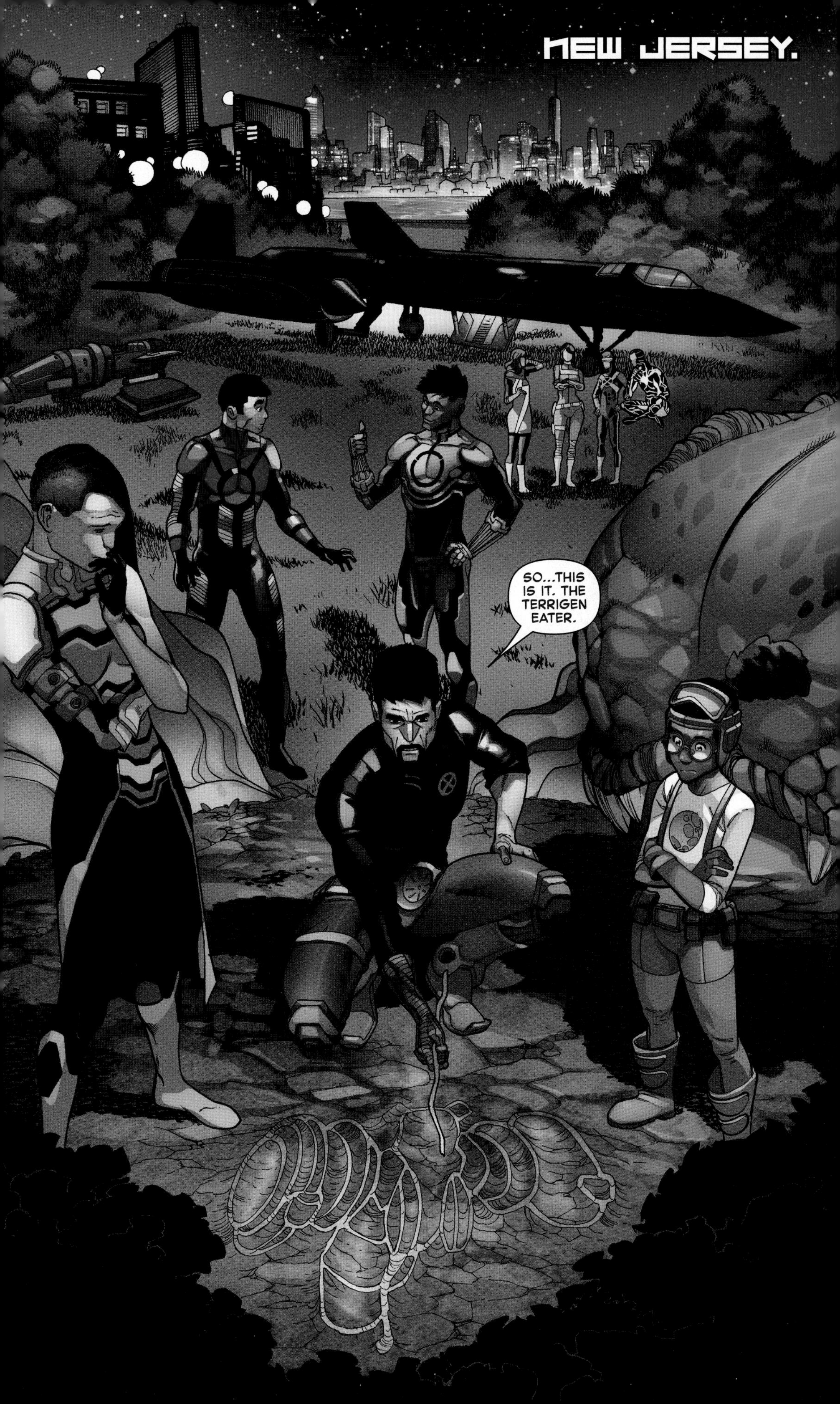
NEW JERSEY.
SO...THIS IS IT. THE TERRIGEN EATER.

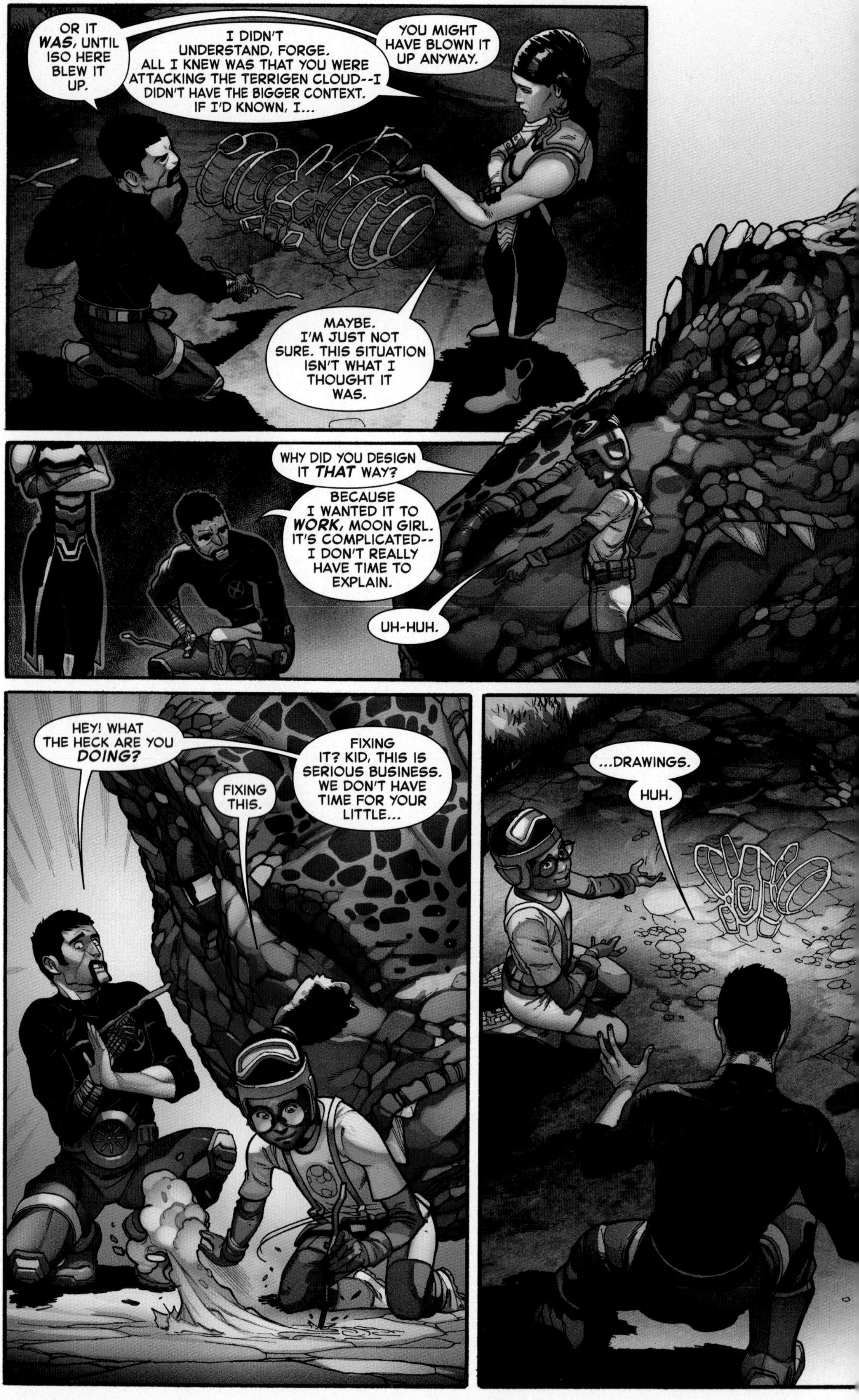
OR IT WAS, UNTIL ISO HERE BLEW IT UP.
I DIDN'T UNDERSTAND, FORGE. ALL I KNEW WAS THAT YOU WERE ATTACKING THE TERRIGEN CLOUD--I DIDN'T HAVE THE BIGGER CONTEXT. IF I'D KNOWN, I...
YOU MIGHT HAVE BLOWN IT UP ANYWAY.
MAYBE. I'M JUST NOT SURE. THIS SITUATION ISN'T WHAT I THOUGHT IT WAS.
WHY DID YOU DESIGN IT THAT WAY?
BECAUSE I WANTED IT TO WORK, MOON GIRL. IT'S COMPLICATED-- I DON'T REALLY HAVE TIME TO EXPLAIN.
UH-HUH.
HEY! WHAT THE HECK ARE YOU DOING?
FIXING THIS.
FIXING IT? KID, THIS IS SERIOUS BUSINESS. WE DON'T HAVE TIME FOR YOUR LITTLE...
...DRAWINGS.
HUH.

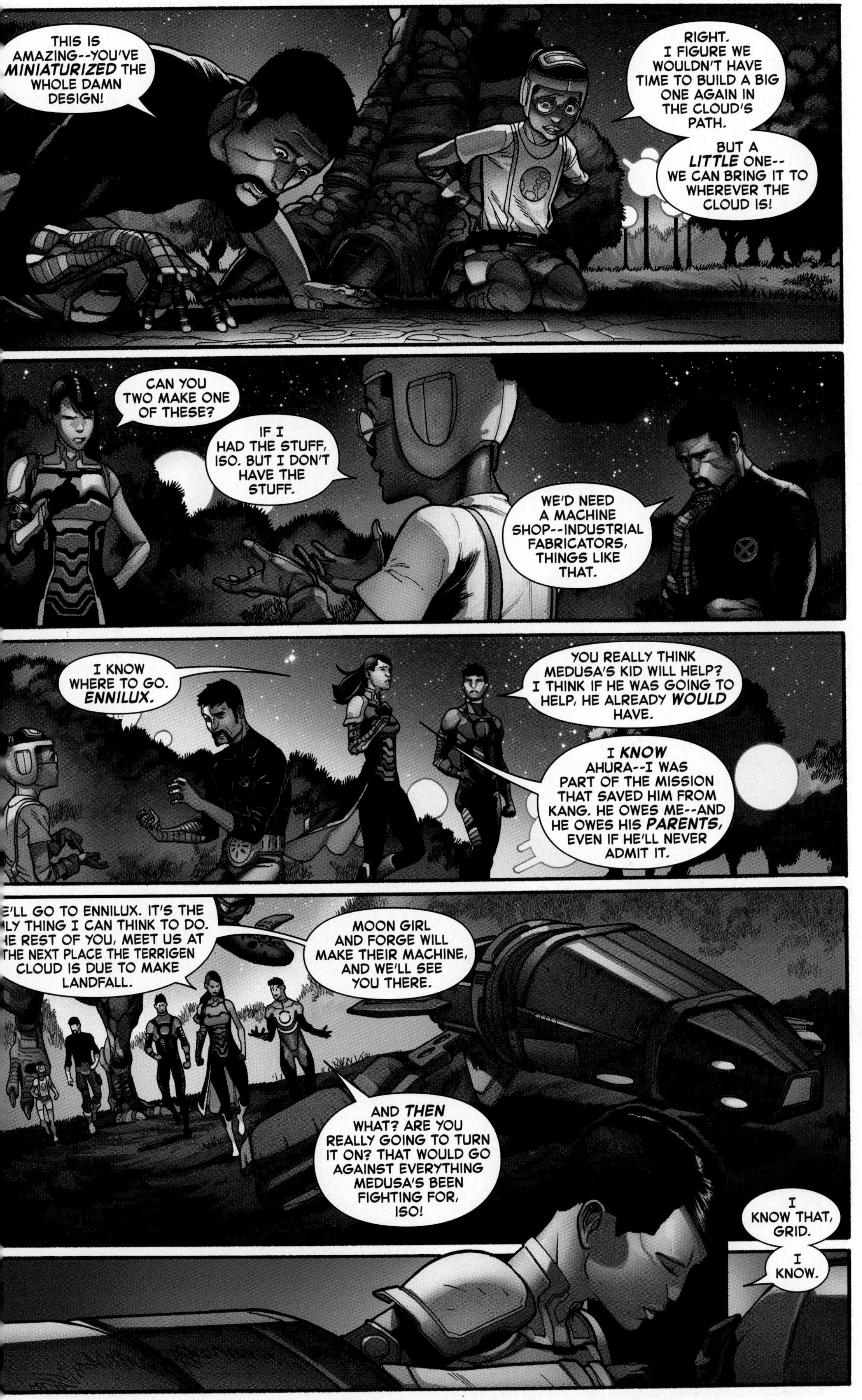
THIS IS AMAZING--YOU'VE *MINIATURIZED* THE WHOLE DAMN DESIGN!
RIGHT. I FIGURE WE WOULDN'T HAVE TIME TO BUILD A BIG ONE AGAIN IN THE CLOUD'S PATH.
BUT A *LITTLE* ONE-- WE CAN BRING IT TO WHEREVER THE CLOUD IS!
CAN YOU TWO MAKE ONE OF THESE?
IF I HAD THE STUFF, ISO. BUT I DON'T HAVE THE STUFF.
WE'D NEED A MACHINE SHOP--INDUSTRIAL FABRICATORS, THINGS LIKE THAT.
I KNOW WHERE TO GO. *ENNILUX.*
YOU REALLY THINK MEDUSA'S KID WILL HELP? I THINK IF HE WAS GOING TO HELP, HE ALREADY *WOULD* HAVE.
I *KNOW* AHURA--I WAS PART OF THE MISSION THAT SAVED HIM FROM KANG. HE OWES ME--AND HE OWES HIS *PARENTS,* EVEN IF HE'LL NEVER ADMIT IT.
E'LL GO TO ENNILUX. IT'S THE LY THING I CAN THINK TO DO. HE REST OF YOU, MEET US AT THE NEXT PLACE THE TERRIGEN CLOUD IS DUE TO MAKE LANDFALL.
MOON GIRL AND FORGE WILL MAKE THEIR MACHINE, AND WE'LL SEE YOU THERE.
AND *THEN* WHAT? ARE YOU REALLY GOING TO TURN IT ON? THAT WOULD GO AGAINST EVERYTHING MEDUSA'S BEEN FIGHTING FOR, ISO!
I KNOW THAT, GRID.
I KNOW.

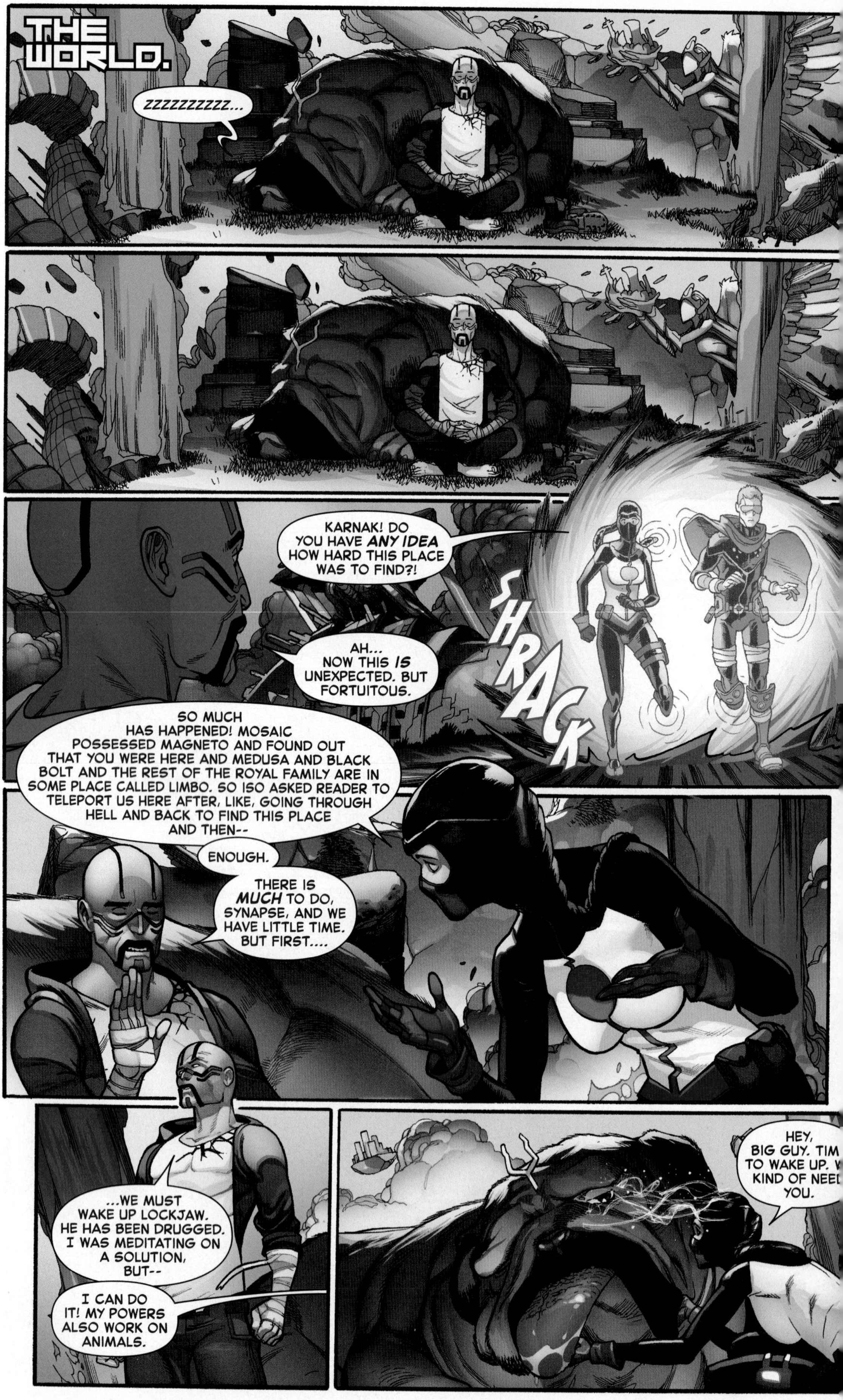
THE WORLD.
ZZZZZZZZZZ...
KARNAK! DO YOU HAVE ANY IDEA HOW HARD THIS PLACE WAS TO FIND?!
SHRACK
AH... NOW THIS IS UNEXPECTED. BUT FORTUITOUS.
SO MUCH HAS HAPPENED! MOSAIC POSSESSED MAGNETO AND FOUND OUT THAT YOU WERE HERE AND MEDUSA AND BLACK BOLT AND THE REST OF THE ROYAL FAMILY ARE IN SOME PLACE CALLED LIMBO. SO ISO ASKED READER TO TELEPORT US HERE AFTER, LIKE, GOING THROUGH HELL AND BACK TO FIND THIS PLACE AND THEN--
ENOUGH.
THERE IS MUCH TO DO, SYNAPSE, AND WE HAVE LITTLE TIME. BUT FIRST....
...WE MUST WAKE UP LOCKJAW. HE HAS BEEN DRUGGED. I WAS MEDITATING ON A SOLUTION, BUT--
I CAN DO IT! MY POWERS ALSO WORK ON ANIMALS.

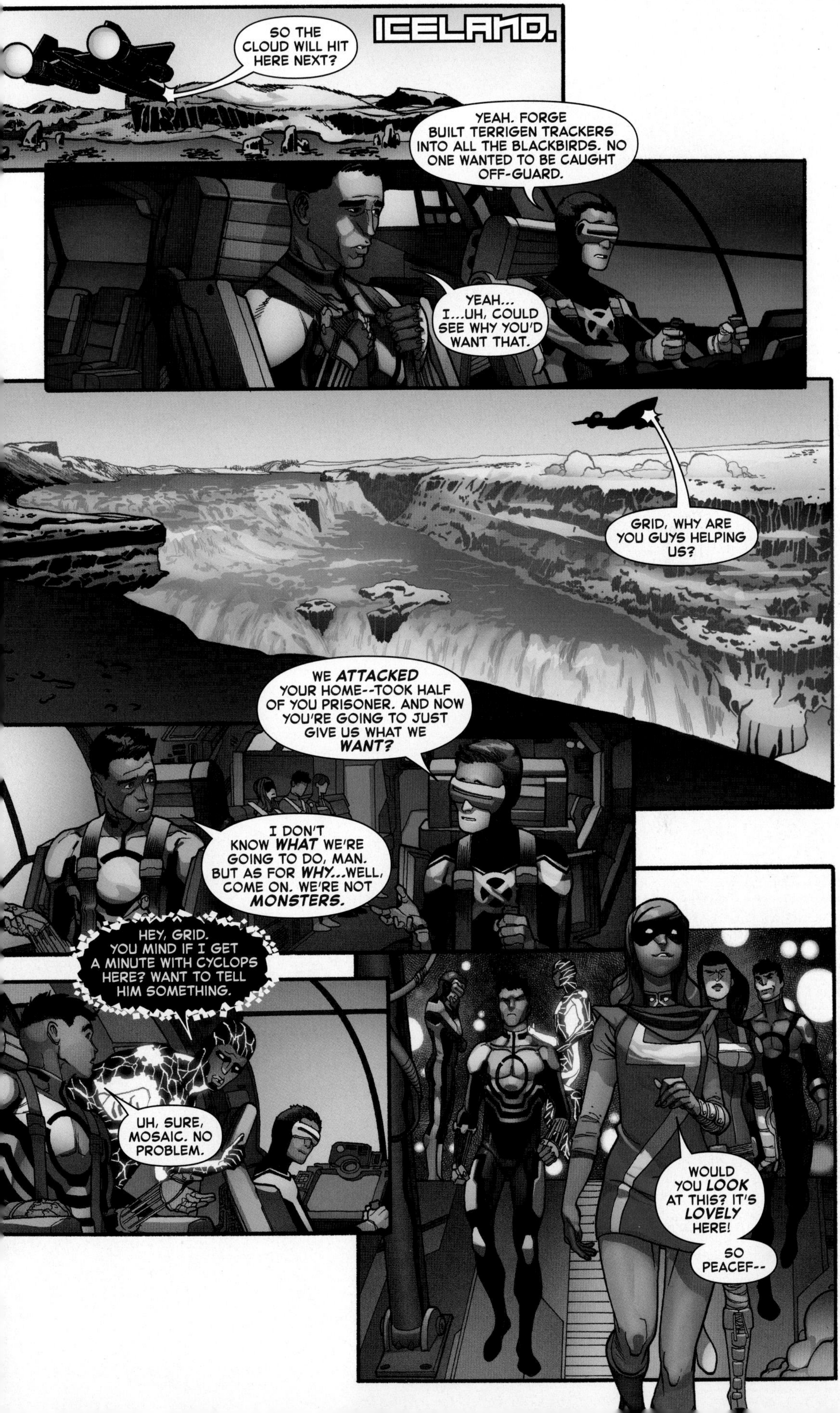
ICELAND.
SO THE CLOUD WILL HIT HERE NEXT?
YEAH. FORGE BUILT TERRIGEN TRACKERS INTO ALL THE BLACKBIRDS. NO ONE WANTED TO BE CAUGHT OFF-GUARD.
YEAH... I...UH, COULD SEE WHY YOU'D WANT THAT.
GRID, WHY ARE YOU GUYS HELPING US?
WE ATTACKED YOUR HOME--TOOK HALF OF YOU PRISONER. AND NOW YOU'RE GOING TO JUST GIVE US WHAT WE WANT?
I DON'T KNOW WHAT WE'RE GOING TO DO, MAN. BUT AS FOR WHY...WELL, COME ON. WE'RE NOT MONSTERS.
HEY, GRID. YOU MIND IF I GET A MINUTE WITH CYCLOPS HERE? WANT TO TELL HIM SOMETHING.
UH, SURE, MOSAIC. NO PROBLEM.
WOULD YOU LOOK AT THIS? IT'S LOVELY HERE!
SO PEACEF--

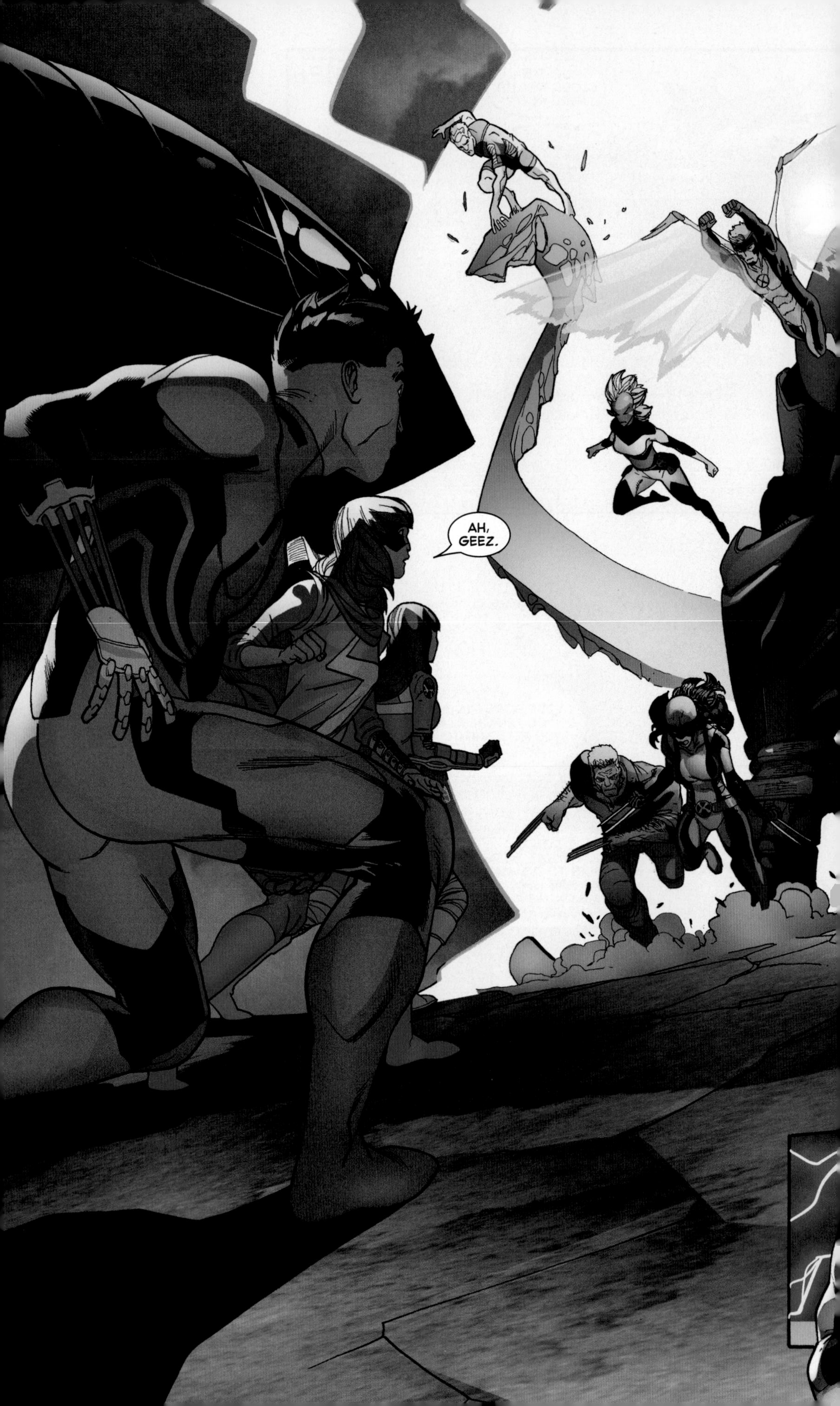
AH, GEEZ.

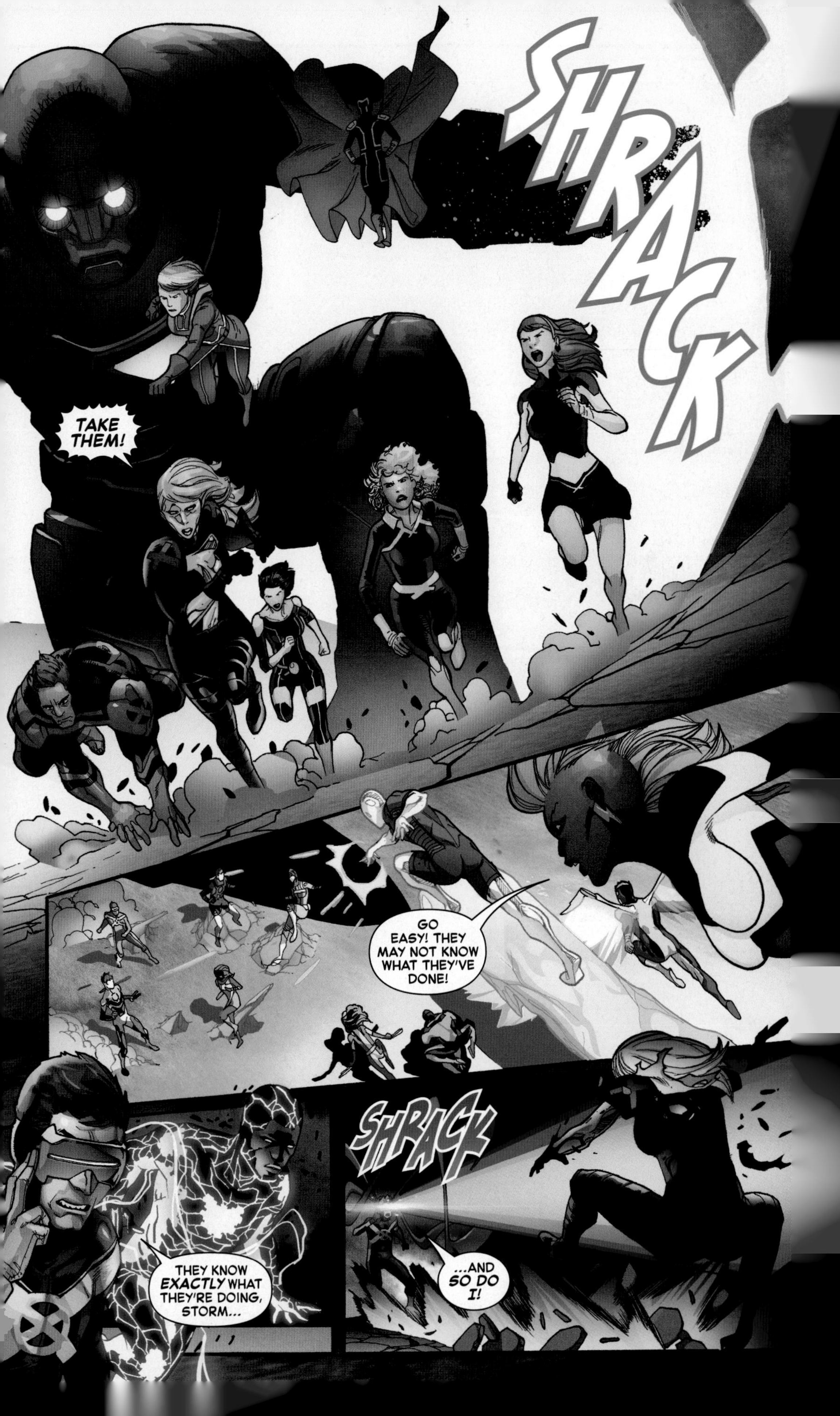
SHRACK
TAKE THEM!
GO EASY! THEY MAY NOT KNOW WHAT THEY'VE DONE!
THEY KNOW EXACTLY WHAT THEY'RE DOING, STORM...
SHRACK
...AND SO DO I!

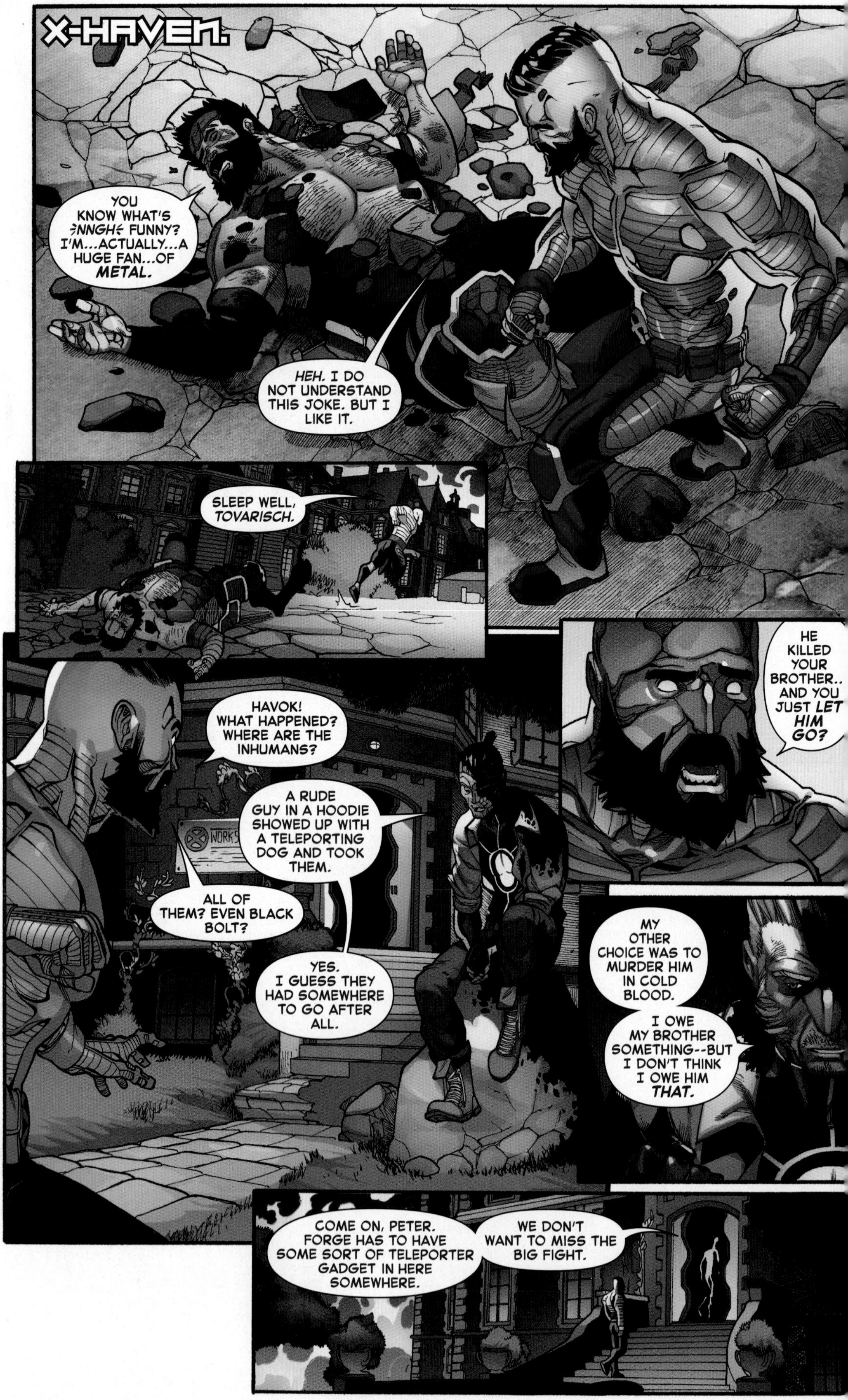
X-HAVEN.
YOU KNOW WHAT'S ⸗NNGH⸗ FUNNY? I'M...ACTUALLY...A HUGE FAN...OF METAL.
HEH. I DO NOT UNDERSTAND THIS JOKE. BUT I LIKE IT.
SLEEP WELL, TOVARISCH.
HAVOK! WHAT HAPPENED? WHERE ARE THE INHUMANS?
A RUDE GUY IN A HOODIE SHOWED UP WITH A TELEPORTING DOG AND TOOK THEM.
ALL OF THEM? EVEN BLACK BOLT?
YES. I GUESS THEY HAD SOMEWHERE TO GO AFTER ALL.
HE KILLED YOUR BROTHER.. AND YOU JUST LET HIM GO?
MY OTHER CHOICE WAS TO MURDER HIM IN COLD BLOOD.
I OWE MY BROTHER SOMETHING--BUT I DON'T THINK I OWE HIM THAT.
COME ON, PETER. FORGE HAS TO HAVE SOME SORT OF TELEPORTER GADGET IN HERE SOMEWHERE.
WE DON'T WANT TO MISS THE BIG FIGHT.

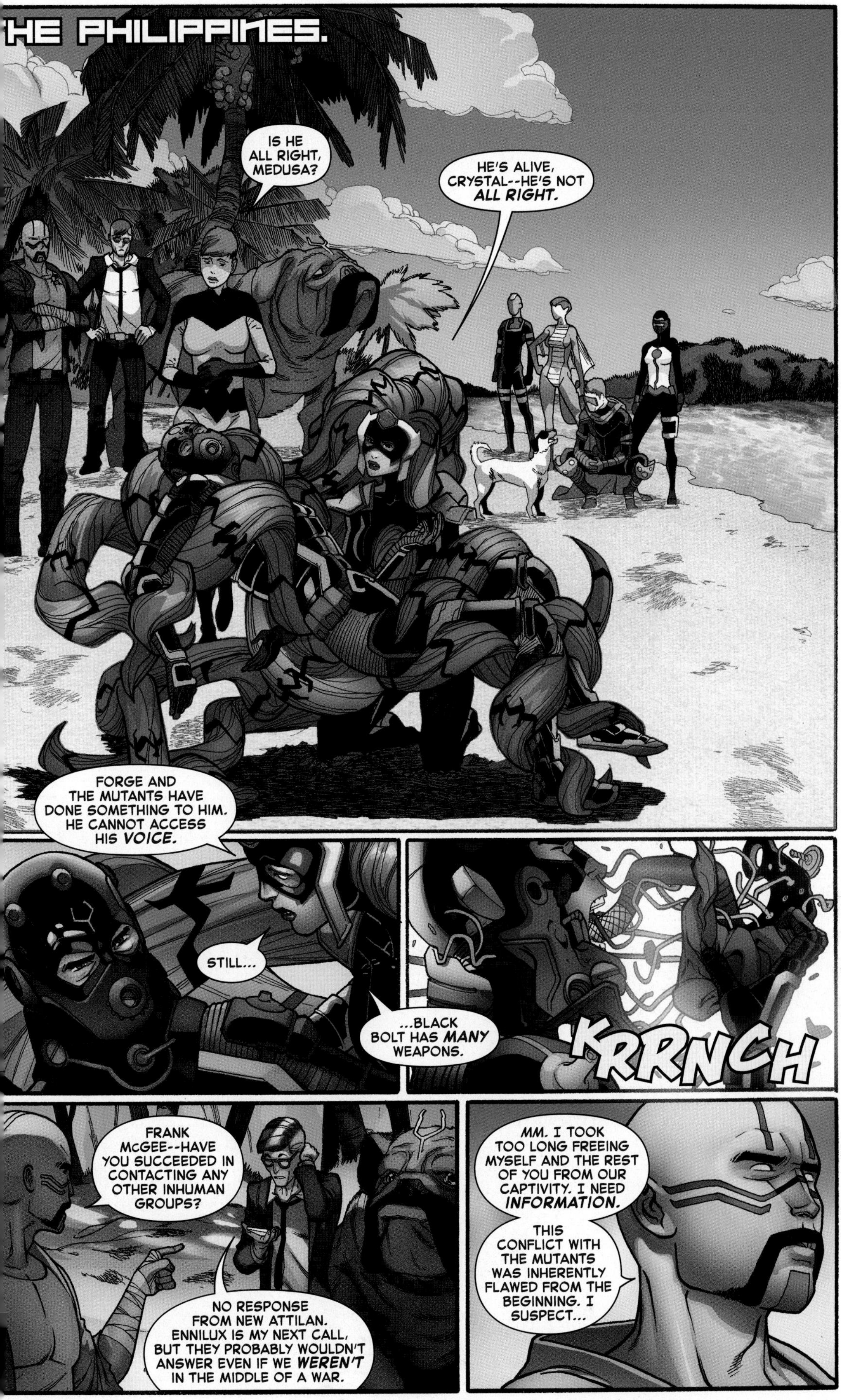

THE PHILIPPINES.
IS HE ALL RIGHT, MEDUSA?
HE'S ALIVE, CRYSTAL--HE'S NOT *ALL RIGHT.*
FORGE AND THE MUTANTS HAVE DONE SOMETHING TO HIM. HE CANNOT ACCESS HIS *VOICE.*
STILL...
...BLACK BOLT HAS *MANY* WEAPONS.
KRRNCH
FRANK McGEE--HAVE YOU SUCCEEDED IN CONTACTING ANY OTHER INHUMAN GROUPS?
NO RESPONSE FROM NEW ATTILAN. ENNILUX IS MY NEXT CALL, BUT THEY PROBABLY WOULDN'T ANSWER EVEN IF WE *WEREN'T* IN THE MIDDLE OF A WAR.
MM. I TOOK TOO LONG FREEING MYSELF AND THE REST OF YOU FROM OUR CAPTIVITY. I NEED *INFORMATION.*
THIS CONFLICT WITH THE MUTANTS WAS INHERENTLY FLAWED FROM THE BEGINNING. I SUSPECT...

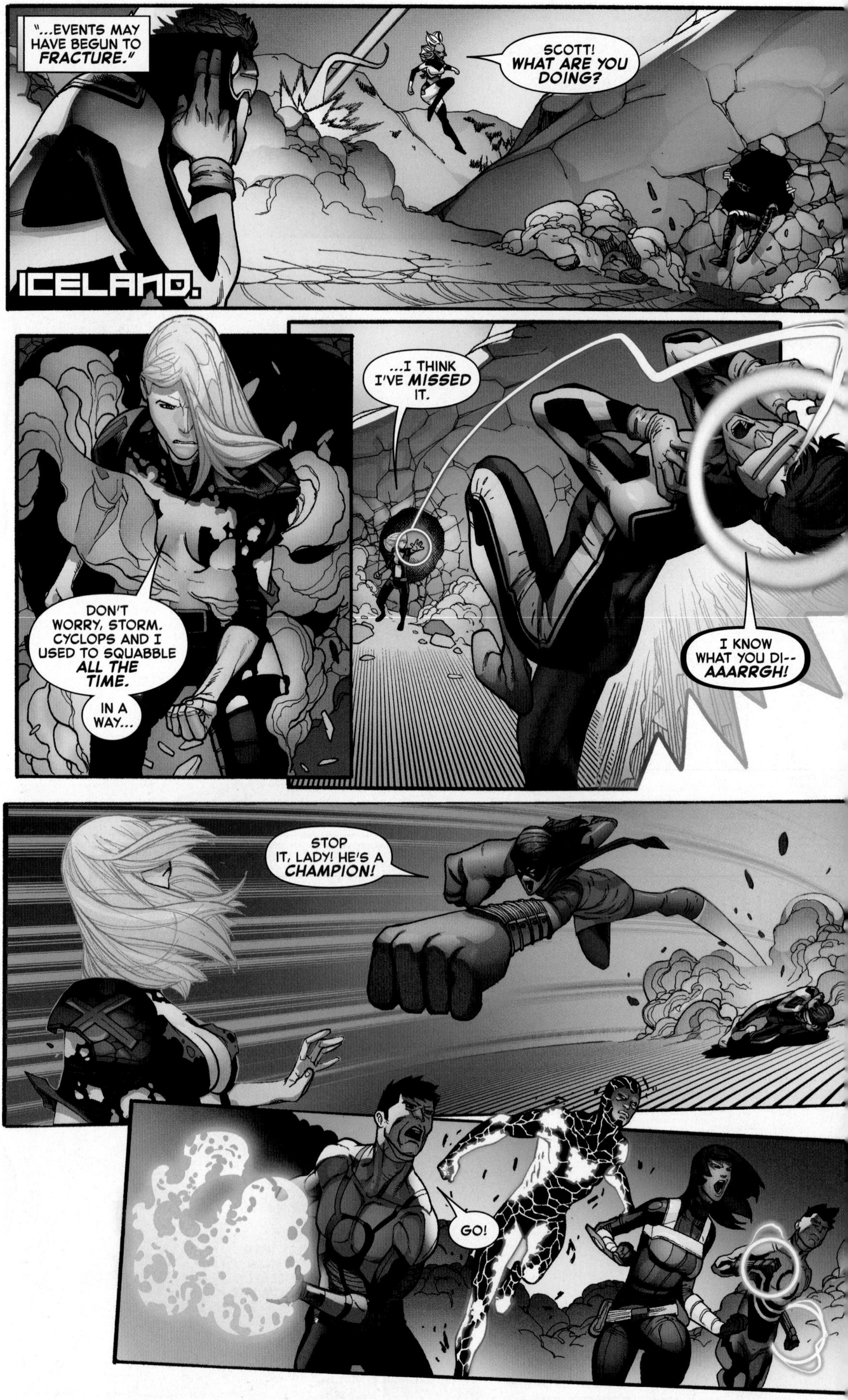
"...EVENTS MAY HAVE BEGUN TO FRACTURE."
SCOTT! WHAT ARE YOU DOING?
ICELAND.
DON'T WORRY, STORM. CYCLOPS AND I USED TO SQUABBLE ALL THE TIME.
IN A WAY...
...I THINK I'VE MISSED IT.
I KNOW WHAT YOU DI-- AAARRGH!
STOP IT, LADY! HE'S A CHAMPION!
GO!

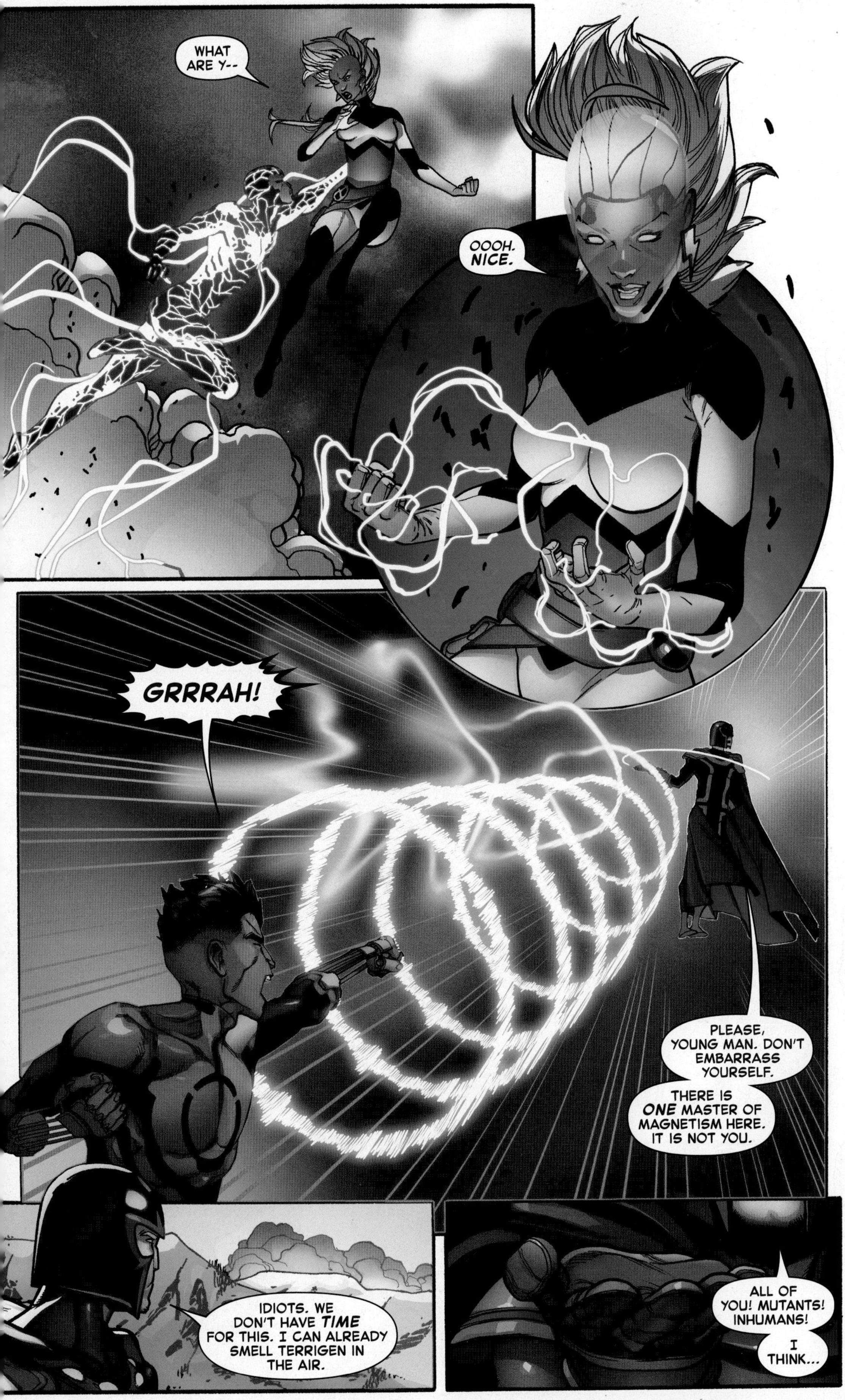
WHAT ARE Y--
OOOH. NICE.
GRRRAH!
PLEASE, YOUNG MAN. DON'T EMBARRASS YOURSELF.
THERE IS ONE MASTER OF MAGNETISM HERE. IT IS NOT YOU.
IDIOTS. WE DON'T HAVE TIME FOR THIS. I CAN ALREADY SMELL TERRIGEN IN THE AIR.
ALL OF YOU! MUTANTS! INHUMANS!
I THINK...

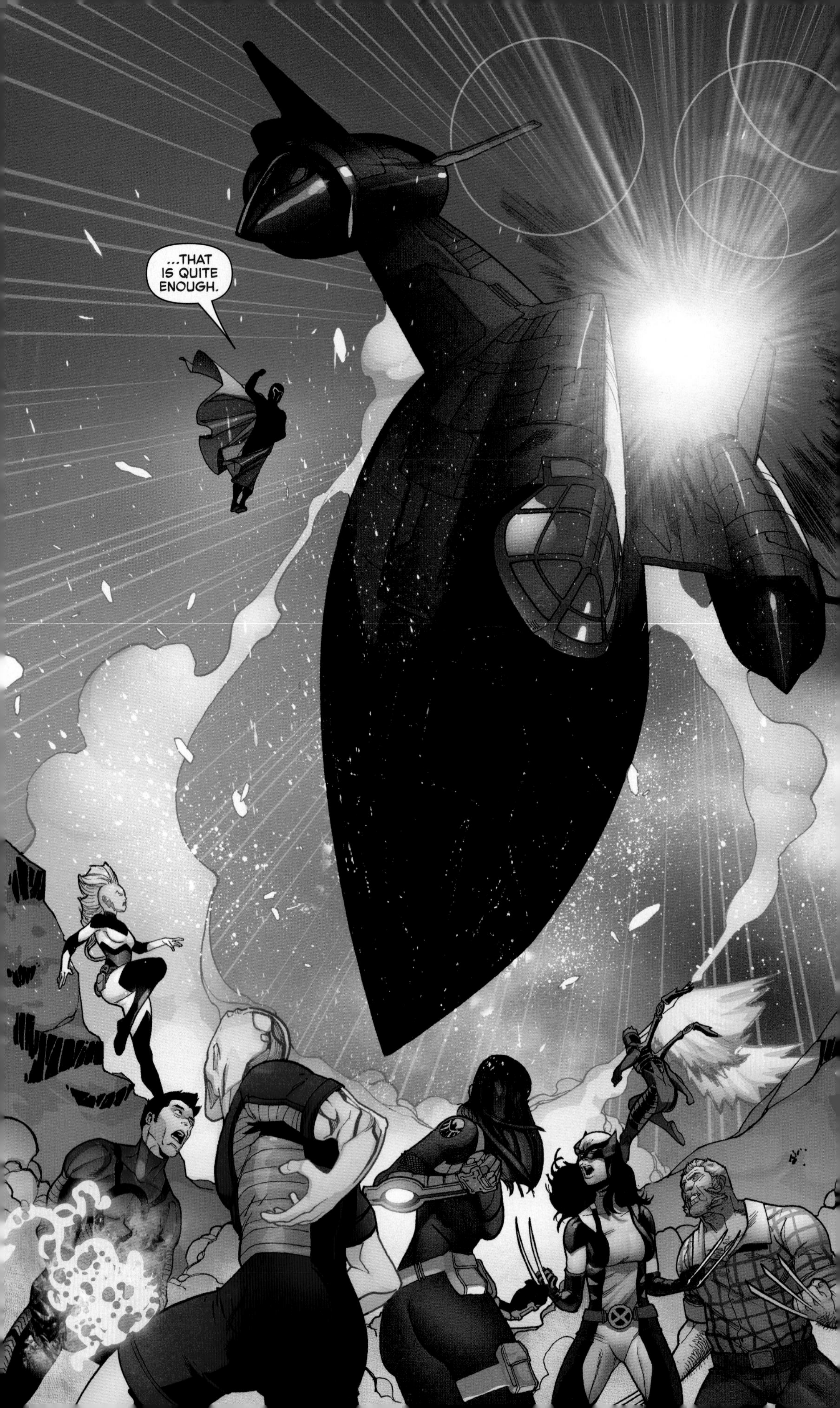

...THAT IS QUITE ENOUGH.

#6 Variant
by Simone Bianchi & Simone Peruzzi

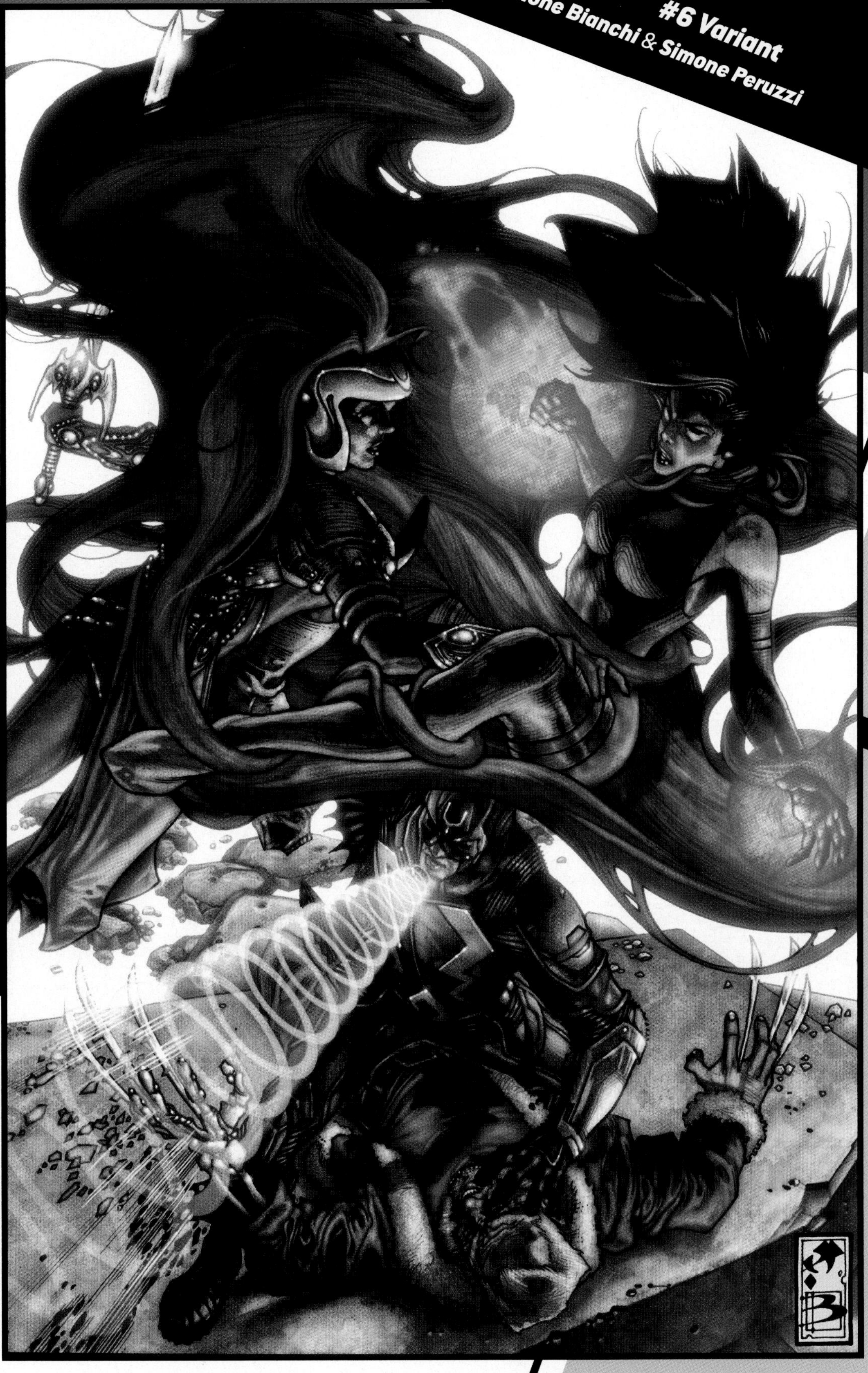

6

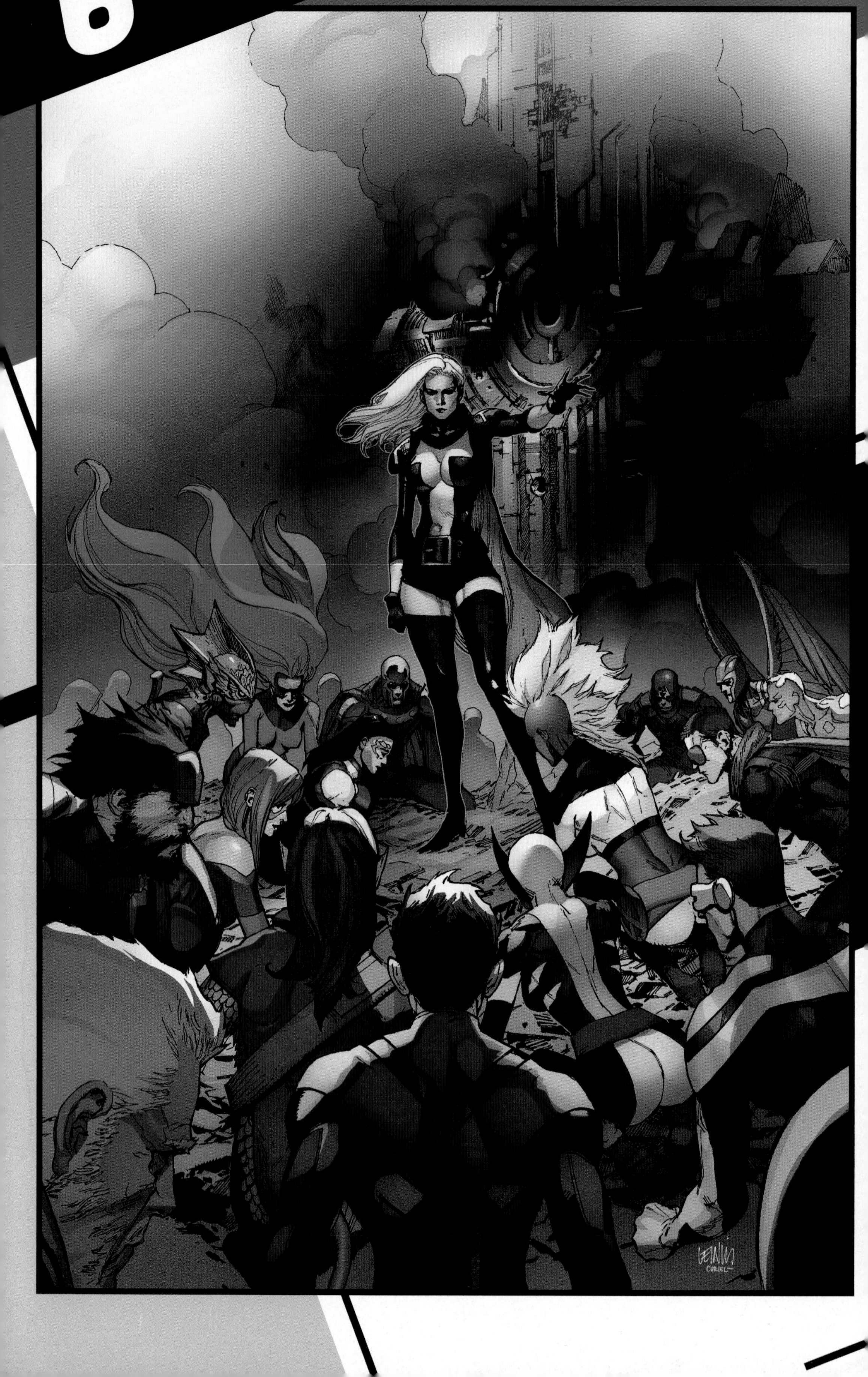

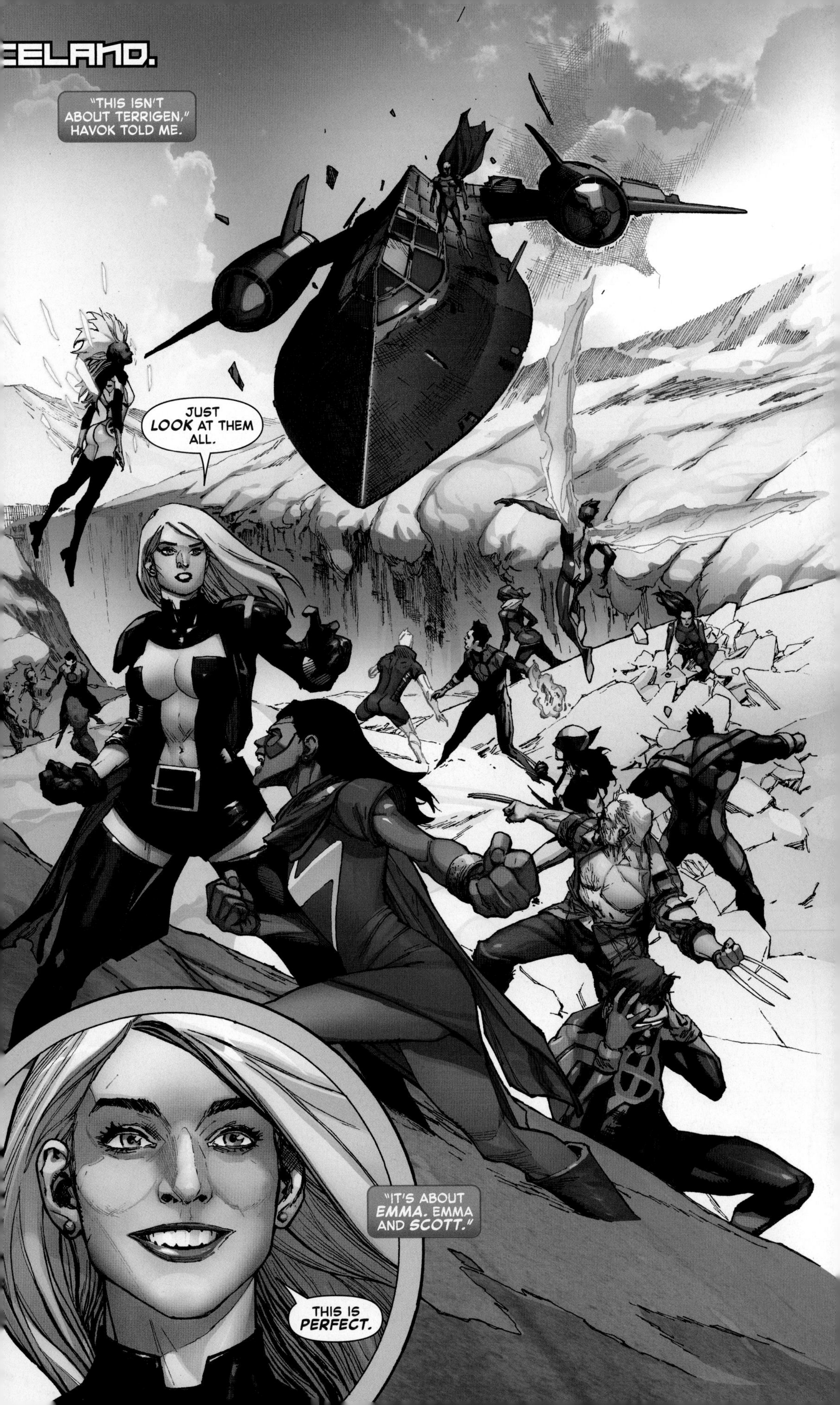

ELAND.
"THIS ISN'T ABOUT TERRIGEN," HAVOK TOLD ME.
JUST LOOK AT THEM ALL.
"IT'S ABOUT EMMA. EMMA AND SCOTT."
THIS IS PERFECT.

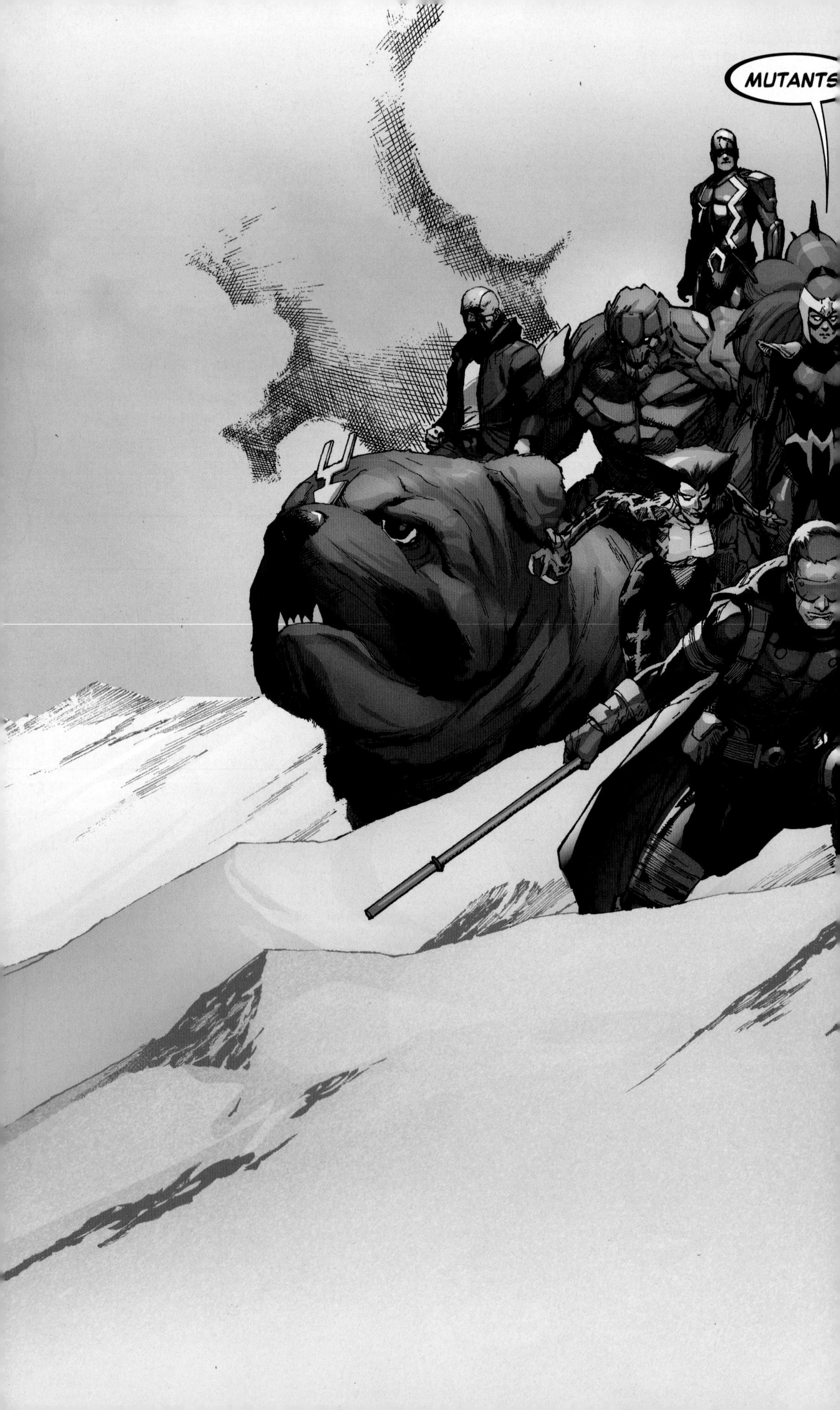
MUTANTS

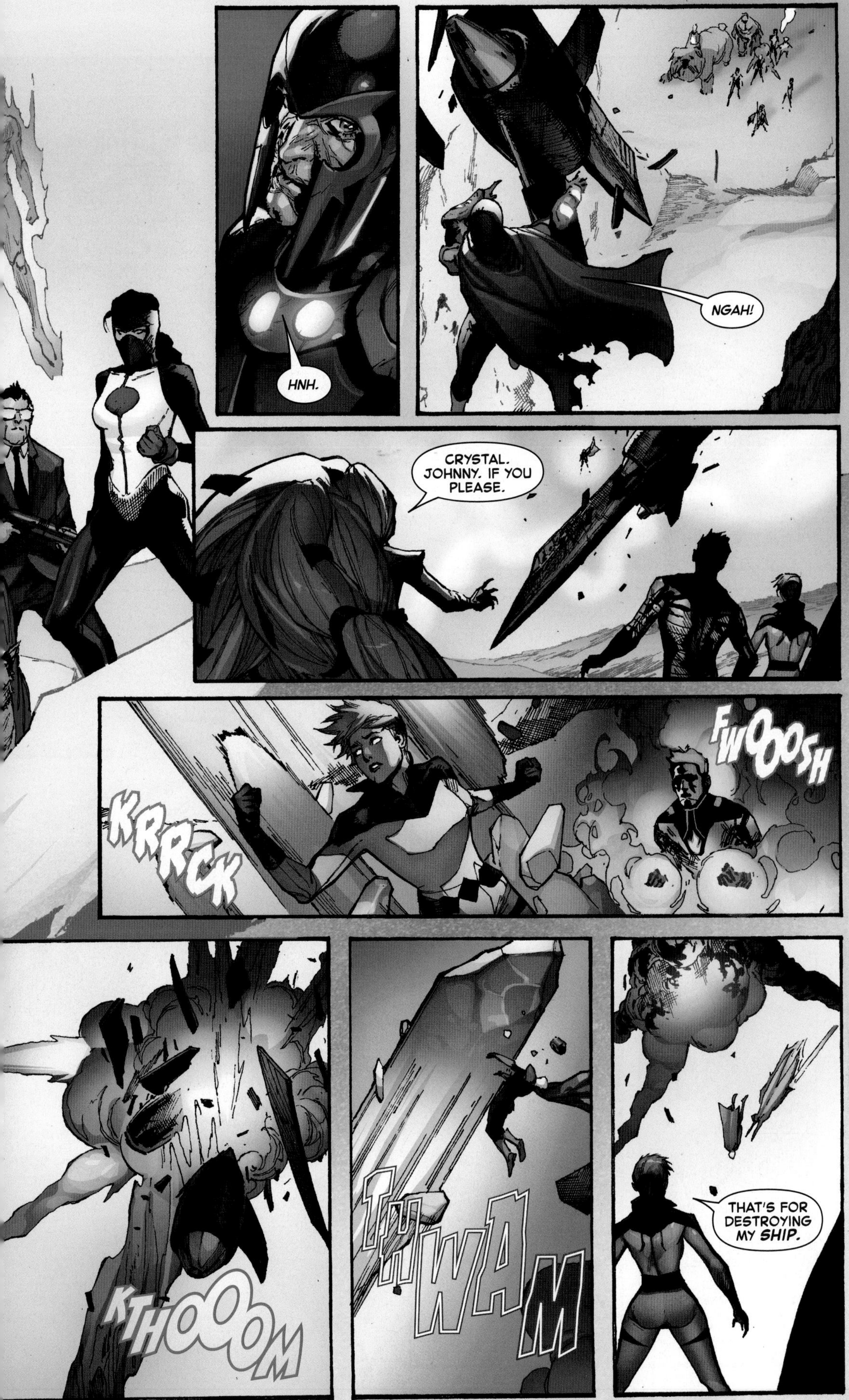
HNH.
NGAH!
CRYSTAL. JOHNNY. IF YOU PLEASE.
KRRRCK
FWOOOSH
KTHOOOOM
THWAM
THAT'S FOR DESTROYING MY SHIP.

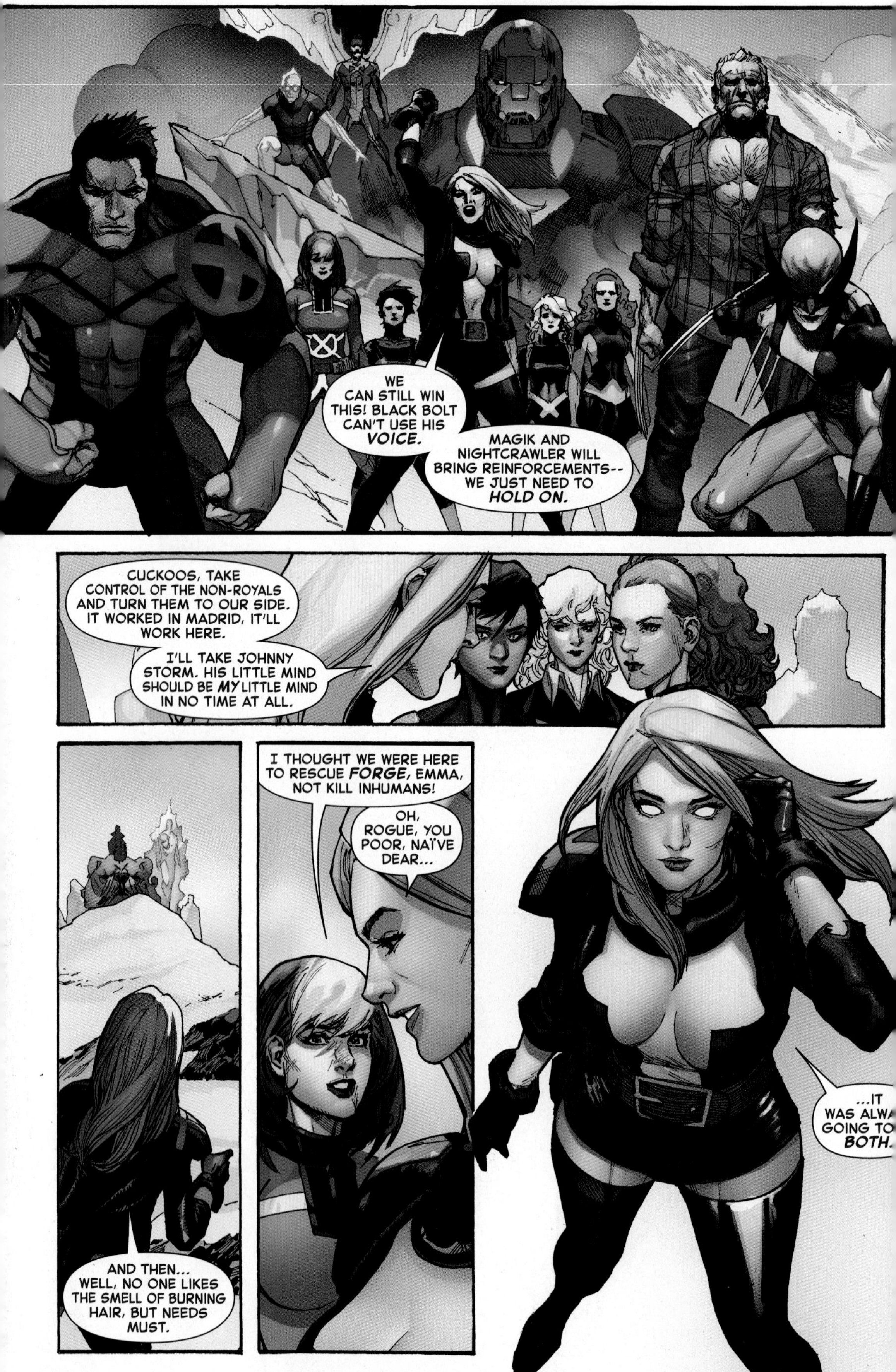
WE CAN STILL WIN THIS! BLACK BOLT CAN'T USE HIS VOICE.
MAGIK AND NIGHTCRAWLER WILL BRING REINFORCEMENTS-- WE JUST NEED TO HOLD ON.
CUCKOOS, TAKE CONTROL OF THE NON-ROYALS AND TURN THEM TO OUR SIDE. IT WORKED IN MADRID, IT'LL WORK HERE.
I'LL TAKE JOHNNY STORM. HIS LITTLE MIND SHOULD BE MY LITTLE MIND IN NO TIME AT ALL.
AND THEN... WELL, NO ONE LIKES THE SMELL OF BURNING HAIR, BUT NEEDS MUST.
I THOUGHT WE WERE HERE TO RESCUE FORGE, EMMA, NOT KILL INHUMANS!
OH, ROGUE, YOU POOR, NAÏVE DEAR...
...IT WAS ALWA GOING TO BOTH.

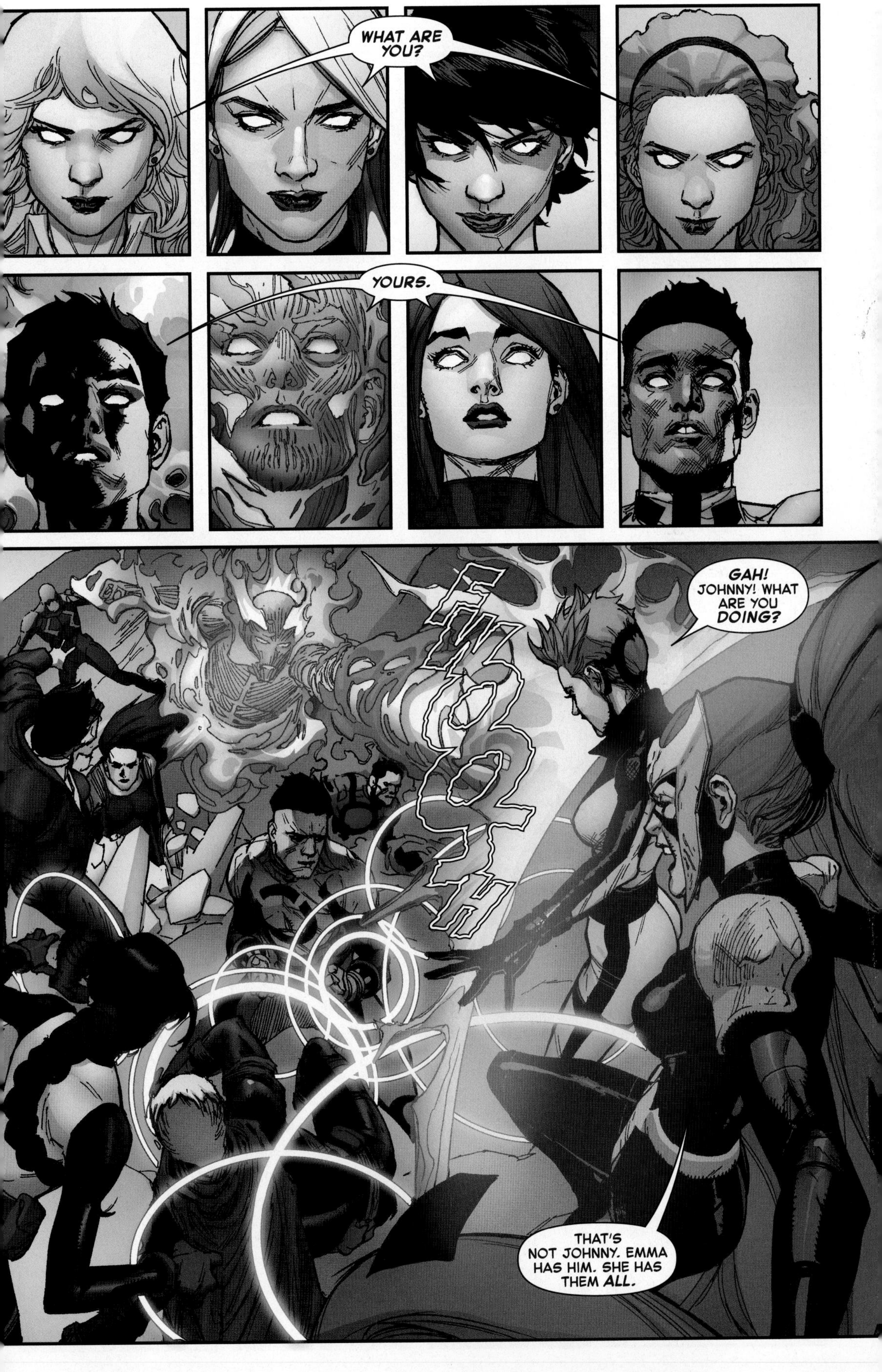
WHAT ARE YOU?
YOURS.
GAH! JOHNNY! WHAT ARE YOU DOING?
FWOOOSH
THAT'S NOT JOHNNY. EMMA HAS HIM. SHE HAS THEM ALL.

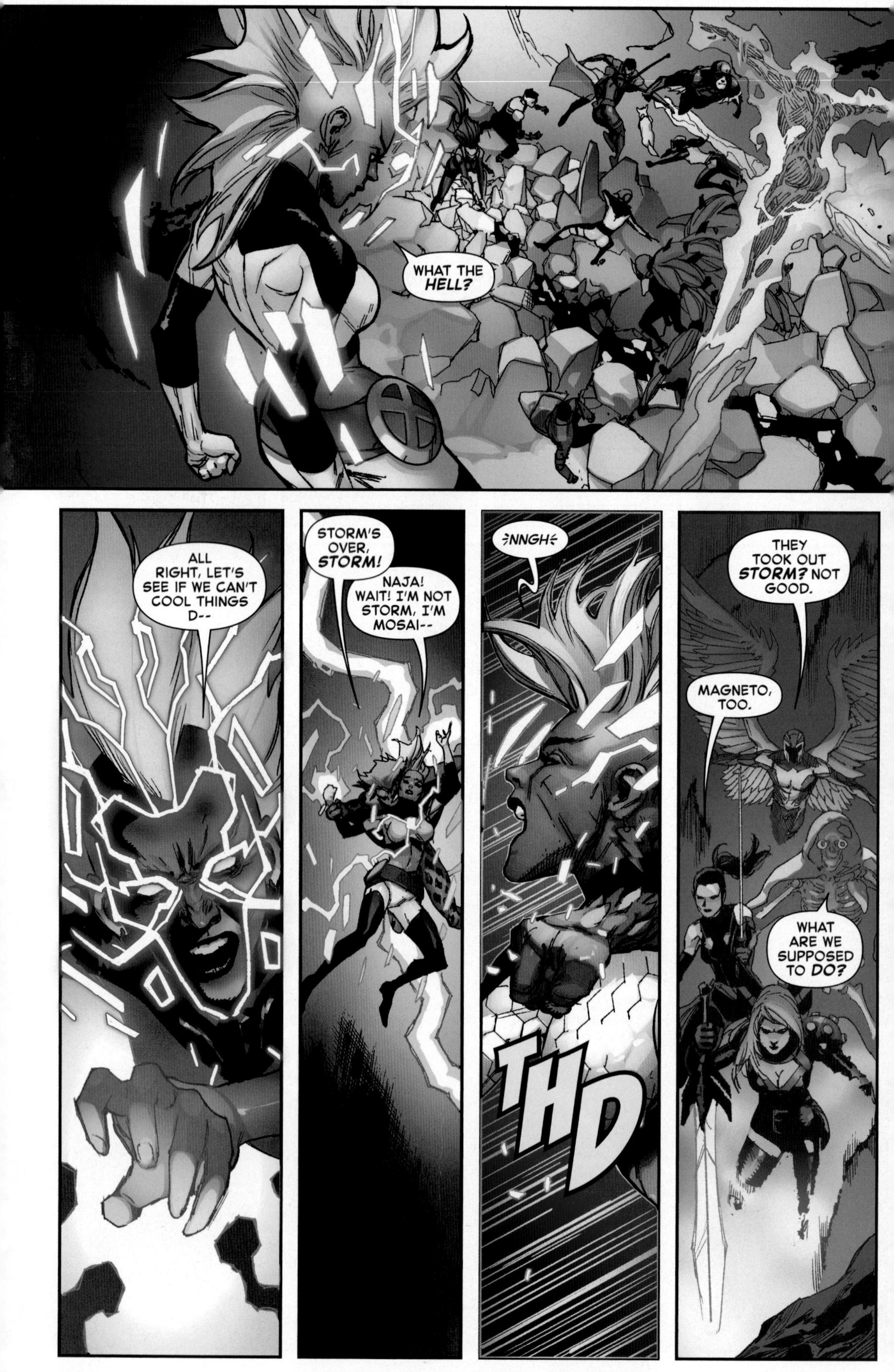
WHAT THE HELL?
ALL RIGHT, LET'S SEE IF WE CAN'T COOL THINGS D--
STORM'S OVER, STORM!
NAJA! WAIT! I'M NOT STORM, I'M MOSAI--
NNGH
THD
THEY TOOK OUT STORM? NOT GOOD.
MAGNETO, TOO.
WHAT ARE WE SUPPOSED TO DO?

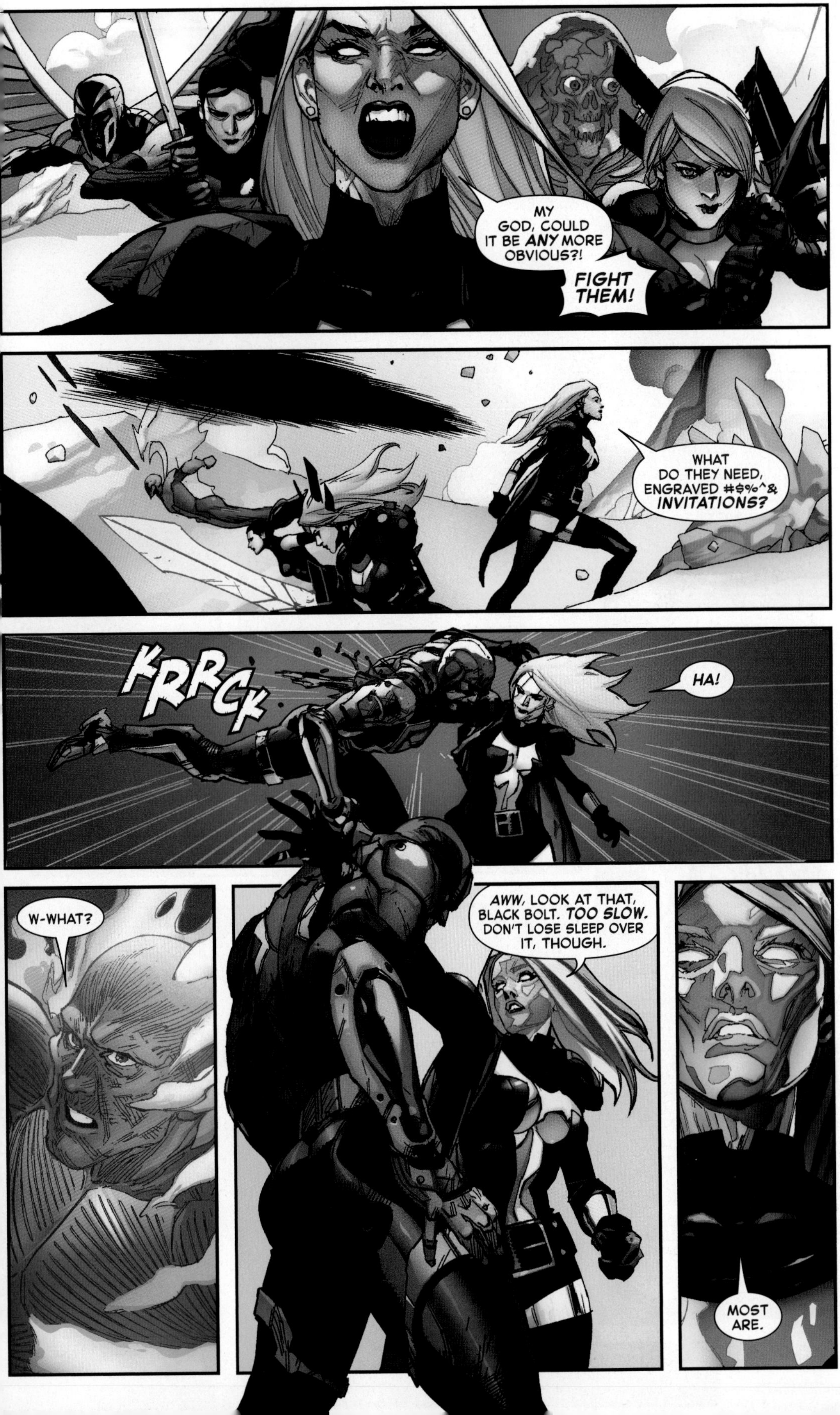

MY GOD, COULD IT BE ANY MORE OBVIOUS?!
FIGHT THEM!
WHAT DO THEY NEED, ENGRAVED #$%^& INVITATIONS?
KRRCK
HA!
W-WHAT?
AWW, LOOK AT THAT, BLACK BOLT. TOO SLOW. DON'T LOSE SLEEP OVER IT, THOUGH.
MOST ARE.

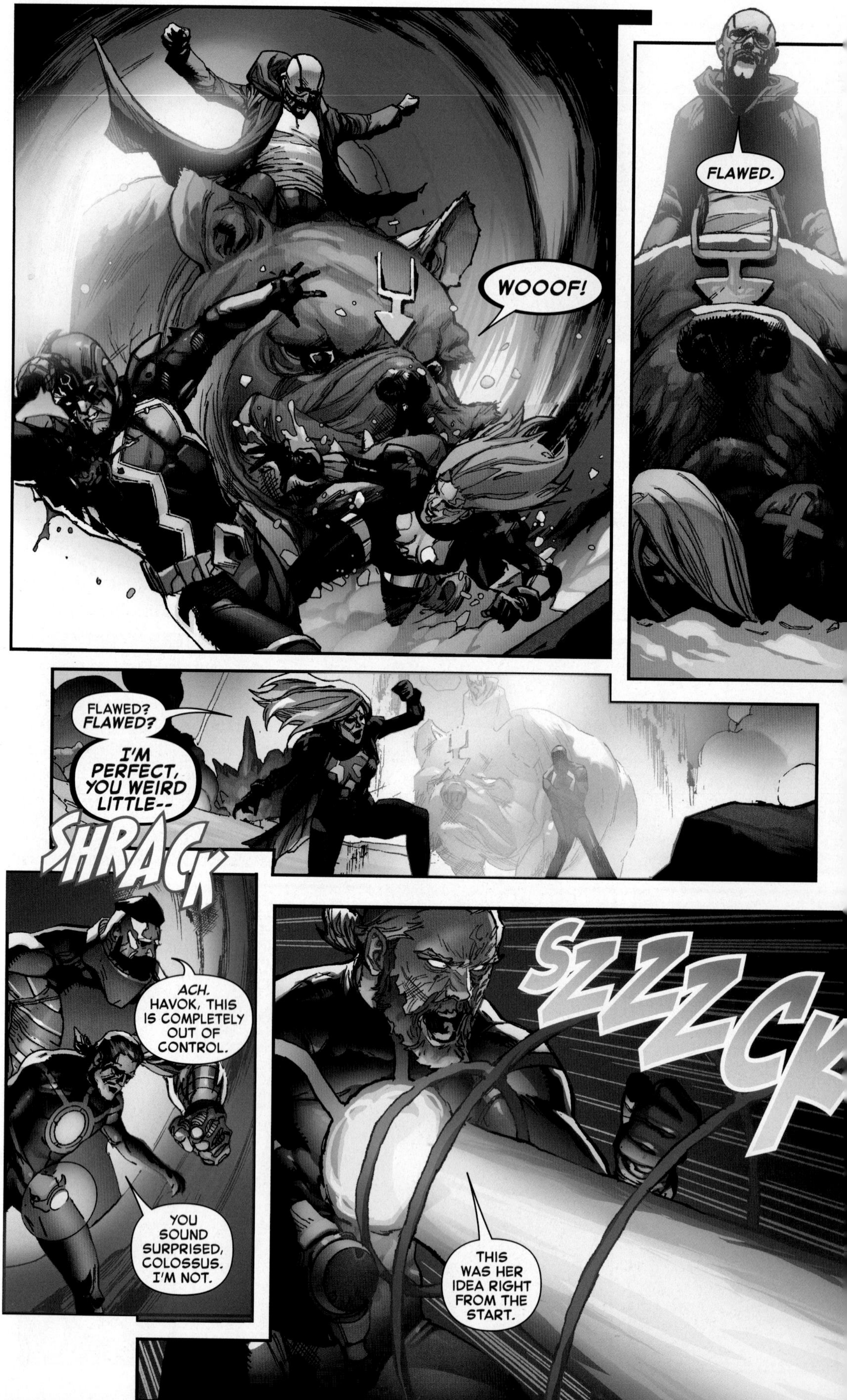
WOOOF!
FLAWED.
FLAWED? FLAWED?
I'M PERFECT, YOU WEIRD LITTLE--
SHRACK
ACH. HAVOK, THIS IS COMPLETELY OUT OF CONTROL.
YOU SOUND SURPRISED, COLOSSUS. I'M NOT.
SZZZCK
THIS WAS HER IDEA RIGHT FROM THE START.

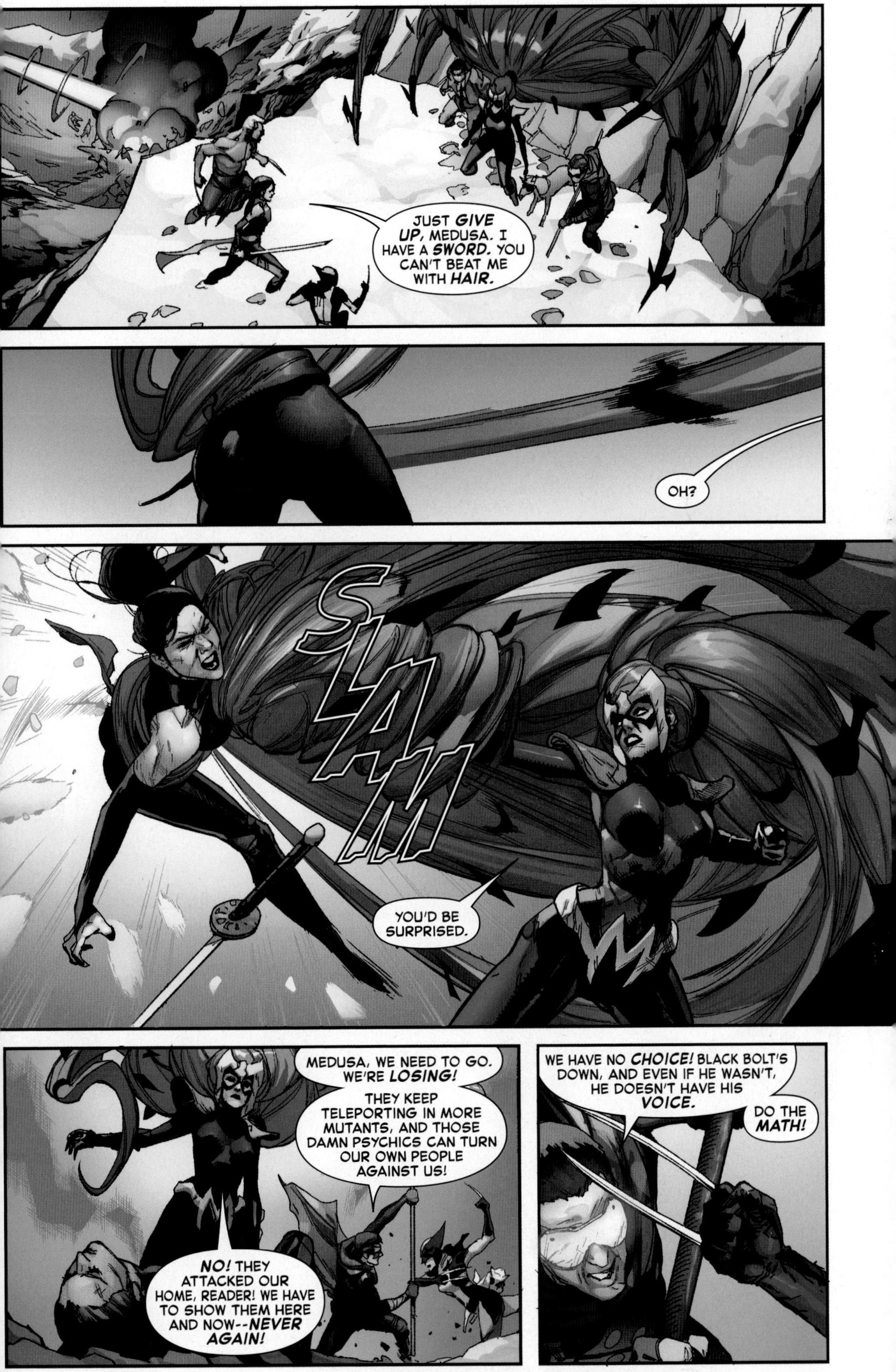

JUST GIVE UP, MEDUSA. I HAVE A SWORD. YOU CAN'T BEAT ME WITH HAIR.
OH?
SLAM
YOU'D BE SURPRISED.
MEDUSA, WE NEED TO GO. WE'RE LOSING!
THEY KEEP TELEPORTING IN MORE MUTANTS, AND THOSE DAMN PSYCHICS CAN TURN OUR OWN PEOPLE AGAINST US!
NO! THEY ATTACKED OUR HOME, READER! WE HAVE TO SHOW THEM HERE AND NOW--NEVER AGAIN!
WE HAVE NO CHOICE! BLACK BOLT'S DOWN, AND EVEN IF HE WASN'T, HE DOESN'T HAVE HIS VOICE.
DO THE MATH!

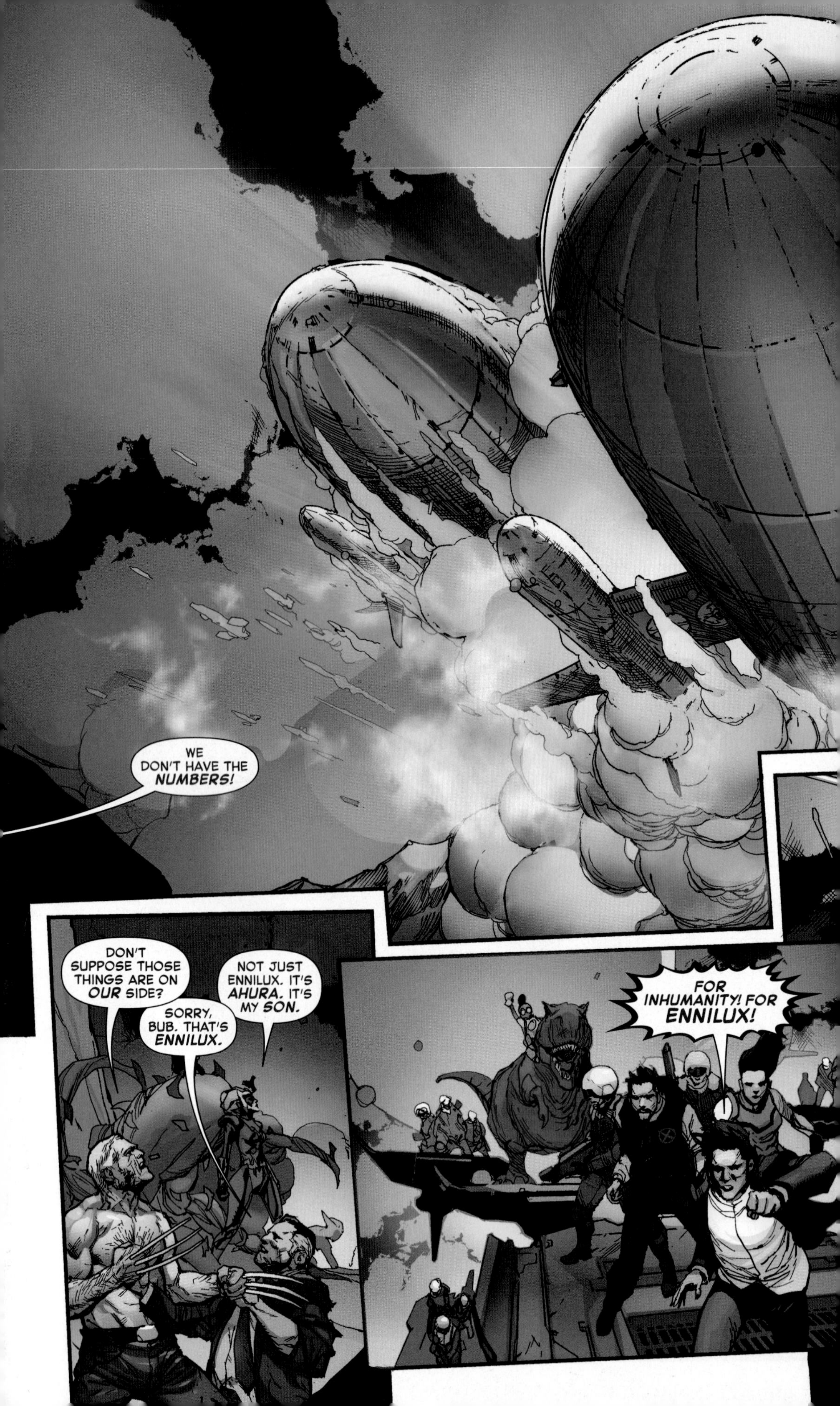
WE DON'T HAVE THE NUMBERS!
DON'T SUPPOSE THOSE THINGS ARE ON OUR SIDE?
SORRY, BUB. THAT'S ENNILUX.
NOT JUST ENNILUX. IT'S AHURA. IT'S MY SON.
FOR INHUMANITY! FOR ENNILUX!

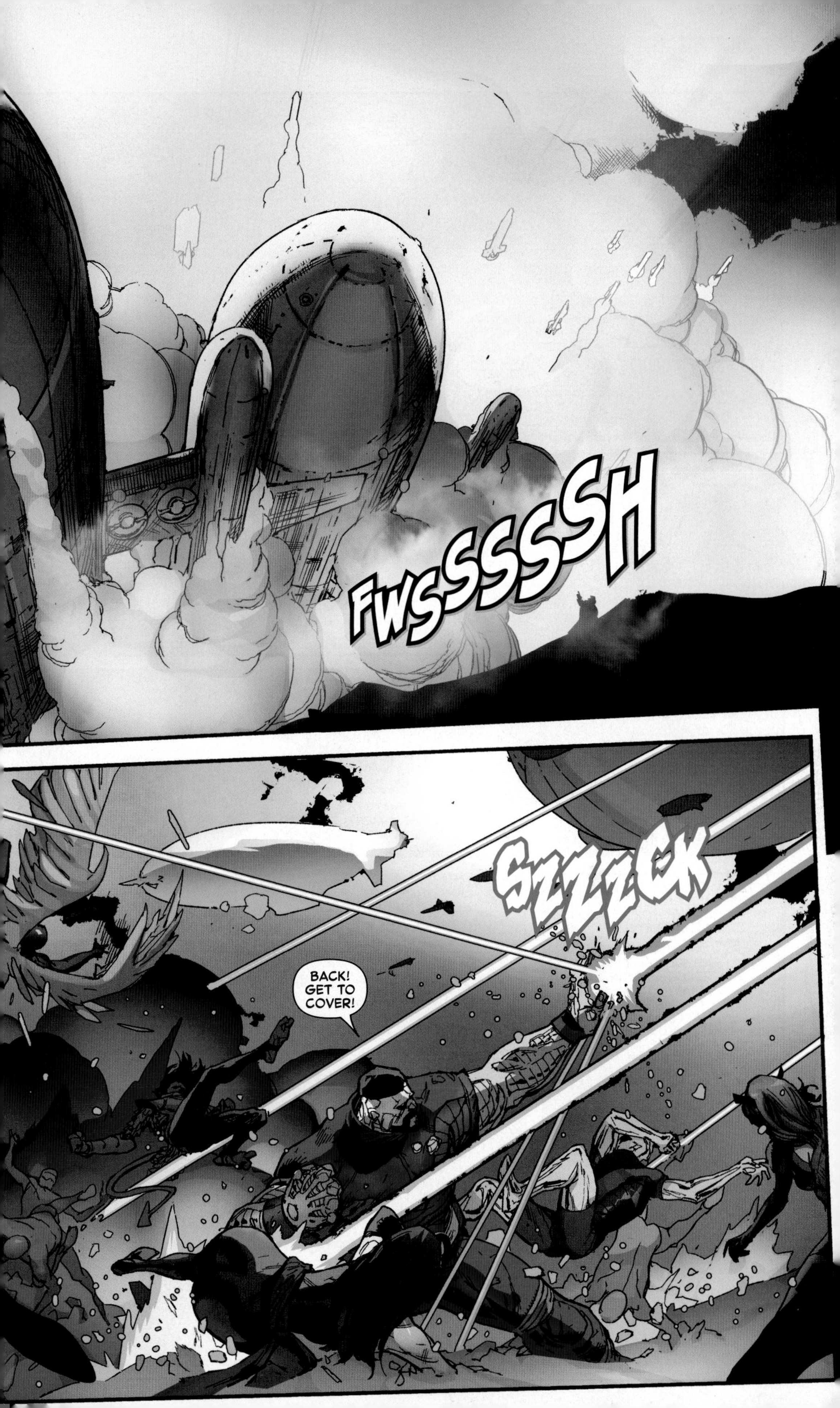
FWSSSSSH
SZZZCK
BACK! GET TO COVER!

HELLO, MOTHER.

AHURA-- THANK YOU. I... DIDN'T THINK YOU WOULD GET INVOLVED.

WHAT CONVINCED YOU TO FINALLY COMMIT ENNILUX TO THE INHUMAN CAUSE?

I ALMOST DIDN'T. I ASSUMED YOU AND FATHER COULD HANDLE YOURSELVES.

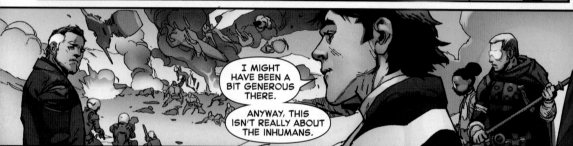

I MIGHT HAVE BEEN A BIT GENEROUS THERE.

ANYWAY, THIS ISN'T REALLY ABOUT THE INHUMANS.

IT'S ABOUT THEM.

WHAT? THE X-MEN? I DON'T--

MEDUSA, THIS ISN'T WHAT YOU THINK. THE MUTANTS DIDN'T ATTACK US FOR REVENGE--OR AT LEAST NOT COMPLETELY.

THE TERRIGEN SATURATION LEVELS ARE REACHING A CRITICAL POINT IN EARTH'S ATMOSPHERE. IF THEY CAN'T DESTROY THE CLOUD NOW, THEY'LL ALL DIE.

WHAT? WHY DIDN'T THEY JUST TELL US, ISO? WE WOULD HAVE FOUND A SOLUTION. IT DIDN'T HAVE TO BECOME...THIS.

THEY DIDN'T THINK THEY HAD TIME TO NEGOTIATE. THEY WEREN'T SURE YOU'D AGREE TO DESTROY THE CLOUD.

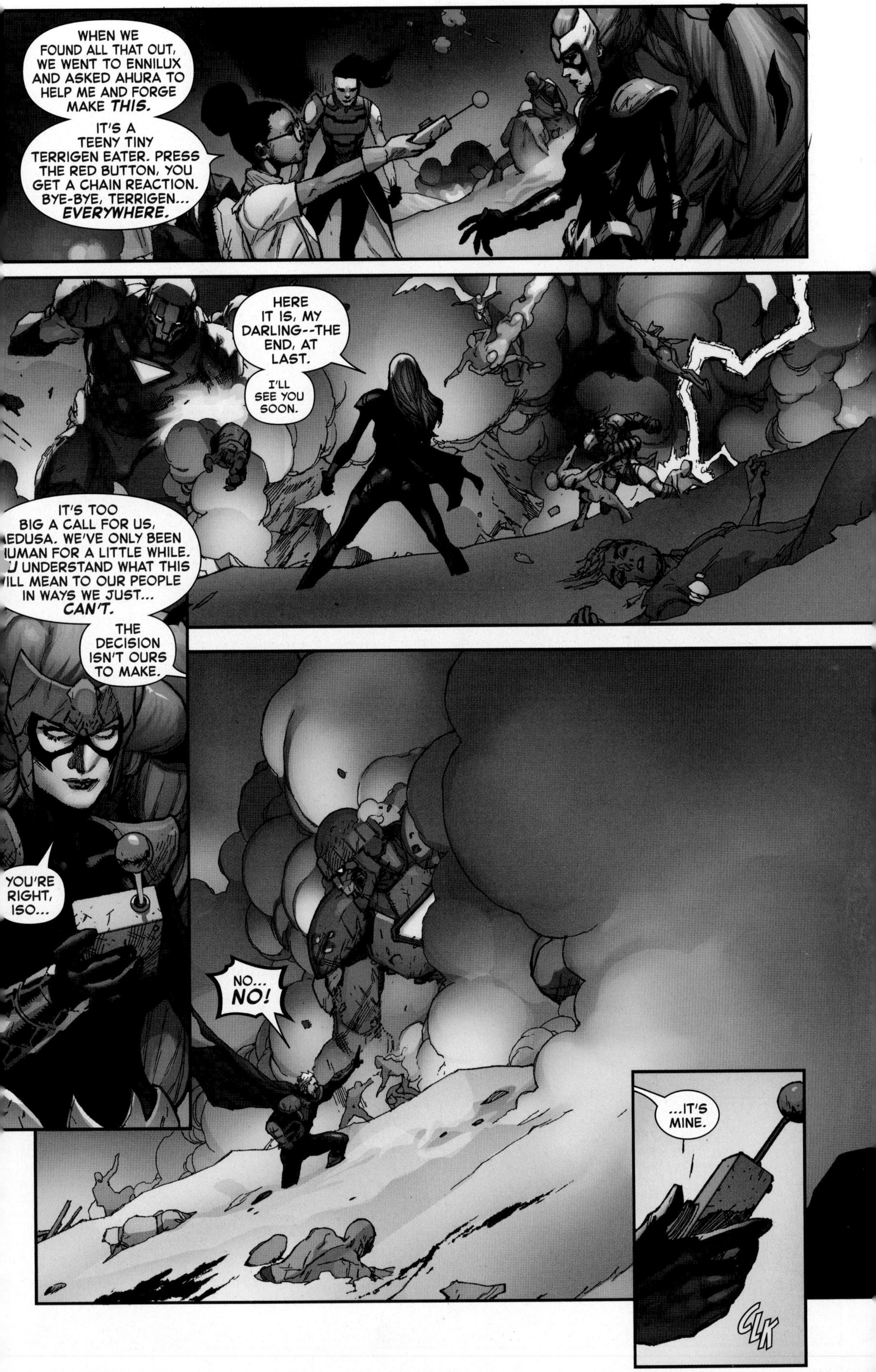
WHEN WE FOUND ALL THAT OUT, WE WENT TO ENNILUX AND ASKED AHURA TO HELP ME AND FORGE MAKE *THIS.*
IT'S A TEENY TINY TERRIGEN EATER. PRESS THE RED BUTTON, YOU GET A CHAIN REACTION. BYE-BYE, TERRIGEN... *EVERYWHERE.*
HERE IT IS, MY DARLING--THE END, AT LAST.
I'LL SEE YOU SOON.
IT'S TOO BIG A CALL FOR US, EDUSA. WE'VE ONLY BEEN UMAN FOR A LITTLE WHILE. U UNDERSTAND WHAT THIS ILL MEAN TO OUR PEOPLE IN WAYS WE JUST... *CAN'T.*
THE DECISION ISN'T OURS TO MAKE.
YOU'RE RIGHT, ISO...
NO... *NO!*
...IT'S MINE.
CLK

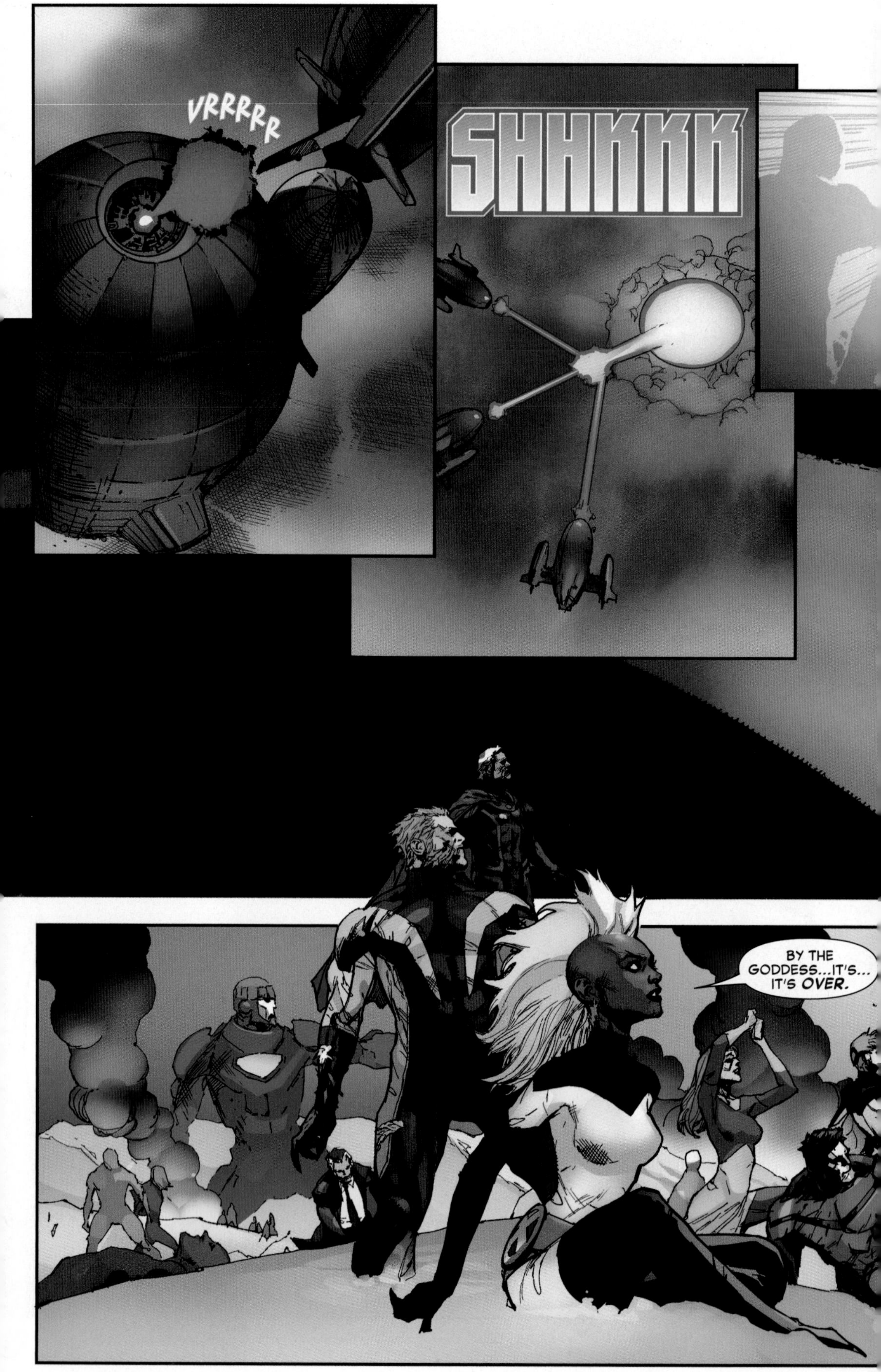
VRRRRR
SHKKKK
BY THE GODDESS...IT'S... IT'S OVER.

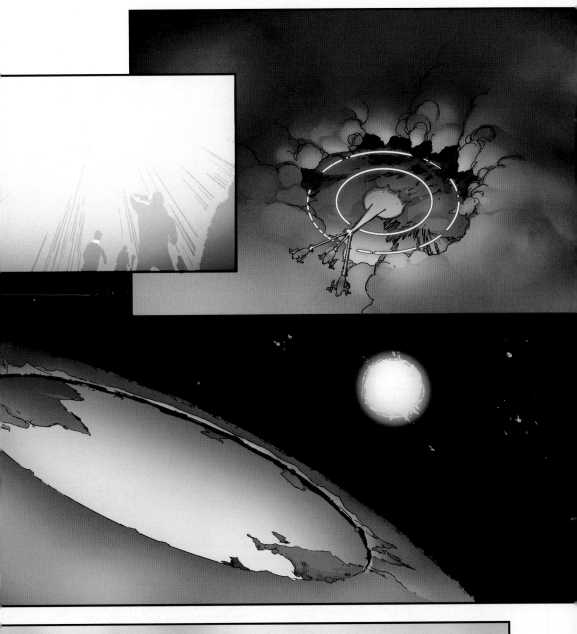

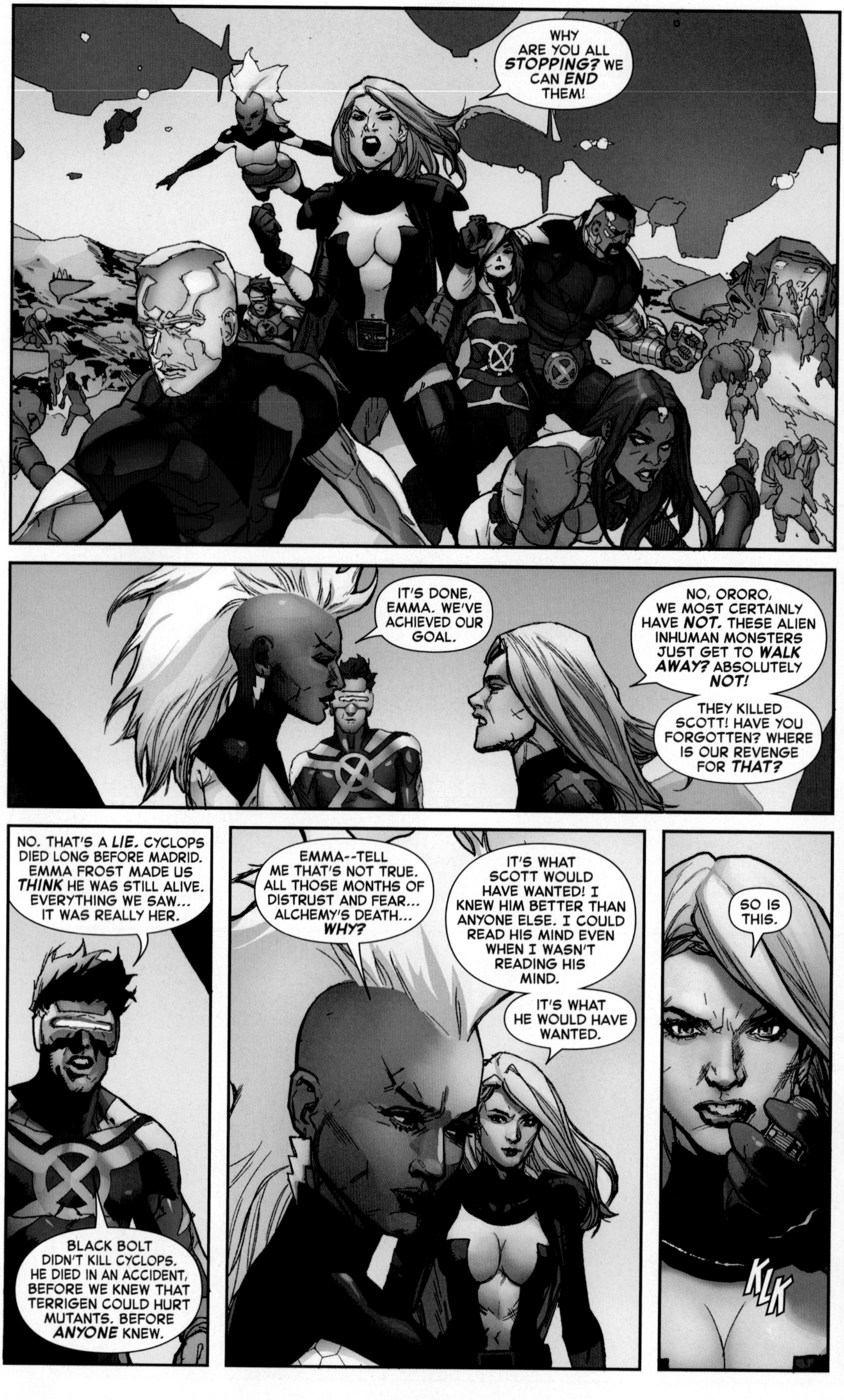

WHY ARE YOU ALL *STOPPING?* WE CAN *END* THEM!
IT'S DONE, EMMA. WE'VE ACHIEVED OUR GOAL.
NO, ORORO, WE MOST CERTAINLY HAVE *NOT.* THESE ALIEN INHUMAN MONSTERS JUST GET TO *WALK AWAY?* ABSOLUTELY *NOT!*
THEY KILLED SCOTT! HAVE YOU FORGOTTEN? WHERE IS OUR REVENGE FOR *THAT?*
NO. THAT'S A *LIE.* CYCLOPS DIED LONG BEFORE MADRID. EMMA FROST MADE US *THINK* HE WAS STILL ALIVE. EVERYTHING WE SAW... IT WAS REALLY HER.
BLACK BOLT DIDN'T KILL CYCLOPS. HE DIED IN AN ACCIDENT, BEFORE WE KNEW THAT TERRIGEN COULD HURT MUTANTS. BEFORE *ANYONE* KNEW.
EMMA--TELL ME THAT'S NOT TRUE. ALL THOSE MONTHS OF DISTRUST AND FEAR... ALCHEMY'S DEATH... *WHY?*
IT'S WHAT SCOTT WOULD HAVE WANTED! I KNEW HIM BETTER THAN ANYONE ELSE. I COULD READ HIS MIND EVEN WHEN I WASN'T READING HIS MIND.
IT'S WHAT HE WOULD HAVE WANTED.
SO IS THIS.
KLK

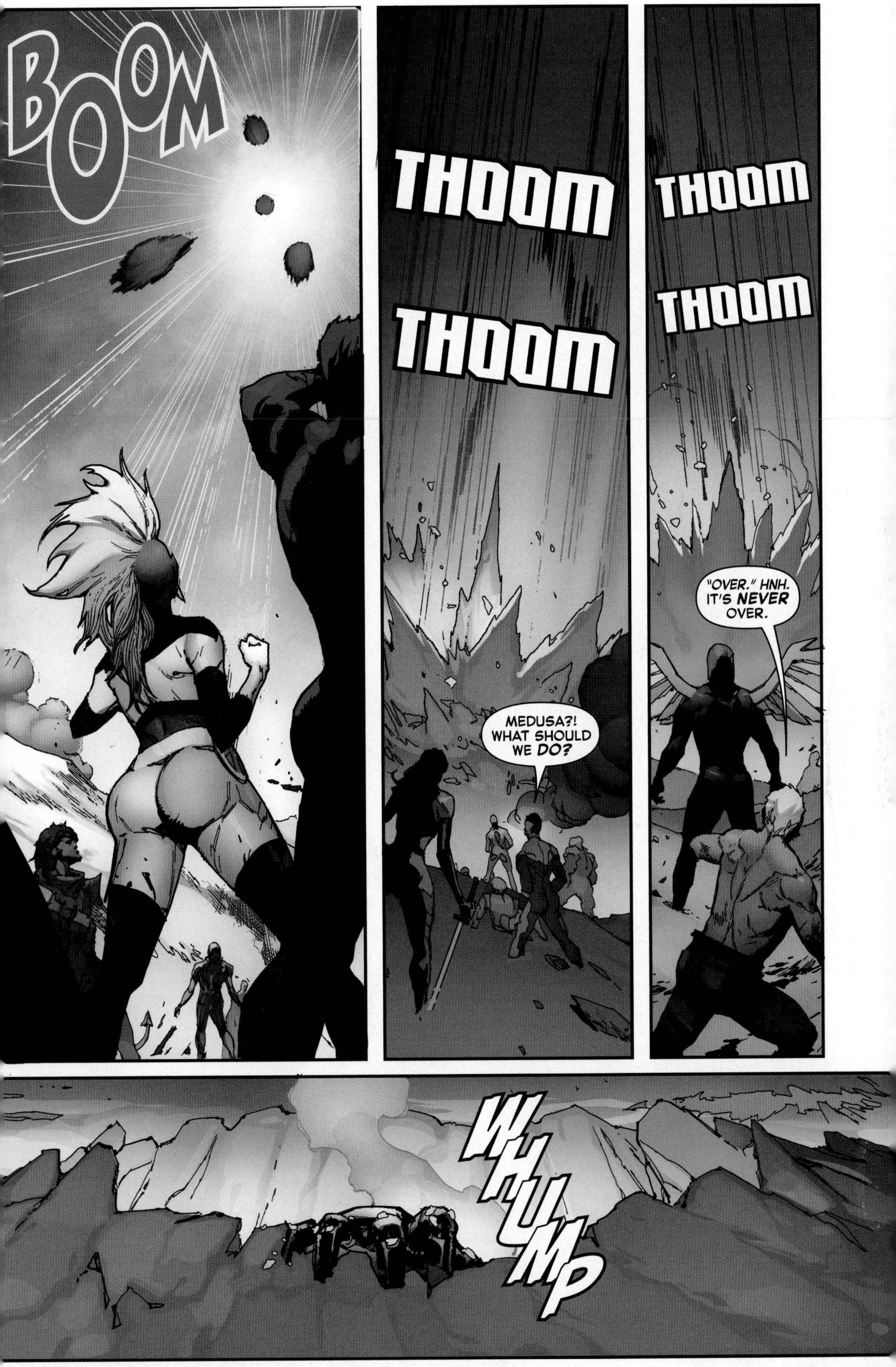
BOOM
THOOM
THOOM
MEDUSA?! WHAT SHOULD WE DO?
THOOM
THOOM
"OVER." HNH. IT'S NEVER OVER.
WHUMP

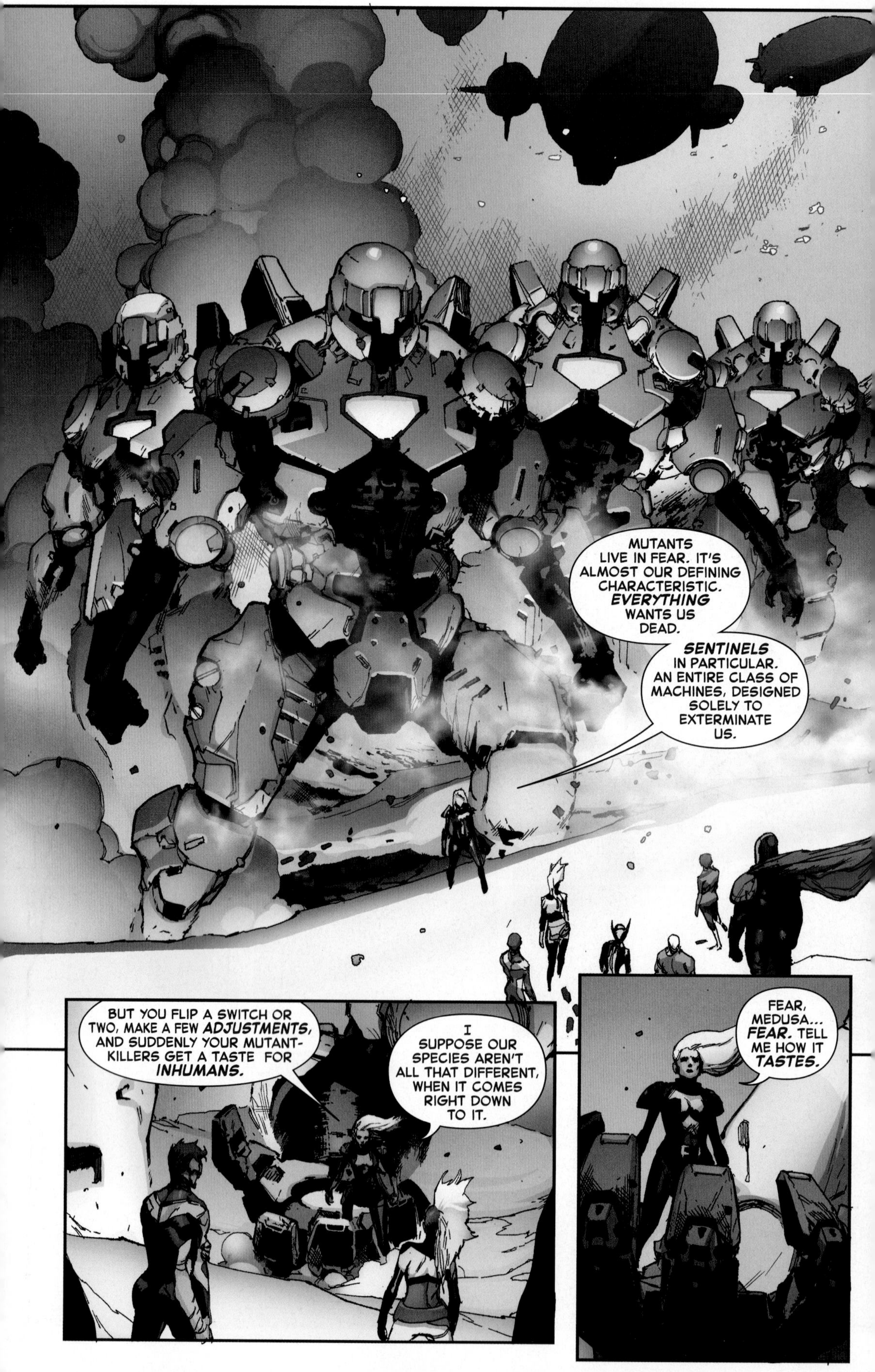
MUTANTS LIVE IN FEAR. IT'S ALMOST OUR DEFINING CHARACTERISTIC. EVERYTHING WANTS US DEAD.
SENTINELS IN PARTICULAR. AN ENTIRE CLASS OF MACHINES, DESIGNED SOLELY TO EXTERMINATE US.
BUT YOU FLIP A SWITCH OR TWO, MAKE A FEW ADJUSTMENTS, AND SUDDENLY YOUR MUTANT-KILLERS GET A TASTE FOR INHUMANS.
I SUPPOSE OUR SPECIES AREN'T ALL THAT DIFFERENT, WHEN IT COMES RIGHT DOWN TO IT.
FEAR, MEDUSA... FEAR. TELL ME HOW IT TASTES.

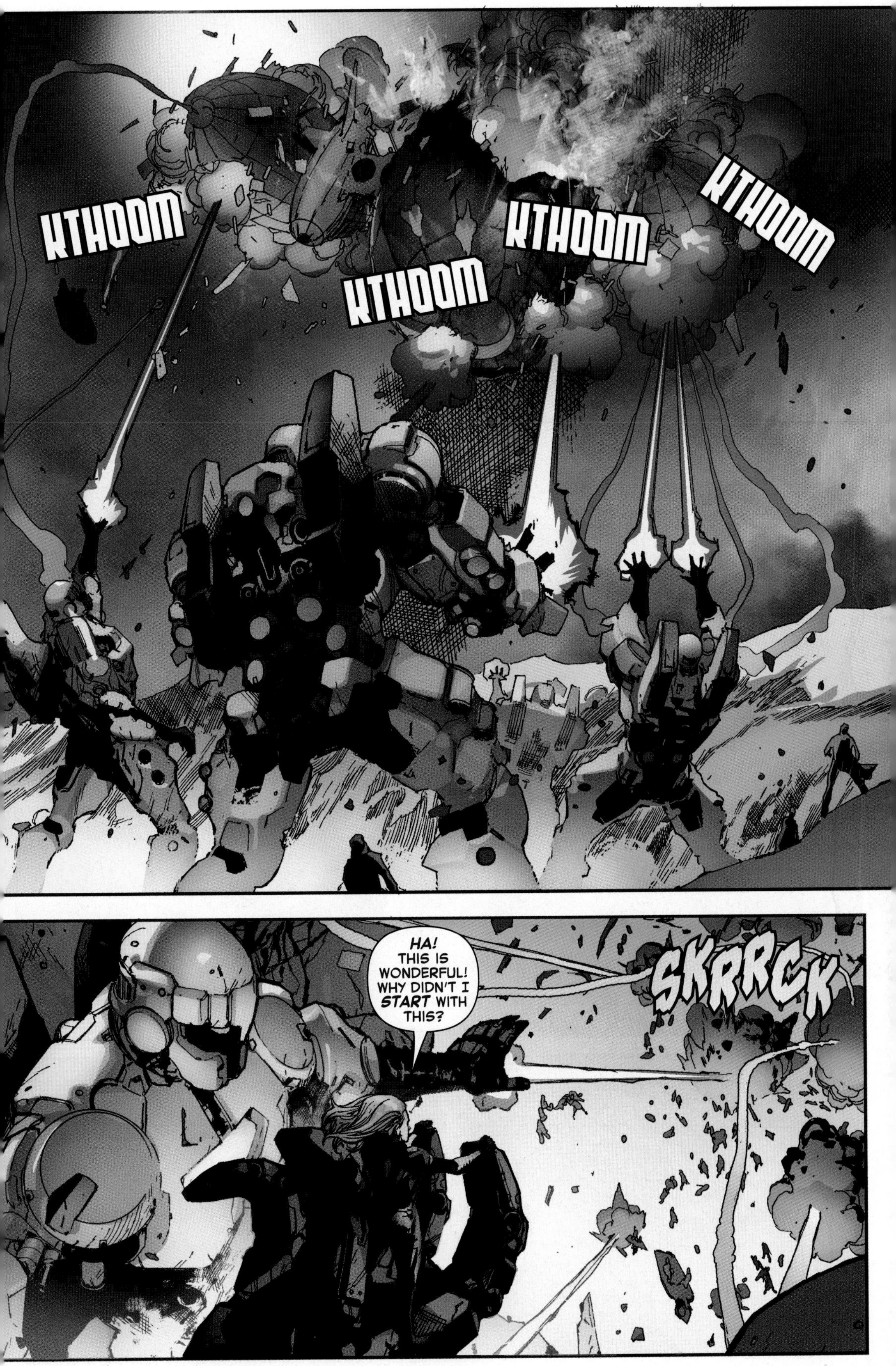
KTHOOM
KTHOOM
KTHOOM
KTHOOM
HA! THIS IS WONDERFUL! WHY DIDN'T I START WITH THIS?
SKRRCK

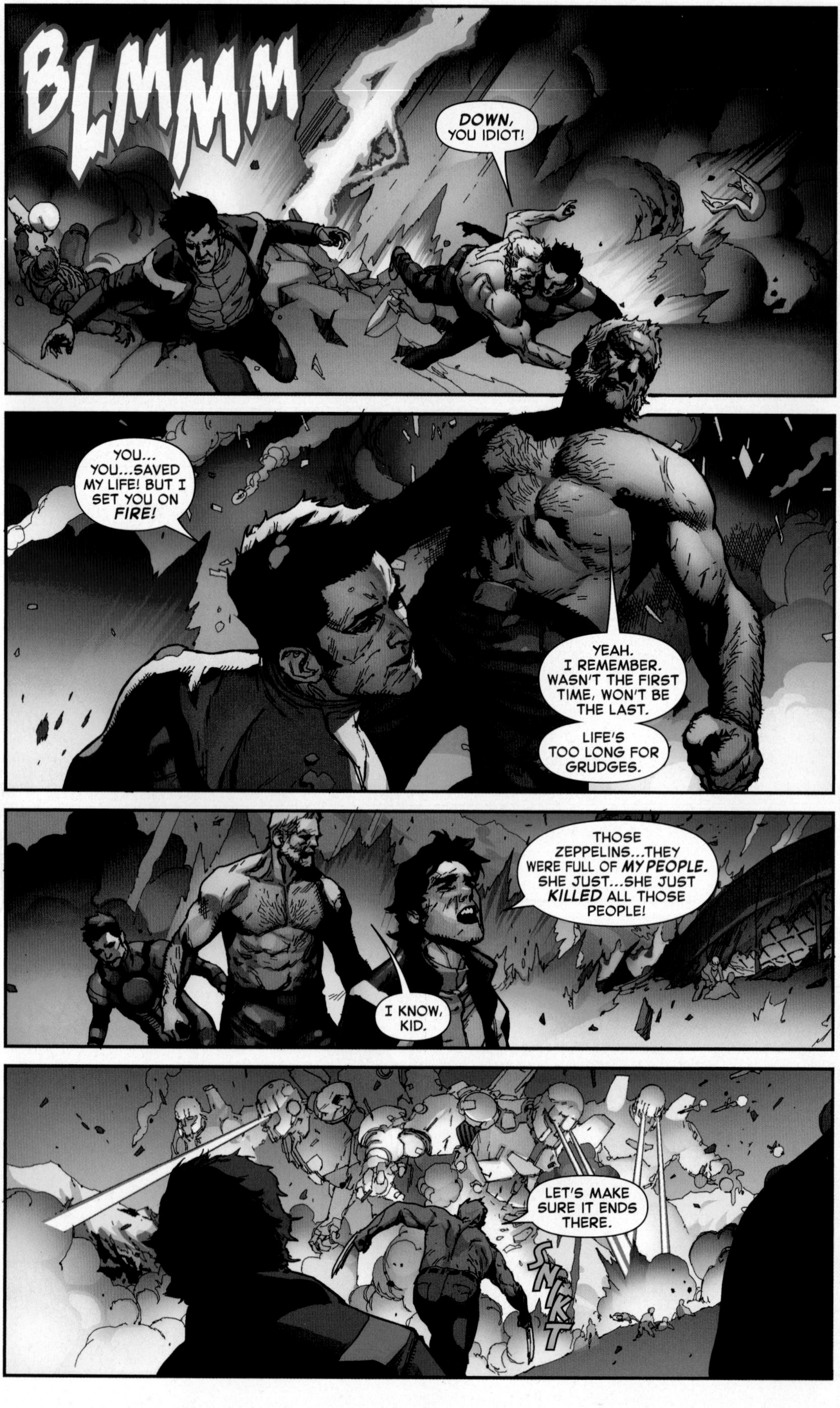
BLMMM
DOWN, YOU IDIOT!
YOU... YOU...SAVED MY LIFE! BUT I SET YOU ON FIRE!
YEAH. I REMEMBER. WASN'T THE FIRST TIME, WON'T BE THE LAST.
LIFE'S TOO LONG FOR GRUDGES.
THOSE ZEPPELINS...THEY WERE FULL OF MY PEOPLE. SHE JUST...SHE JUST KILLED ALL THOSE PEOPLE!
I KNOW, KID.
LET'S MAKE SURE IT ENDS THERE.
SNIKT

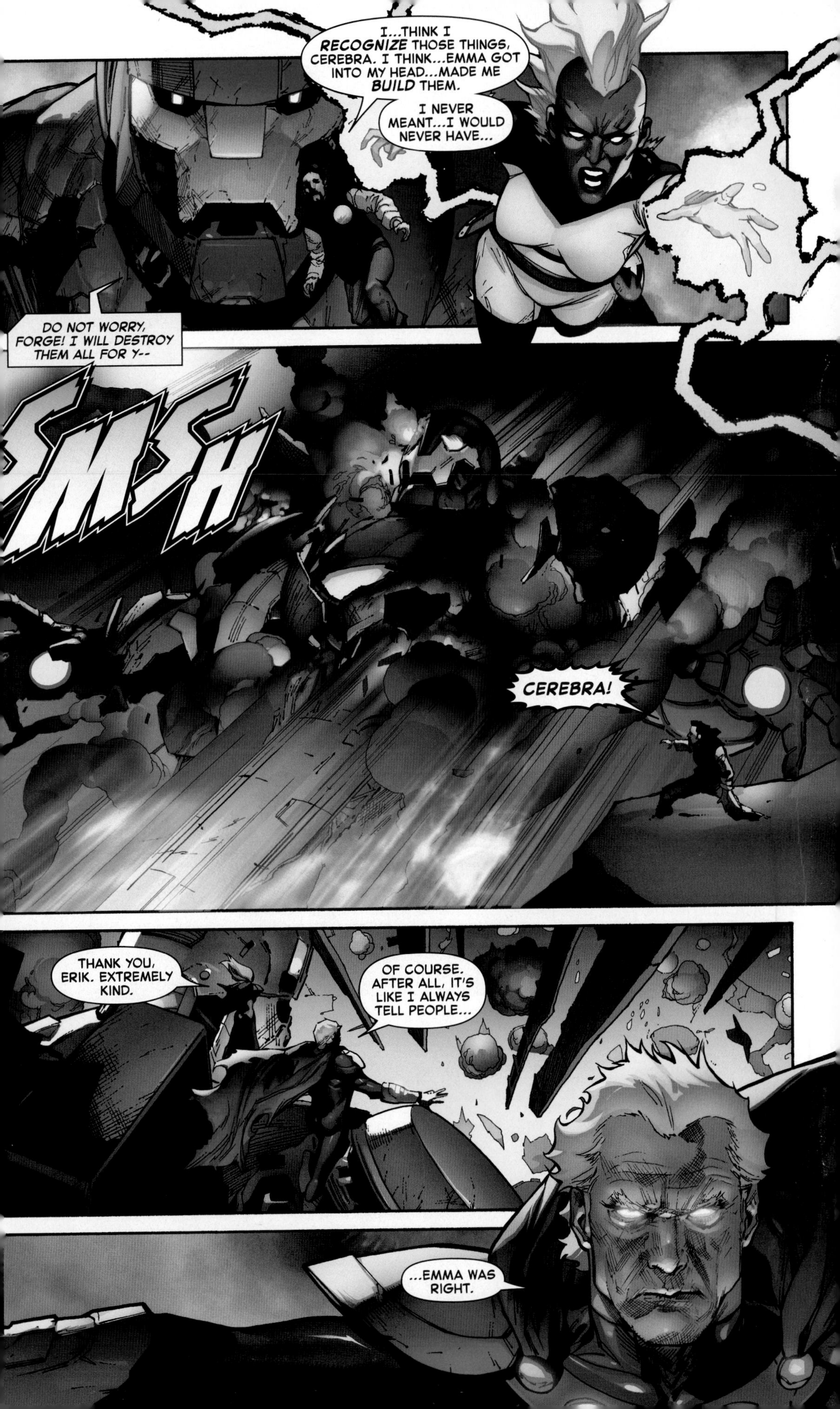
I...THINK I RECOGNIZE THOSE THINGS, CEREBRA. I THINK...EMMA GOT INTO MY HEAD...MADE ME BUILD THEM.
I NEVER MEANT...I WOULD NEVER HAVE...
DO NOT WORRY, FORGE! I WILL DESTROY THEM ALL FOR Y--
SMSH
CEREBRA!
THANK YOU, ERIK. EXTREMELY KIND.
OF COURSE. AFTER ALL, IT'S LIKE I ALWAYS TELL PEOPLE...
...EMMA WAS RIGHT.

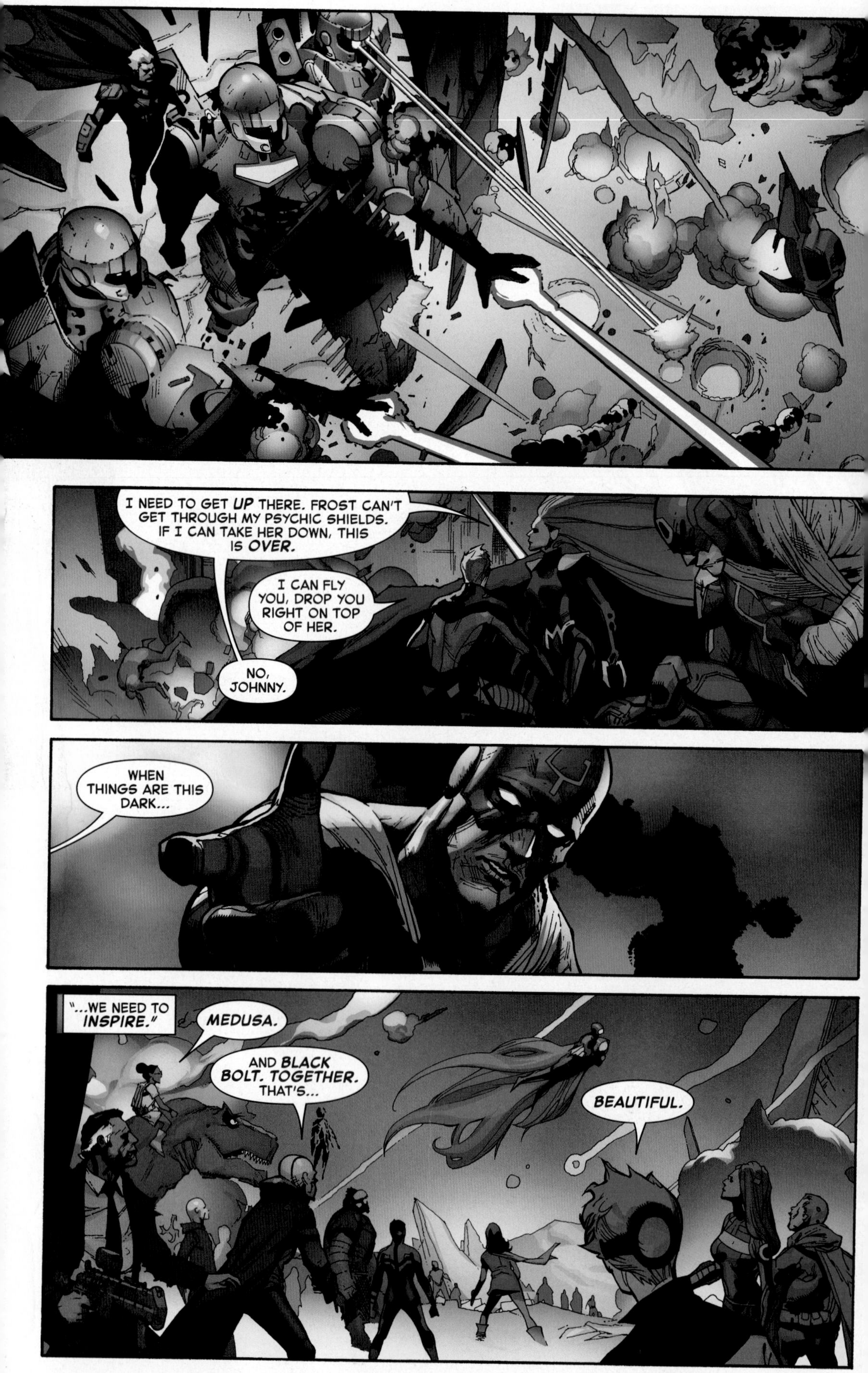
I NEED TO GET UP THERE. FROST CAN'T GET THROUGH MY PSYCHIC SHIELDS. IF I CAN TAKE HER DOWN, THIS IS OVER.
I CAN FLY YOU, DROP YOU RIGHT ON TOP OF HER.
NO, JOHNNY.
WHEN THINGS ARE THIS DARK...
"...WE NEED TO INSPIRE."
MEDUSA.
AND BLACK BOLT. TOGETHER. THAT'S...
BEAUTIFUL.

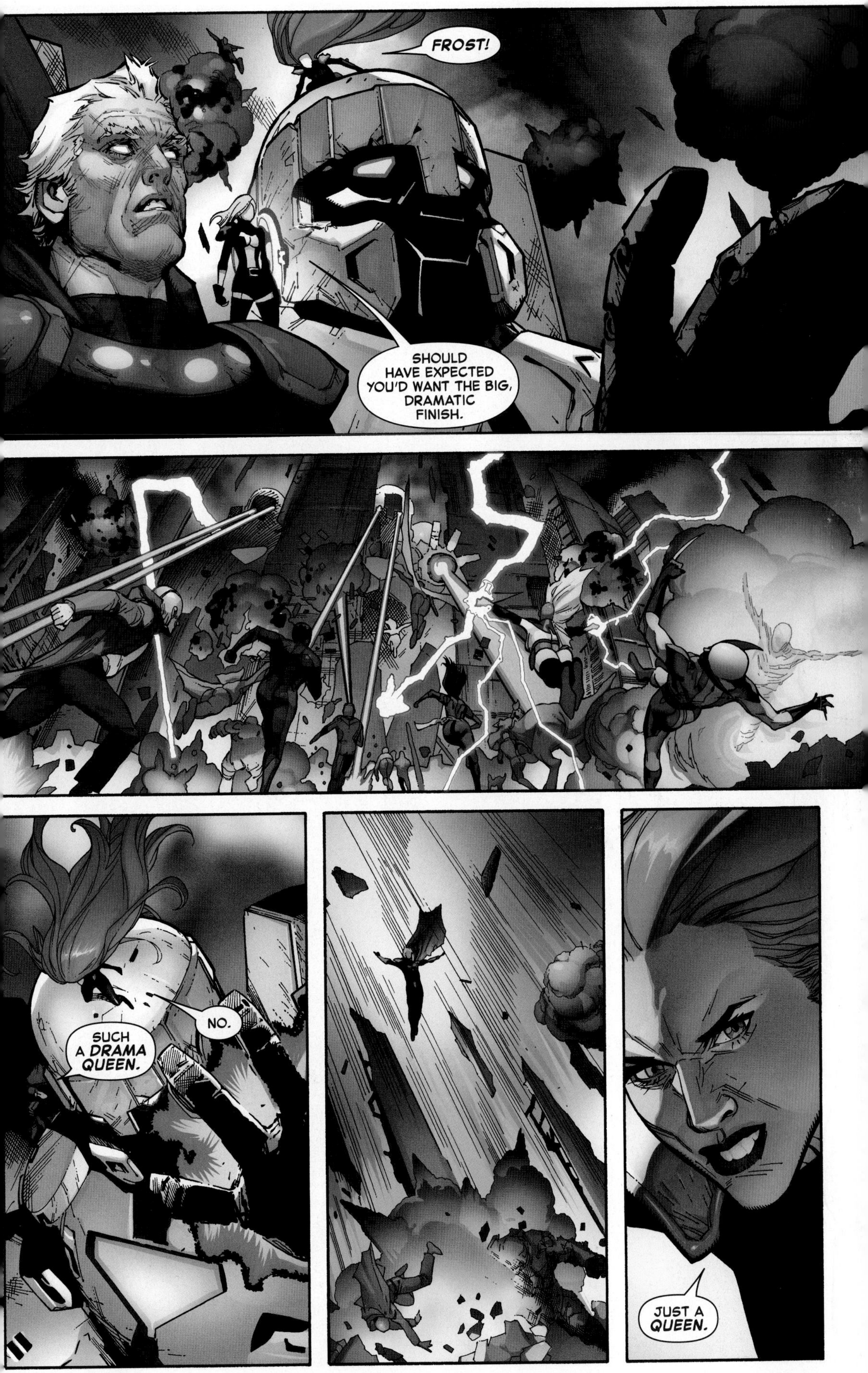
FROST!
SHOULD HAVE EXPECTED YOU'D WANT THE BIG, DRAMATIC FINISH.
SUCH A DRAMA QUEEN.
NO.
JUST A QUEEN.

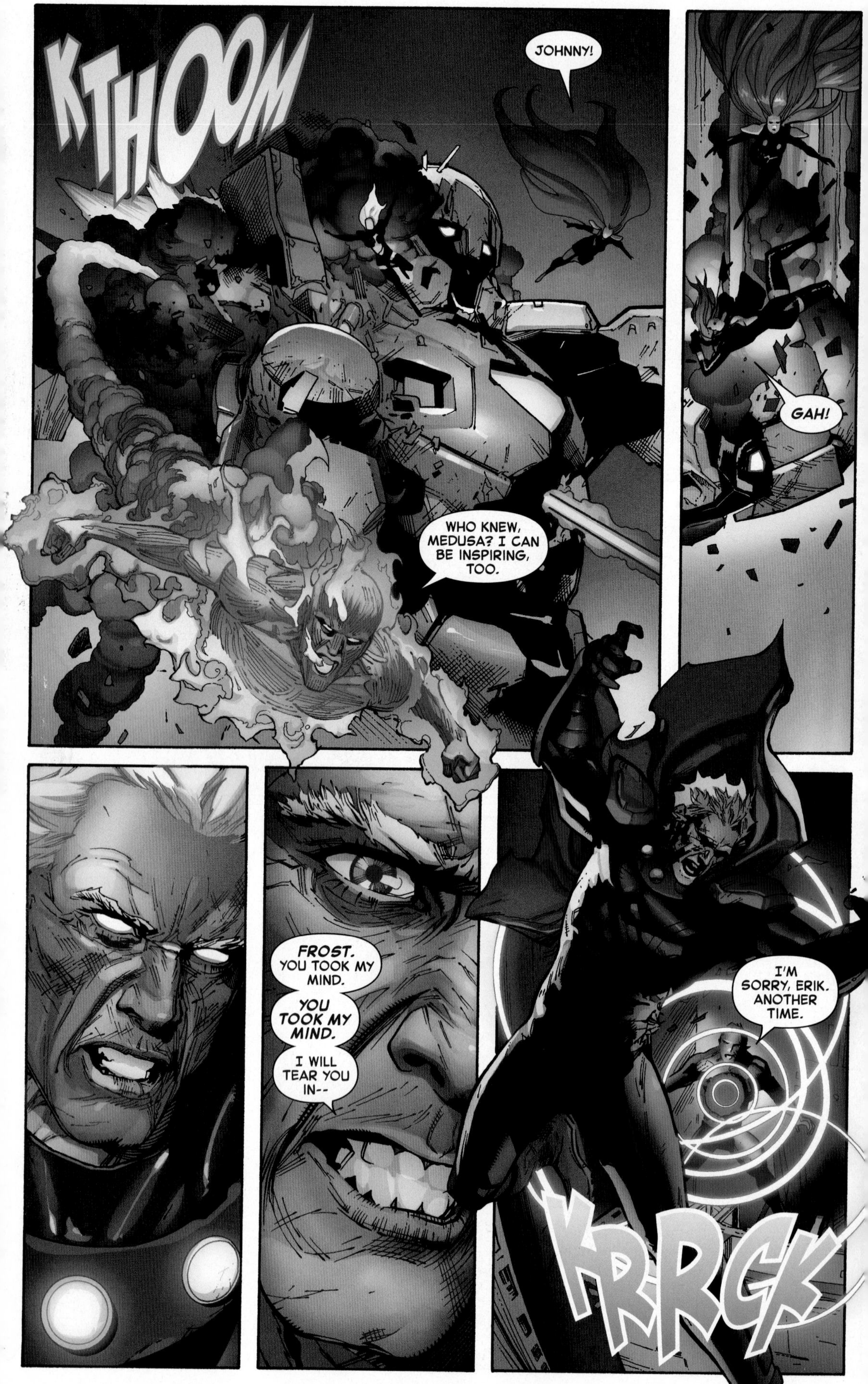
KTHOOM
JOHNNY!
GAH!
WHO KNEW, MEDUSA? I CAN BE INSPIRING, TOO.
FROST. YOU TOOK MY MIND.
YOU TOOK MY MIND.
I WILL TEAR YOU IN--
I'M SORRY, ERIK. ANOTHER TIME.
KRRCK

YOU GAVE THE ORDER. *YOU TOLD BLACK BOLT TO KILL SCOTT.*

I WAS IN YOUR HEAD, REMEMBER? I SAW WHAT YOU WERE THINKING-- THAT IT WOULD BE SO MUCH *SIMPLER* IF CYCLOPS WAS DEAD...

KZZZZCK

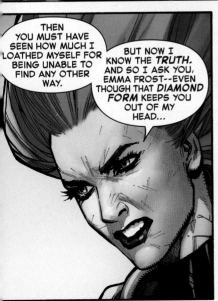

THEN YOU MUST HAVE SEEN HOW MUCH I LOATHED MYSELF FOR BEING UNABLE TO FIND ANY OTHER WAY.

BUT NOW I KNOW THE *TRUTH.* AND SO I ASK YOU, EMMA FROST--EVEN THOUGH THAT *DIAMOND FORM* KEEPS YOU OUT OF MY HEAD...

KRRCK

...WHAT AM I THINKING *RIGHT NOW?*

ARRGH!

TNK

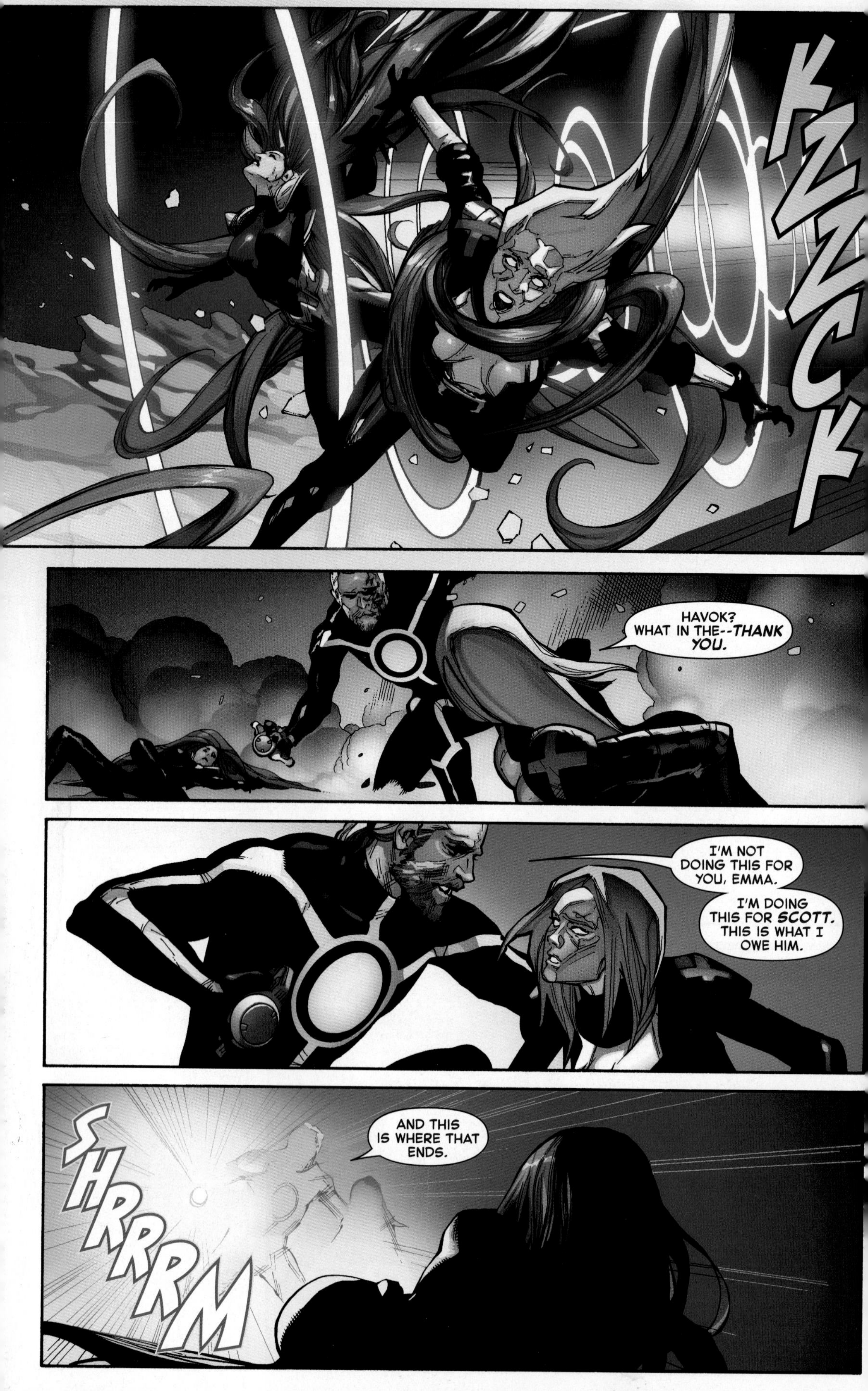
KZZZCK
HAVOK? WHAT IN THE--THANK YOU.
I'M NOT DOING THIS FOR YOU, EMMA.
I'M DOING THIS FOR SCOTT. THIS IS WHAT I OWE HIM.
AND THIS IS WHERE THAT ENDS.
SHRRRM

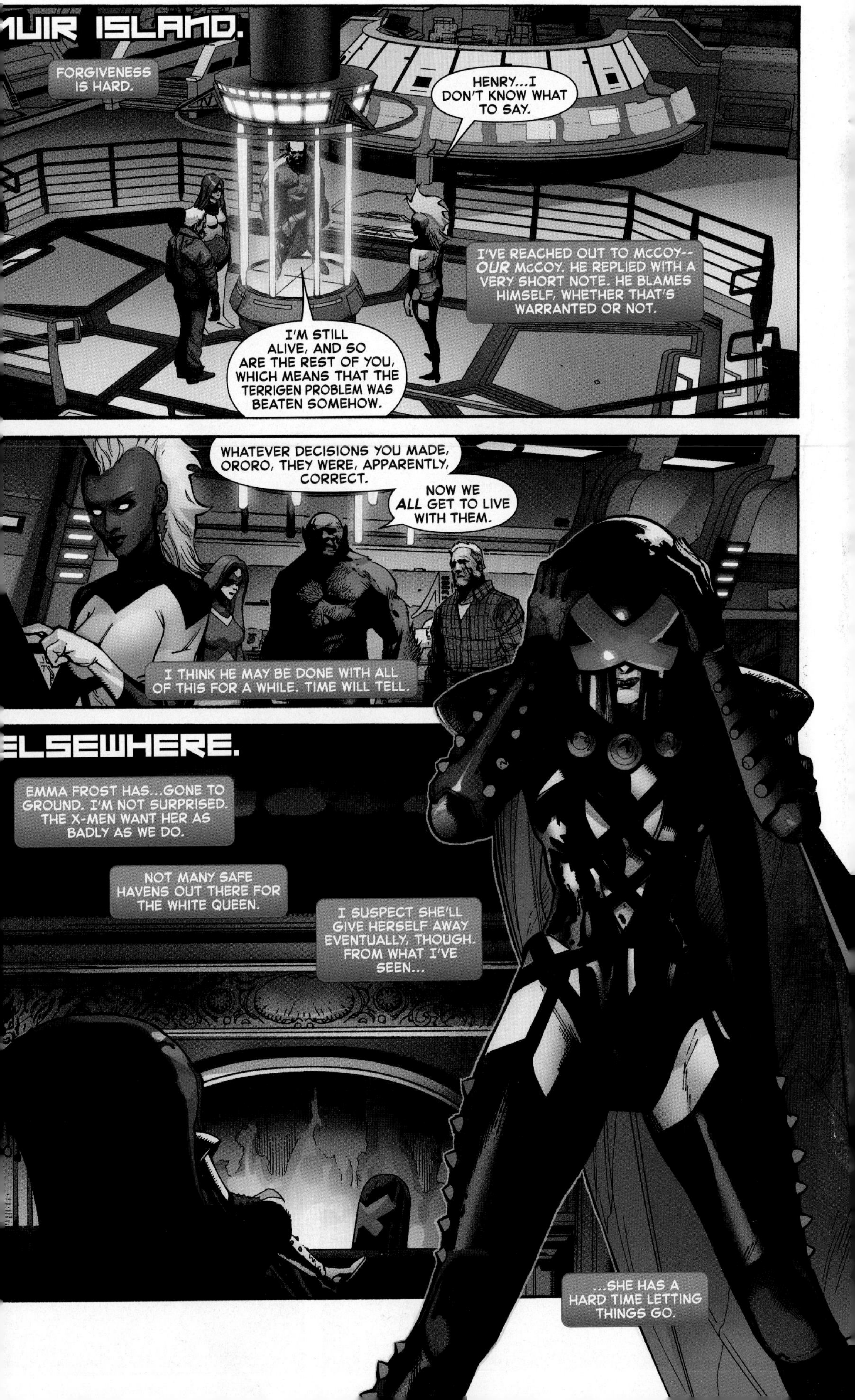

MUIR ISLAND.
FORGIVENESS IS HARD.
HENRY...I DON'T KNOW WHAT TO SAY.
I'VE REACHED OUT TO McCOY-- OUR McCOY. HE REPLIED WITH A VERY SHORT NOTE. HE BLAMES HIMSELF, WHETHER THAT'S WARRANTED OR NOT.
I'M STILL ALIVE, AND SO ARE THE REST OF YOU, WHICH MEANS THAT THE TERRIGEN PROBLEM WAS BEATEN SOMEHOW.
WHATEVER DECISIONS YOU MADE, ORORO, THEY WERE, APPARENTLY, CORRECT.
NOW WE ALL GET TO LIVE WITH THEM.
I THINK HE MAY BE DONE WITH ALL OF THIS FOR A WHILE. TIME WILL TELL.
ELSEWHERE.
EMMA FROST HAS...GONE TO GROUND. I'M NOT SURPRISED. THE X-MEN WANT HER AS BADLY AS WE DO.
NOT MANY SAFE HAVENS OUT THERE FOR THE WHITE QUEEN.
I SUSPECT SHE'LL GIVE HERSELF AWAY EVENTUALLY, THOUGH. FROM WHAT I'VE SEEN...
...SHE HAS A HARD TIME LETTING THINGS GO.

AND THEN THERE'S ME.

THERE IS NO QUESTION IN MY MIND THAT I DID THE RIGHT THING.

OUR SPECIES' ABILITY TO TRANSFORM THROUGH TERRIGENESIS DOES NOT OUTWEIGH THE LIVES OF EVEN A SINGLE MUTANT, MUCH LESS *ALL* OF THEM.

MANY INHUMANS DID NOT UNDERSTAND. *YEARS* SPEN[T] TELLING THEIR CHILDREN OF THE GLORY OF EMERGENCE INTO THEIR TRUE FORMS...

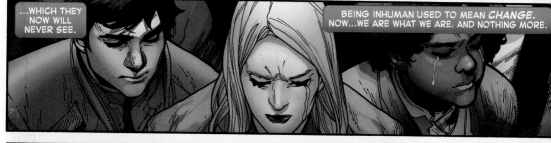

...WHICH THEY NOW WILL NEVER SEE.

BEING INHUMAN USED TO MEAN *CHANGE.* NOW...WE ARE WHAT WE ARE, AND NOTHING MORE.

IT HAD TO BE DONE, AND THE WEIGHT OF IT HAD TO LAND ON ME. I AM THE QUEEN.

OR...I WAS. I *ABDICATED.*

I GAVE *ISO* MY AUTHORITY OVER NEW ATTILAN. SHE HAS EARNED THE PEOPLE'S TRUST.

SHE WILL GOVERN WELL. ALTHOUGH, SHE SAID SOMETHING TO ME ABOUT HOLDING *ELECTIONS,* IF YOU CAN BELIEVE THAT.

ELECTIONS! THE FIRST IN ATTILAN IN TWO HUNDRED CENTURIES.

PERHAPS THE INHUMANS ARE NOT FINISHED WITH CHANGE AFTER ALL.

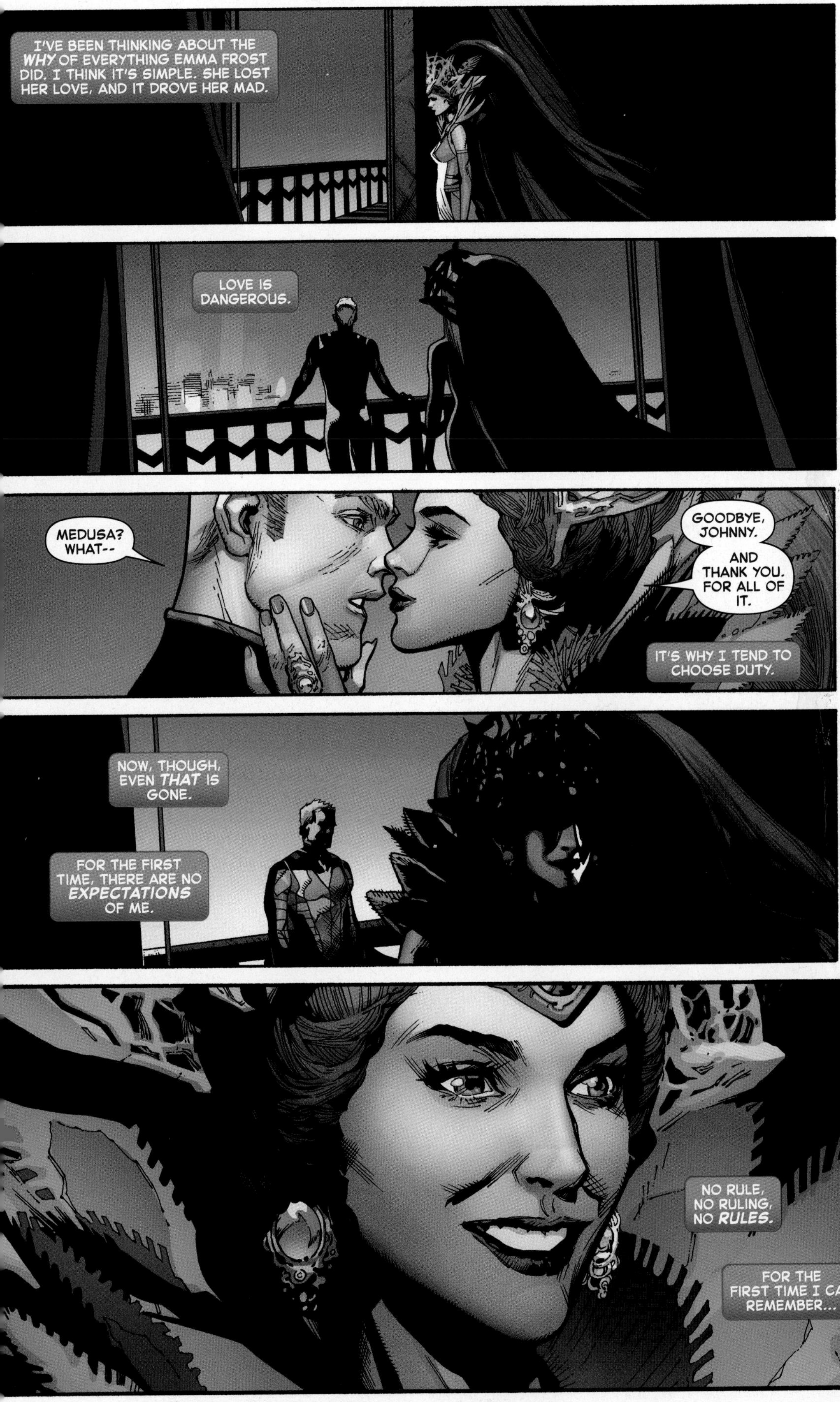
I'VE BEEN THINKING ABOUT THE *WHY* OF EVERYTHING EMMA FROST DID. I THINK IT'S SIMPLE. SHE LOST HER LOVE, AND IT DROVE HER MAD.
LOVE IS DANGEROUS.
MEDUSA? WHAT--
GOODBYE, JOHNNY.
AND THANK YOU. FOR ALL OF IT.
IT'S WHY I TEND TO CHOOSE DUTY.
NOW, THOUGH, EVEN *THAT* IS GONE.
FOR THE FIRST TIME, THERE ARE NO *EXPECTATIONS* OF ME.
NO RULE, NO RULING, NO *RULES.*
FOR THE FIRST TIME I CAN REMEMBER...

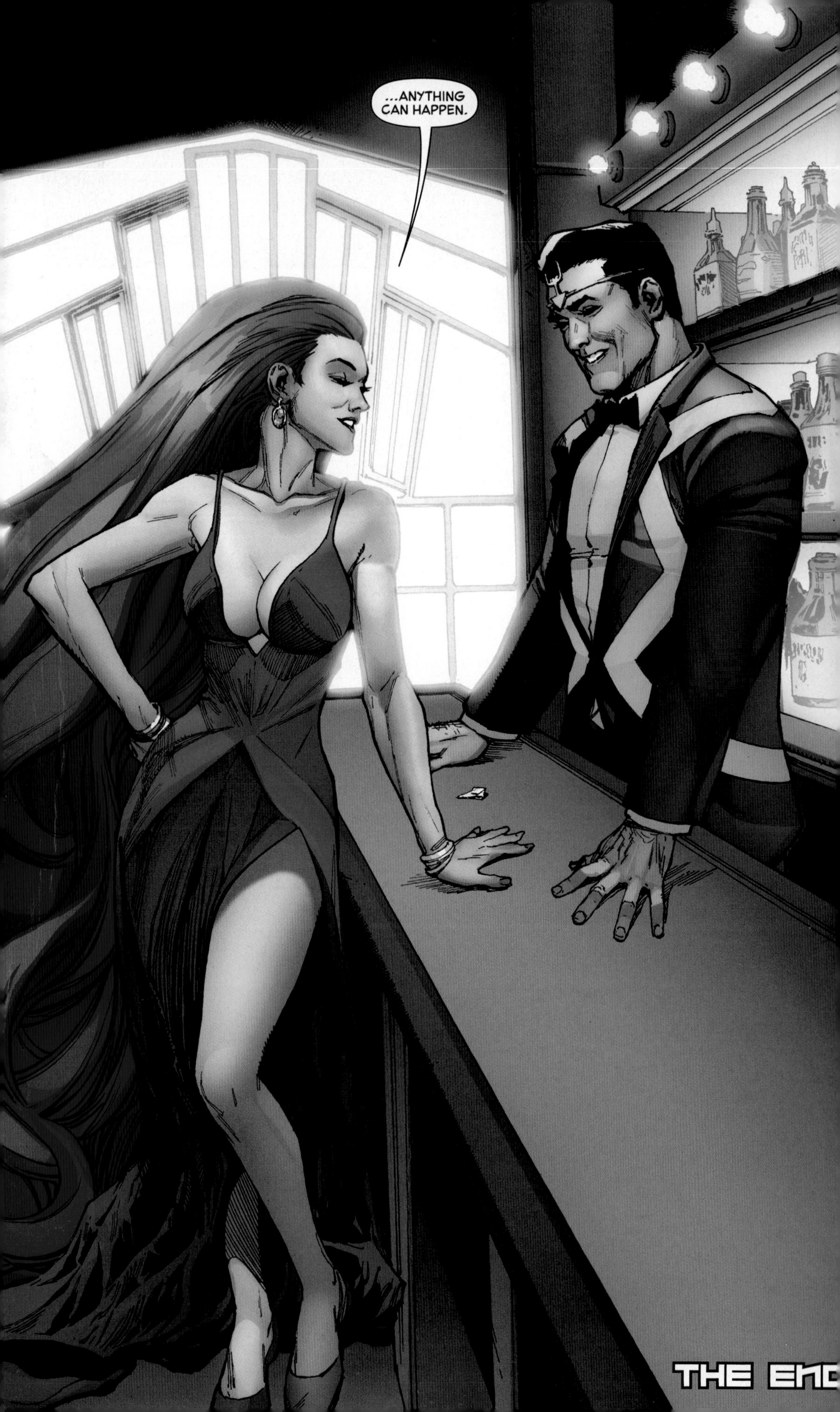
...ANYTHING CAN HAPPEN.
THE END

#0 Variant

by **Ron Lim, Andy Smith** & **Rachelle Rosenberg**

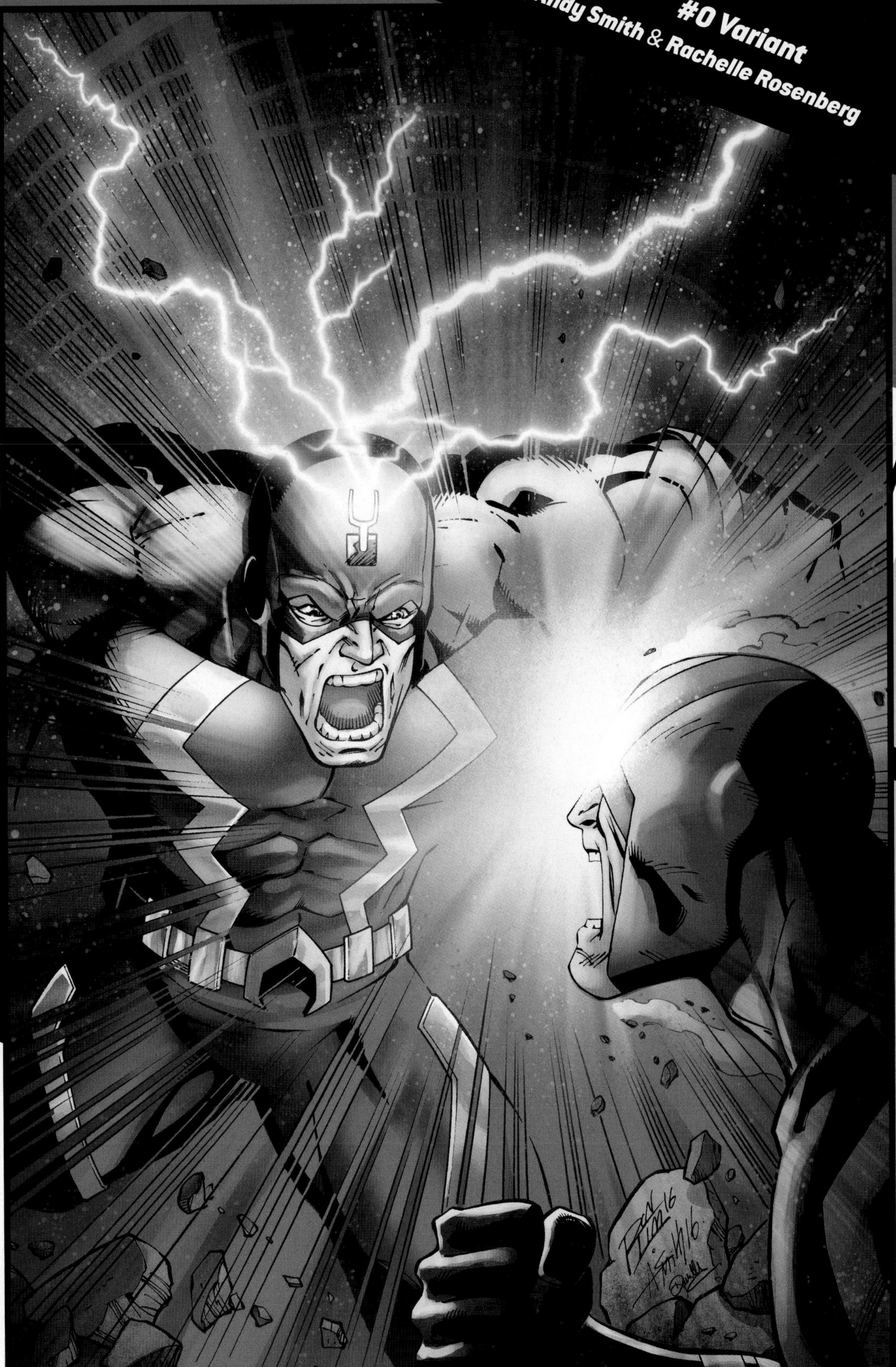

#0 Variant
by **Alan Davis, Mark Farmer** & **Matt Hollingsworth**

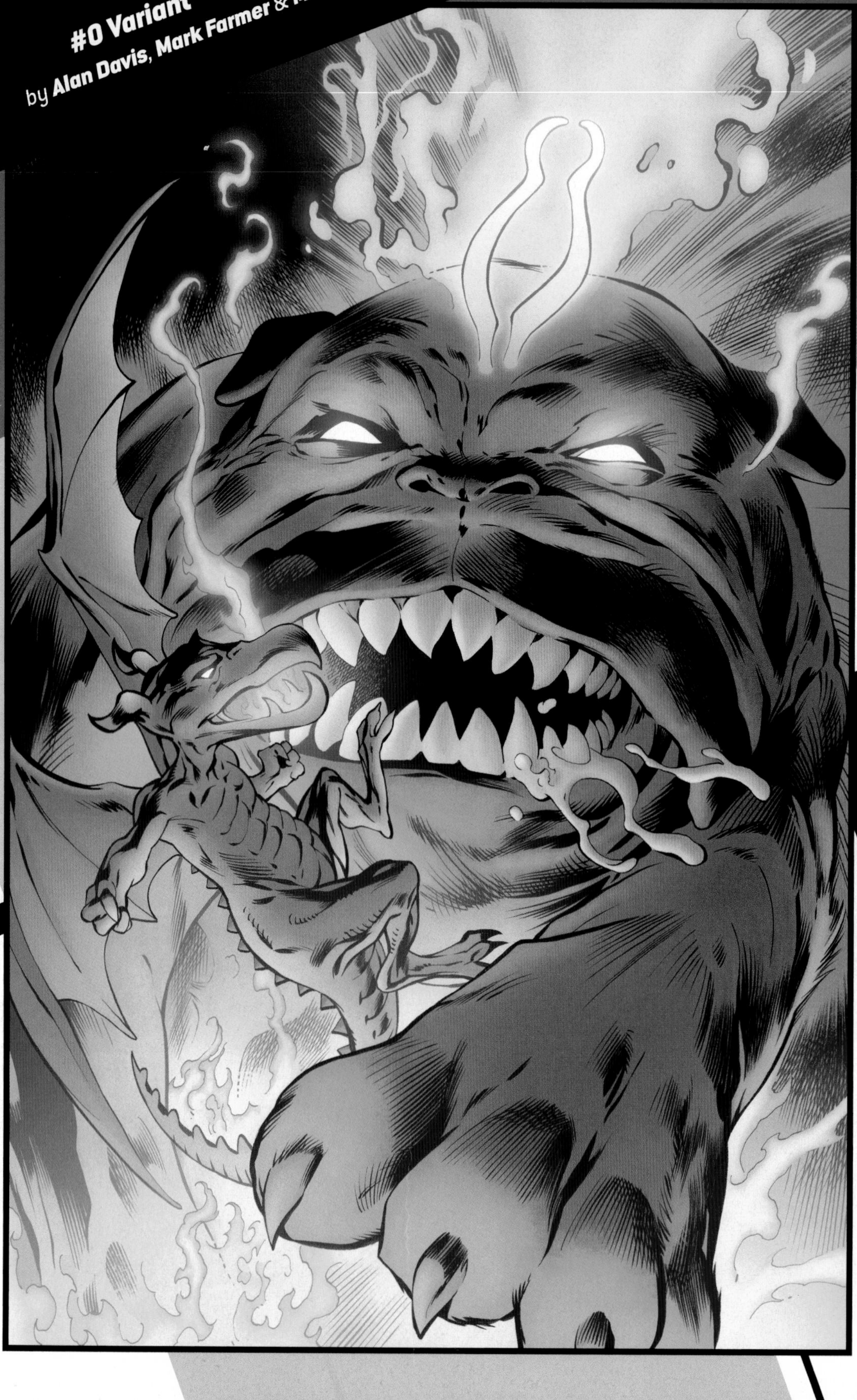

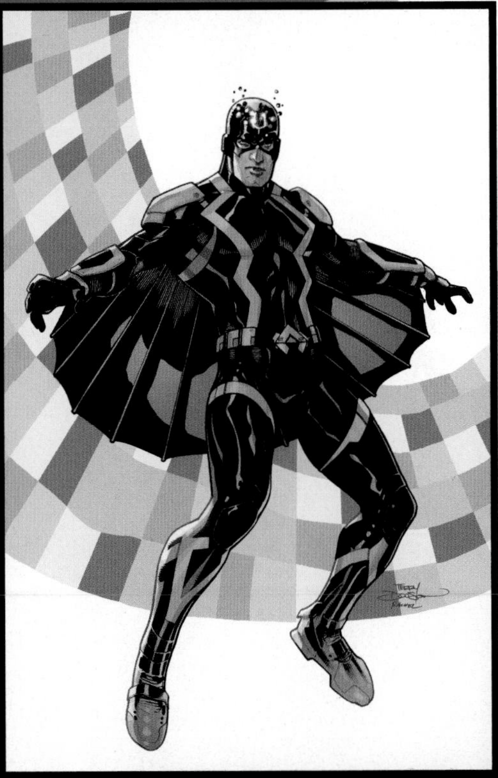

#1 Inhumans Variant
by **Terry Dodson** & **Rachel Dodson**

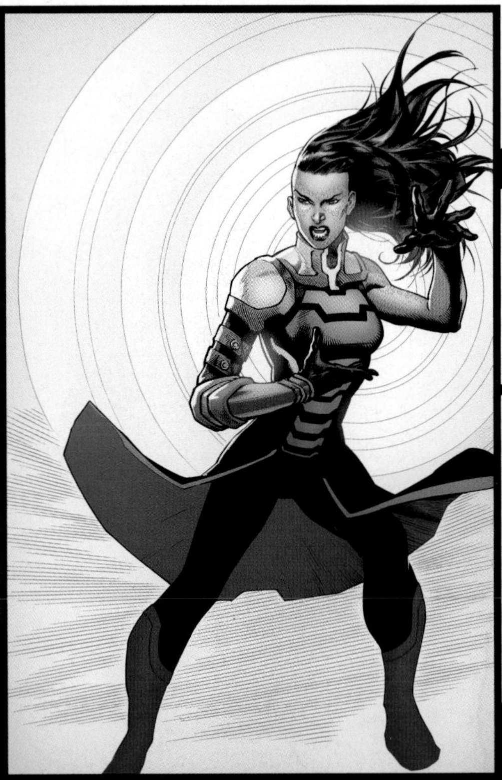

#2 Inhumans Variant
by **Ardian Syaf, Dexter Vines**
& **Edgar Delgado**

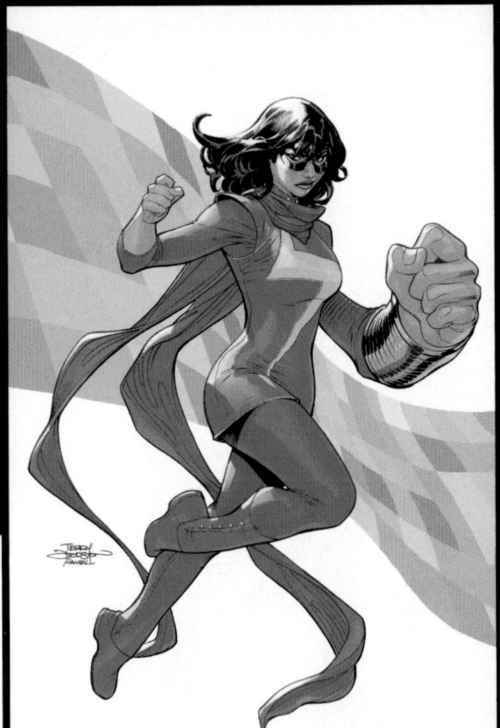

#3 Inhumans Variant
by **Terry Dodson** & **Rachel Dodson**

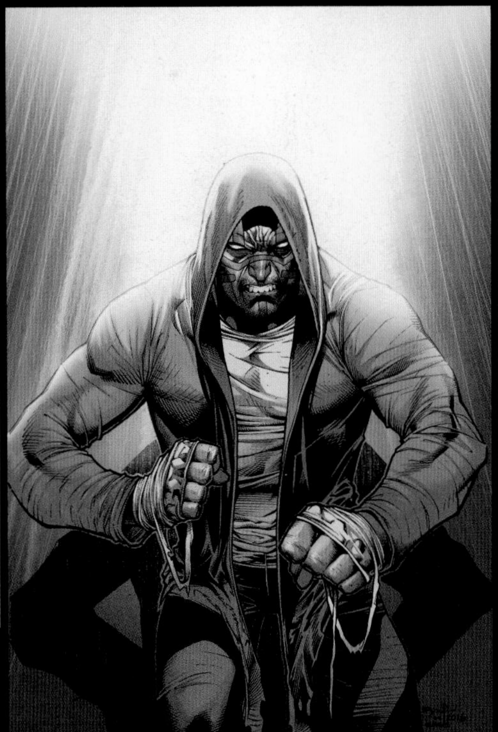

#4 Inhumans Variant
by **Ardian Syaf, Mark Morales**

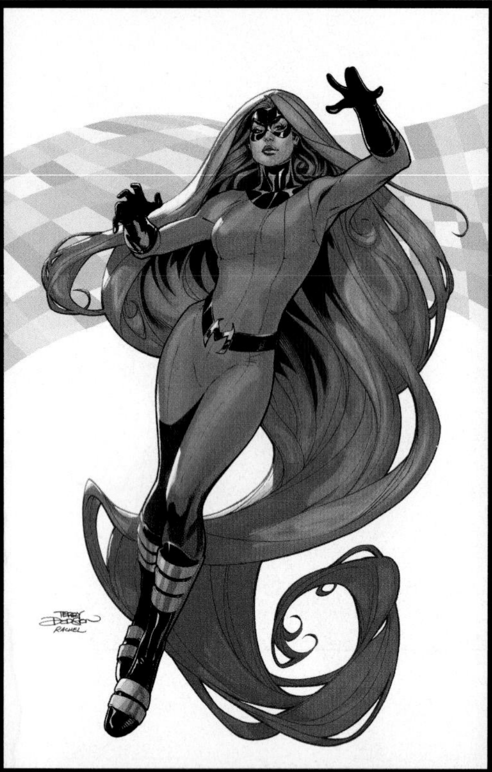

#5 Inhumans Variant

by **Terry Dodson** & **Rachel Dodson**

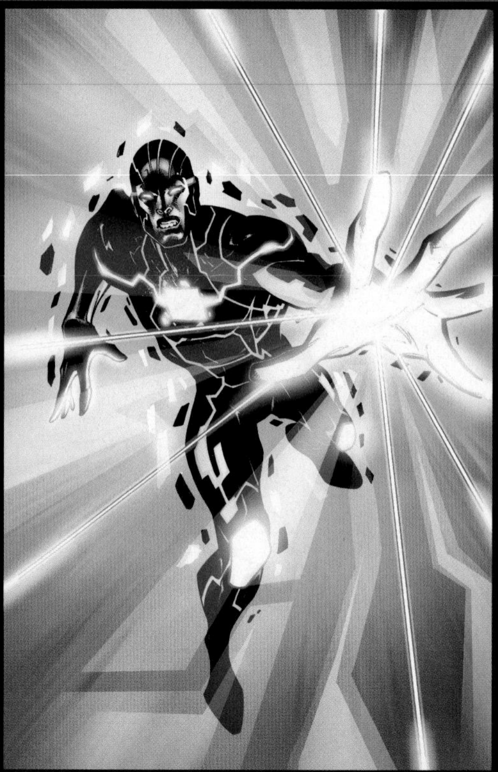

#6 Inhumans Variant

by **Ardian Syaf, Craig Yeung** & **Ulises Arreola**

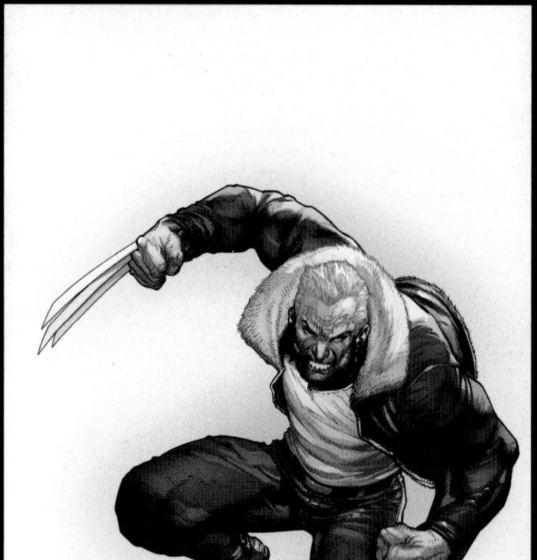

#1 X-Men Variant

by **Ardian Syaf, Dexter Vines** & **David Curiel**

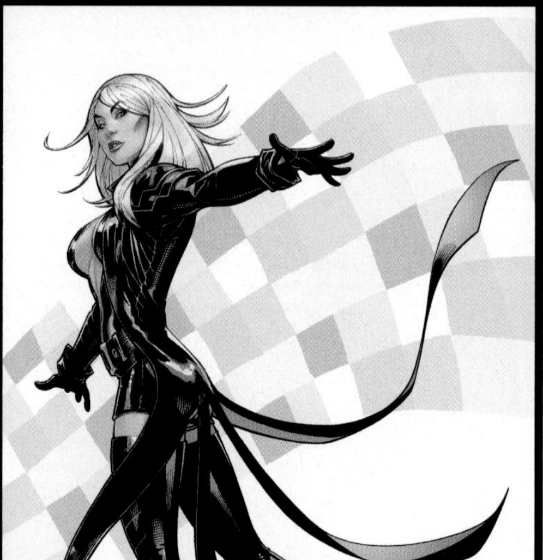

#2 X-Men Variant

by **Terry Dodson** & **Rachel Dodson**

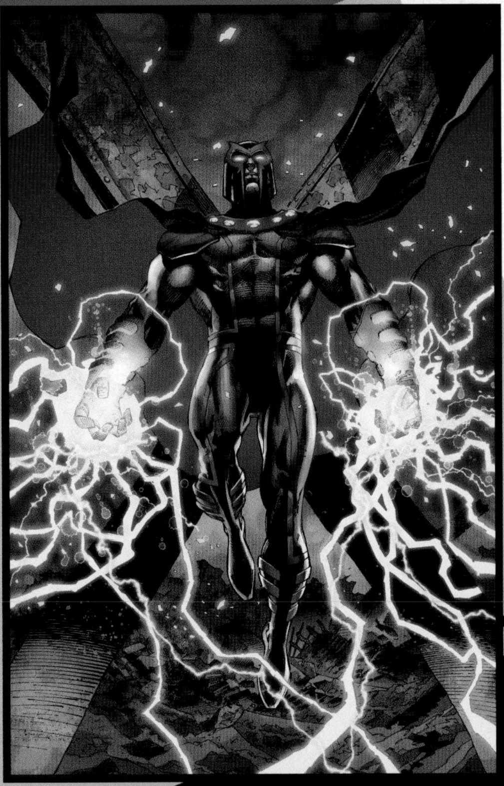

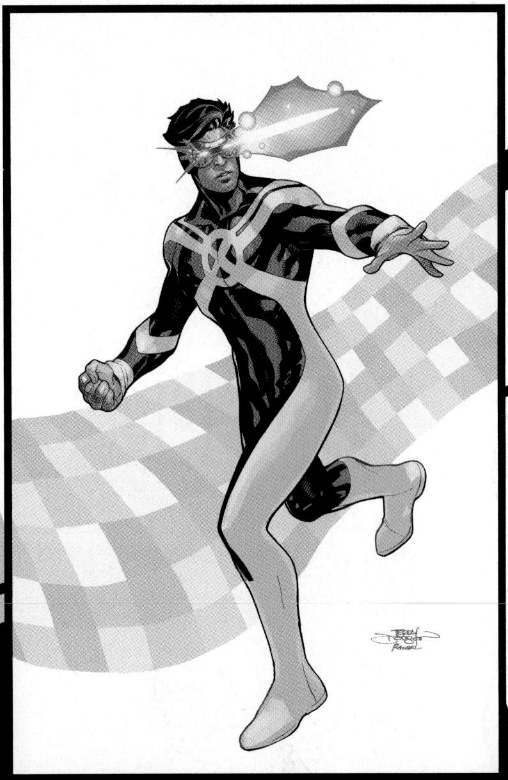

#3 X-Men Variant

by **Ardian Syaf**, **Jay Leisten** & **Paul Mounts**

#4 X-Men Variant

by **Terry Dodson** & **Rachel Dodson**

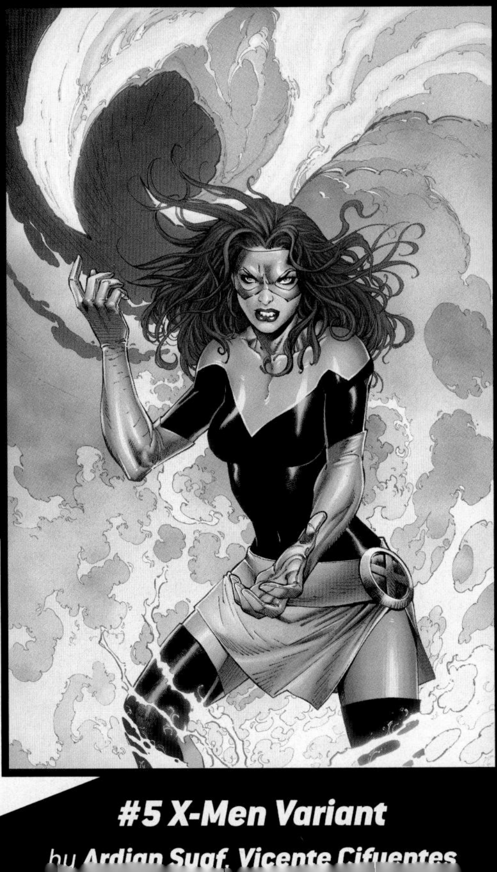

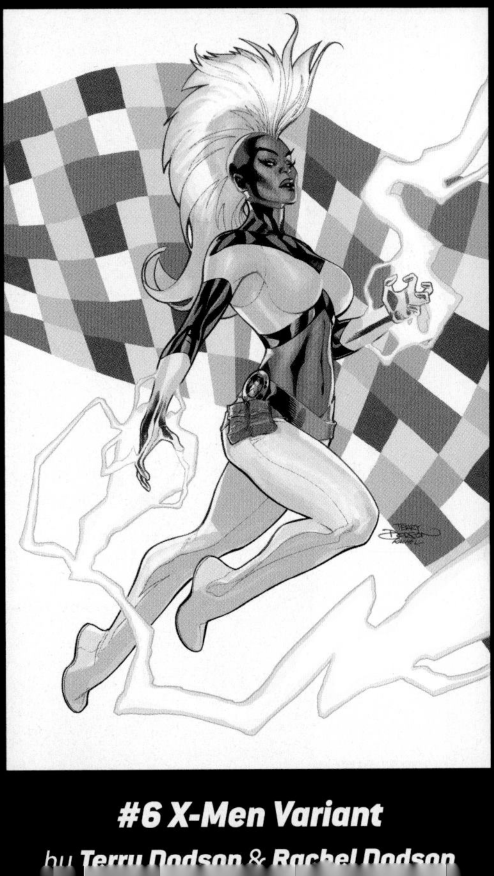

#5 X-Men Variant

by **Ardian Syaf**, **Vicente Cifuentes**

#6 X-Men Variant

by **Terry Dodson** & **Rachel Dodson**

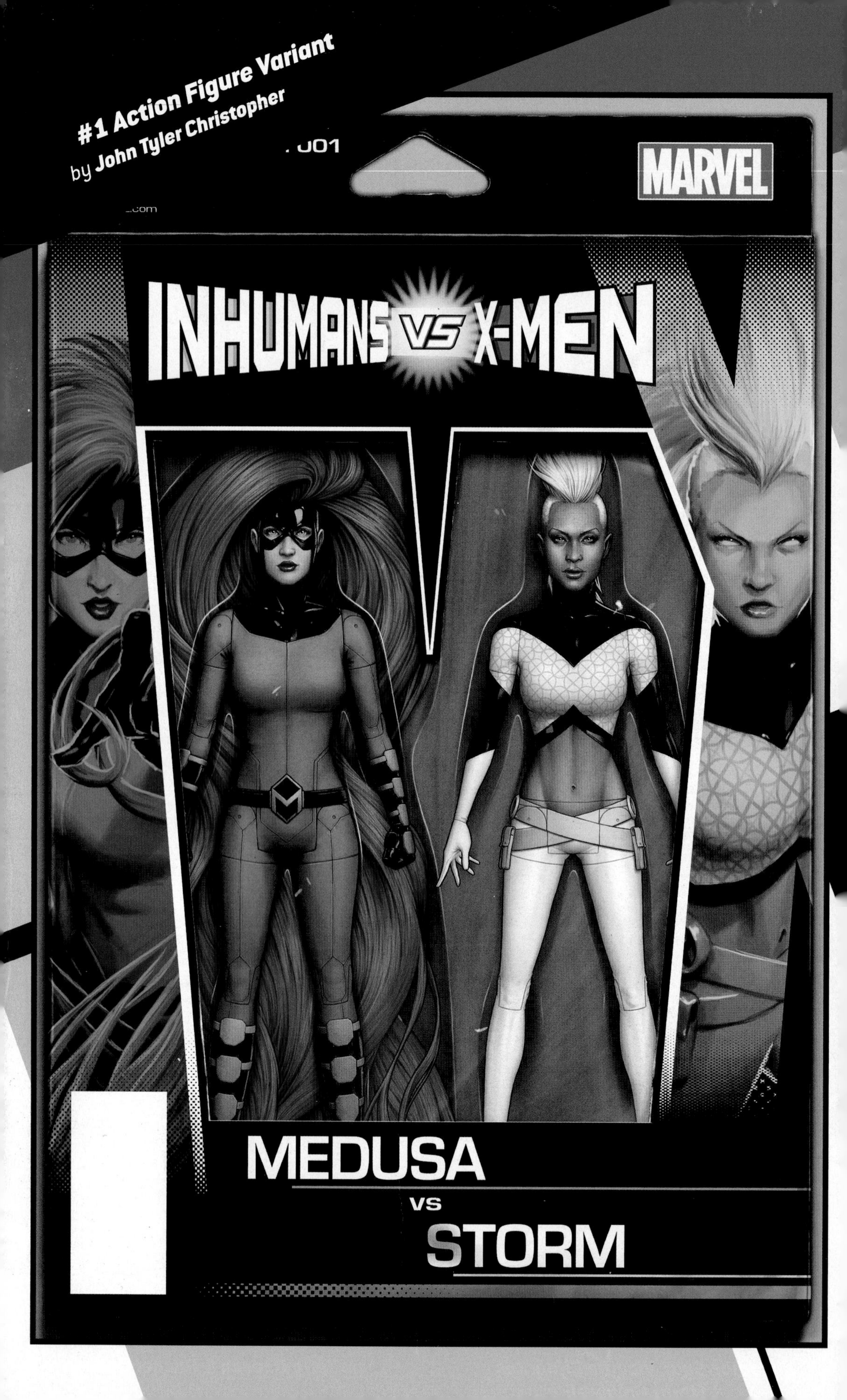

MARVEL
INHUMANS VS X-MEN
MEDUSA
VS
STORM

#1 Action Figure Variant
by John Tyler Christopher

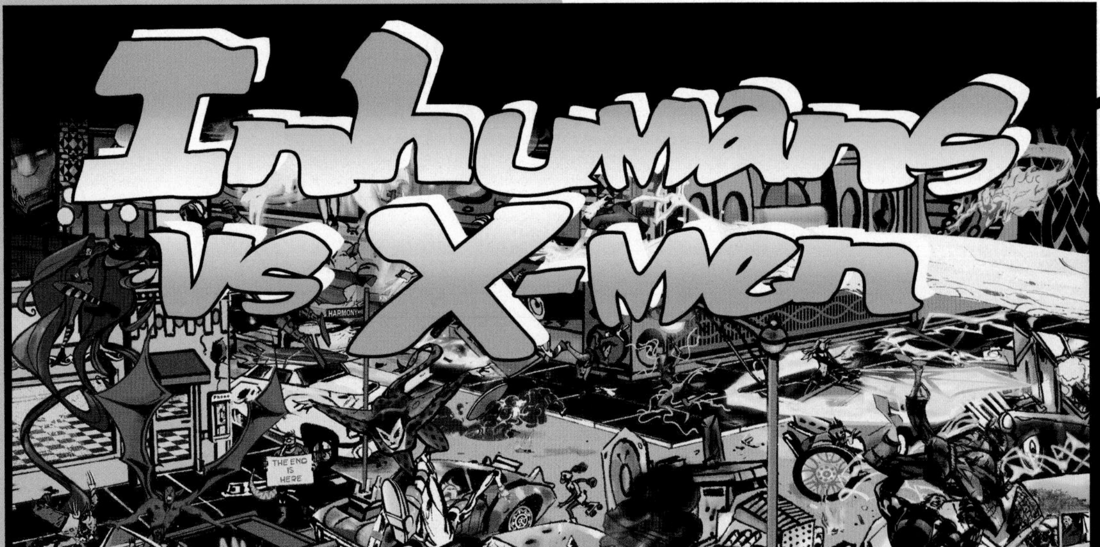
Inhumans
vs X-Men
THE END IS HERE
Sittin' In Mist

#1 Hip-Hop Variant

by ***Wilfred Santiago***

#1 Party Variant
by Chip Zdarsky

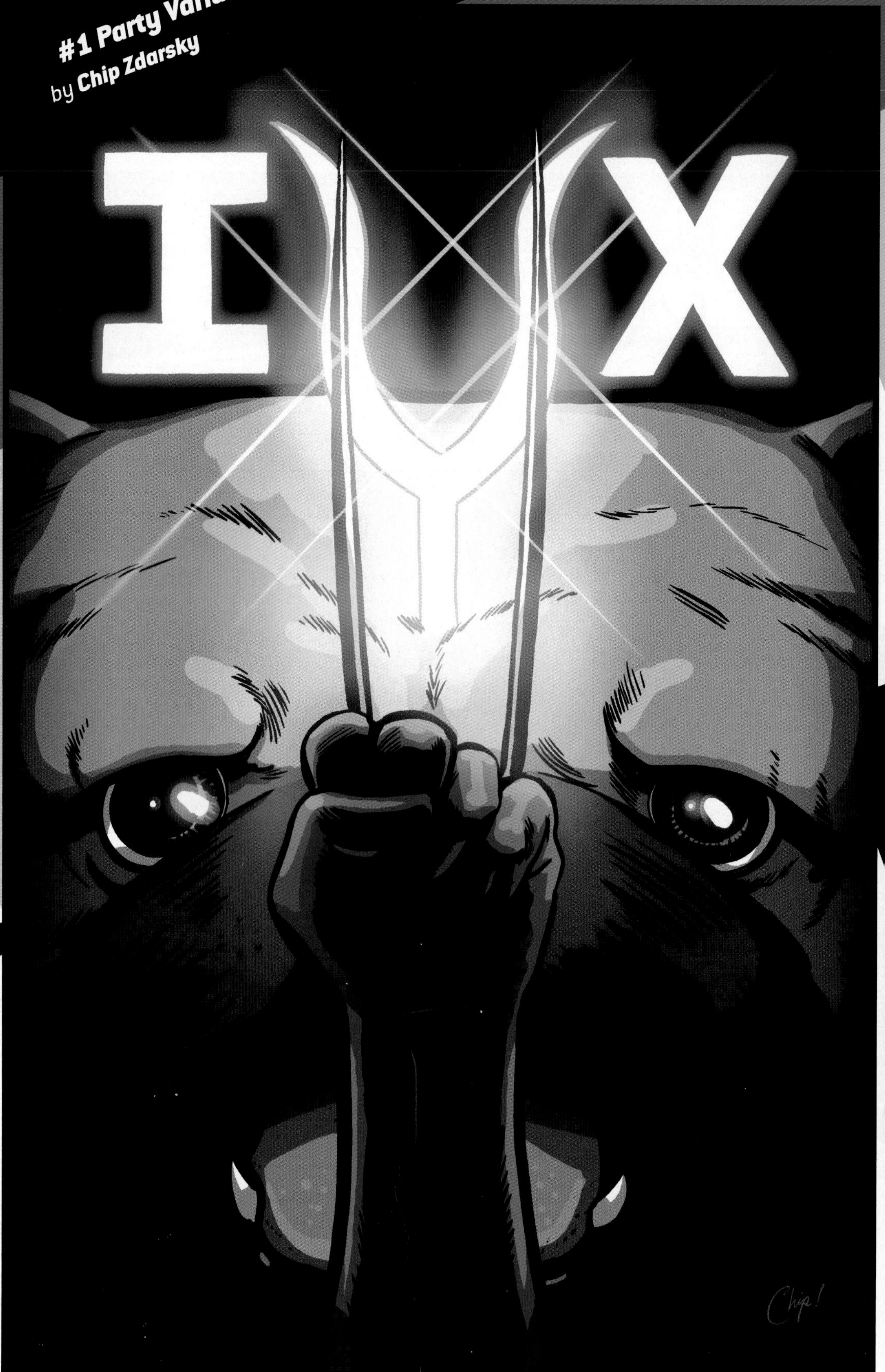
Chip!

#2 Variant
by **Arthur Adams** & **Paul Mounts**

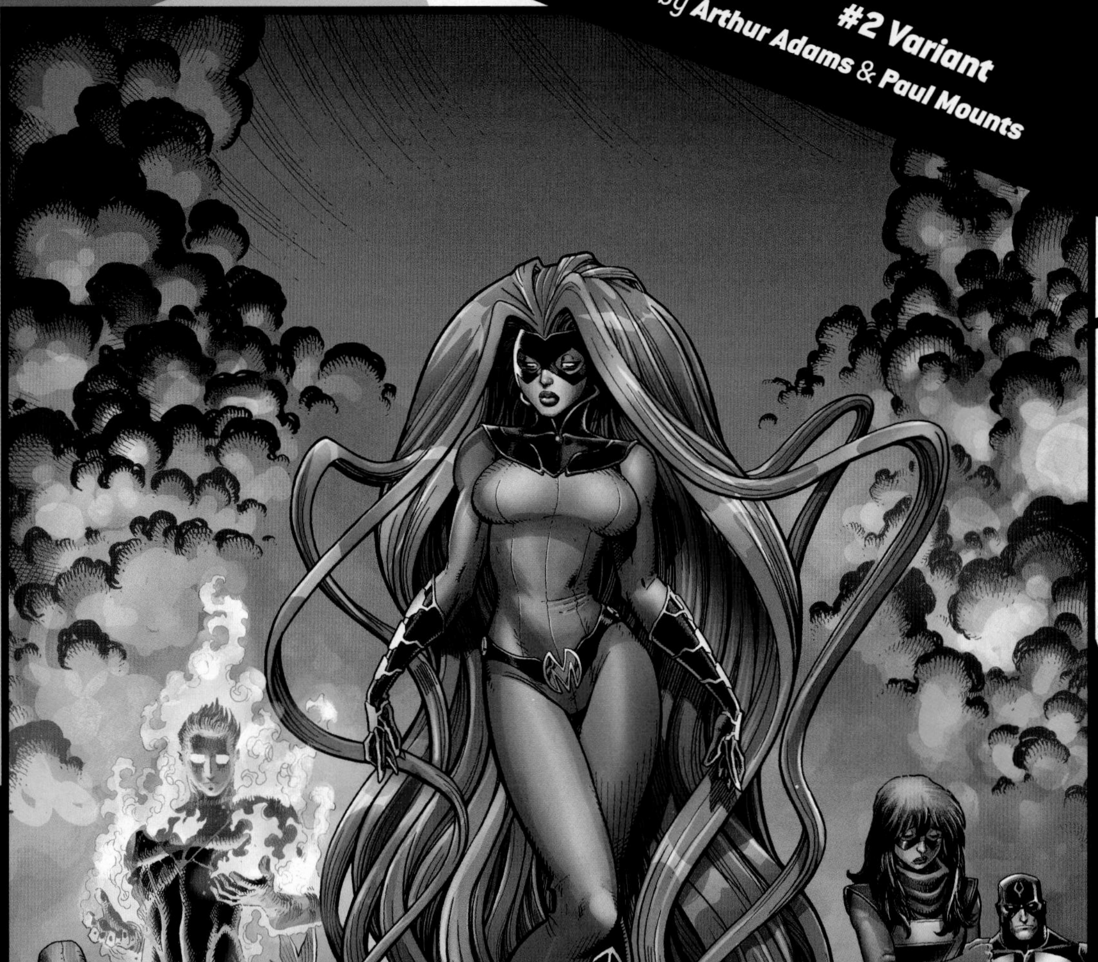

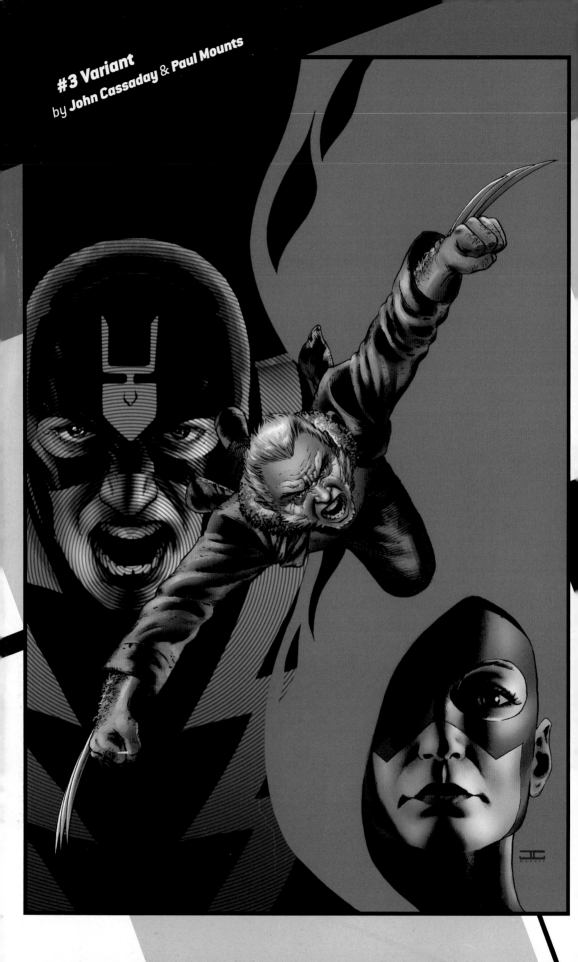

#3 Variant
by John Cassaday & Paul Mounts

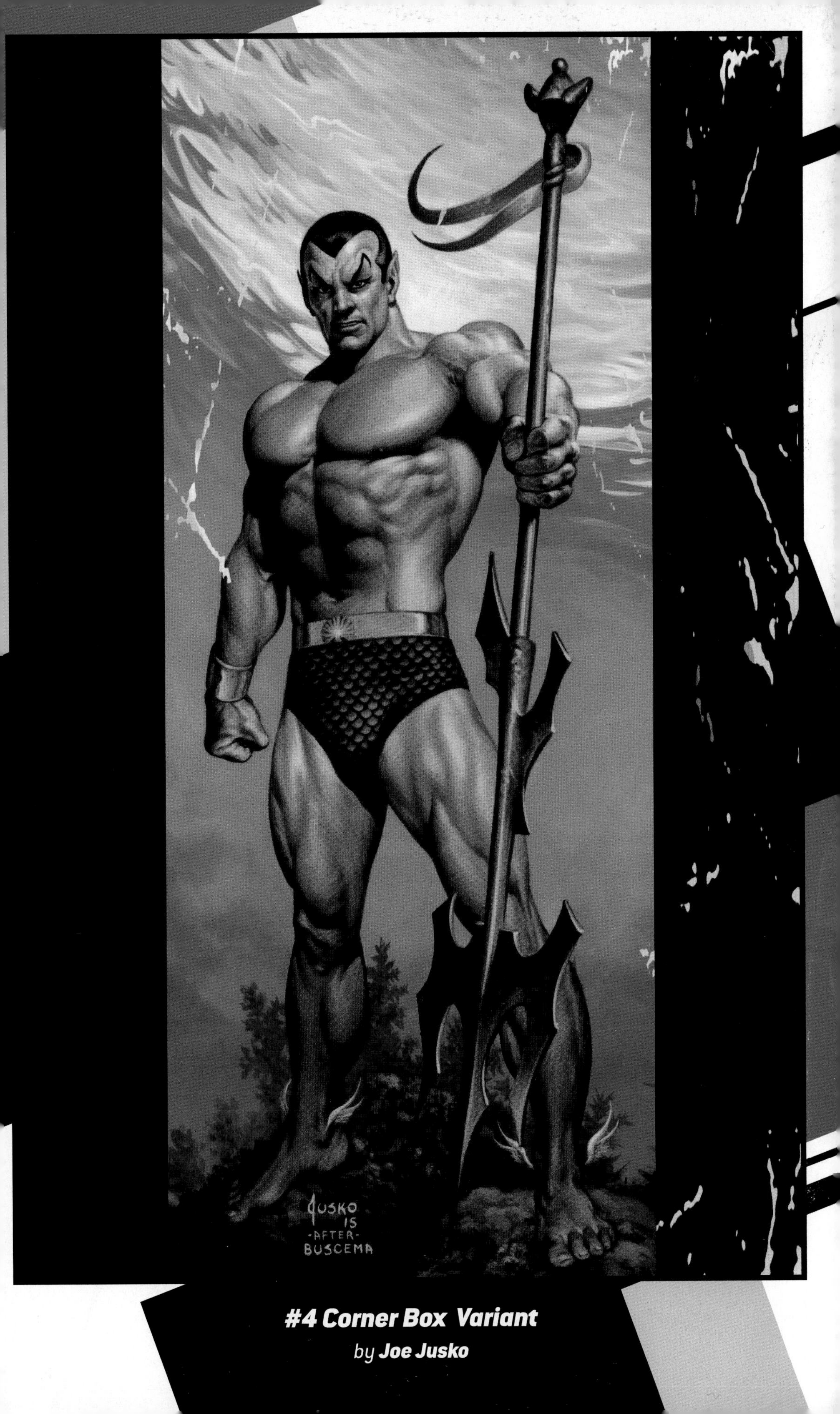
JUSKO
15
-AFTER-
BUSCEMA

#4 Corner Box Variant

by **Joe Jusko**

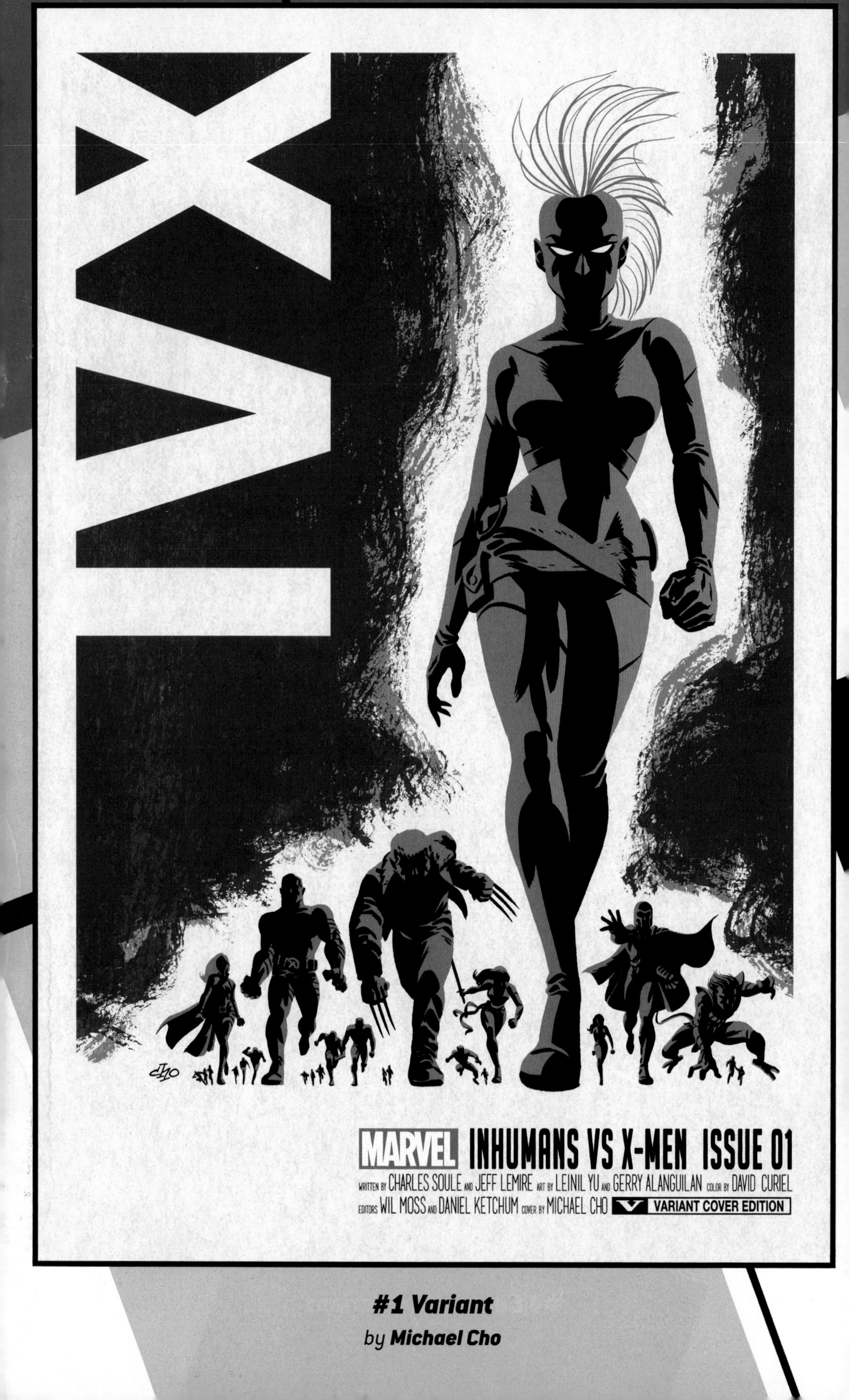
IVX
MARVEL INHUMANS VS X-MEN ISSUE 01
WRITTEN BY CHARLES SOULE AND JEFF LEMIRE ART BY LEINIL YU AND GERRY ALANGUILAN COLOR BY DAVID CURIEL
EDITORS WIL MOSS AND DANIEL KETCHUM COVER BY MICHAEL CHO
VARIANT COVER EDITION

#1 Variant

by **Michael Cho**

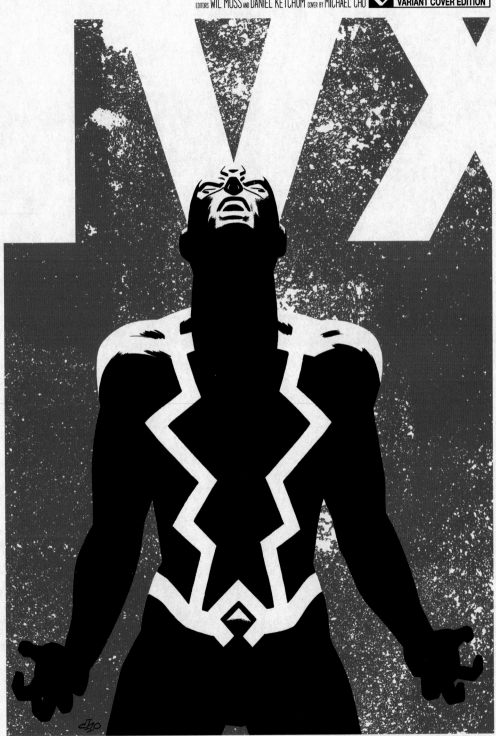

MARVEL INHUMANS VS X-MEN ISSUE 02

WRITTEN BY JEFF LEMIRE AND CHARLES SOULE ART BY LEINIL YU AND GERRY ALANGUILAN COLORS BY DAVID CURIEL

EDITORS WIL MOSS AND DANIEL KETCHUM COVER BY MICHAEL CHO   **V VARIANT COVER EDITION**

#2 Variant
by *Michael Cho*

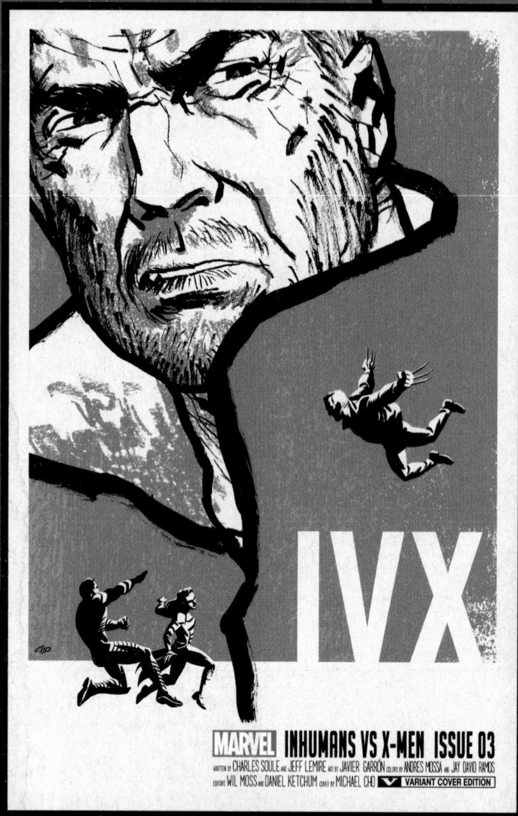
IVX
MARVEL INHUMANS VS X-MEN ISSUE 03
CHARLES SOULE JEFF LEMIRE JAVIER GARRÓN ANDRES MOSSA JAY DAVID RAMOS
WIL MOSS DANIEL KETCHUM MICHAEL CHO
VARIANT COVER EDITION

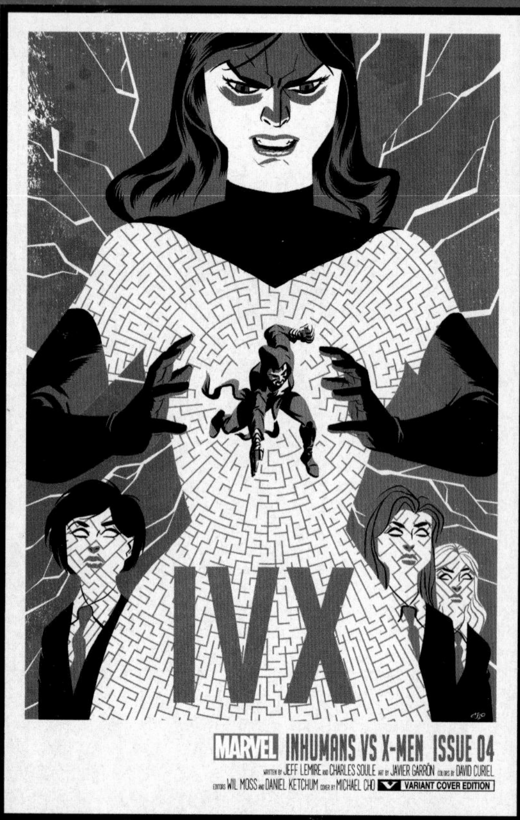
IVX
MARVEL INHUMANS VS X-MEN ISSUE 04
JEFF LEMIRE CHARLES SOULE JAVIER GARRÓN DAVID CURIEL
WIL MOSS DANIEL KETCHUM MICHAEL CHO
VARIANT COVER EDITION

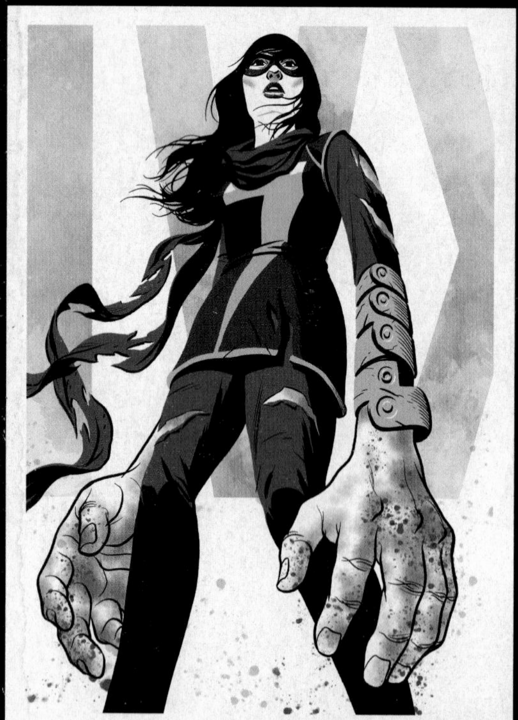
MARVEL INHUMANS VS X-MEN ISSUE 05
CHARLES SOULE JEFF LEMIRE JAVIER GARRÓN DAVID CURIEL
WIL MOSS DANIEL KETCHUM MICHAEL CHO
VARIANT COVER EDITION

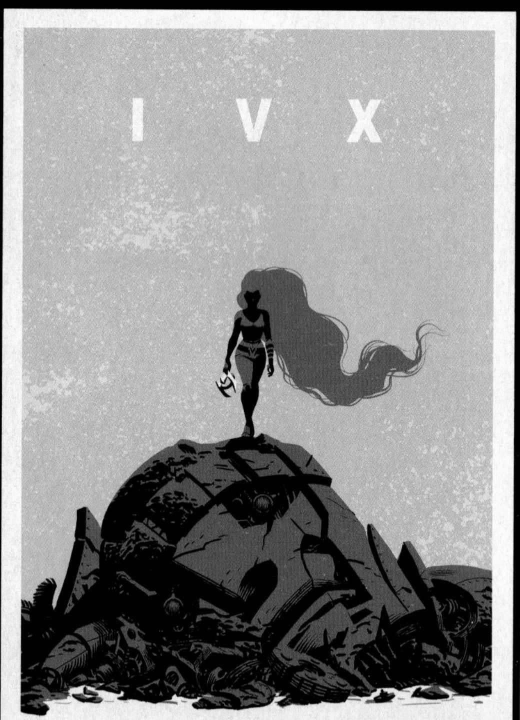
I V X
MARVEL INHUMANS VS X-MEN ISSUE 06
JEFF LEMIRE CHARLES SOULE LEINIL YU GERRY ALANGUILAN DAVID CURIEL
WIL MOSS DANIEL KETCHUM MICHAEL CHO
VARIANT COVER EDITION

#3-6 Variants

by **Michael Cho**